Functional Software Size Measurement Methodology with Effort Estimation and Performance Indication

About IEEE Computer Society

IEEE Computer Society is the world's leading computing membership organization and the trusted information and career-development source for a global workforce of technology leaders including: professors, researchers, software engineers, IT professionals, employers, and students. The unmatched source for technology information, inspiration, and collaboration, the IEEE Computer Society is the source that computing professionals trust to provide high-quality, state-of-the-art information on an on-demand basis. The Computer Society provides a wide range of forums for top minds to come together, including technical conferences, publications, and a comprehensive digital library, unique training webinars, professional training, and the TechLeader Training Partner Program to help organizations increase their staff's technical knowledge and expertise, as well as the personalized information tool myComputer. To find out more about the community for technology leaders, visit http://www.computer.org.

IEEE/Wiley Partnership

The IEEE Computer Society and Wiley partnership allows the CS Press authored book program to produce a number of exciting new titles in areas of computer science, computing, and networking with a special focus on software engineering. IEEE Computer Society members continue to receive a 15% discount on these titles when purchased through Wiley or at wiley.com/ieeecs.

To submit questions about the program or send proposals, please contact Mary Hatcher, Editor, Wiley-IEEE Press: Email: mhatcher@wiley.com, Telephone: 201-748-6903, John Wiley & Sons, Inc., 111 River Street, MS 8-01, Hoboken, NJ 07030-5774.

Functional Software Size Measurement Methodology with Effort Estimation and Performance Indication

Jasveer Singh

Published by John Wiley & Sons, Inc., Hoboken, New Jersey.
Published simultaneously in Canada.

Library of Congress Cataloging-in-Publication Data:

Names: Singh, Jasveer, 1955- author.
Title: Functional software size measurement methodology with effort
estimation and performance indication / Jasveer Singh.
Description: Hoboken, New Jersey : John Wiley & Sons, Inc., [2017] | Includes
bibliographical references and index.
Identifiers: LCCN 2016037106| ISBN 9781119238058 (pbk.) | ISBN 9781119238119 (epub)
Subjects: LCSH: Software measurement. | Computer software–Evaluation.
Classification: LCC QA76.76.S65 S56 2017 | DDC 005.1/4–dc23 LC record available at
https://lccn.loc.gov/2016037106

Printed in the United States of America.

10 9 8 7 6 5 4 3 2 1

This book is dedicated to all the software and management professionals and students, and those keen to expand their knowledge on the topic of software size measurement.

Contents

Part Three FSSM: Measurements

Part Four FSSM: Estimations and Indications

Preface

PRELUDE

Software Size Measurement is an extremely important and highly specialized part of the software life cycle. It is needed for determining the effort and cost estimations for project planning purposes of the software projects' execution, and/or for other costing/charging/productivity analysis purposes of the software projects. The software size measurement part has not received proper attention and has been neglected till now as it is well known that many software projects exceed their allocated budget limits because the currently available methodologies for software size measurement present many areas for improvements whereby better and more accurate estimations for effort can be obtained. These methodologies measure only a very limited part of the software to determine the complete software's size which is an inaccurate way for the measurement of most of the software applications because of the reasons explained later in the book.

The available standards in this area, for example, ISO/IEC 14143-1[1], ISO/IEC 14143-2[2], do not specify what the constituents of the software are, which need to be measured. So it is left to the methodologies what to measure.

Project leaders and project managers depend on the size measurement specialists for measuring the software size. Specialists measure the size based on the current techniques. Then, various multiplier factors depending on the environmental factors such as the area of application software and assumptions about the complexity of the software are used to expand the size of the remaining unmeasured parts to get the complete software size in order to include the size of the parts missing in the measurements. Using non-specific multipliers would result in an assumed measurement size for the project. Project leaders, project managers, and specialists are aware of these facts but are obliged to continue using these measurements because no other thorough technique is available.

The new software size measurement methodology presented in this book, "Functional Software Size Measurement Methodology with Effort Estimation and Performance Indication (FSSM)", overcomes these deficiencies, and is a comprehensive, elaborate, and complete software Functional Size Measurement[1] methodology, which can help enterprises to estimate the size and required effort for all their software projects developed in High Level Languages, quite accurately. Hence, these projects can be completed within the defined budget limits because of accurate estimations obtained by using the detailed and complete approach of the FSSM.

SOFTWARE SIZE MEASUREMENT

"Functional Size Measurement (FSM)"[1] is a very effective method to measure the software "size in terms of the functions required by the user"[1] in which the functional "size of the software derived by quantifying the Functional User Requirements (FUR)"[1] is measured. Extra care should be taken to select a specific FSM[1] method. A method which measures only very few of the various types of functions available in the software should not be selected but one which measures all the important types of functions should be selected, for the reasons explained later in the book. Many currently available, popular FSM[1] methodologies can be improved in this respect. The most desired improvement would be to increase the coverage of the measurement regarding the number of the measured type of functions. The very small number of the type of functions measured – a small subset of the complete set of various available types of measurable functions – should be increased to a more extensive functional range.

Software consists of several constituent parts or components which can be named as "Base Functional Components (BFCs)"[1]. These components have no fixed proportional relationships amongst themselves or with respect to the complete software concerning their size in different applications or in the sub-programs (modules) of the same application. Moreover, the BFCs[1] have sub-types which are called "BFC Type"[1]. Most of these sub-types have no fixed proportional relationships amongst themselves for a particular BFC[1] or with the sub-types of other BFCs[1] regarding their size. Therefore, if only one or a few BFC types[1] of one or a few BFCs[1] are measured – so only a partial measurement – the size of the other remaining sub-types and components cannot be determined correctly based on this aforementioned measured part and some multiplication factors. However, this is how the current software sizing methodologies approach the estimation.

ABOUT THE BOOK

Software has become so ubiquitous that the importance of the software projects and their timely completion cannot be overlooked. Timely completion is dependent on correct planning which requires realistic effort estimates. Effort estimates can be realistic only if accurate and complete software size measurements are available.

Many medium- and big-sized software projects are unable to be completed within the planned limits of time, money, and resources. This book pinpoints one of the major, originating, basic root causes of the erroneous planning by disclosing the hidden errors that are made in the software size measurement, and consequently in the effort estimates and project planning. It then reveals the simple and correct manner of accurate software size measurement whereby realistic effort estimates can be obtained based on which precise project planning can be done, and successful execution of the projects can be achieved within the planned limits.

The "Functional Software Size Measurement Methodology with Effort Estimation and Performance Indication (FSSM)" presented in this book provides comprehensive and precise measurements of the complete software whereby factual software size determination, development effort estimation, and performance indications are obtained. The methodology is elaborate, effective, and accurate for software size measurement and development effort estimation. Consequently, misconstrued project planning of the software projects can be avoided.

All the major, relevant, and important aspects of the software size measurement are taken into consideration in the FSSM and are presented to the reader. They are the software's measurable components, software component's measurable features, software component's feature points, software component's feature point counts, software component's feature measurements, software component's measurements, software size and effort estimations, and software performance quality indicators. Also included are a worked-out example with counting table, explanation, and results; software diagnostics based on the software component's feature measurements and software performance quality indicators; comparison with and advantages over some of the currently available methodologies; convertibility to another FSM[1] methodology; effort estimation for applying the FSSM methodology; and details of the full compliance with the ISO/IEC 14143-1[1] standards.

The book is destined and recommended for all the management/software professionals/students, and those interested in the field of software size measurement. It is intended to be used as a text book for the full or part of the advanced, specialized course of "Software Size Measurement" at the level of Master of Technology/Engineering/Science in the curriculum of the Computer Science/Engineering/Technology courses.

It is recommended that the reader already has some exposure to the software concepts/architecture from the point of view of applications, requirements, analysis, design, coding, and testing; DBMS, object-oriented technology; and acquaintance with the existing software size measurement/estimation techniques such as COSMIC[3] and IFPUG[4].

The book comprises:

1. Introduction to Functional Software Size Measurement;
2. Synopsis of the Functional Software Size Measurement Methodology with Effort Estimation and Performance Indication;
3. Software's Measurable Components;
4. Software Component's Measurable Features;
5. Software Component's Feature Points;
6. Software Component's Feature Point Counts;
7. Software Component's Measurements through Software Component's Feature Measurements;
8. Software Size Determination and Effort Estimations;
9. Software Performance Quality Indicators for Static Structure and Dynamic Characteristics;
10. Summary Charts;
11. Software Diagnostics;
12. Convertibility and ISO/IEC Standards Compliance;
13. Strengths and Comparison: Methodology Coverage and Advantages;
14. A Worked-Out Example with Functional Requirements Specifications, Counting Table and Explanations, and Results;
15. Methodology Usage Effort;
16. Examples, Exercises, and Glossary.

The presentation of the contents of FSSM is organized in the chapters in the following manner:

1. Distinct parts of group of chapters:
   a. The book is divided into distinct parts of groups of chapters. The chapters in a group are related and linked amongst themselves. The parts follow a pattern of flow of information convenient for understanding.

2. Flow of information in the chapter contents:
   a. The sequence of chapters with respect to their contents follows an orderly flow according to the flow scheme of proceedings in applying the FSSM.
3. Organization of contents of the chapters:
   a. In all the chapters:
      i. The descriptions in the chapters are divided under different relevant topics.
      ii. The summary of the contents of the chapter is presented at the end of the chapter.
4. Use of examples and exercises:
   a. Suitable examples and exercises are included at the end of the chapters where appropriate. Some examples presented in the chapters are part of a large example which is presented completely in a separate chapter.
5. References:
   a. Superscripted numbers point to the references of which a list is presented at the end of the book.
6. Use of new terms and acronyms:
   a. Since the methodology is new and comprehensive, there is an abundance of terms which are associated with the methodology and are used in the book. To convey the meaning of the terms properly, the names of some of them are long. To make the use of terms simple, acronyms are utilized.
   b. A complete acronym list is presented at the beginning of the book. Most of the acronyms used in the example chapter are not included in the complete list because their use is limited to the example chapter only and not elsewhere in the book.
   c. In order to get familiar with the acronyms and terms, and get used to them, an attempt is made to adhere to the following conventions for their use in the text of the chapters: if the terms are used many times in a paragraph or a series of sequentially connected paragraphs, their first time use in the paragraph(s) utilizes the full-term name followed by the acronym in parentheses, the next time use utilizes the acronym followed by the full-term name in parentheses, and the further uses afterward utilize the acronym only. This way, it is easier to get familiarized with and get used to the terms and acronyms.

Acknowledgments

Special contribution and help, in the form of meticulous reviews, valuable suggestions for improvements in the structure and contents of the book throughout the period of book preparation, of the author's son, Seenu Singh, who is a concert pianist (Master of Music, Royal Conservatory of Flanders, Antwerp, Belgium) and holder of Master of Information Management degree (Katholieke Universiteit Leuven, Leuven, Belgium) and Master of Business Administration degree (IE Business School, Madrid, Spain), deserve special thanks and acknowledgment from the author who appreciates enormously their value and importance.

At the same time, the author is very thankful to the reviewers, amongst whom are Anupam Kumar (Senior Manager, Capgemini, Belgium), Bernard Tinant (ICT Consultant, Belgium), and Ramesh Dhar (IT Principal, Cigna Inc., USA), of the book at the proposal and final manuscript stages for their critical, valuable, and useful comments which helped to improve significantly the contents of the book. Also, the author is sincerely thankful to Mary Hatcher and Melissa Yanuzzi of Wiley/IEEE Press and all others involved in the publication of this book for their excellent professional support without which the publication of this book would not be possible.

Equally important are the permissions granted for using the material from the following organizations for which the author is very thankful:

1. ISO/IEC: The authorization to reproduce text from the ISO/IEC standards is given by NBN, the Belgian national standardization body. The standards can be obtained from ISO and any ISO member. NBN.
2. IFPUG: This book contains material which has been extracted from the IFPUG Counting Practices Manual. It is reproduced in this book with permission of IFPUG.
3. UKSMA: This book is based on the concepts in the presentation "Software Comprehensive Count with Quality Indicators (SCCQI)" made at the UKSMA/COSMIC 23rd Annual Conference 2012.
4. SMEF: This book is based on the concepts presented in the paper "Software Comprehensive Count with Quality Indicators (SCCQI)" published in the Proceedings of the 9th Software Measurement European Forum, Rome, 2012.
5. NESMA: This book is based on the concepts in the presentation "Software Comprehensive Count with Quality Indicators (SCCQI) for Software Size Measurement" made at the NESMA November 2012 najaarsbijeenkomst (Autumn Meeting).

About the Author

The author of this book, Mr. Jasveer Singh, holds a Master of Technology degree in Computer Technology from the Indian Institute of Technology, Delhi, and has studied Executive Master in Management at École de Commerce Solvay, Brussels, Belgium.

He has about 30 years of valuable senior-level international experience in the Information and Communication Technology area and has worked in the top Information Technology/Telecom equipment manufacturer, operator, consultancy, and service companies in different countries (Bharat Electronics Limited, Alcatel, Siemens Business Services, WorldCom, Logica, and Keynote Sigos in India, France, Australia, Belgium, and Germany). A significant part of this experience has been in the management of software development (analysis, design, coding, testing), system design, quality assurance/control, and project management while working with different programming languages, object-oriented technology, database management systems, etc. His in-depth experience in these software domains led him to realize the improvements needed in the currently available methodologies for software size measurement and to develop the Functional Software Size Measurement Methodology with Effort Estimation and Performance Indication (FSSM) which is a thorough methodology and great help for software projects.

Currently, he is based in Belgium. He has extensive experience of working in multicultural environments and has very good communication skills in multiple languages. He has had the opportunity to visit about 25 countries for his work, enriching his knowledge both professionally and individually.

List of Acronyms

AECP	Action Execution Content Proportion
AEL	Action Execution Level
AEO	Action Execution Operations
ASD	Application Software Development
BFC Type	Base Functional Component Type[1]
BFC	Base Functional Component[1]
CFD	Software's Measurable Component 'Functional Data'
CFDM	Software Component 'Functional Data' Measurement
CFE	Software's Measurable Component 'Functionality Execution'
CFEM	Software Component 'Functionality Execution' Measurement
CFP	COSMIC Function Point[3]
CM	Class Method
CMDE	Class Method Entities
CME	Software's Measurable Component 'Message Exchange'
CMEM	Software Component 'Message Exchange' Measurement
CNC	Computer Numerical Control (machine)
CO	Computational Operations
COCP	Computational Operation Content Proportion
COL	Computational Operations Level
COSMIC	Common Software Measurement International Consortium[3]
CRDM	Software Components Requirement Deficiency Measurement
CUI	Software's Measurable Component 'User Interface'
CUIM	Software Component 'User Interface' Measurement
DAE	Data Class Attribute Entities
DBMS	Data Base Management System
DCE	Data Class Entities
DCL	Data Collection
DECP	Decision Execution Content Proportion
DEL	Decision Execution Level
DEO	Decision Execution Operations
DFE	Data Class Field Entities
ECDL	External Communication Functional Data Level
ECL	External Communication Level
ECP	External Communication Proportion
EFCCP	Execution Flow Control Content Proportion
EFCL	Execution Flow Control Level

EFCO	Execution Flow Control Operations
EHC	Error Handling Capability
EHO	Error Handling Operations
EHP	Error Handling Proportion
EI	External Input[4]
EIF	External Interface File[4]
EO	External Output[4]
EOFE	Message Exchange Operations Functional Data Entities
EODP	Message Exchange Operations Functional Data Proportion
EQ	External Inquiry[4]
ERP	Enterprise Resource Planning
FCCM	Software Component's Feature Point Count for 'Class Method'
FCDA	Software Component's Feature Point Count for 'Data Attribute'
FCDC	Software Component's Feature Point Count for 'Data Class'
FCDF	Software Component's Feature Point Count for 'Data Field'
FCDI	Software Component's Feature Point Count for 'Data Input'
FCDM	Software Component's Feature Point Count for 'Data Missing'
FCDO	Software Component's Feature Point Count for 'Data Output'
FCDR	Software Component's Feature Point Count for 'Data Read'
FCDW	Software Component's Feature Point Count for 'Data Write'
FCFA	Software Component's Feature Point Count for 'Function Action Execution'
FCFC	Software Component's Feature Point Count for 'Function Computational Operation'
FCFD	Software Component's Feature Point Count for 'Function Decision Execution'
FCFE	Software Component's Feature Point Count for 'Function Error Handling'
FCFL	Software Component's Feature Point Count for 'Function Logical Operation'
FCFM	Software Component's Feature Point Count for 'Functionality Missing'
FCFO	Software Component's Feature Point Count for 'Function Execution Flow Control'
FCFR	Software Component's Feature Point Count for 'Function Repeat Execution'
FCLG	Software Component's Feature Point Count for 'General Operations Functional Data'
FCLI	Software Component's Feature Point Count for 'Input/Output Operations Functional Data'
FCLM	Software Component's Feature Point Count for 'Memory Operations Functional Data'
FCLS	Software Component's Feature Point Count for 'Message Exchange Operations Functional Data'
FCM	Software Component's Measurable Feature 'Class Method'
FCMF	Software Component's Feature Point Count for 'Message Field'
FCMM	Software Component's Feature Point Count for 'Message Missing'
FCMR	Software Component's Feature Point Count for 'Message Receive'
FCMS	Software Component's Feature Point Count for 'Message Send'
FCNM	Software Component's Feature Point Count for 'Notifying Message'

FCUF	Software Component's Feature Point Count for 'User Screen Field'
FCUI	Software Component's Feature Point Count for 'User Screen Input Link'
FCUM	Software Component's Feature Point Count for 'User Screen Missing'
FCUO	Software Component's Feature Point Count for 'User Screen Output Link'
FCUS	Software Component's Feature Point Count for 'User Screen'
FD	Functional Data
FDA	Software Component's Measurable Feature 'Data Attribute'
FDC	Software Component's Measurable Feature 'Data Class'
FDCP	Functional Data Component Proportion
FDCS	Functional Data Complexity and Size
FDF	Software Component's Measurable Feature 'Data Field'
FDI	Software Component's Measurable Feature 'Data Input'
FDM	Software Component's Measurable Feature 'Data Missing'
FDME	Functional Data Missing Entities
FDO	Software Component's Measurable Feature 'Data Output'
FDR	Software Component's Measurable Feature 'Data Read'
FDW	Software Component's Measurable Feature 'Data Write'
FE	Functionality Execution
FECP	Functionality Execution Component Proportion
FECS	Functionality Execution Complexity and Size
FEDM	Functionality Execution Data Manipulation Measurement
FEME	Functionality Execution Missing Entities
FEODM	Functionality Execution Operations Dynamic Measurement
FEOM	Functionality Execution Operations Measurement
FFA	Software Component's Measurable Feature 'Function Action Execution'
FFC	Software Component's Measurable Feature 'Function Computational Operation'
FFD	Software Component's Measurable Feature 'Function Decision Execution'
FFE	Software Component's Measurable Feature 'Function Error Handling'
FFL	Software Component's Measurable Feature 'Function Logical Operation'
FFM	Software Component's Measurable Feature 'Functionality Missing'
FFO	Software Component's Measurable Feature 'Function Execution Flow Control'
FFR	Software Component's Measurable Feature 'Function Repeat Execution'
FLG	Software Component's Measurable Feature 'General Operations Functional Data'
FLI	Software Component's Measurable Feature 'Input/Output Operations Functional Data'
FLM	Software Component's Measurable Feature 'Memory Operations Functional Data'
FLS	Software Component's Measurable Feature 'Message Exchange Operations Functional Data'
FMF	Software Component's Measurable Feature 'Message Field'
FMM	Software Component's Measurable Feature 'Message Missing'
FMR	Software Component's Measurable Feature 'Message Receive'
FMS	Software Component's Measurable Feature 'Message Send'
FNM	Software Component's Measurable Feature 'Notifying Message'
FP	Function Point[4]

FPCM	Software Component's Feature Point for 'Class Method'
FPDA	Software Component's Feature Point for 'Data Attribute'
FPDC	Software Component's Feature Point for 'Data Class'
FPDF	Software Component's Feature Point for 'Data Field'
FPDI	Software Component's Feature Point for 'Data Input'
FPDM	Software Component's Feature Point for 'Data Missing'
FPDO	Software Component's Feature Point for 'Data Output'
FPDR	Software Component's Feature Point for 'Data Read'
FPDW	Software Component's Feature Point for 'Data Write'
FPFA	Software Component's Feature Point for 'Function Action Execution'
FPFC	Software Component's Feature Point for 'Function Computational Operation'
FPFD	Software Component's Feature Point for 'Function Decision Execution'
FPFE	Software Component's Feature Point for 'Function Error Handling'
FPFL	Software Component's Feature Point for 'Function Logical Operation'
FPFM	Software Component's Feature Point for 'Functionality Missing'
FPFO	Software Component's Feature Point for 'Function Execution Flow Control'
FPFR	Software Component's Feature Point for 'Function Repeat Execution'
FPLG	Software Component's Feature Point for 'General Operations Functional Data'
FPLI	Software Component's Feature Point for 'Input/Output Operations Functional Data'
FPLM	Software Component's Feature Point for 'Memory Operations Functional Data'
FPLS	Software Component's Feature Point for 'Message Exchange Operations Functional Data'
FPMF	Software Component's Feature Point for 'Message Field'
FPMM	Software Component's Feature Point for 'Message Missing'
FPMR	Software Component's Feature Point for 'Message Receive'
FPMS	Software Component's Feature Point for 'Message Send'
FPNM	Software Component's Feature Point for 'Notifying Message'
FPUF	Software Component's Feature Point for 'User Screen Field'
FPUI	Software Component's Feature Point for 'User Screen Input Link'
FPUM	Software Component's Feature Point for 'User Screen Missing'
FPUO	Software Component's Feature Point for 'User Screen Output Link'
FPUS	Software Component's Feature Point for 'User Screen'
FRS	Functional Requirements Specifications
FS	Functional Size[1]
FSM	Functional Size Measurement[1]
FSSM	Functional Software Size Measurement Methodology with Effort Estimation and Performance Indication
FSU	Functional Size Unit
FUF	Software Component's Measurable Feature 'User Screen Field'
FUI	Software Component's Measurable Feature 'User Screen Input Link'
FUM	Software Component's Measurable Feature 'User Screen Missing'
FUO	Software Component's Measurable Feature 'User Screen Output Link'
FUR	Functional User Requirements[1]
FUS	Software Component's Measurable Feature 'User Screen'

GODL	General Operations Execution Functional Data Level
GODP	General Operations Functional Data Proportion
GOFE	General Operations Functional Data Entities
GPS	Global Positioning System
ICT	Information and Communications Technology
IE	Instituto de Empresa
IEC	International Electrotechnical Commission
IFPUG	International Function Point Users Group[4]
ILF	Internal Logical File[4]
IODP	Input/Output Operations Functional Data Proportion
IOFE	Input/Output Operations Functional Data Entities
IOO	Input/Output Operations
ISO	International Organization for Standardization
KSI	Key Software Indicator
LDM	Logical Data Model
LO	Logical Operations
LOCP	Logical Operation Content Proportion
LOL	Logical Operations Level
ME	Message Exchange
MECP	Message Exchange Component Proportion
MECS	Message Exchange Complexity and Size
MEME	Message Exchange Missing Entities
MEO	Message Exchange Operations
MFE	Message Field Entities
MO	Memory Operations
MODP	Memory Operations Functional Data Proportion
MOFE	Memory Operations Functional Data Entities
MTDL	Memory Traffic Functional Data Level
MTL	Memory Traffic Level
MTP	Memory Transaction Proportion
N/L/M/H/VH	Nil/Low/Medium/High/Very High
NESMA	Netherlands Software Metrics Users Association[7]
NME	Notifying Message Entities
QR	Quality Requirements
QRS	Quality Requirements Specifications
RDG	Requirements Deficiency Grade
RECP	Repeat Execution Content Proportion
REL	Repeat Execution Level
REO	Repeat Execution Operations

SADCE	Software Analysis, Design, and Coding Effort
SCCM	Software Comprehensive Count Method
SCCQI	Software Comprehensive Count with Quality Indicators
SCDS	Software Code Statements
SCE	Software Code Effort
SCFP	Software Component's Feature Point
SCFPC	Software Component's Feature Point Count
SCM	Software Component's Measurement
SCFM	Software Component's Feature Measurement
SCMF	Software Component's Measurable Feature
SCS	Software Comment Statements
SDADE	Software Data Analysis and Design Effort
SDS	Software Data Statements
SFADE	Software Functional Analysis and Design Effort
SLS	Software Logical Size
SMC	Software's Measurable Component
SMEF	Software Measurement European Forum[6]
SOA	Service-Oriented Architecture
SOI	Software Operational Indicator[5–7]
SPQI	Software Performance Quality Indicator
SSEE	Software Size and Effort Estimation
SSI	Software Structural Indicator[5–7]
STCM	Software Total Components Measurement
STDE	Software Total Development Effort
STE	Software Testing Effort
TDS	Technical Design Specifications
TR	Technical Requirements
UI	User Interface
UICP	User Interface Component Proportion
UICS	User Interface Complexity and Size
UIDL	User Interaction Functional Data Level
UIFE	User Interface Field Entities
UIIE	User Interface Input Link Entities
UIL	User Interaction Level
UIME	User Interface Missing Entities
UIOE	User Interface Output Link Entities
UIP	User Interaction Proportion
UISE	User Interface Screen Entities
UKSMA	United Kingdom Software Metrics Association[5]
URL	Uniform Resource Locator

About the Companion Websites

This book is accompanied by a companion website hosted by Wiley:

http://booksupport.wiley.com

The website includes:

- FSSM 1.0 Calculations Template for Results Tables and Graphs, containing the Calculations, and Results Tables/Graphs for the Mini FSSM Example.

There is also an official FSSM website hosted by the author:

www.fssm.software

It provides additional interesting and relevant information related to the methodology presented in this book.

Part One

FSSM: Introduction

Chapter 1

Introduction to Functional Software Size Measurement

1.1 INTRODUCTION

For software projects, it is very important to determine the size of the software for development effort estimation, project planning, and cost/productivity analysis.

How much effort will be spent on the software development – analysis, design, coding, testing, and documentation – for a particular application depends on the size of the software to be developed.

The size of the software to be developed depends on the functionality required by the application, and the effort is spent to develop all the required functionality.

The functionality required by the application is described in the Functional User Requirements (FUR)[1] which are the specifications of the required functionality and hence are also known as the Functional Requirements Specifications (FRS). These terms – FUR (Functional User Requirements)[1] and FRS (Functional Requirements Specifications) – denote the same thing, that is, the specifications of the user functionality required by the application.

1.2 FUNCTIONAL SIZE MEASUREMENT AND EFFORT ESTIMATION

Functional Size Measurement (FSM)[1] is an effective method for measuring the size of the software because it is meant to measure the functionality which is described in the FRS and on which the effort is spent for analysis, design, coding, testing, documentation, and maintenance.

All the functionality of the application is distributed in different constituent components of the software. These components are defined as Base Functional Components (BFCs)[1] in the ISO/IEC 14143-1[1] standards. Measurement of the size of software is achieved by measuring the size of the BFCs[1] and computing the total size based on the sizes of the BFCs[1].

The constituent components, that is, the BFCs[1], of the software comprise sub-types of the BFCs[1], defined as the Base Functional Component Types (BFC Types)[1] in the

Functional Software Size Measurement Methodology with Effort Estimation and Performance Indication, First Edition. Jasveer Singh.

Companion website: http://booksupport.wiley.com

ISO/IEC 14143-1[1] standards. Measurement of the size of the BFCs[1] is achieved by measuring the size of the BFC Types[1] and computing the size of the BFCs[1] from the sizes of the BFC Types[1].

After deciding the boundaries which define the limits of the software measurement to a particular area of functionality specified in the FUR[1], the functional size of the BFC Types[1] is calculated by assigning the Units of Functional Size[2] to the BFC Types[1]. The functional size unit is defined in the methodologies mostly as Function Point[4]. Function Points[4] are thus assigned to various BFC Types[1] and are summed up for the entire functionality within the defined boundaries to produce the total software size of the corresponding BFCs[1], and then the sum of the Function Points[4] of the BFCs[1] produces the total software size.

Because of some substantial limitations (details of which are described in this and later chapters), in some of the popular and widely used software size measurement methodologies available, various multiplication factors which are different according to the type/field and functional contents of applications are used subsequently in order to estimate the effort required for development. The use of multiplication factors is required because a very limited part of all the measurable BFC Types[1] of a part of all the measurable BFCs[1] is measured, and from that small partial measurement, an attempt is made to estimate the effort of development for the whole software based on the assumption that the multiplication factors will take care of the unmeasured part and will thus produce the correct effort estimation. This approach may give erroneous results as clarified in further description. The FSSM is specially designed to overcome such limitations.

1.3 IMPORTANT CONSIDERATIONS FOR THE SOFTWARE SIZE MEASUREMENT AND EFFORT ESTIMATION

Care should be taken while selecting a methodology to use for the Functional Size Measurement[1]. The methodology should be such that it measures all the major, relevant functionality on which the effort is required to be spent on development; otherwise – in case of measurement of only a small part of the software functionality – the significance of measurement is lost. The methodology should be simple and easy to use as well. Hence, there is a need of an integral software size measurement methodology which is presented in this book.

The following are some important facts that should be considered regarding the Functional Size Measurement[1], and methodologies to measure the functional size:

1. Software is composed of several distinct components which are inter-related but do not have any obligatory fixed size proportion relationship with respect to one another in any software application. That means, if there are four components: c1, c2, c3 and c4, their size may have any proportion according to the functional requirements concerning these components in different applications. So the magnitude of c1 may be much greater (measured by any method, e.g., counts, units) than c2 in one software application but it may be the opposite in another application. Similarly, the size proportion of c1 to other components in one application may be entirely different than in another application.
2. Each component has several features. For example, component c1 may have two features: c1f1, c1f2; component c2 may have three features: c2f1, c2f2, c2f3; component c3 may have four features: c3f1, c3f2, c3f3, c3f4; and component c4 may

have one feature: c4f1. The size of different features varies according to the application. For most of the features, there is no fixed size relationship of different features of a component amongst themselves and with the features of other components. For example, in one application, the size of one feature c1f1 may be about 10 times bigger (measured by any method, e.g., counts, units) than the size of c2f3, but in another application, it may be of approximately the same size or even of opposite proportion.

3. If an application is made of several sub-programs or modules, the sub-programs have different proportions of different features of the components and may not have any similar size proportionate relationship with respect to one another or with respect to the whole software.
4. Size and complexity of a software component are interrelated.

   What is meant by the complexity of the software components here is the level and degree of effort and time required for understanding, analyzing, designing, coding, testing, and maintaining the components.

   The more the effort and time are required for these activities, the more complex the component is. For example, regarding data component, 1 table with 10 columns in a database application, or 1 data record with 10 fields in a program is quite simple, but 20 tables with 15–20 columns each, or 20 data records with 15–20 fields each, respectively, are more complex, and 80 tables with 20 columns each, or 80 data records with 20 fields each, respectively, are highly complex as far as the effort and time required for their understanding, analyzing, designing, coding, testing, and maintaining are concerned. The same is true for other components – functionality execution, user interfaces, and message communication.

   As a general rule, the bigger the size of the component, the more the effort and time required to understand, analyze, design, code, test, and maintain it; and the more the effort and time required to understand, analyze, design, test, and maintain it, the more complex the component is.
5. Effort for software life cycle activities – development (analysis, design, coding, and testing), maintenance, documentation, etc. – is spent on all the features of all the components. Of course, not all the minute details of all the functionality can be taken into account for measurement, but it is important that the most relevant, major components and all their important features should be considered for size determination, effort estimation, and performance indication. If an accurate estimation of the total software size is needed for correct project planning, the size of all the measurable features for all the components should be computed. Hence, no major and relevant component and at the same time, no major and relevant feature should be ignored for measurement and estimation.
6. If we consider various application programs in different domains and see the magnitude of the presence of different features of the constituent components, it will vary from one application to the other. Not only that, the magnitude will vary in different sub-programs or modules of these applications programs with respect to one another.

   The relationship of size between the components and their features depends on only the functionality required and it varies from one application to the other, and from one sub-program (module) to the other of any particular application.

   For example, in the signaling part of the application of telecom call handling (call handling would normally consist of signaling, call control, number analysis, routing, charging, subscriber data, etc.), there will be much more amount of input/output operations from the input/output devices and much more message communication to/from other modules than the disk memory read/write operations. On the other hand, subscriber data will have more disk memory read operations to access the subscriber data, and message communication to/from call control module than computational/logical and decision operations. Routing may have more proportion of decision operations to decide about the routing.

In the radar application which will normally consist of input/output for image data, image extraction, filtering, etc., there will be high amount of input/output operations, high amount of computational operations, and medium amount of disk memory read/write operations in the complete application.

In a data warehouse report preparation application, there will be high amount of disk memory read/write operations and high amount of computational operations.

Table 1 shows the approximate magnitude (size) of some software constituents – components, features, and operations – and their size and complexity in terms of very low, low, medium, high, and very high depending on the number of functional operations or number of functional data elements being almost none, very few, a few, many, and too many, respectively, for the sub-programs of two applications: Telecom Call Handling and Radar. In this table, the sub-programs (or modules) of these applications are considered separately and individually, and their interactions with the other sub-programs (or modules) of the same application program are considered. The table contents are a rough estimate based on practical experience and assessment, and not based on any measurements.

Table 2 shows the approximate magnitude (size) of different components and features of components in different applications. In this table, the whole applications are considered and not separate sub-programs (modules) of the applications individually. For example, for the application Telecom Call Handling, all the sub-programs (modules) for signaling, call control, number analysis, routing, and charging are considered together as a whole application. Similarly, for radar application, all the sub-programs (modules) for input data, image extraction, filtering, and output display are considered together as a whole application. Only one instance of the program execution is considered and not the execution and operations for multi-users with multi-instances of the program running simultaneously. The table contents are a rough estimate based on practical experience and assessment, and not based on any measurements.

The purpose of Tables 1 and 2 is just to show how various applications differ in the size of the components and in the size of the features of the components.

7. If only a few features of one component or of a few components are measured (by any method, e.g., counts, units) and based on that the complete software size is calculated by using various multiplication factors, it may give unreliable results because there is no fixed proportional relationship of the size of one feature to the other feature(s) of the same component or of the other components for the majority of features as explained before. For example,

Example 1 In one application, there may be 50 data tables for which there may be one memory data read and write operation each from/to disk for each table, so the count for memory data read/write operations will be 100. In another application, there may be 2 data tables of which there may be 25 memory data read and write operations each from/to disk for each table, so the count for memory data

Table 1 Software Constituents' Approximate Relative Magnitude (Size) in Different Applications Sub-programs

Approximate Relative Magnitude (Size) of Some Software Constituents in the Sub-programs of Two Different Applications								
Sl. No.	**Software Application Sub-program**	**Memory Read/Write Operations**	**User Interface Input/ Output Operations**	**Message Communication with Internal Modules, External Application Programs**	**Functionality Execution: Computa-tional Operations**	**Functionality Execution: Logical Operations**	**Functionality Execution: Actions, Decisions, Repeat Operations, Execution Flow Control Operations**	**Functional Data Size and Complexity: Diversity, Variety and Width (Number of Classes, Their Attributes and Fields)**
1.	Telecom Call Handling: Signaling	Very low	High	High	Very low	Low	High	Medium
2.	Telecom Call Handling: Subscriber Data	High	Very low	Medium	Very low	Medium	High	High
3.	Telecom Call Handling: Routing	High	Very low	Medium	Medium	High	High	High
4.	Radar: Input Data	Low	High	High	Low	Low	Low	Medium
5.	Radar: Image Extraction	Low	Low	High	High	High	High	Medium
6.	Radar: Filtering	Low	Low	High	High	High	High	Medium
7.	Radar: Output Image	Medium	High	High	Low	Low	Low	Medium

Table 2 Software Constituents' Approximate Relative Magnitude (Size) in Different Applications

Approximate Relative Magnitude (Size) of Some Software Constituents in a Few Applications						
Sl. No.	**Software Application**	**Memory Read/Write Operations**	**User Interface Input/Output Operations**	**Message Communication with Internal Modules, External Application Programs**	**Functionality Execution: Actions, Decisions/ Repeat/Execution Flow Control Operations, Computational/Logical Operations**	**Functional Data Size and Complexity: Diversity, Variety and Width (Number of Classes, Their Attributes and Fields)**
1.	Telecom Call Handling	Low	Medium	Medium	High	High
2.	Telecom Billing	High	Low	Low	High	High
3.	Video Games	Low	High	Low	High	Medium
4.	ERP – Inventory, Sales, Marketing, HR Management	High	High	High	High	Very high
5.	Radar – Image Extraction, Filtering, Input, Output	Low	High	Medium	High	High
6.	Online Shopping	High	High	Medium	Low	High
7.	Data Warehousing	High	Medium	Medium	High	Very high
8.	Text Processing	High	High	Low	Low	Low
9.	Computer Numerical Control (CNC) Machine	High	High	Low	High	Medium

read/write operations will be 100. In both the applications, the number of memory data read/write operations is the same but the data complexity and effort required from the point of view of development is much more in the former application. If we do the measurement of only memory data read and write operation, we would not know how big and complex the data part is, and whether database expertise is required for the development.

Example 2 In an application, there may be 2 user screens, one for input data and the other for output data, being used for input/output data 50 times each, so there will be 100 input/output operations. In another application, there may be 50 user screens for input data being used for 1 input operation each and 50 user screens for output data being used for 1 output operation each, so the total number of input/output operations will be 100. In both the applications, the number of input/output operations is the same but the user interface design in the latter application is more effort-consuming than the former. Only the size of input/output operations does not give a right indication about the input/output interface size and complexity, and thus the effort required for designing the screens, that is, screen structures, cannot be estimated based on the size of the input/output operations.

Moreover, in the aforementioned examples, the size of memory data read/write and input/output operations, respectively, does not indicate the magnitude of other operations in the program, for example, computational, logical, decision, repeat, execution flow control, and message exchange operations, and thus the effort required for these operations cannot be estimated.

8. The existing methodologies of software size measurements measure only a few features of a few components and try to estimate the total software size with the help of some multipliers based on type/field of applications and past experience with similar projects. Effort estimation done in this manner may be inaccurate in most of the cases.
9. Different skills and expertise may be needed for different activities of the software life cycle; for example, for an application which uses huge amount of data deploying databases, database skills would be required. Hence, it is necessary/desirable to know the size and complexity of different components of the software which can help in project planning activities from the point of view of human expertise and skills required.
10. Real effort depends on many factors such as expertise, experience, knowledge, productivity, and efficiency of the project team members but the average effort which has, more or less, approximate fixed proportionate relationships with the type of components to be developed, tested, and maintained can be calculated taking into consideration the average productivity, efficiency, and knowledge.
11. Static and dynamic (run-time) characteristics of any software application may be different. For example, in a program, there may be one disk memory read operation which is in a loop of one thousand times. While counting the Function Points[4] for the memory read operation, it will be counted as one Function Point[4] which is correct from the point of view of software development because it will lead to the effort for writing the statement(s) for one such operation, but at run-time, it will create high disk memory read traffic. If it is desired to assess the run-time characteristics based

on the Function Points[4], careful selection of the right kind of parameters (Function Points[4]) will be required.

12. Real run-time performance characteristics can best be obtained by capturing data at real run-time and analyzing that to find out what type of operations are being performed because the analysis based on static structure of data may not indicate the true performance due to the presence of decision operations. For example, if in a program there is one decision statement which leads to many:
    a. memory data write operations if it is evaluated true;
    b. data output operations for data display if it is evaluated false;

    and if, at the execution time, the possibility of its being true is about 75%, the result will be high memory write traffic in about 75% of the cases and high output traffic for data display in the other 25% of the cases whenever the program is run. Based on the static structure analysis only, we will assess the program to have high memory as well as high output traffic which is also correct from the point of view of design because care will have to be taken to provide suitable design for both high memory traffic as well as high output traffic since both the situations can occur.

1.4 INTRODUCTION TO THE FUNCTIONAL SOFTWARE SIZE MEASUREMENT METHODOLOGY WITH EFFORT ESTIMATION AND PERFORMANCE INDICATION (FSSM)

The methodology presented in this book – Functional Software Size Measurement Methodology with Effort Estimation and Performance Indication (FSSM) – is based on the principles of Functional Size Measurement (FSM)[1] and is fully compliant with the ISO/IEC 14143-1[1] standards. It also takes into account all the important considerations concerning size measurement and effort estimation mentioned earlier in Section 1.3.

In this methodology, the size of the software is measured based on the Functional Requirements Specifications which contain mainly the:

a. description of the functionality, error handling, messages, and user interfaces;
b. logical data model providing high-level information about the data.

Among the available software size measurement methodologies at present, some of them give an estimation of the software size by counting the Function Points[4] and are extensively used but they use very limited software measurability features (only a small percentage of the complete features) for measurement. For example, some currently available methodologies take into account only some of the following types of operations for the data movements:

a. memory read/write operations used for reading/writing the data from/to the data storage devices;
b. input/output operations used for receiving/sending the input/output data from/to the input/output devices;
c. messages to external application programs;

and data fields.

In other methodologies, other counts such as the count of business rules are used but in no methodology, all the following aspects which are the main constituents of

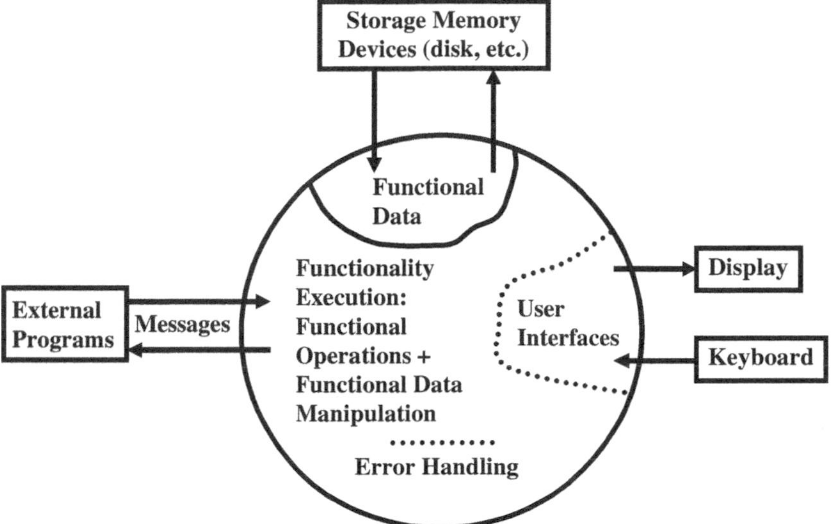

Figure 1 Software size determination model. Adapted from Software Comprehensive Count with Quality Indicators (SCCQI), Jasveer Singh, UKSMA/COSMIC Conference 2012[5], SMEF 2012[6], NESMA Autumn Meeting 2012[7].

software, as shown in Figure 1, are considered and taken into account for the software size measurement[5–7]:

a. size and complexity of the functional data;
b. size, type, and complexity of all the functionality;
c. magnitude of the functional data handling in all the functionality;
d. error handling;
e. number, size, and complexity of the user interfaces;
f. quantity, size, and complexity of the messages for communication with the external application programs and/or sub-programs of the same application program.

All these aspects – the main constituents of software – are considered and taken into account for the software size measurement in the FSSM.

In most of the existing methodologies, a number of constants with complicated assumptions based on the area of the software application are used as multiplication factors, which makes the software size measurement and effort estimation dependent on assumptions. Project planning done based on such estimations may not result in correct time schedules in many cases. In the FSSM, no such multiplication factors are required.

Because of the approach in the existing methodologies that neither all the major components of the software nor all the measureable features of the components are considered for measurement, it cannot be possible to assess the complete size of the software reliably by using them. In the FSSM, these limitations are not there.

It is clear that all the functionality of the application is distributed in different constituent components of the software, these components are called the Software's Measurable Components (SMCs) in the FSSM and are defined as Base Functional Components (BFCs)[1] in the ISO/IEC 14143-1[1] standards. The terms BFC (Base Functional Component)[1] and SMC (Software's Measurable Component) denote the same thing, that is, the constituent components of the software, and they are used interchangeably in this book henceforth. Measurement of the size of software is achieved by measuring the size of the SMCs (i.e., BFCs)[1] and computing the total size.

The constituent components, that is, the BFCs[1], of the software comprise sub-types of the BFCs[1], defined as the BFC Type[1] in the ISO/IEC 14143-1[1] standards. The BFC Types[1] are, in fact, the features of the SMCs. These features of the SMCs are different for each of the SMC, and are denoted as Software Component's Measurable Features (SCMFs) in the FSSM, that is, the BFC Types[1]. Thus, each Software's Measurable Component (SMC), that is, the BFC[1], has several Software Component's Measurable Features (SCMFs), that is, the BFC Types[1]. The terms BFC Type (Base Functional Component Type)[1] and SCMF (Software Component's Measurable Feature) denote the same thing, that is, different features of the constituent components of the software, and they are used interchangeably in this book henceforth. Measurement of the size of the SMCs (i.e., the BFCs[1]) is achieved by measuring the size of the SCMFs (i.e., the BFC Types[1]), and then computing the size of the SMCs based on the size of the SCMFs. The complete size of the software is calculated based on the size of the SMCs.

The functional size of the SCMFs (BFC Types[1]) is calculated by assigning the Units of Functional Size[2], called Functional Size Units (FSUs) in the FSSM, to the SCMFs. The Functional Size Unit (FSU) in the FSSM is defined as the Software Component's Feature Point (SCFP). Hence, the SCFPs (Software Component's Feature Points) are assigned to various SCMFs (Software Component's Measurable Features) of different SMCs (Software's Measurable Components). All the assigned SCFPs are summed up correspondingly for each SCMF (i.e., the BFC Type[1]) of different SMCs (i.e., the BFCs[1]), and the sums are called the Software Component's Measurable Feature Point Counts (SCFPCs). The SCFPCs form the basis of the Software Component's Feature Measurements (SCFMs). The SCFMs are used for further measurement calculations, estimations, and indications, which are the Software Component's Measurements (SCMs), Software Size and Effort Estimations (SSEEs), and Software Performance Quality Indicators (SPQIs) of 2 types – Software Structural Indicators (SSIs)[5–7] and Software Operational Indicators (SOIs)[5–7] – respectively, as explained in the subsequent chapters.

1.5 CHAPTER SUMMARY

Software is composed of different components which have many features associated with them. The sizes of the components and their features are dependent on the functionality required, and they do not have any fixed proportional size relationship amongst themselves. Functional Size Measurement (FSM)[1] measures the size of the software based on the functionality.

It is highly desirable and advisable that all the relevant and major software components, that is, the BFCs[1], and their features, that is, the BFC Types[1], are taken into account properly in the FSM (Functional Size Measurement)[1] methodology in order to have a realistic measurement of the software size and, consequently, a correct estimation of the effort required for software development to be used for project planning/cost analysis purposes.

In the Functional Software Size Measurement Methodology with Effort Estimation and Performance Indication (FSSM):

a. The Software's Measurable Components (SMCs) are the constituent components of the software. They are the same as the BFCs (Base Functional Components)[1] defined in the ISO/IEC 14143-1[1] standards.

b. The Software Component's Measurable Features (SCMFs) are the different features of the SMCs and are equivalent of the BFC Types[1] defined in the ISO/IEC 14143-1[1] standards.

c. All the major and relevant Software's Measurable Components (SMCs), that is, the BFCs[1], and Software Component's Measurable Features (SCMFs), that is, the BFC Types[1], are taken into account to provide the software size measurements, effort estimations, and performance indications.

d. The Software Component's Feature Points (SCFPs) are assigned to the SCMFs in the Functional Requirements Specifications (FRS) which are the same as the Functional User Requirements (FUR)[1] defined in the ISO/IEC 14143-1[1] standards.

e. The SCFP is the Functional Size Unit (FSU), which is the Unit of Functional Size[2] according to the ISO/IEC 14143-2[2] standards.

f. Summing up the assigned SCFPs correspondingly for different SCMFs produces the Software Component's Feature Point Counts (SCFPCs).

g. SCFPCs form the basis of the Software Component's Feature Measurements (SCFMs).

h. All the Software Component's Measurements (SCMs), Software Size and Effort Estimations (SSEEs), and Software Performance Quality Indicators (SPQIs) of 2 types – Software Structural Indicators (SSIs)[5–7] and Software Operational Indicators (SOIs)[5–7] – are computed from the SCFMs.

i. Full compliance with the ISO/IEC 14143-1[1] standards exists.

EXERCISES

1.1 Which of the following in the FSSM is the equivalent of the BFC (Base Functional Component)[1] of the ISO/IEC 14143-1[1] standards?

A. SMC (Software's Measurable Component).

B. SCMF (Software Component's Measurable Feature).

C. SCFP (Software Component's Feature Point).

1.2 Which of the following in the FSSM is the equivalent of the BFC Type (Base Functional Component Type)[1] of the ISO/IEC 14143-1[1] standards?

A. SMC (Software's Measurable Component).

B. SCMF (Software Component's Measurable Feature).

C. SCFP (Software Component's Feature Point).

1.3 Which of the methods below can be considered as the best practice for software size measurement?

A. Do not use any formal software size measurement methodology and estimate the effort by experience of the experts.

B. Use a software size measurement methodology which measures only a tiny part of the software which has no fixed proportion to the other software parts, nor to the complete software, and estimate the development effort based on the partial and deficient measurement.

C. Use a software size measurement methodology which measures all the major and relevant features of all the components of the software for complete software measurement, and estimate the development effort based on that.

1.4 Which of the following is true for all the software applications?

A. The number of input/output operations is always approximately equal to the number of memory read/write operations in all the software applications.

B. The number of computational operations is always double the number of input/output operations in all the software applications.

C. There is no fixed size proportion relationship between the various types of functionality operations in the different software applications.

1.5 Which of the following relationships exist between the effort required for analyzing, designing, and coding of the functionality and the effort required for data analysis, design, and coding of the data structures (or data tables) in different software applications?

A. Both the efforts – functionality and data – are always equal in all the software applications.

B. The effort for functionality is always 3 times the effort for data in all the software applications.

C. The efforts vary from application to application depending upon the functional requirements.

Chapter 2

Synopsis of the Functional Software Size Measurement Methodology with Effort Estimation and Performance Indication (FSSM)

2.1 SALIENT CHARACTERISTICS OF THE FSSM

2.1.1 Purpose of the FSSM

The purpose of the Functional Software Size Measurement Methodology with Effort Estimation and Performance Indication (FSSM) is to measure the size of the complete software in a comprehensive manner based on the Functional Size Measurement[1] principles, and to provide the software development effort estimation and software performance quality indication of the software static structure and software dynamic (run-time) characteristics.

2.1.2 Mapping of the Usage of the FSSM in the Software Life Cycle, and Source of Input Information for the FSSM

In the software life cycle which consists mainly of the Requirements, Development (analysis, design, coding, and testing), Deployment, Operations, and Maintenance phases, all the phases are accompanied and covered by Project Management. The Requirement phase consists of preparing the Business Requirements first, and then, the Functional Requirements Specifications (FRS) based on the Business Requirements.

The software measurement can be performed by applying the FSSM as soon as the functional requirements are ready in the Requirements phase.

All the information needed for software measurement in the FSSM is identified in and is derived and collected from the Functional Requirements Specifications (FRS) which are the source of input information for the FSSM. In this regard, the FSSM is not dependent

Functional Software Size Measurement Methodology with Effort Estimation and Performance Indication, First Edition. Jasveer Singh.

Companion website: http://booksupport.wiley.com

on Technical Requirements (TR), nor Technical Design Specifications (TDS), nor Quality Requirements (QR) (also known as Quality Requirements Specifications (QRS)).

The output of the software size estimation and other outputs of the measurements can be used for project planning purpose by the Project Management.

The FSSM provides the effort estimates for the Development activities, does not cover the effort estimates for the Deployment and Maintenance activities although the measurements give sufficient information about the size of the software which can be helpful for understanding the enormity of work for the Deployment and Maintenance activities. The effort for Project Management is also not covered.

It is possible to apply the FSSM after the development work is finished, this being done for the purposes of cost/productivity analysis mainly, or for future reference of software projects.

2.1.3 Functional Domain

The FSSM is useful and can be applied for all the types of Application Software – business applications, real-time applications, etc. – developed in High-Level Languages. A few examples of the type of applications are

a. data processing applications;
b. data acquisition system applications;
c. financial applications for banking, insurance, etc.;
d. ERP applications – inventory management, sales and marketing management, human resources management, product planning, manufacturing, etc.;
e. telecom applications – call handling, billing, etc.;
f. radar system application;
g. embedded software systems applications for equipment and appliances;
h. online sale systems applications;
i. online reservations systems applications, for example, for airlines, trains, and hotels;
j. vehicle navigational systems applications;
k. meteorological systems applications.

The aforementioned list is an example list only and not exhaustive.

In general, all the software applications which have the types of characteristics described in the next sub-section are eligible to be used for applying the FSSM for Functional Size Measurement (FSM)[1].

2.1.3.1 Software Applications Characteristics for the Usage of the FSSM

In order to use the FSSM, the software applications should have the following general characteristics.

2.1.3.1.1 Functional Requirements Description Contents The functional requirements of the applications are specified in the Functional Requirements Specifications (FRS) type of document. They contain the description of the

1. Functional Data in the form of class structures describing the classes, subclasses, attributes of the classes and subclasses, fields of the attributes, and methods of the classes and subclasses;
2. Functionality Execution where the following types of operations and the data handled in the operations can be identified:
   a. functional operations of the type:
      i. memory data read/write operations used for reading/writing the data from/to the memory devices;
      ii. input/output operations used for receiving/sending the input/output data from/to the input/output devices;
      iii. message exchange operations used for sending/receiving the messages to/from the external application programs or sub-programs (modules) of the same application program;
      iv. general functional operations of the type:
         - computational;
         - logical;
         - action performance;
         - decision;
         - repeat;
         - execution flow control;
      v. error handling operations;
   b. Functional Data handled in the
      i. data read/write operations;
      ii. input/output operations;
      iii. message exchange operations;
      iv. general functional operations of the type:
         - computational;
         - logical;
         - decision;
         - repeat;
         - execution flow control;
3. User Interface (screens) in the form of screen layouts, their fields, and input/output navigational links;
4. Message Exchange in the form of message structures with their fields.

2.1.3.1.2 Functional Requirements Description Level In order to collect all the necessary information for the FSSM, the functionality requirement description in the Functional Requirements Specifications (FRS) should be as detailed as possible. The more detailed the description of the FRS, the easier it is to gather the necessary information for measurement by the FSSM. The quality and accuracy of the software size measurement by the FSSM is directly related with the description level of the functional requirements, the lower (more detailed) the level of the requirements description, the better it is for the size measurement by the FSSM. This can also be understood as the granularity level of the functional requirements description. The smaller the granularity level of the functional requirements description, the better it is for the size measurement by the FSSM. The minimum information and the way of its presentation which the FRS should contain corresponding to the information required for the Functional Size Measurement[1] by the FSSM is described in the previous sub-section and next chapters. A few examples about the functional requirements are presented at the end of this chapter.

2.1.4 Scope and Borderline Definition

The scope of the measurement of software is decided by defining the boundary[1] of the software to be measured. Normally, the boundary[1], that is, the borderline, to determine the scope of measurement should be defined where the communication from the software to be measured takes place for the following items:

1. communication with the Operating Systems functions by using the operating systems execution operations;
2. communication with the non-volatile, permanent memory storage devices, for example, disks, by using the memory data read/write operations for reading/writing from/to the memory devices;
3. communication with the input/output devices, for example, keyboard and display, by using the input/output operations for receiving/sending the input/output data from/to the input/output devices;
4. communication with the other external application programs by using the message send/receive operations for sending/receiving the messages to/from the external application programs;
5. communication with the sub-programs (modules) of the same application program by using the message send/receive operations for sending/receiving the messages to/from the sub-programs (modules) of the same application program.

All the aforementioned operations reside in the software to be measured.

2.1.5 Development Methodology and Programming Language Independence

Software Size Measurement, Effort Estimation, and Performance Indication in the FSSM are independent of the development methodology/platform and high-level programming language used for the execution of the project. The measurements, estimations, and indications are determined based on the information identified, collected, and derived about the Software Component's Measurable Features (SCMFs) of the Software's Measurable Components (SMCs) in the Functional Requirements Specifications (FRS) and are not based on the development methodology or platform, for example, Agile development methodology or any other, nor on any particular high-level language used for the development.

2.1.6 Methodology Users Background

It is advised and recommended that the user of the FSSM should have certain minimum level of background knowledge and experience in the following areas of the software domain: programming languages, requirements analysis, software architecture/structure and development (analysis, design, coding, and testing), database management systems, object-oriented technology, and software size measurement techniques.

2.1.7 ISO/IEC 14143-1 Compliance

The FSSM is fully compliant with the ISO/IEC 14143-1[1] standards. The compliance details are presented in Section 12.2.

2.1.8 Coverage

The FSSM is quite comprehensive in nature and covers all the important and relevant software components and their important and relevant features for the measurement. Thus, it measures the complete, actual functionality in reality and does not make assumptive measurements – a significant improvement over the existing software size measurement methodologies. At the same time, the software development effort estimation and software performance indication are an integral part of the FSSM.

2.1.9 Convertibility

The FSSM is fully convertible to another software measurement methodology – COSMIC[3]. This is described in detail in Section 12.1.

2.1.10 Name, Version, and Localization

The name of the methodology is "Functional Software Size Measurement Methodology with Effort Estimation and Performance Indication" for which the acronym is FSSM. The current version of the FSSM which is described in this book is 1.0. Hence, the methodology is known as FSSM 1.0. Any local customization will be known as FSSM 1.0cx where x = 1, 2, 3, etc. Hence, the local customization (if any in the future) will be denoted as FSSM 1.0c1, FSSM 1.0c2, etc.

2.1.11 Synonym Terms of the ISO/IEC 14143-1/-2 and the FSSM

Table 3 shows the terms used in the FSSM which have the same meaning and significance as the indicated terms of the ISO/IEC 14143-1/-2[1,2] standards. Hence, they are treated as synonyms.

Table 3 Synonym Terms Used in the ISO/IEC 14143-1/-2 Standards and the FSSM

ISO/IEC 14143-1/-2[1,2] Standards Terms and their Synonym FSSM Terms	
ISO/IEC 14143-1[1] and ISO/IEC 14143-2[2] Terms	**FSSM Terms**
Base Functional Component (BFC)[1]	Software's Measurable Component (SMC)
Base Functional Component Type (BFC Type)[1]	Software Component's Measurable Feature (SCMF)
Units of Functional Size[2]	Functional Size Unit (FSU)
Functional User Requirements (FUR)[1]	Functional Requirements Specifications (FRS)
Boundary[1]	Borderline

From now onwards, the FSSM terms will be used in the book mostly.

2.1.12 Effort Estimation Assumption

Effort estimations are calculated in the FSSM in person days with the assumption of normal 8 hours of work per person day.

2.1.13 Usage and Significance of Some General Terms Utilized in the FSSM

2.1.13.1 Memory Operations

All the 'memory operations' or 'memory read/write operations' or 'memory data read/write operations' or simply 'data read/write operations' mentioned hereafter mean data reading/writing from/to the non-volatile permanent type of memory storage devices such as disks.

2.1.13.2 Data Collection (DCL)

Data Collection (DCL) means a group of data that can be handled together independently for memory read/write, input/output, message exchange, or general functional – computational, logical, decision, repeat, or execution flow control – operations. This group of data may be either whole class data, or whole subclass data, or single attribute data of a class or subclass, or group of attributes data of a class or subclass.

2.1.13.3 User

As far as the users of the software are concerned, they can be human beings, an instrument, embedded software in machines/instruments/equipment, or software modules/programs. For example, in software architectures which are based on services, where the service software modules provide services to the other software modules/programs/applications, such as SOA (Service-Oriented Architecture), user can be another software module using the services of a particular software service module. So the software service module offering the services can be measured as well as the software module using its services provided they fulfil the general conditions described in Sections 2.1.3 – in particular in Section 2.1.3.1 – and 2.1.4.

2.2 DISTINGUISHING UNIQUE KEY FEATURES OF THE FSSM

The FSSM offers the following unique features which distinguish it from the current existing software measurement methodologies.

2.2.1 Comprehensive Coverage and Completeness

For correct and comprehensive measurement of the complete software, all the important, relevant Software Component's Measurable Features (SCMFs) of all the Software's Measurable Components (SMCs) are measured to obtain the correct size of the complete software. These measurements – the Software Component's Feature Measurements

(SCFMs) – form the basis of all the component measurements, software size determination, effort estimations, and performance indications. Hence, obtaining the correct size of the complete software is accomplished by measuring the complete, actual functionality in reality, and not by making the measurements for a tiny part of the functionality and making assumptions for the major non-measured part of the functionality by using some experimental multiplication factors.

Thus, comprehensive measurement of the complete software is one of the major distinguishing features of the FSSM as compared to the other existing software size measurement methodologies.

2.2.2 Effort Estimation

Comprehensive measurement of the complete software is directly linked with the real software constituent parts on which the effort is spent on the development. Based on the elaborate measurements, the effort estimation for the software development activities is calculated in a realistic and reliable manner in the FSSM. So, there is no need to search the statistical data about the past projects and find out the correct multiplier factors to apply, dependent on the type, field and complexity of the application, in order to get the estimations about the development effort. Development effort estimate is directly obtained from the effort estimation formulae which are based on the generalized real software model, hence avoiding assumption errors.

2.2.3 Performance Indication

Many useful software performance indications are provided that help in understanding the software characteristics from the point of view of the software static structure and dynamic run-time properties, and thus better project planning can be achieved.

2.2.4 Software Diagnostics

Based on the software component's features measurements, and software performance indicators, many software diagnostics can be performed to determine the weak areas and so, improvements can be planned and made. For example, the absence or degree of the error handling capability in the software; the degree of the memory traffic to/from the memory devices, the input/output flow from/to the input/output devices, or the message flow to/from the other programs can be determined with the help of the performance indicators and can be used for improving the quality of requirements, software/hardware architecture/design, and planning activities.

2.2.5 Detection of Deficiencies in the Functional Requirements Specifications (FRS)

Most of the obvious and apparent deficiencies in the descriptions of the functional requirements are determined that helps in improving the requirements and thus the quality of the software. For example, the apparent missing items in the Functional Data, missing functional operations, missing user screens/screen information, or missing messages/message information are found out.

2.2.6 Simple Mathematical Calculations

Only simple addition, multiplication, and division calculations are used in the FSSM for the measurements, effort estimations, and performance indications. No complex computations involving advanced mathematics are used. Hence, no advanced mathematics knowledge is required.

2.2.7 Significant Advantages over Other Existing Software Size Measurement Methodologies Including COSMIC and IFPUG.

There are many advantages over the other existing software size measurement methodologies including COSMIC[3] and IFPUG[4] regarding the coverage, completeness, and useful features. They are described in detail in Section 13.2.

2.3 SYNOPTIC DESCRIPTION OF THE FSSM

The Functional Software Size Measurement Methodology with Effort Estimation and Performance Indication (FSSM) is an elaborate and comprehensive methodology which takes into account all the major, important, relevant components of the software and similarly, the measurable features of the components, for the size measurement in compliance with the ISO/IEC 14143-1[1] standards.

For using it, the application software scope and boundaries for the software to be measured should be decided and defined in the beginning, and then, the methodology should be applied.

Figure 2 presents the FSSM information/procedure flow diagram. As depicted in the flow diagram, the functional requirements are contained in the Functional Requirements Specifications (FRS). The software comprises software components which are measurable and are called the Software's Measurable Components (SMCs). Each SMC has several measurable features which are called the Software Component's Measurable Features (SCMFs). The Software Component's Feature Points (SCFPs), which are the Functional Size Units (FSUs), are assigned to the features of the software components, that is, to the SCMFs, according to the defined rules in the methodology. A detailed SCFP counting procedure is applied to determine the complete size of the software by considering all the SCFPs. Summation of the corresponding SCFPs are known as the Software Component's Feature Point Counts (SCFPCs).

These SCFPCs are used to arrive at the Software Component's Feature Measurements (SCFMs).

The SCFMs (Software Component's Feature Measurements) are used to calculate the Software Component's Measurements (SCMs) indicating different aspects of the software size.

The SCFMs and SCMs are used for the following further calculations:

a. Software Size and Effort Estimations (SSEEs) about the Software Logical Size (SLS) and effort required for the development of the software;

b. Software Performance Quality Indicators (SPQIs) of the type:

  i. Software Structural Indicators (SSIs)[5–7];

  ii. Software Operational Indicators (SOIs)[5–7].

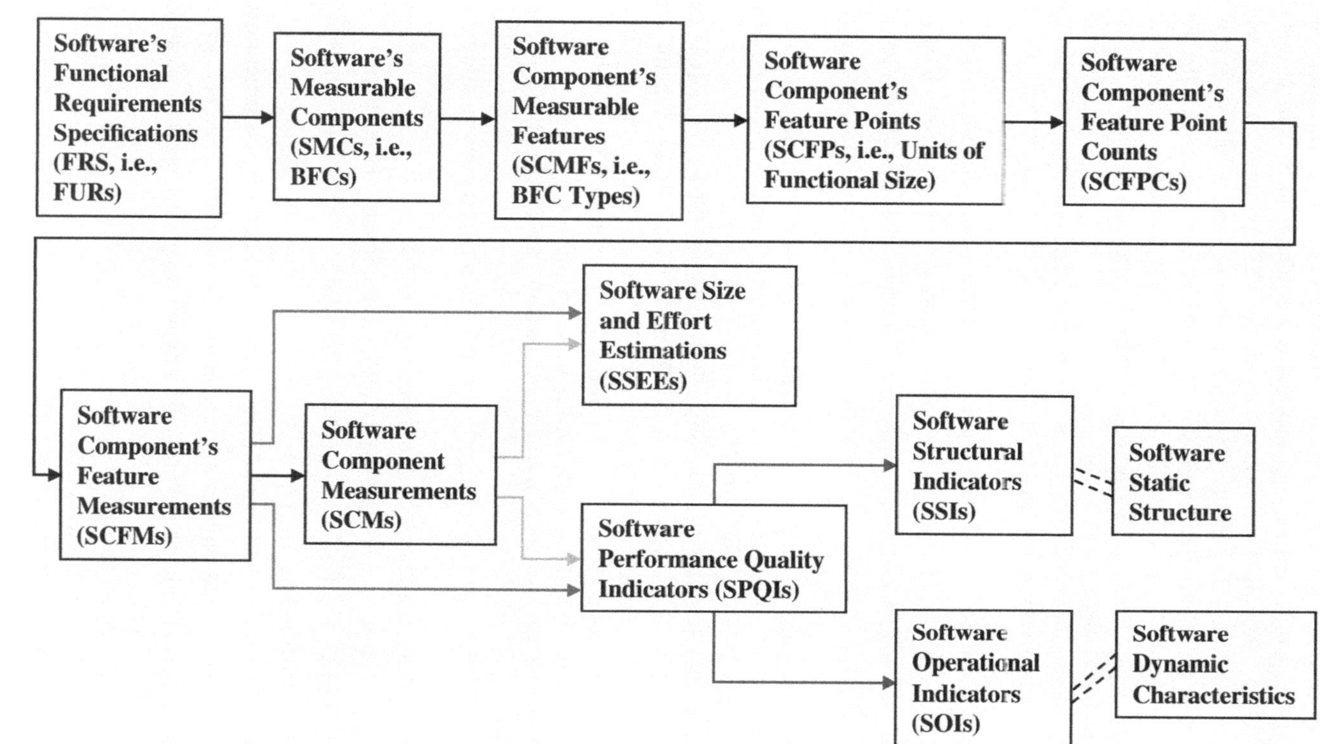

Figure 2 The FSSM information/procedure flow diagram.

Hence, in the FSSM, elaborate Software Component's Feature Measurement (SCFM), Software Component's Measurement (SCM), Software Size and Effort Estimation (SSEE) of the complete software along with major Software Performance Quality Indicators (SPQIs) are obtained. The SPQIs are divided into 2 categories: the Software Structural Indicators (SSIs)[5–7] related to the software static structure and Software Operational Indicators (SOIs)[5–7] related to the software dynamic characteristics.

The complete information about the SCFPCs and as a result about the SCFMs is collected and derived from the Functional Requirements Specifications and is not dependent on any Technical Requirements (TR), nor Technical Design Specifications (TDS), nor Quality Requirements (QR) (also known as Quality Requirements Specifications (QRS)).

Figures 3–13 present the summary of the FSSM. Figures 3–8 provide a summarized overview of the FSSM, and the description of these figures follows in this chapter. Figures 9–13 show the summarized contents of the FSSM constituents, and the description of these figures is available in the later chapters. Various types of lines (continuous/dotted/dashed) with arrows are used in these figures to make the source(s)/destination(s) of the information flow distinctly clear.

As shown in Figures 3–8, the Functional Requirements Specifications (FRS) which contain the descriptions of the

1. Functional Data (FD) in the Logical Data Model (LDM) part;
2. functionality in the Functionality Execution (FE) description part;
3. user interfaces/screens in the User Interface (UI) description part;
4. message communication in the Message Exchange (ME) description part;

are used to gather the information about 31 relevant and important measurable features known as the Software Component's Measurable Features (SCMFs) of the 4 Software's Measurable Components (SMCs).

Next, the Software Component's Feature Points (SCFPs) are assigned to the SCMFs and thus, 31 types of corresponding SCFPs are obtained. Adding together the corresponding 31 types of SCFPs, respectively, produces 31 Software Component's Feature Point Counts (SCFPCs) for the corresponding 31 Software Component's Measurable Features (SCMFs) of the 4 Software's Measurable Components (SMCs).

These SCFPCs are used to calculate the Software Component's Feature Measurements (SCFMs).

The SCFPCs and consequently the SCFMs reflect the information about the[5–7]

a. size and complexity of the Functional Data;
b. size, type, and complexity of all the Functionality Execution;
c. magnitude of the functional data handling in all the functionality;
d. error handling;
e. number, size, and complexity of the User Interface part structure elements;
f. quantity, size, and complexity of the Message Exchange part structure elements;
g. apparent deficiencies in the Functional Requirements Specifications of the
    i. data model;
    ii. functionalities;
    iii. user interfaces/screens;
    iv. messages.

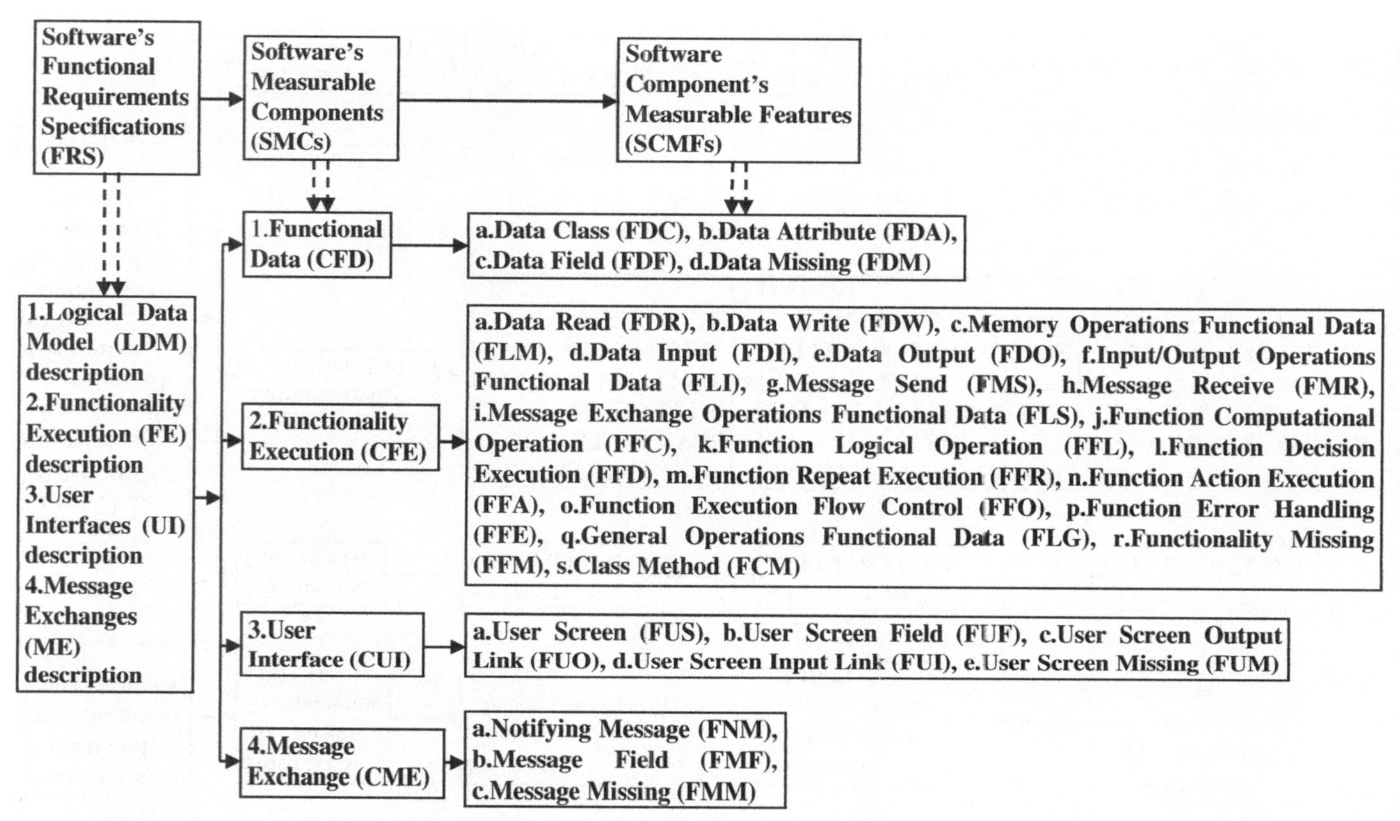

Figure 3 FSSM summary diagram (part 1/5) – general overview (1/6) FRS, SMCs, and SCMFs.

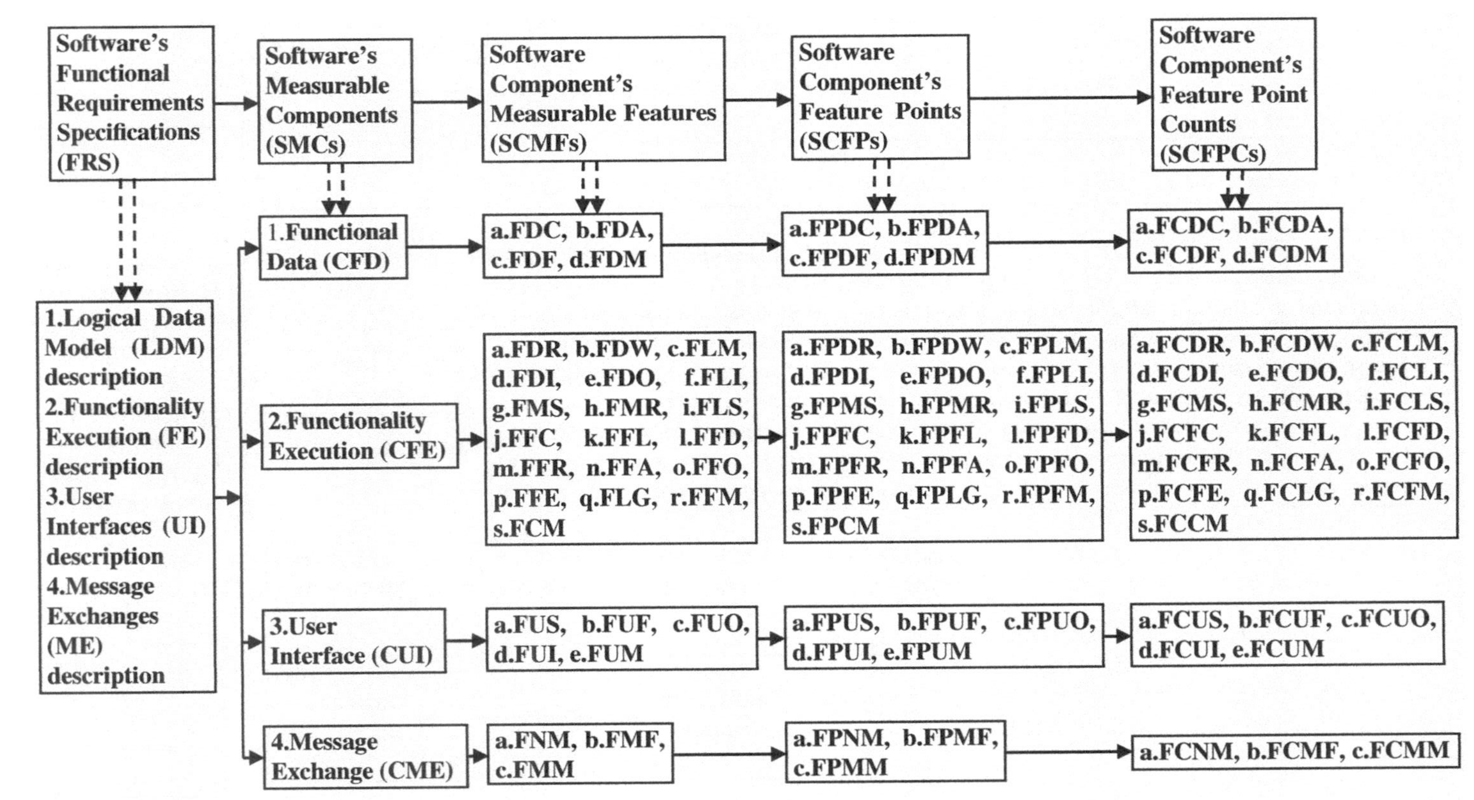

Figure 4 FSSM summary diagram (part 1/5) – general overview (2/6) FRS, SMCs, SCMFs, SCFPs, and SCFPCs.

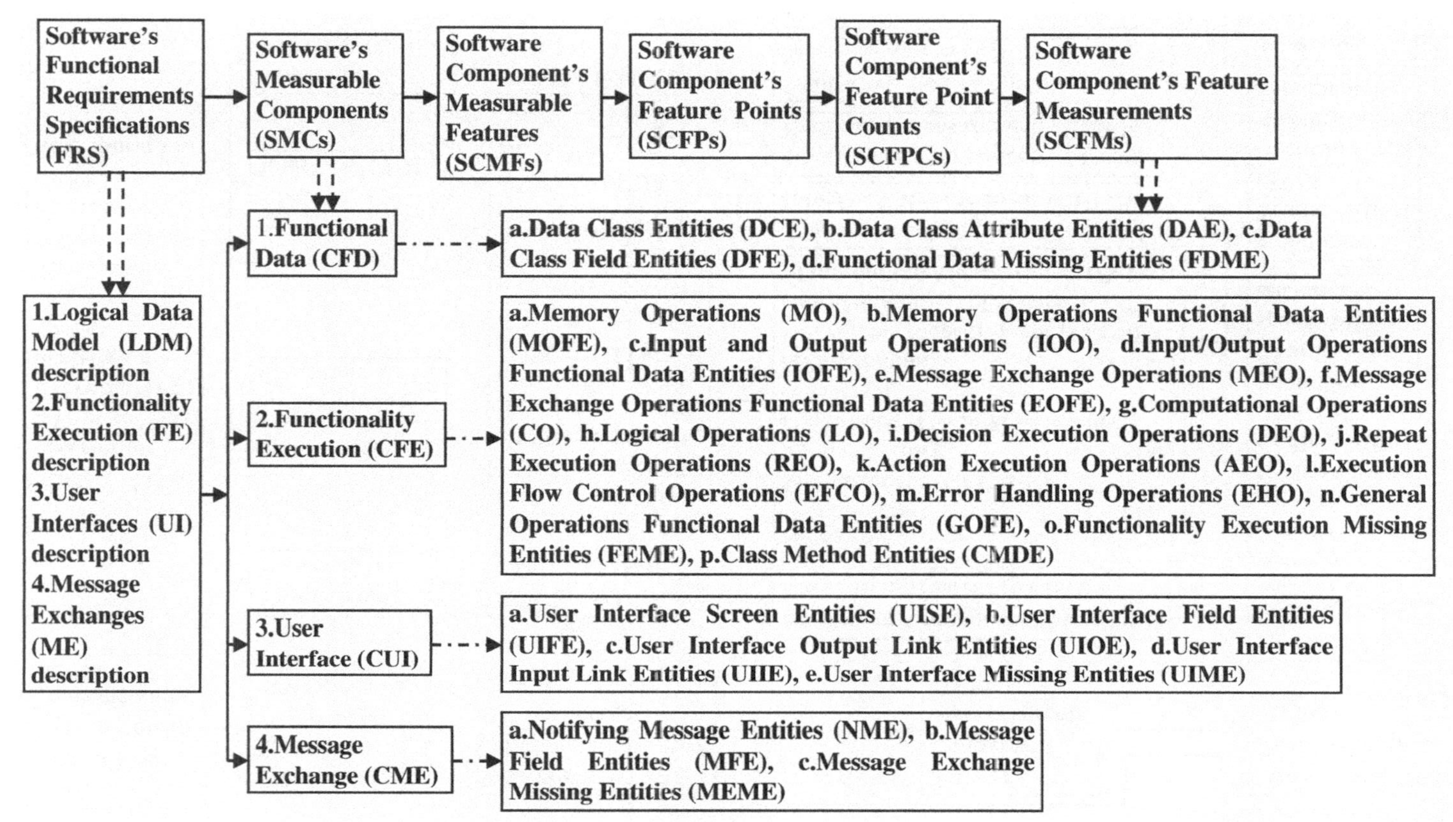

Figure 5 FSSM summary diagram (part 1/5) – general overview (3/6) FRS, SMCs, and SCFMs.

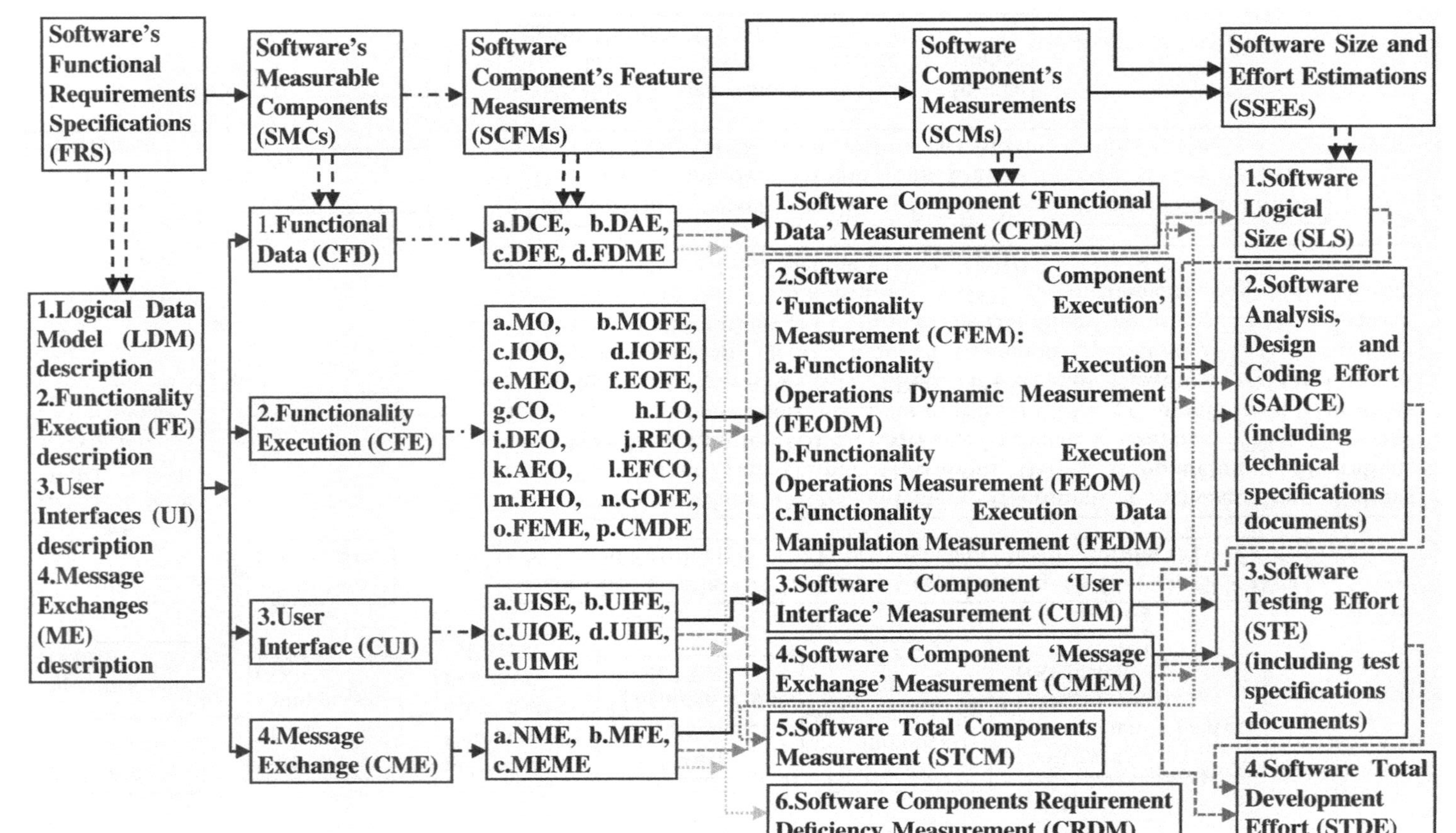

Figure 6 FSSM summary diagram (part 1/5) – general overview (4/6) FRS, SMCs, SCFMs, SCMs, and SSEEs.

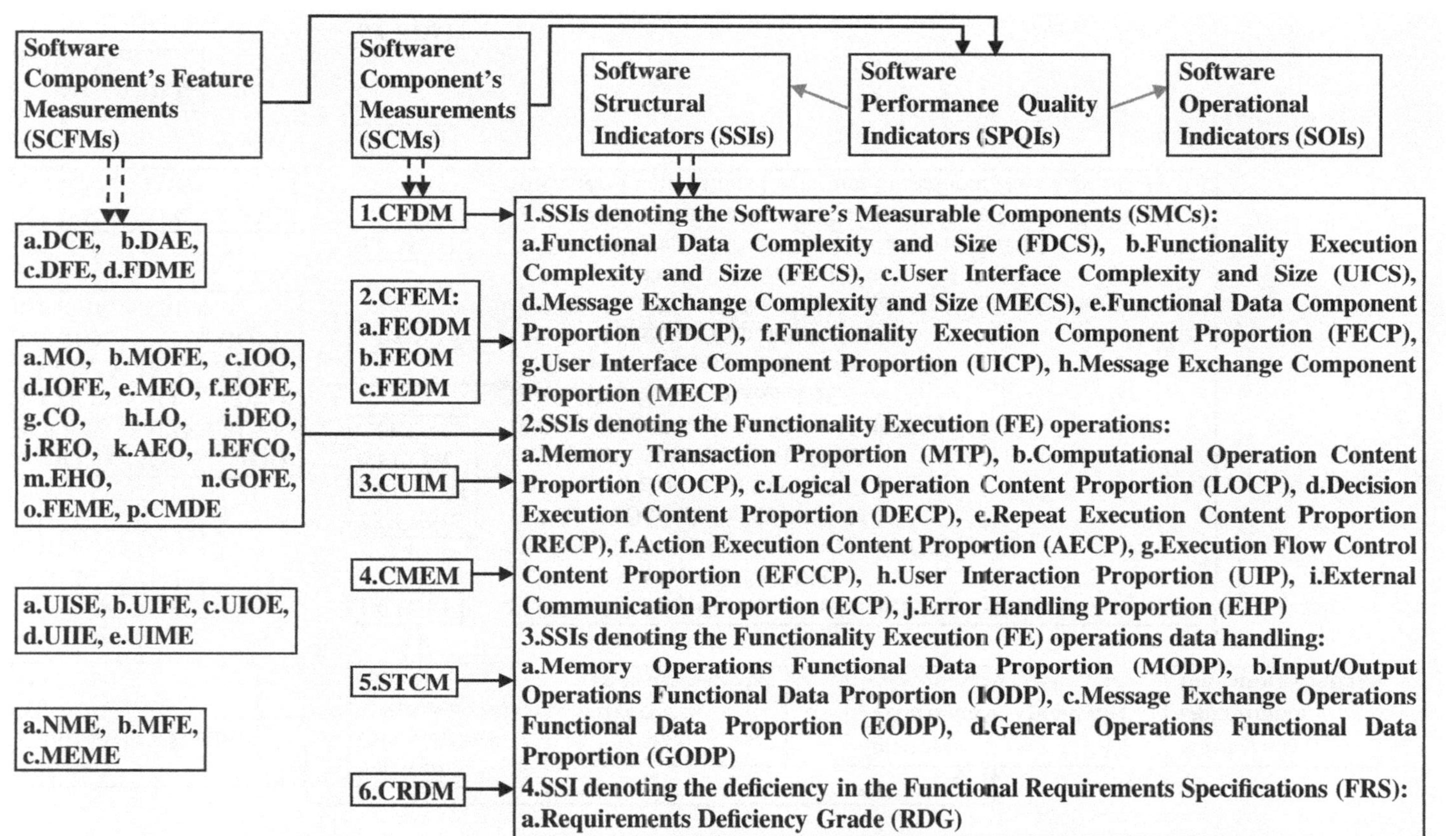

Figure 7 FSSM summary diagram (part 1/5) – general overview (5/6) SCFMs, SCMs, and SPQIs-SSIs.

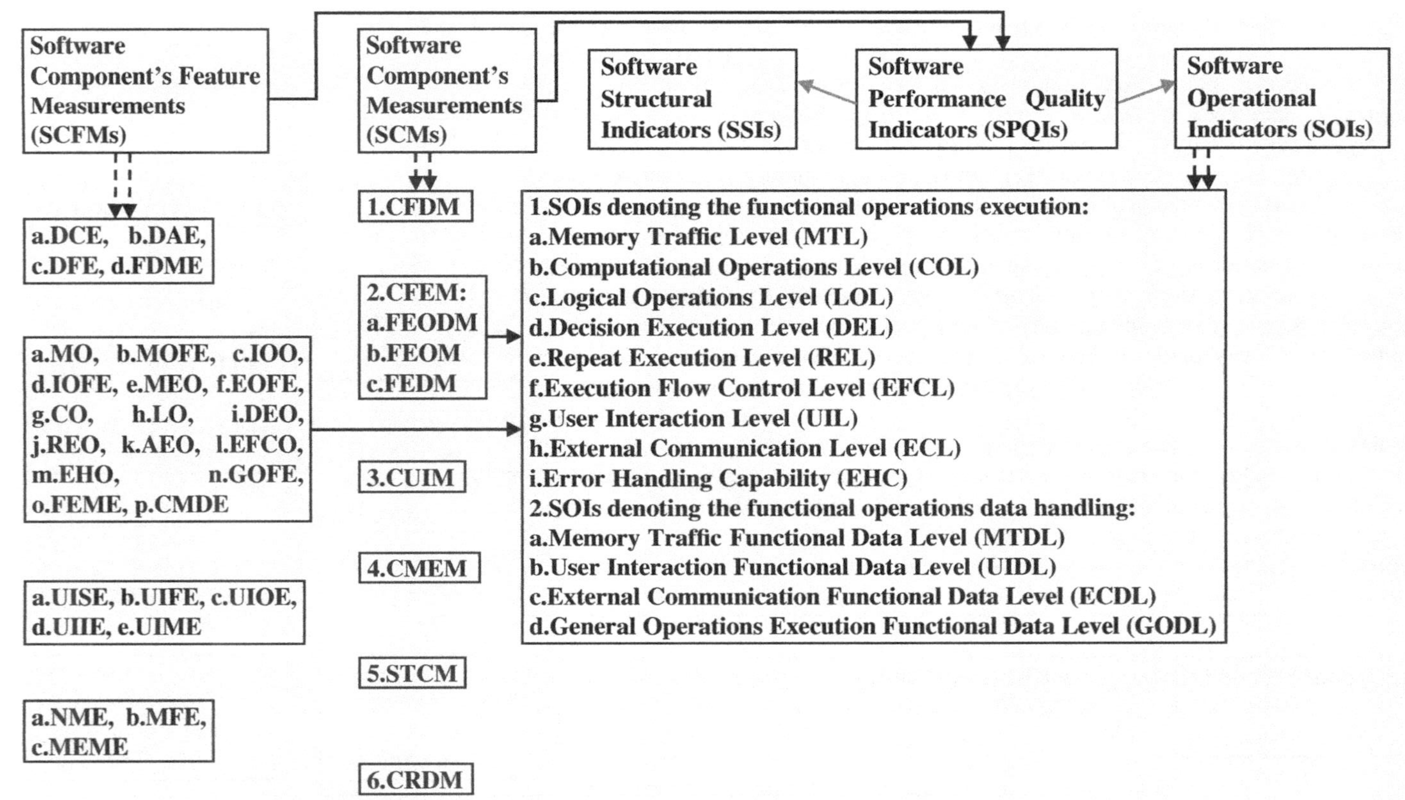

Figure 8 FSSM summary diagram (part 1/5) – general overview (6/6) SCFMs, SCMs, and SPQIs-SOIs.

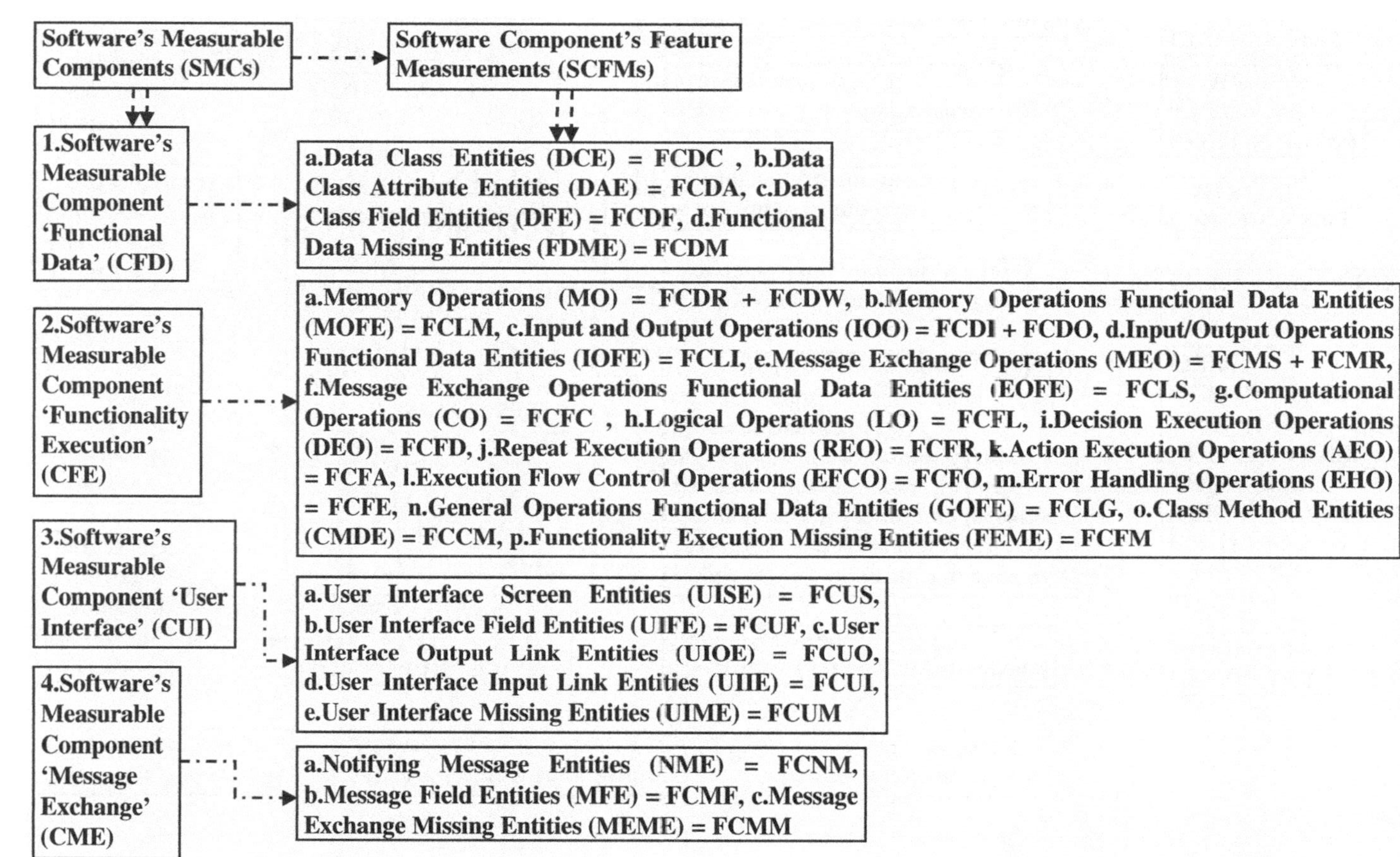

Figure 9 FSSM summary diagram (part 2/5) – SCFMs.

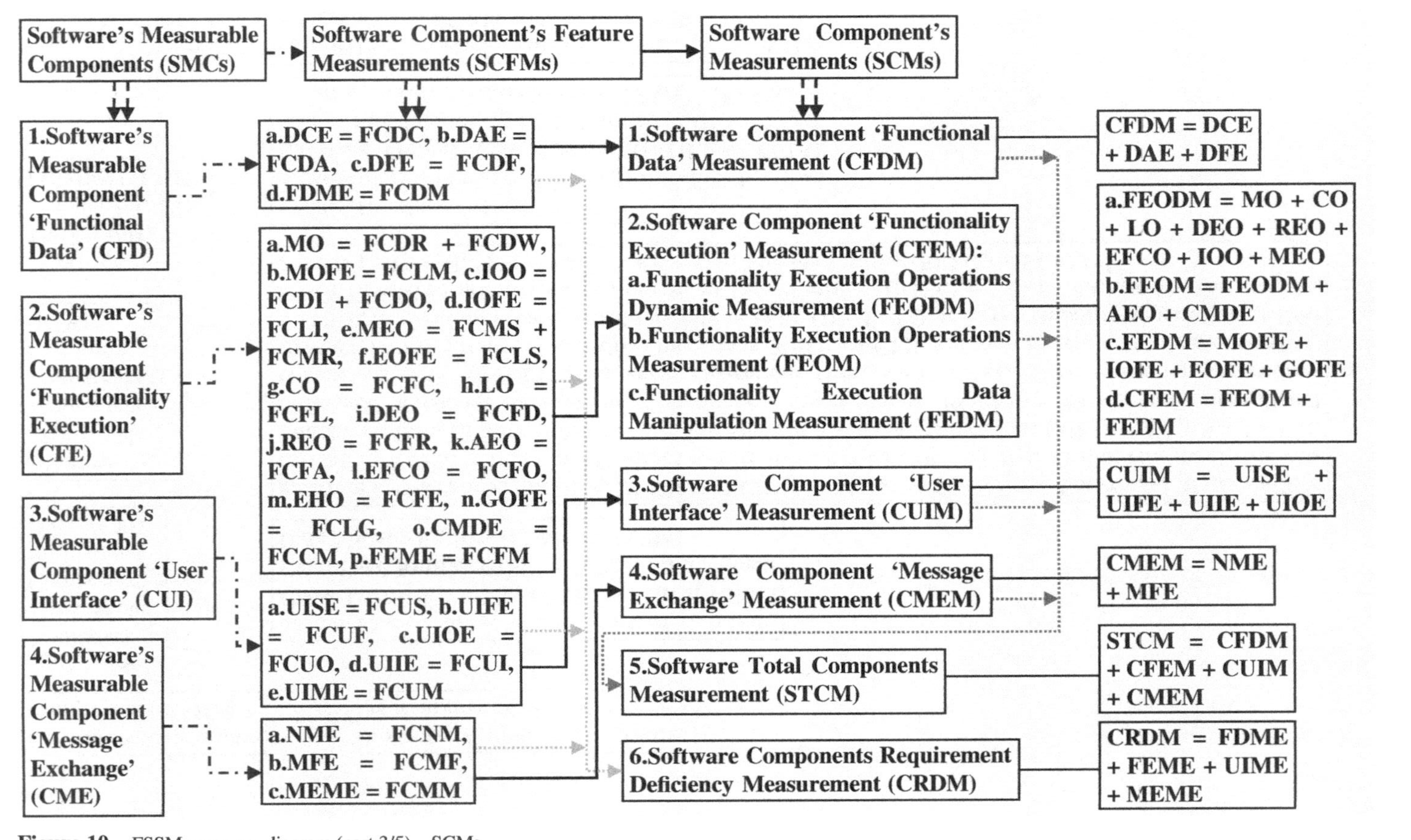

Figure 10 FSSM summary diagram (part 3/5) – SCMs.

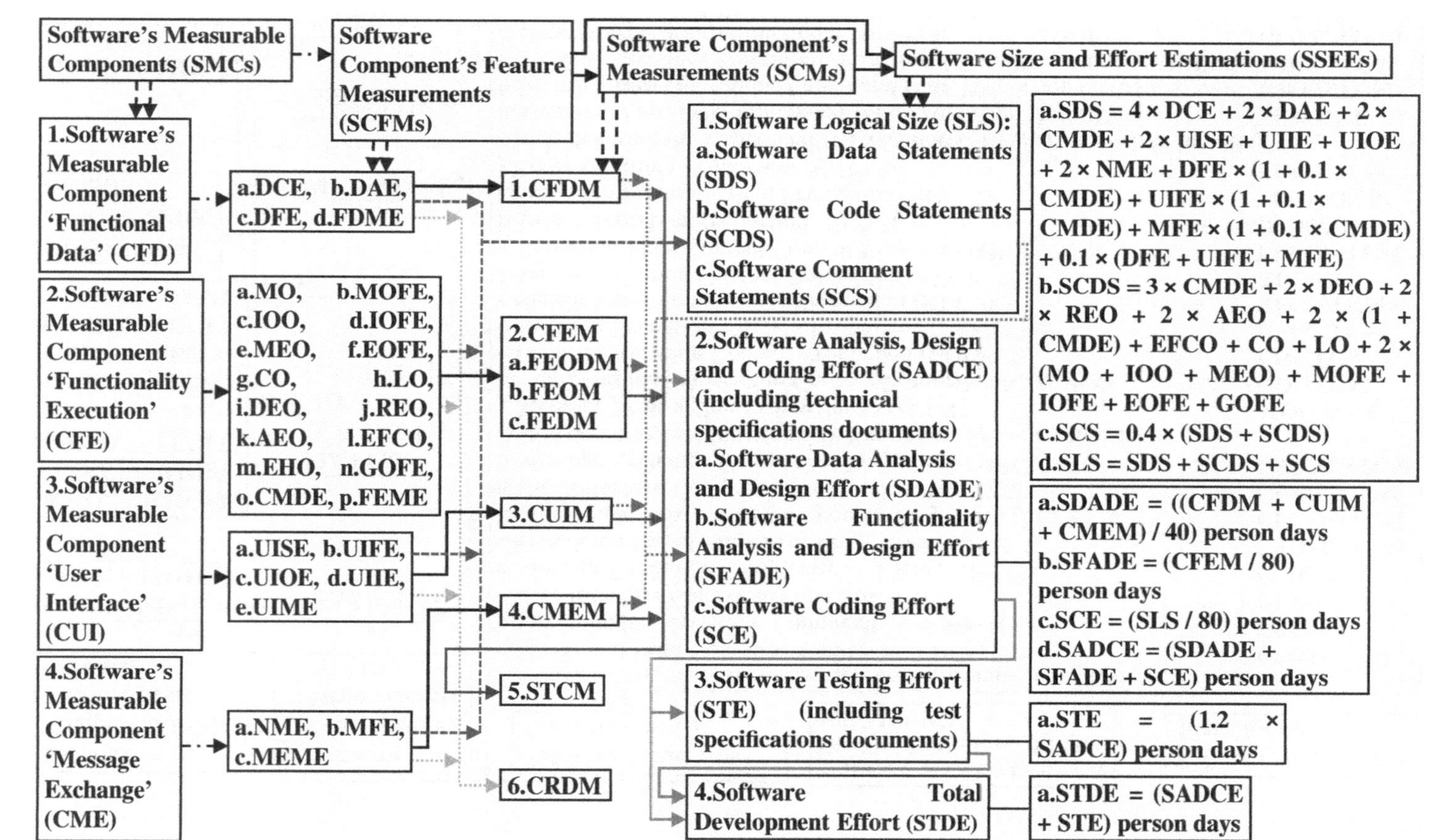

Figure 11 FSSM summary diagram (part 4/5) – SSEEs.

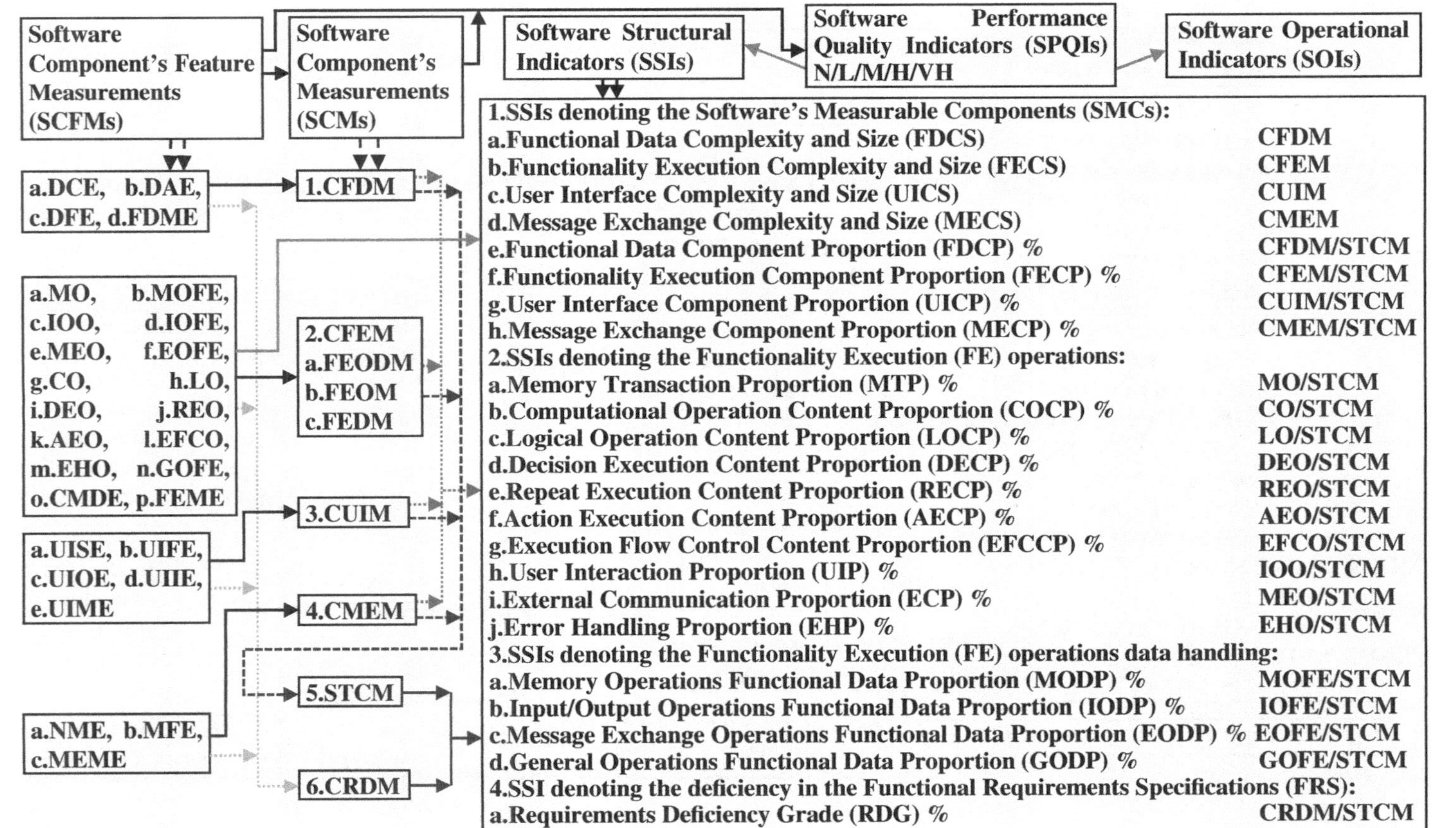

Figure 12 FSSM summary diagram (part 5/5) – SPQIs (1/2) of the type SSIs.

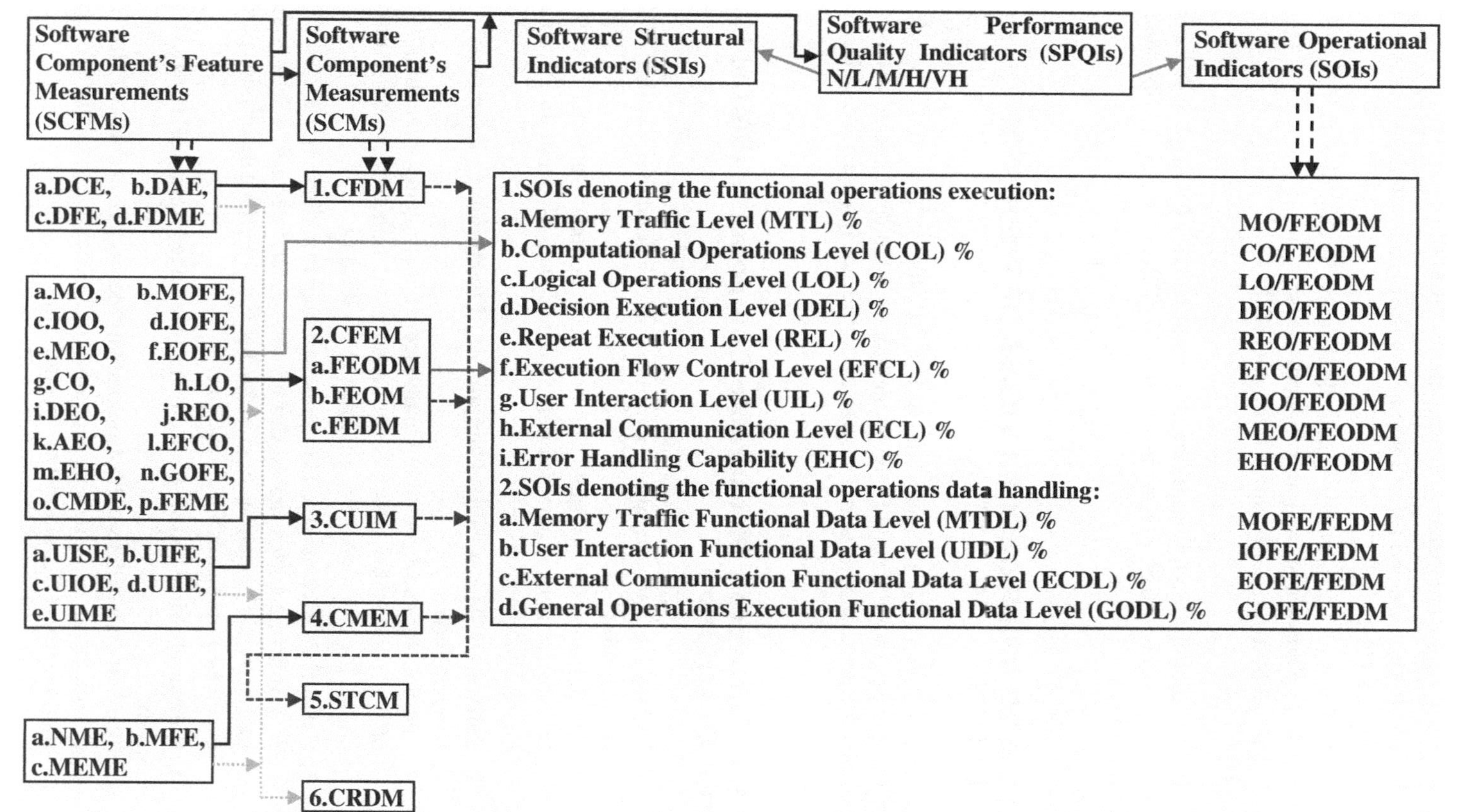

Figure 13 FSSM summary diagram (part 5/5) – SPQIs (2/2) of the type SOIs.

The SCFMs are the basis of the calculations for the following measurements, estimations, and indications:

a. 6 Software Component's Measurements (SCMs);

b. 4 Software Size and Effort Estimations (SSEEs) about the software size and development effort;

c. 36 Software Performance Quality Indicators (SPQIs) of which:
   i. 23 Software Structural Indicators (SSIs)[5–7];
   ii. 13 Software Operational Indicators (SOIs)[5–7].

Lists and brief descriptions of the aforementioned 4 SMCs, 31 SCMFs, 31 SCFPs, 31 SCFPCs, 28 SCFMs, 6 SCMs, 4 SSEEs, and 36 SPQIs of which 23 SSIs and 13 SOIs are presented next.

2.4 LISTS AND BRIEF DESCRIPTIONS OF THE FSSM CONSTITUENTS

The lists and brief descriptions of the SMCs, SCMFs, SCFPs, SCFPCs, SCFMs, SCMs, SSEEs, and SPQIs – SSIs and SOIs – which all form the constituents of the FSSM and are determined/calculated with a high degree of confidence in the FSSM follow.

2.4.1 Software's Measurable Components (SMCs) List with Brief Description

1. **Software's Measurable Component 'Functional Data' (CFD) Brief Description:**
   The Software's Measurable Component 'Functional Data' (CFD) is the Functional Data part which is contained in the Logical Data Model of the Functional Requirements Specifications.
2. **Software's Measurable Component 'Functionality Execution' (CFE) Brief Description:**
   The Software's Measurable Component 'Functionality Execution' (CFE) consists of the functionality which is contained in the Functionality Execution description part of the Functional Requirements Specifications.
3. **Software's Measurable Component 'User Interface' (CUI) Brief Description:**
   The Software's Measurable Component 'User Interface' (CUI) is the user interface/screen information contained in the User Interface description part of the Functional Requirements Specifications.
4. **Software's Measurable Component 'Message Exchange' (CME) Brief Description:**
   The Software's Measurable Component 'Message Exchange' (CME) is the message communication information contained in the Message Exchange description part of the Functional Requirements Specifications.

2.4.2 Software Component's Measurable Features (SCMFs) List

The list of 31 Software Component's Measurable Features (SCMFs) for the aforementioned 4 Software's Measurable Components (SMCs) – 4 SCMFs for the CFD, 19 SCMFs for the CFE, 5 SCMFs for the CUI, and 3 SCMFs for the CME – follows.

2.4.2.1 Software Component's Measurable Features (SCMFs) List for the Software's Measurable Component 'Functional Data' (CFD)

The Software Component's Measurable Features (SCMFs) of the Software's Measurable Component 'Functional Data' (CFD) are the following:

1. Software Component's Measurable Feature 'Data Class' (FDC);
2. Software Component's Measurable Feature 'Data Attribute' (FDA);
3. Software Component's Measurable Feature 'Data Field' (FDF);
4. Software Component's Measurable Feature 'Data Missing' (FDM).

2.4.2.2 Software Component's Measurable Features (SCMFs) List for the Software's Measurable Component 'Functionality Execution' (CFE)

The Software Component's Measurable Features (SCMFs) of the Software's Measurable Component 'Functionality Execution' (CFE) are the following:

1. Software Component's Measurable Feature 'Data Read' (FDR);
2. Software Component's Measurable Feature 'Data Write' (FDW);
3. Software Component's Measurable Feature 'Memory Operations Functional Data' (FLM);
4. Software Component's Measurable Feature 'Data Input' (FDI);
5. Software Component's Measurable Feature 'Data Output' (FDO);
6. Software Component's Measurable Feature 'Input/Output Operations Functional Data' (FLI);
7. Software Component's Measurable Feature 'Message Send' (FMS);
8. Software Component's Measurable Feature 'Message Receive' (FMR);
9. Software Component's Measurable Feature 'Message Exchange Operations Functional Data' (FLS);
10. Software Component's Measurable Feature 'Function Computational Operation' (FFC);
11. Software Component's Measurable Feature 'Function Logical Operation' (FFL);
12. Software Component's Measurable Feature 'Function Decision Execution' (FFD);
13. Software Component's Measurable Feature 'Function Repeat Execution' (FFR);
14. Software Component's Measurable Feature 'Function Action Execution' (FFA);
15. Software Component's Measurable Feature 'Function Execution Flow Control' (FFO);
16. Software Component's Measurable Feature 'Function Error Handling' (FFE);

17. Software Component's Measurable Feature 'General Operations Functional Data' (FLG);
18. Software Component's Measurable Feature 'Class Method' (FCM);
19. Software Component's Measurable Feature 'Functionality Missing' (FFM).

2.4.2.3 Software Component's Measurable Features (SCMFs) List for the Software's Measurable Component 'User Interface' (CUI)

The Software Component's Measurable Features (SCMFs) of the Software's Measurable Component 'User Interface' (CUI) are the following:

1. Software Component's Measurable Feature 'User Screen' (FUS);
2. Software Component's Measurable Feature 'User Screen Field' (FUF);
3. Software Component's Measurable Feature 'User Screen Output Link' (FUO);
4. Software Component's Measurable Feature 'User Screen Input Link' (FUI);
5. Software Component's Measurable Feature 'User Screen Missing' (FUM).

2.4.2.4 Software Component's Measurable Features (SCMFs) List for the Software's Measurable Component 'Message Exchange' (CME)

The Software Component's Measurable Features (SCMFs) of the Software's Measurable Component 'Message Exchange' (CME) are the following:

1. Software Component's Measurable Feature 'Notifying Message' (FNM);
2. Software Component's Measurable Feature 'Message Field' (FMF);
3. Software Component's Measurable Feature 'Message Missing' (FMM).

2.4.3 Software Component's Feature Points (SCFPs) List

By assigning the Software Component's Feature Points (SCFPs), that is, the Functional Size Units (FSUs), to the aforementioned 31 Software Component's Measurable Features (SCMFs), there are 31 Software Component's Feature Points (SCFPs) which are obtained corresponding to the 31 SCMFs, respectively. The list of the SCFPs follows.

2.4.3.1 Software Component's Feature Points (SCFPs) List for the Software's Measurable Component 'Functional Data' (CFD)

The Software Component's Feature Points (SCFPs) for the Software's Measurable Component 'Functional Data' (CFD) are the following:

1. Software Component's Feature Point 'Data Class' (FPDC);
2. Software Component's Feature Point 'Data Attribute' (FPDA);
3. Software Component's Feature Point 'Data Field' (FPDF);
4. Software Component's Feature Point 'Data Missing' (FPDM).

2.4.3.2 Software Component's Feature Points (SCFPs) List for the Software's Measurable Component 'Functionality Execution' (CFE)

The Software Component's Feature Points (SCFPs) for the Software's Measurable Component 'Functionality Execution' (CFE) are the following:

1. Software Component's Feature Point for 'Data Read' (FPDR);
2. Software Component's Feature Point for 'Data Write' (FPDW);
3. Software Component's Feature Point for 'Memory Operations Functional Data' (FPLM);
4. Software Component's Feature Point for 'Data Input' (FPDI);
5. Software Component's Feature Point for 'Data Output' (FPDO);
6. Software Component's Feature Point for 'Input/Output Operations Functional Data' (FPLI);
7. Software Component's Feature Point for 'Message Send' (FPMS);
8. Software Component's Feature Point for 'Message Receive' (FPMR);
9. Software Component's Feature Point for 'Message Exchange Operations Functional Data' (FPLS);
10. Software Component's Feature Point for 'Function Computational Operation' (FPFC);
11. Software Component's Feature Point for 'Function Logical Operation' (FPFL);
12. Software Component's Feature Point for 'Function Decision Execution' (FPFD);
13. Software Component's Feature Point for 'Function Repeat Execution' (FPFR);
14. Software Component's Feature Point for 'Function Action Execution' (FPFA);
15. Software Component's Feature Point for 'Function Execution Flow Control' (FPFO);
16. Software Component's Feature Point for 'Function Error Handling' (FPFE);
17. Software Component's Feature Point for 'General Operations Functional Data' (FPLG);
18. Software Component's Feature Point for 'Class Method' (FPCM);
19. Software Component's Feature Point for 'Functionality Missing' (FPFM).

2.4.3.3 Software Component's Feature Points (SCFPs) List for the Software's Measurable Component 'User Interface' (CUI)

The Software Component's Feature Points (SCFPs) for the Software's Measurable Component 'User Interface' (CUI) are the following:

1. Software Component's Feature Point for 'User Screen' (FPUS);
2. Software Component's Feature Point for 'User Screen Field' (FPUF);
3. Software Component's Feature Point for 'User Screen Output Link' (FPUO);
4. Software Component's Feature Point for 'User Screen Input Link' (FPUI);
5. Software Component's Feature Point for 'User Screen Missing' (FPUM).

2.4.3.4 Software Component's Feature Points (SCFPs) List for the Software's Measurable Component 'Message Exchange' (CME)

The Software Component's Feature Points (SCFPs) for the Software's Measurable Component 'Message Exchange' (CME) are the following:

1. Software Component's Feature Point for 'Notifying Message' (FPNM);
2. Software Component's Feature Point for 'Message Field' (FPMF);
3. Software Component's Feature Point for 'Message Missing' (FPMM).

2.4.4 Software Component's Feature Point Counts (SCFPCs) List

From the aforementioned set of 31 Software Component's Feature Points (SCFPs), the set of 31 Software Component's Feature Point Counts (SCFPCs) are obtained corresponding to the 31 SCMFs, respectively. The list of the SCFPCs follows.

2.4.4.1 Software Component's Feature Point Counts (SCFPCs) List for the Software's Measurable Component 'Functional Data' (CFD)

The Software Component's Feature Point Counts (SCFPCs) for the Software's Measurable Component 'Functional Data' (CFD) are the following:

1. Software Component's Feature Point Count for 'Data Class' (FCDC);
2. Software Component's Feature Point Count for 'Data Attribute' (FCDA);
3. Software Component's Feature Point Count for 'Data Field' (FCDF);
4. Software Component's Feature Point Count for 'Data Missing' (FCDM).

2.4.4.2 Software Component's Feature Point Counts (SCFPCs) List for the Software's Measurable Component 'Functionality Execution' (CFE)

The Software Component's Feature Point Counts (SCFPCs) for the Software's Measurable Component 'Functionality Execution' (CFE) are the following:

1. Software Component's Feature Point Count for 'Data Read' (FCDR);
2. Software Component's Feature Point Count for 'Data Write' (FCDW);
3. Software Component's Feature Point Count for 'Memory Operations Functional Data' (FCLM);
4. Software Component's Feature Point Count for 'Data Input' (FCDI);
5. Software Component's Feature Point Count for 'Data Output' (FCDO);
6. Software Component's Feature Point Count for 'Input/Output Operations Functional Data' (FCLI);
7. Software Component's Feature Point Count for 'Message Send' (FCMS);
8. Software Component's Feature Point Count for 'Message Receive' (FCMR);
9. Software Component's Feature Point Count for 'Message Exchange Operations Functional Data' (FCLS);

10. Software Component's Feature Point Count for 'Function Computational Operation' (FCFC);
11. Software Component's Feature Point Count for 'Function Logical Operation' (FCFL);
12. Software Component's Feature Point Count for 'Function Decision Execution' (FCFD);
13. Software Component's Feature Point Count for 'Function Repeat Execution' (FCFR);
14. Software Component's Feature Point Count for 'Function Action Execution' (FCFA);
15. Software Component's Feature Point Count for 'Function Execution Flow Control' (FCFO);
16. Software Component's Feature Point Count for 'Function Error Handling' (FCFE);
17. Software Component's Feature Point Count for 'General Operations Functional Data' (FCLG);
18. Software Component's Feature Point Count for 'Class Method' (FCCM);
19. Software Component's Feature Point Count for 'Functionality Missing' (FCFM).

2.4.4.3 Software Component's Feature Point Counts (SCFPCs) List for the Software's Measurable Component 'User Interface' (CUI)

The Software Component's Feature Point Counts (SCFPCs) for the Software's Measurable Component 'User Interface' (CUI) are the following:

1. Software Component's Feature Point Count for 'User Screen' (FCUS);
2. Software Component's Feature Point Count for 'User Screen Field' (FCUF);
3. Software Component's Feature Point Count for 'User Screen Output Link' (FCUO);
4. Software Component's Feature Point Count for 'User Screen Input Link' (FCUI);
5. Software Component's Feature Point Count for 'User Screen Missing' (FCUM).

2.4.4.4 Software Component's Feature Point Counts (SCFPCs) List for the Software's Measurable Component 'Message Exchange' (CME)

The Software Component's Feature Point Counts (SCFPCs) for the Software's Measurable Component 'Message Exchange' (CME) are the following:

1. Software Component's Feature Point Count for 'Notifying Message' (FCNM);
2. Software Component's Feature Point Count for 'Message Field' (FCMF);
3. Software Component's Feature Point Count for 'Message Missing' (FCMM).

2.4.5 Software Component's Feature Measurements (SCFMs) List

From the aforementioned set of 31 Software Component's Feature Points Counts (SCFPCs), there are 28 Software Component's Feature Measurements (SCFMs) which are calculated. The list of the SCFMs follows.

2.4.5.1 Software Component's Feature Measurements (SCFMs) List for the Software's Measurable Component 'Functional Data' (CFD)

The Software Component's Feature Measurements (SCFMs) for the Software's Measurable Component 'Functional Data' (CFD) are the following:

1. Data Class Entities (DCE);
2. Data Class Attribute Entities (DAE);
3. Data Class Field Entities (DFE);
4. Functional Data Missing Entities (FDME).

2.4.5.2 Software Component's Feature Measurements (SCFMs) List for the Software's Measurable Component 'Functionality Execution' (CFE)

The Software Component's Feature Measurements (SCFMs) for the Software's Measurable Component 'Functionality Execution' (CFE) are the following:

1. Memory Operations (MO);
2. Computational Operations (CO);
3. Logical Operations (LO);
4. Decision Execution Operations (DEO);
5. Repeat Execution Operations (REO);
6. Action Execution Operations (AEO);
7. Execution Flow Control Operations (EFCO);
8. Error Handling Operations (EHO);
9. Input/Output Operations (IOO);
10. Message Exchange Operations (MEO);
11. Class Method Entities (CMDE);
12. Memory Operations Functional Data Entities (MOFE);
13. Input/Output Operations Functional Data Entities (IOFE);
14. Message Exchange Operations Functional Data Entities (EOFE);
15. General Operations Functional Data Entities (GOFE);
16. Functionality Execution Missing Entities (FEME).

2.4.5.3 Software Component's Feature Measurements (SCFMs) List for the Software's Measurable Component 'User Interface' (CUI)

The Software Component's Feature Measurements (SCFMs) for the Software's Measurable Component 'Message Exchange' (CME) are the following:

1. User Interface Screen Entities (UISE);
2. User Interface Field Entities (UIFE);
3. User Interface Input Link Entities (UIIE);
4. User Interface Output Link Entities (UIOE);
5. User Interface Missing Entities (UIME).

2.4.5.4 Software Component's Feature Measurements (SCFMs) List for the Software's Measurable Component 'Message Exchange' (CME)

The Software Component's Feature Measurements (SCFMs) for the Software's Measurable Component 'Message Exchange' (CME) are the following:

1. Notifying Message Entities (NME);
2. Message Field Entities (MFE);
3. Message Exchange Missing Entities (MEME).

2.4.6 Software Component's Measurements (SCMs) List with Brief Description

The Software Component's Feature Measurements (SCFMs) are used to calculate the following 6 Software Component's Measurements (SCMs):

1. **Software Component 'Functional Data' Measurement (CFDM) Brief Description:**
   The Software Component 'Functional Data' Measurement (CFDM) is the measurement for the Software's Measurable Component 'Functional Data' (CFD). It indicates the Functional Data size and complexity
   a. taking into account the classes, their attributes, and their fields;
   b. based on 3 SCFMs obtained from the corresponding 3 SCFPCs.
2. **Software Component 'Functionality Execution' Measurement (CFEM) Brief Description:**
   The Software Component 'Functionality Execution' Measurement (CFEM) is the measurement for the Software's Measurable Component 'Functionality Execution' (CFE). It indicates the Functionality Execution size and complexity, taking into account
   a. all the operations of the
      i. software processing which are the following:
         - computational;
         - logical;
         - decision;
         - repeat action;
         - action execution;
         - execution flow control;
      ii. error handling;
      iii. memory transactions;
      iv. input/output device interactions;
      v. communications with external application programs;
   b. data handled during the following operations:
      i. memory transactions;
      ii. input/output device interactions;
      iii. communications with external application programs;
      iv. software processing operations which are the following:
         - computational;
         - logical;
         - decision;

- repeat action;
- execution flow control;

c. class methods;

involved in the functionality, based on 14 SCFMs obtained from the corresponding 17 SCFPCs.

3. **Software Component 'User Interface' Measurement (CUIM) Brief Description:**
The Software Component 'User Interface' Measurement (CUIM) is the measurement for the Software's Measurable Component 'User Interface' (CUI). It indicates the User Interface size and complexity
a. taking into account the screens, their size, and navigation links connecting the screen;
b. based on 4 SCFMs obtained from the corresponding 4 SCFPCs.
4. **Software Component 'Message Exchange' Measurement (CMEM) Brief Description:**
The Software Component 'Message Exchange' Measurement (CMEM) is the measurement for the Software's Measurable Component 'Message Exchange' (CME). It indicates the Message Exchange size and complexity
a. taking into account the messages and their fields;
b. based on 2 SCFMs obtained from the corresponding 2 SCFPCs.
5. **Software Total Components Measurement (STCM) Brief Description:**
The Software Total Components Measurement (STCM) is the composite measurement of all the software comprising all the aforementioned 4 Software's Measurable Components (SMCs) – Software's Measurable Component 'Functional Data' (CFD), 'Functionality Execution' (CFE), 'User Interface' (CUI), and 'Message Exchange' (CME). It indicates the total software size and complexity. It is calculated based on the CFDM, CFEM, CUIM, and CMEM.
6. **Software Components Requirement Deficiency Measurement (CRDM) Brief Description:**
The Software Components Requirement Deficiency Measurement (CRDM) indicates apparently missing items
a. taking into account the apparent missing items for the
 i. Functional Data;
 ii. Functionality Execution;
 iii. User Interface;
 iv. Message Exchange;
b. based on 4 SCFMs obtained from the corresponding 4 SCFPCs.

2.4.7 Software Size and Effort Estimations (SSEEs) List with Brief Description

The Software Component's Feature Measurements (SCFMs) and Software Component's Measurements (SCMs) are used for the calculations of the following 4 Software Size and Effort Estimations (SSEEs):

1. **Software Logical Size (SLS) Brief Description:**
The Software Logical Size (SLS) is the logical statement size of the software which is developed according to the functional requirements. It is a complex function

of various Functional Data, Functionality Execution, User Interface, and Message Exchange measurements, and is used to calculate the effort required for software coding.

2. **Software Analysis, Design, and Coding Effort (SADCE) Brief Description:**
   The Software Analysis, Design, and Coding Effort (SADCE) is the effort needed for analyzing, designing, coding, and preparing the technical specifications documents.
   The SADCE (Software Analysis, Design, and Coding Effort) is a function of the Software Logical Size (SLS), Software Component 'Functional Data' Measurement (CFDM), Software Component 'Functionality Execution' Measurement (CFEM), Software Component 'User Interface' Measurement (CUIM), Software Component 'Message Exchange' Measurement (CMEM), and average productivity for the analysis, design, and coding activities.
3. **Software Testing Effort (STE) Brief Description:**
   The Software Testing Effort (STE) is the effort needed for testing and preparing the test specifications documents.
   The STE (Software Testing Effort) is a function of the Software Analysis, Design, and Coding Effort (SADCE) and average productivity for the testing activity.
4. **Software Total Development Effort (STDE) Brief Description:**
   The Software Total Development Effort (STDE) is calculated based on the Software Analysis, Design, and Coding Effort (SADCE), and Software Testing Effort (STE).

2.4.8 Software Performance Quality Indicators (SPQIs) List

The Software Component's Feature Measurements (SCFMs) and Software Component's Measurements (SCMs) are also used for the calculations of the 36 Software Performance Quality Indicators (SPQIs) which are divided into 2 categories:

1. Software Structural Indicators (SSIs)[5–7];
2. Software Operational Indicators (SOIs)[5–7].

2.4.8.1 Software Structural Indicators (SSIs) List

The Software Structural Indicators (SSIs)[5–7] are the indicators to express the software's static structural characteristics, and are categorized as Nil, Low, Medium, High, or Very High. They are divided into 4 sub-categories:

A. **SSIs denoting the Software's Measurable Components (SMCs):**
   1. Functional Data Complexity and Size (FDCS);
   2. Functionality Execution Complexity and Size (FECS);
   3. User Interface Complexity and Size (UICS);
   4. Message Exchange Complexity and Size (MECS);
   5. Functional Data Component Proportion (FDCP);
   6. Functionality Execution Component Proportion (FECP);
   7. User Interface Component Proportion (UICP);
   8. Message Exchange Component Proportion (MECP);

B. **SSIs denoting the Functionality Execution (FE) Operations:**
   1. Memory Transaction Proportion (MTP);

2. Computational Operation Content Proportion (COCP);
3. Logical Operation Content Proportion (LOCP);
4. Decision Execution Content Proportion (DECP);
5. Repeat Execution Content Proportion (RECP);
6. Action Execution Content Proportion (AECP);
7. Execution Flow Control Content Proportion (EFCCP);
8. User Interaction Proportion (UIP);
9. External Communication Proportion (ECP);
10. Error Handling Proportion (EHP);

C. **SSIs denoting the Functionality Execution (FE) Operations Data Handling:**
1. Memory Operations Functional Data Proportion (MODP);
2. Input/Output Operations Functional Data Proportion (IODP);
3. Message Exchange Operations Functional Data Proportion (EODP);
4. General Operations Functional Data Proportion (GODP);

D. **SSI denoting the deficiency in the Functional Requirements Specifications (FRS):**
1. Requirements Deficiency Grade (RDG).

2.4.8.2 Software Operational Indicators (SOIs) List

The Software Operational Indicators (SOIs)[5–7] are the indicators to express the software's dynamic run-time characteristics, and are categorized as Nil, Low, Medium, High, or Very High. They are divided into 2 sub-categories:

A. **SOIs denoting the Functional Operations Execution:**
1. Memory Traffic Level (MTL);
2. Computational Operations Level (COL);
3. Logical Operations Level (LOL);
4. Decision Execution Level (DEL);
5. Repeat Execution Level (REL);
6. User Interaction Level (UIL);
7. Execution Flow Control Level (EFCL);
8. External Communication Level (ECL);
9. Error Handling Capability (EHC);

B. **SOIs denoting the Functional Operations Data Handling:**
1. Memory Traffic Functional Data Level (MTDL);
2. User Interaction Functional Data Level (UIDL);
3. External Communication Functional Data Level (ECDL);
4. General Operations Execution Functional Data Level (GODL).

2.5 SOURCE OF INFORMATION FOR THE FSSM CONSTITUENTS

All the information regarding the

- SMCs (Software's Measurable Components);
- SCMFs (Software Component's Measurable Features);
- SCFPs (Software Component's Feature Points);

- SCFPCs (Software Component's Feature Point Counts);
- SCFMs (Software Component's Feature Measurements);
- SCMs (Software Component's Measurements);
- SSEEs (Software Size and Effort Estimations);
- SPQIs (Software Performance Quality Indicators) of the type:
  - SSIs (Software Structural Indicators)[5–7];
  - SOIs (Software Operational Indicators)[5–7];

is collected and extracted from the Functional Requirements Specifications (FRS) document which describes the

- Logical Data Model;
- functionalities;
- user interfaces/screens;
- messages.

Detailed descriptions of all the aforementioned FSSM constituents are presented in the next chapters. Suitable examples have been included wherever helpful for better understanding. Some of the examples which are spread over in various chapters have been presented in a later Example chapter as a consolidated example.

2.6 EXAMPLES

The following are some examples of the Functional Requirements Specifications (FRS):

1. The desired and advised level of details of the Functional Requirements Specifications is illustrated by the following example for log on procedure.

The functional requirements about log on can be specified in one of the following manners in the Functional Requirements Specifications (FRS):

A. A very high level requirements statement: User logs on.

B. Slightly more descriptive way: A screen is displayed with the user-id and password fields to be entered, and the user enters the user-id and password to log on.

C. Detailed procedure to log on in which all the following with basic minimum required details is specified:

a. In User Interface description part, the following screen is defined:

i. A Log-on screen is defined with layout diagram, 2 output text fields to display the texts 'user-id' and 'password'; one output text field to display the error messages; 2 input text fields where the user will type the user-id and password; 2 text fields for screen output navigational links 'Enter' and 'Cancel'; one input link to indicate from where the Log-on screen is reached from.

b. In the class structure diagram/description in the Logical Data Model, the following classes are defined:

i. Class user with attributes identifier, password, e-mail address.

ii. Class screen with relevant attributes and fields.

iii. Class error message with various error message instances: 'please enter both the user-id and password correctly'; 'user-id is not registered'; 'password is not correct'; 'log in not allowed because the limit of 3 trials is crossed.'

c. In the functionality description, full procedure about log on is described as presented next:
Log-on screen is displayed. There are 3 possibilities:
i. User clicks on 'Cancel' and the previous screen is presented.
ii. User clicks on 'Enter' without having entered anything, or after having entered only user-id, or after having entered only password, the error message 'please enter both the user-id and password correctly' is displayed in the Log-on screen.
iii. User enters the user-id and password. Both are checked. If the user-id is not correct, the error message 'user-id is not registered' is displayed in the Log-on screen. If the password is not correct, the error message 'password is not correct' is displayed in the Log-on screen. If both are correct, the log on is successful.
iv. If user-id is correct and the password is entered incorrectly more than 3 times, the error message 'log in not allowed because the limit of 3 trials is crossed' is displayed and an e-mail is sent to the user.

Out of the aforementioned 3 manners of specifying the functional requirements, the last (third) manner is the best way with respect to the level of details. It is not only the best way from the point of view of using the FSSM methodology for measurement, size estimation, and performance indication, but it is also very much desirable from the point of view of development because it gives sufficient details at a deeper and lower level ensuring a better quality of development.

2. The following functional requirement will be part of the User Interface description part of the Functional Requirements Specifications (FRS): "Log-on screen displaying the fields user-id and password to log on".

3. The following functional requirement will be part of the Logical Data Model description part of the Functional Requirements Specifications (FRS): "Class: KSI (Key Software Indicator)[5–7]; Attributes: memory traffic level, computational level, logical operations level, decision execution level, repeat execution level, action execution level, user interaction level, external communication level, error handling capability, data complexity and size, code complexity and size, data operation and transaction proportion, decision content proportion, repeat content proportion, action content proportion, external communication proportion, and error handling proportion (there are a total of 18 attributes); Fields: each attribute has one field".
(*Note*: The aforementioned functional requirement is part of Chapter 14);

4. All the following functional requirements will be part of the Functionality Execution description part of the Functional Requirements Specifications (FRS).
(*Note*: The functional requirements that follow in this example are part of Chapter 14.)
A. "Application opens a window Option screen and asks if it is a new count estimate or continue working from an old estimate file. If user clicks on new, it is a new estimate, open a new window New Entry screen for New Entry".

B. "Enter identifier (any text, maximum 20 char), description (any text, maximum 2000 char)".
C. "In new entry, if text limit is crossed or count is not integer, display error".
D. "Calculate Data Count = DC + DA + DF".
E. "Calculate Comment Lines = 0.4 × (code lines)".

2.7 CHAPTER SUMMARY

The Functional Software Size Measurement Methodology with Effort Estimation and Performance Indication (FSSM) is a new, comprehensive Software Size Measurement methodology which is based on the Functional Size Measurement[1] principles, and is compliant with the ISO/IEC 14143-1[1] standards. The distinguishing unique key features of the FSSM are its comprehensive coverage and completeness to measure the size of software, inclusion of effort estimation and performance indication of the software, software diagnosis, detection of deficiencies in the Functional Requirements Specifications, simple calculations, and significant advantages over the existing software size measurement methodologies.

An information/procedure flow diagram of the methodology is presented in Figure 2, and summary overview diagrams are presented in Figures 3–8. It is explained briefly that the information about the Software's Measurable Components (SMCs) – Software's Measurable Component 'Functional Data' (CFD), 'Functionality Execution' (CFE), 'User Interface' (CUI), and 'Message Exchange' (CME) – is available in the different description parts – Logical Data Model (LDM), Functionality Execution (FE), User Interface (UI), and Message Exchange (ME) – of the Functional Requirements Specifications (FRS). From these description parts of the FRS, the Software Component's Measurable Features (SCMFs) for all the SMCs are identified, and the Software Component's Feature Points (SCFPs, i.e., FSUs) are assigned to them according to the defined rules. Summation of the respective SCFPs produces the Software Component's Feature Point Counts (SCFPCs) for the corresponding SCMFs. The SCFPCs are utilized to calculate the Software Component's Feature Measurements (SCFMs). The SCFMs are the basis for the calculations of the Software Component's Measurements (SCMs), Software Size and Effort Estimations (SSEEs), and Software Performance Quality Indicators (SPQIs) of the 2 types – Software Structural Indicators (SSIs)[5–7] and Software Operational Indicators (SOIs)[5–7].

Quantitatively, in the FSSM, 31 Software Component's Measurable Features (SCMFs) for 4 Software's Measurable Components (SMCs) are identified in the Functional Requirements Specifications (FRS) to assign the Software Component's Feature Points (SCFPs, i.e., FSUs) that make corresponding 31 types of Software Component's Feature Points (SCFPs) and consequently the corresponding 31 Software Component's Feature Point Counts (SCFPCs). The SCFPCs are used for the calculations of 28 Software Component's Feature Measurements (SCFMs) which are utilized to calculate 6 Software Component's Measurements (SCMs), 4 Software Size and Effort Estimations (SSEEs) and 36 Software Performance Quality Indicators (SPQIs) of which 23 Software Structural Indicators (SSIs)[5–7] and 13 Software Operational Indicators (SOIs)[5–7].

EXERCISES

2.1 Which of the following document is used in the FSSM for collecting the information about the SCFPCs?

A. Technical Design Specifications (TDS).
B. Functional Requirements Specifications (FRS).
C. Quality Requirements Specifications (QRS).

2.2 Which of the following is a Software's Measurable Component (SMC) in the FSSM?
A. Memory Traffic Level (MTL).
B. User Interface Component Proportion (UICP).
C. Software's Measurable Component 'Functional Data' (CFD).

2.3 Which of the following does not belong to the group of Software Operational Indicators (SOIs)[5–7] in the FSSM?
A. Memory Traffic Level (MTL).
B. Decision Execution Level (DEL).
C. User Interaction Level (UIL).
D. Software Logical Size (SLS).
E. Memory Traffic Functional Data Level (MTDL).

2.4 In the FSSM, the Software Component's Feature Points (SCFPs) are assigned to which of the following?
A. Software's Measurable Components (SMCs).
B. Software Component's Measurable Features (SCMFs).
C. Software Structural Indicators (SSIs)[5–7].

2.5 In the FSSM, the Software Component's Feature Point Counts (SCFPCs) are obtained by summing up which of the following?
A. Software Component's Feature Points (SCFPs).
B. Software Component's Measurements (SCMs).
C. All the Software Component's Feature Measurements (SCFMs).

Part Two

FSSM: Software View

Chapter 3

Software's Measurable Components in the FSSM

Software comprises different components – the Software's Measurable Components (SMCs) – that all need to be measured in order to achieve a reliable and accurate measurement. The information about the SMCs (Software's Measurable Components) is present in the Logical Data Model, Functionality Execution, User Interface, and Message Exchange description parts of the Functional Requirements Specifications (FRS) document. There are 4 SMCs corresponding to the aforementioned 4 parts of the FRS. These 4 SMCs are presented in this chapter.

3.1 SOFTWARE'S MEASURABLE COMPONENT (SMC) DESCRIPTION

Software is constituted of several components. As explained earlier, all the components of the software should be measured in order to have a correct measurement based on which an accurate estimation of effort can be obtained because their size relationship with respect to one another is variable in various software applications (see Section 1.3). Hence, it is very important to measure them separately and completely for each application to get the measurement of the complete software. As shown in Figure 1 and Figure 3, the major, important, relevant components of the software which should be measured for comprehensive software size measurement are the Software's Measurable Component 'Functional Data' (CFD), Software's Measurable Component 'Functionality Execution' (CFE), Software's Measurable Component 'User Interface' (CUI), and Software's Measurable Component 'Message Exchange' (CME). The description of these Software's Measurable Components (SMCs) follows.

3.1.1 Software's Measurable Component 'Functional Data' (CFD) Description

Most of the software operations are performed on the Functional Data (FD). Effort is spent on the Functional Data analysis, design, coding, and testing as part of the effort of the

Functional Software Size Measurement Methodology with Effort Estimation and Performance Indication, First Edition. Jasveer Singh.

Companion website: http://booksupport.wiley.com

development of the total application program. Hence, the Software's Measurable Component 'Functional Data' (CFD) is one of the important components which needs to be measured. This component contains the Functional Data to be operated upon. Normally, it is described in the Logical Data Model (LDM) of the Functional Requirements Specifications (FRS) document with the help of class structure diagrams and suitable text descriptions.

What we need about the CFD in the FSSM is the information about the following, either in the diagrams or in the text form in the LDM of the FRS:

a. all the data classes and subclasses used for the functionality required;

b. all the attributes of all the data classes and subclasses;

c. all the fields of all the attributes of all the data classes and subclasses.

So, these details are the minimum details which should be present in the data description part of the Functional Requirements Specifications concerning the measurement, size and effort estimation, and performance indication by the FSSM.

3.1.2 Software's Measurable Component 'Functionality Execution' (CFE) Description

Another important component of the software which needs to be measured is the Software's Measurable Component 'Functionality Execution' (CFE). It contains the functionality to be executed which needs to be designed in the program code. The functionality includes the error handling and also includes the functional data handling during the functionality execution. Normally, the functionality of the software is described in the Functionality Execution (FE) description part of the Functional Requirements Specifications (FRS).

Effort is spent on the functionality analysis, design, coding, and testing as part of the effort of the development of the total application program. Hence, it is important to measure the CFE (Software's Measurable Component 'Functionality Execution').

Concerning the CFE in the FSSM, it should be possible to collect the following information about the Functionality Execution from the functionality description part of the FRS:

1. information about the following functionality execution operations:
   - **a.** memory data read/write used for reading/writing the data from/to the memory devices;
   - **b.** input/output used for receiving/sending data from/to the input/output devices;
   - **c.** message exchange (message send/receive) used for sending/receiving the messages to/from the external application programs or sub-programs (modules) of the same application program;
   - **d.** general functionality execution operations which are the following:
      - **i.** computational;
      - **ii.** logical;
      - **iii.** decision execution;
      - **iv.** repeat execution;
      - **v.** action execution;
      - **vi.** execution flow control;
      - **vii.** error handling;

2. information about the following functional data handling during the functionality execution operations indicated:

a. functional data handled in the memory read/write operations;
b. functional data handled in the input/output operations;
c. functional data handled in the message exchange operations;
d. functional data handled in the general functionality execution operations for the following types of functional operations:
   i. computational;
   ii. logical;
   iii. decision execution;
   iv. repeat execution;
   v. execution flow control;

and from the Logical Data Model part of the FRS:

1. information about all the class methods (operations or procedures).

3.1.3 Software's Measurable Component 'User Interface' (CUI) Description

The Software's Measurable Component 'User Interface' (CUI), another important component of the software, contains the user interfaces/screens for communication with the input/output devices. These devices may be keyboard, display, and/or other input/output devices such as instruments and equipment. Normally, the User Interface (UI) component functionality is described in the User Interface (UI) description part of the Functional Requirements Specifications (FRS) in the form of user screens structures: the layouts and details of the screens.

Effort is spent on the user interface/screens analysis, design, coding, and testing as part of the effort of the development of the total application program. Hence, it is important to measure the CUI (Software's Measurable Component 'User Interface').

The information required in the FSSM for the CUI is the structure of the input/output screens: the screens layouts, fields contained in the screens and information about the input and output navigation links of the screens. For this, it is preferable that the User Interface (UI) description part of the FRS contains the layout of all the input/output screens with their fields and input/output navigation links. Regarding the input/output navigation links, a complete screens interconnection diagram showing all the connections between the input/output navigation links is highly desirable from the quality point of view because it is not only helpful for gathering the information about the CUI in the FSSM but is also helpful for designing and testing the software in later phases.

3.1.4 Software's Measurable Component 'Message Exchange' (CME) Description

The Software's Measurable Component 'Message Exchange' (CME) is also an important software component. It contains the notifying messages which are exchanged with the external application programs or with the sub-programs (modules) of the same application program. Normally, the Message Exchange (ME) component description is available in the Message Exchange (ME) description part of the Functional Requirements Specifications (FRS) in the form of the message structures and relevant message details.

Effort is spent on the analysis, design, coding, and testing of the messages and their structure as part of the effort of the development of the total application program. Hence, it is important to measure the CME (Software's Measurable Component 'Message Exchange').

The information about the messages, their structure including their fields should be possible to be found in the Message Exchange description part of the FRS regarding what is required in the FSSM about the CME.

3.2 SOFTWARE'S MEASURABLE COMPONENTS (SMCs) CHARACTERISTICS

All the Software's Measurable Components which are the following:

a. Software's Measurable Component 'Functional Data' (CFD);

b. Software's Measurable Component 'Functionality Execution' (CFE);

c. Software's Measurable Component 'User Interface' (CUI);

d. Software's Measurable Component 'Message Exchange' (CME);

have different distinct Software Component's Measurable Features (SCMFs). All the major, important, relevant Software Component's Measurable Features (SCMFs) of all the aforementioned 4 Software's Measurable Components (SMCs) are taken into consideration for reliable software size measurement in the FSSM. The SCMFs of the SMCs are presented in Chapter 4.

The complete information about the SMCs and SCMFs is derived from the Functional Requirements Specifications (FRS) and is not dependent on any Technical Requirements (TR), nor Technical Design Specifications (TDS), nor Quality Requirements (QR) (also known as Quality Requirements Specifications (QRS)).

The SMCs are assessed by their measurements known as the Software Component's Measurements (SCMs). The SCMs are based on the Software Component's Feature Measurements (SCFMs). Both the SCMs and SCFMs are used further for the calculations of the Software Size and Effort Estimations (SSEEs) and Software Performance Quality Indicators (SPQIs) of the two types: Software Structural Indicators (SSIs)[5–7] and Software Operational Indicators (SOIs)[5–7]. The SCMs and SCFMs are presented in Chapter 7.

3.3 SOFTWARE'S MEASURABLE COMPONENTS (SMCs) PRESENCE AND SIZE

The absence, or presence and size of the different Software's Measurable Components (SMCs) depend on the type of applications and thus, on the Functional Requirements Specifications (FRS) of the applications.

It may be possible that certain SMCs are absent, or present in small size, but some others may be present with bigger size.

In fact, the total size of the software is dependent on the varying sizes of the Software's Measurable Components (SMCs) – Software's Measurable Component 'Functional Data' (CFD), 'Functionality Execution' (CFE), 'User Interface' (CUI), and 'Message Exchange' (CME) – which are present. The size of the SMCs is measured by the Software Component's Measurements (SCMs), and thus, the total size of the software is determined based on the SCMs.

There is no limit or restriction on the size of the SMCs which are present.

3.4 EXAMPLES

The following examples are all valid:

1. The functional requirement "Display error message 'Name not correct' ":
   A. Is one of the Functional Requirements Specifications;
   B. Is normally part of the Functionality Execution (FE) description part of the Functional Requirements Specifications (FRS);
   C. Forms part of the Software's Measurable Component 'Functionality Execution' (CFE).
2. The functional requirement "Message Identifier: 1356; Message Fields: id_1356, source_module_1, destination_module_2, function_add_name; Message Description: request from module_1 to module_2 to add name in the list":
   A. Is normally part of the Message Exchange (FE) description part of the Functional Requirements Specifications (FRS);
   B. Forms part of the Software's Measurable Component 'Message Exchange' (CME).
3. The functional requirement "Get user-id and password to log on":
   A. Is normally part of the Functionality Execution (FE) description part of the Functional Requirements Specifications (FRS);
   B. Forms part of the Software's Measurable Component 'Functionality Execution' (CFE).

3.5 CHAPTER SUMMARY

3.5.1 Software's Measurable Component (SMC): Summary

Software comprises 4 Software's Measurable Components (SMCs) corresponding to the 4 parts – Logical Data Model, Functionality Execution description, User Interface description, and Message Exchange description – of the Functional Requirements Specifications (FRS) document.

The 4 Software's Measurable Components (SMCs) are the Software's Measurable Component 'Functional Data' (CFD), 'Functionality Execution' (CFE), 'User Interface' (CUI), and 'Message Exchange' (CME). They contain the Functional Data which are used and are operated upon by the functionality; functionality operations and data handling during these operations; user interfaces/screens for the input/output communications; and notifying messages for communications with the other programs, respectively.

All the SMCs comprise several Software Component's Measurable Features (SCMFs) that need to be measured for complete software measurement.

3.5.2 Presence and Size of the Software's Measurable Components (SMCs): Summary

The presence and size of the SMCs depend on the Functional Requirements Specifications (FRS) of the applications. There is no restriction on the size of the SMCs which are present.

EXERCISES

3.1 To which of the following Software's Measurable Component (SMC) does the functional requirement about data "Class: Result; Attributes: data count, memory operations, computational operations, logical operations, decision execution operations, repeat execution operations, action execution operations, input/output operations, message exchange operations, error handling operations, class methods, code count, user interface count, message count, total software count, program lines, design effort, test effort, and total effort (there are a total of 19 attributes); Fields: each attribute has one field" described in the Logical Data Model part belong?

A. Software's Measurable Component 'Functional Data' (CFD).

B. Software's Measurable Component 'Functionality Execution' (CFE).

C. Software's Measurable Component 'User Interface' (CUI).

D. Software's Measurable Component 'Message Exchange' (CME).

(*Note*: The aforementioned functional requirement is part of Chapter 14.)

3.2 To which of the following Software's Measurable Component (SMC) does the functional requirement about user screen "Option screen to ask if a new count estimate or continue working from an old estimate file" described in the User Interface part belong?

A. Software's Measurable Component 'Functional Data' (CFD).

B. Software's Measurable Component 'Functionality Execution' (CFE).

C. Software's Measurable Component 'User Interface' (CUI).

D. Software's Measurable Component 'Message Exchange' (CME).

(*Note*: The aforementioned functional requirement is part of Chapter 14.)

3.3 To which of the following Software's Measurable Component (SMC) does the functional requirement about the functionality "Calculate Data Count = DC+DA+DF" described in the functionality description part belong?

A. Software's Measurable Component 'Functional Data' (CFD).

B. Software's Measurable Component 'Functionality Execution' (CFE).

C. Software's Measurable Component 'User Interface' (CUI).

D. Software's Measurable Component 'Message Exchange' (CME).

(*Note*: The aforementioned functional requirement is part of Chapter 14.)

3.4 To which of the following Software's Measurable Component (SMC) do the Functional Requirements Specifications about the definition and structure of screens with field and input/output navigational links belong?

A. Software's Measurable Component 'Functional Data' (CFD).

B. Software's Measurable Component 'Functionality Execution' (CFE).

C. Software's Measurable Component 'User Interface' (CUI).

D. Software's Measurable Component 'Message Exchange' (CME).

3.5 To which of the following Software's Measurable Component (SMC) do the Functional Requirements Specifications about the memory read/write operations and input/output operations belong?

A. Software's Measurable Component 'Functional Data' (CFD).

B. Software's Measurable Component 'Functionality Execution' (CFE).

C. Software's Measurable Component 'User Interface' (CUI).

D. Software's Measurable Component 'Message Exchange' (CME).

Chapter 4

Software Component's Measurable Features in the FSSM

The Software's Measurable Component 'Functional Data' (CFD), 'Functionality Execution' (CFE), 'User Interface' (CUI), and 'Message Exchange' (CME) comprise several Software Component's Measurable Features (SCMFs) that need to be measured for complete software measurement. These SCMFs are described in the present chapter.

4.1 SOFTWARE COMPONENT'S MEASURABLE FEATURE (SCMF) DESCRIPTION

Each Software's Measurable Component (SMC) has several Software Component's Measurable Features (SCMFs) which are the attributes of the SMCs. Development effort is spent on all the SCMFs. Therefore, it is very important to take all of them into consideration for measurement. As explained in earlier chapters, most of these SCMFs do not have any fixed size–proportion relationship amongst themselves for the same software component and with the features of the other software components. Thus, for correct and comprehensive measurement of the complete software, all the important, relevant SCMFs should be measured so that the correct size of the complete software and consequently, an accurate estimation of the development effort are obtained. That is precisely what is done in the FSSM and is therefore, one of the major distinguishing factors of this methodology as compared to the other existing software size measurement methodologies.

All the Software Component's Measurable Features (SCMFs) of all the Software's Measurable Components (SMCs) are shown in Figure 3.

They are all considered to be measured in the FSSM and their description follows.

4.1.1 Description of the Software Component's Measurable Features (SCMFs) of the Software's Measurable Component 'Functional Data' (CFD)

Functional Data is normally described as data class structures in the Logical Data Model (LDM) with the help of diagrams and text description in the Functional Requirements Specifications (FRS) document. This structure contains the information about and relationships

Functional Software Size Measurement Methodology with Effort Estimation and Performance Indication, First Edition. Jasveer Singh.

Companion website: http://booksupport.wiley.com

amongst the data classes, their subclasses, attributes of the classes and subclasses, fields of the attributes, methods (operations or procedures) of the classes and subclasses, and other relevant descriptions/diagrams related to the data classes.

Class structure of the Functional Data consisting of classes, subclasses, class attributes, fields of the class attributes, and class methods to be used in the application, is a very important aspect to be considered for the effort spent in the software program development. The effort in the development regarding this is required for analyzing, designing, coding, and testing the data structures in normal programs or data tables in database management programs; various initializations of the data at different stages of the functional operations; use of the data for various operations and for processing in the software; and so, the effort needs to be spent on their development and consequently, the effort required for the development needs to be estimated. The amount of effort depends on the quantity of classes, subclasses, their attributes, fields of the attributes, and class methods. Hence, they are all – each one of every class, subclass, attribute, field of the attributes, class method – important to be taken into account for the measurement. They are all – each one of them – measured and form part of the measurements in the FSSM.

Corresponding to three of the aforementioned functional data features which are data classes/subclasses, class attributes, and attribute fields, there are 4 Software Component's Measurable Features (SCMFs) of the Software's Measurable Component 'Functional Data' (CFD). All these 4 SCMFs of the CFD are important and are taken into account for measurement in the FSSM. They are all measured, and their measurements contribute to the component measurements, size and effort estimations, and performance indications in the FSSM. The information concerning 3 SCMFs of the CFD is normally available in the Logical Data Model (LDM) description part of the Functional Requirements Specifications (FRS). Concerning the remaining 1 SCMF of the CFD, the other parts of the FRS provide the information.

The description of the 4 Software Component's Measurable Features (SCMFs) which are considered in the FSSM for the measurement of the Software's Measurable Component 'Functional Data' (CFD) follows.

4.1.1.1 Software Component's Measurable Feature 'Data Class' (FDC), 'Data Attribute' (FDA), and 'Data Field' (FDF) Description

All the classes (data entity) and subclasses of the Functional Data defined in the class structure description in the Logical Data Model part are important for the software development and effort estimate, as they contribute to the effort spent in the software development, and the effort needs to be estimated.

The classes and subclasses have attributes, and attributes of the classes (data entity) and subclasses have fields. All the attributes and fields are mentioned as part of the class structure description in the Logical Data Model part. They contribute to the effort spent in the software development, and the effort needs to be estimated.

Hence, all the classes and subclasses in the Logical Data Model are considered as Software Component's Measurable Feature 'Data Class' (FDC). And all the attributes and fields of the attributes of all the classes and subclasses in the Logical Data Model are considered as Software Component's Measurable Feature 'Data Attribute' (FDA) and 'Data Field' (FDF), respectively.

All the FDCs, FDAs, and FDFs are measured and form part of the measurements in the FSSM. Their measurements contribute to the component measurements, size and effort estimations, and performance indications in the FSSM.

4.1.1.2 Software Component's Measurable Feature 'Data Missing' (FDM) Description

It may be possible that there are some missing data items – classes, subclasses; attributes of the classes and subclasses; fields of the attributes of the classes and subclasses – in the Logical Data Model, and these missing items are easily identifiable while analyzing the functional requirements for performing the measurement. They are important because they reveal the deficiencies in the description of the Logical Data Model.

All the apparent and obvious deficiencies in data or missing data items – classes and subclasses, attributes of the classes and subclasses, and fields of the attributes of the classes and subclasses – for all the data described in the class structures in the Logical Data Model part of the FRS are considered as the Software Component's Measurable Feature 'Data Missing' (FDM).

All the FDMs are measured and form part of the measurements in the FSSM. Their measurements contribute to the component measurements and performance indications in the FSSM.

The measurement of the Software Component's Measurable Feature 'Data Missing' (FDM) is not included in the size and effort estimation calculations. It is used to indicate the improvements required in the Functional Requirements Specifications (FRS).

4.1.2 Common Characteristics of the Software Component's Measurable Features (SCMFs) of the Software's Measurable Component 'Functional Data' (CFD)

All the aforementioned 4 Software Component's Measurable Features (SCMFs) of the Software's Measurable Component 'Functional Data' (CFD) contribute to the effort spent in the software development. They are derived mainly from the Logical Data Model (LDM) description part of the Functional Requirements Specifications (FRS).

All the SCMFs of the CFD are measured. Their measurements form part of the Software Component's Feature Measurements (SCFMs) of the CFD, and are used for the calculations of the Software Component's Measurements (SCMs), Software Size and Effort Estimations (SSEEs), and Software Performance Quality Indicators (SPQIs).

4.1.3 Description of the Software Component's Measurable Features (SCMFs) of the Software's Measurable Component 'Functionality Execution' (CFE)

The Functionality Execution (FE) description part of the Functional Requirements Specifications (FRS) contains the information about the functionality to be executed.

Three types of information are required from the Functionality Execution (FE) description part.

First, the information about the following types of functional operations:

1. Memory operations: these are the data read/write operations from/to the non-volatile permanent type of memory storage devices such as disks. Example of data read is when some data is needed to be processed or checked, it needs to be read from the disk memory first, before processing or checking. Example of data write is when a data save or update action is performed, data gets written to the disk memory.

All the memory operations or memory data read/write operations or simply data read/write operations mentioned hereafter mean data reading/writing from/to non-volatile permanent type of memory storage devices such as disks.

2. Input/output operations: these are the data input/output operations used for receiving/sending the input/output data from/to the input/output devices, such as input device keyboard, and output display devices, or any other types of input/output devices such as digital thermometer device for reading temperature for meteorological applications, input operations of reading instruments for automatic measurement applications, and output operations of sending outputs to the control devices for controlling them.
3. Message communication operations: these are the message exchange operations, that is, message send/receive operations, which are used for communicating with either the external application programs or with the sub-programs (modules) of the same application program with the help of suitable messages.
4. Computational operations involving computations such as addition, subtraction, multiplication, division, power, log, and equals.
5. Logical operations such as AND, OR, NOT, and XOR.
6. Decision operations which specify that some decision is taken and particular actions are performed if the decision is true and some other actions are performed if the decision is false.
7. Repeat operations which specify the actions of repeating the execution of some functionality a certain number of times.
8. The actions which are performed for executing the functional operations or groups of functional operations.
9. Operations which are used for the flow control of the execution of the application program, for example, operations which call the execution of a particular part of the functionality, such as performing the functionality of a class method; and which get translated in the program as calling the execution of a subroutine or function or class method.
10. Operations or group of operations which can be categorized as error handling operations.

Second, the information about the following types of functional data handling during the functional operations:

1. Functional data handled during the memory data read/write operations from/to the non-volatile permanent type of memory storage devices such as disks; these are the Data Collections read/written from/to the memory devices.
2. Functional data handled during the input/output operations from/to the various types of input/output devices; these are the Data Collections that are received/sent from/to the input/output devices such as keyboard, display, and instruments; these Data Collections can be related to the fields, links, or parameters of the screens.
3. Functional data handled during the message exchange operations to communicate either with the external application programs or with the sub-programs (modules) of the same application program; the Data Collections handled can be related to the message fields, parameters, etc.

4. Functional data handled during the following functional operations:
   a. computational – the Data Collections involved in the computations;
   b. logical – the Data Collections involved in the logical operations;
   c. decision – the Data Collections used in the decision actions;
   d. repeat – the Data Collections used in the repeat instructions/operations;
   e. execution flow control – the Data Collections used for controlling the flow of execution; the Data Collections can be some parameters used for flow control.

Functional data handling is considered as handling of Data Collections (DCLs) for various types of operations. Data Collection (DCL) means a group of data that can be handled together independently for memory read/write operations, input/output operations, message exchange operations, or general functional operations – computational, logical, decision, repeat, or execution flow control – that may be either whole class data; or whole subclass data; or single attribute data of a class or subclass; or group of attributes data of a class or subclass.

Third, in addition to the functional operations and functional data handling information in the Functionality Execution description part, the information about the class methods described as part of the class structures in the Logical Data Model part is required because class methods form part of the Functionality Execution.

All the aforementioned functional operations and functional data handled in the operations described in the Functionality Execution description part of the Functional Requirements Specifications (FRS), and class methods described in the Logical Data Model part of the FRS need to be developed: their analysis, design, coding, and testing, all contribute to the effort spent on development. Thus the effort needs to be estimated. Hence, they are all important to be taken into account for the measurement. They are all measured and form part of the measurements in the FSSM.

Corresponding to the aforementioned functional operations and functional data handled in the operations, there are 19 Software Component's Measurable Features (SCMFs) of the Software's Measurable Component 'Functionality Execution' (CFE). All these 19 SCMFs of the CFE are important and are taken into account for measurement in the FSSM. They are all measured and their measurements contribute to the component measurements, size and effort estimations, and performance indications. The information concerning 17 SCMFs of the CFE is normally available in the Functionality Execution (FE) description part of the Functional Requirements Specifications (FRS). Regarding one SCMF of the CFE, the information is available in the Logical Data Model (LDM) of the FRS. Concerning the remaining one SCMF of the CFE, the other parts of the FRS provide the information.

The description of the 19 Software Component's Measurable Features (SCMFs) which are considered in the FSSM for the measurement of the Software's Measurable Component 'Functionality Execution' (CFE) follows.

Wherever 'data collection' or 'Data Collection' is mentioned in the description that follows in this chapter, and in the description in later chapters, it means a group of data that can be handled together independently that may be either whole class data, or whole subclass data, or single attribute data of a class or subclass, or group of attributes data of a class or subclass, for that particular operation.

4.1.3.1 Software Component's Measurable Feature 'Data Read' (FDR) and 'Data Write' (FDW) Description

All the memory read operations in the functionality description that read the functional data collections from the data storage devices such as disks are considered as Software Component's Measurable Feature 'Data Read' (FDR).

These operations can be the storage memory read operations for displaying the data, or for modifying the data, or for any other purpose.

All the memory write operations in the functionality description that write the functional data collections on to the data storage devices such as disks are considered as the Software Component's Measurable Feature 'Data Write' (FDW).

These operations can be the storage memory write operations for saving the data after the entry of data from the input devices, or after modifying the data, or after any other operation.

All the FDRs and FDWs are measured and form part of the measurements in the FSSM because they contribute to the effort spent in the software development, and the effort needs to be estimated. Their measurements contribute to the component measurements, size and effort estimations, and performance indications in the FSSM.

4.1.3.2 Software Component's Measurable Feature 'Data Input' (FDI) and 'Data Output' (FDO) Description

All the data input operations in the functionality description that receive the input data collections from the input devices such as keyboard, measurement devices, and instruments, are considered as the Software Component's Measurable Feature 'Data Input' (FDI).

These operations can be all the types of data input operations for either saving or further processing the data from keyboard, instruments/equipment, etc.

All the data output operations in the functionality description that send the output data collections to the output devices such as displays, measurement devices, and instruments, are considered as the Software Component's Measurable Feature 'Data Output' (FDO).

These operations can be all the types of data output operations for either displaying or controlling/instructing the equipment/instruments.

All the FDIs and FDOs are measured and form part of the measurements in the FSSM because they contribute to the effort spent in the software development, and the effort needs to be estimated. Their measurements contribute to the component measurements, size and effort estimations, and performance indications in the FSSM.

4.1.3.3 Software Component's Measurable Feature 'Message Send' (FMS) and 'Message Receive' (FMR) Description

All the message send/receive operations in the functionality description that send/receive the messages to/from the external application programs are considered as the Software Component's Measurable Feature 'Message Send' (FMS)/'Message Receive' (FMR), respectively.

The external programs can be either other application programs or sub-programs (modules) of the same application program.

All the FMSs and FMRs are measured and form part of the measurements in the FSSM because they contribute to the effort spent in the software development, and the effort needs to be estimated. Their measurements contribute to the component measurements, size and effort estimations, and performance indications in the FSSM.

4.1.3.4 Software Component's Measurable Feature 'Function Computational Operation' (FFC), 'Function Logical Operation' (FFL), and 'Function Error Handling' (FFE) Description

All the computational operations – addition, subtraction, multiplication, division, power, log, equals, etc. – in the functionality description are considered as the Software Component's Measurable Feature 'Function Computational Operation' (FFC).

All the logical operations – AND, OR, NOT, XOR – in the functionality description are considered as the Software Component's Measurable Feature 'Function Logical Operation' (FFL).

All the error handling operations or error handling operations groups in the functionality description are considered as the Software Component's Measurable Feature 'Function Error Handling' (FFE).

All the FFCs, FFLs, and FFEs are measured and form part of the measurements in the FSSM because they contribute to the effort spent in the software development, and the effort needs to be estimated. The measurements of the FFCs and FFLs contribute to the calculations of the component measurements, size and effort estimations, and performance indications in the FSSM. The measurements of the FFEs contribute to the calculations of the performance indications only.

4.1.3.5 Software Component's Measurable Feature 'Function Decision Execution' (FFD), 'Function Repeat Execution' (FFR), 'Function Action Execution' (FFA), and 'Function Execution Flow Control' (FFO) Description

All the conditions checking and taking decisions (e.g., if the condition is true, take the action) in the functionality description are considered as the Software Component's Measurable Feature 'Function Decision Execution' (FFD).

All the repeats for action(s) in the functionality description are considered as the Software Component's Measurable Feature 'Function Repeat Execution' (FFR).

Action execution functions are all the actions that are performed. It can be a single action or group of actions. It can be interpreted as follows.

- **a.** It can be a do type of action or instruction such as:
  - **i.** do action(s);
  - **ii.** do some processing;
  - **iii.** do some error handling operations.
- **b.** It can be a take action(s) type of instruction, such as take some decision.
- **c.** It can be a perform action(s) type of instruction, such as:
  - **i.** perform repeat operation;
  - **ii.** perform data read/write operations;
  - **iii.** perform message send/receive operation;
  - **iv.** perform data input/output operation;
  - **v.** perform computational/logical operation.

All the actions or groups of actions to be performed in the functionality description are considered as the Software Component's Measurable Feature 'Function Action Execution' (FFA).

All the execution flow control operations such as transfer to some other part of functionality execution in the functionality description are considered as the Software Component's Measurable Feature 'Function Execution Flow Control' (FFO).

All the FFDs, FFRs, FFAs, and FFOs are measured and form part of the measurements in the FSSM because they contribute to the effort spent in the software development, and the effort needs to be estimated. Their measurements contribute to the component measurements, size and effort estimations, and performance indications in the FSSM.

4.1.3.6 Software Component's Measurable Feature 'Memory Operations Functional Data' (FLM), 'Input/Output Operations Functional Data' (FLI), 'Message Exchange Operations Functional Data' (FLS), and 'General Operations Functional Data' (FLG) Description

All the Data Collections handled during memory read/write operations in the functionality description are considered as the Software Component's Measurable Feature 'Memory Operations Functional Data' (FLM).

Similarly, all the Data Collections handled during input/output, message send/receive, and general functional – computational, logical, decision, repeat, and execution flow control – operations, in the functionality description are considered as the Software Component's Measurable Feature 'Input/Output Operations Functional Data' (FLI), 'Message Exchange Operations Functional Data' (FLS), and 'General Operations Functional Data' (FLG), respectively.

All the FLMs, FLIs, FLSs, and FLGs are measured and form part of the measurements in the FSSM because they contribute to the effort spent in the software development, and the effort needs to be estimated. Their measurements contribute to the component measurements, size and effort estimations, and performance indications in the FSSM.

4.1.3.7 Software Component's Measurable Feature 'Class Method' (FCM) Description

The classes (data entity) and subclasses of the functional data defined in the class structure description in the Logical Data Model part have methods (operations or procedures). Software corresponding to the functionality required by these methods needs to be developed and so, effort is required to be spent for this, and thus needs to be estimated.

Hence, all the methods of all the classes and subclasses in the Logical Data Model are considered as the Software Component's Measurable Feature 'Class Method' (FCM).

All the FCMs are measured and form part of the measurements in the FSSM. Their measurements contribute to the component measurements, size and effort estimations, and performance indications in the FSSM.

4.1.3.8 Software Component's Measurable Feature 'Functionality Missing' (FFM) Description

It may be possible that there are some missing functionality items in the Functionality Execution description, and these missing items are easily identifiable while performing the measurement. The following functionality items are the type of operations and data handled that may be deficient or missing:

- **a.** memory read/write operations;
- **b.** functional data handled during the memory read/write operations;
- **c.** input/output operations;
- **d.** functional data handled during the input/output operations;
- **e.** message exchange operations;
- **f.** functional data handled during the message exchange operations;
- **g.** computational operations;
- **h.** logical operations;

i. decision execution operations;
j. repeat execution operations;
k. action execution operations;
l. execution flow control operations;
m. error handling operations;
n. functional data handled during the general computational, logical, decision, repeat, and execution flow control operations.

Also, it may be possible that there are missing class methods (operations or procedures) in the Logical Data Model.

All the aforementioned type of apparent and obvious deficiencies in the functionality, or missing functionality items for all the functionality described in the Functionality Execution description part, and the missing class methods in the Logical Data Model part, of the FRS are considered as the Software Component's Measurable Feature 'Functionality Missing' (FFM).

All the FFMs are measured and form part of the measurements in the FSSM. Their measurements contribute to the component measurements and performance indications in the FSSM.

The measurement of the Software Component's Measurable Feature 'Functionality Missing' (FFM) is not included in the size and effort estimation calculations. It is used to indicate the improvements required in the Functional Requirements Specifications (FRS).

4.1.4 Common Characteristics of the Software Component's Measurable Features (SCMFs) of the Software's Measurable Component 'Functionality Execution' (CFE)

All the aforementioned 19 Software Component's Measurable Features (SCMFs) of the Software's Measurable Component 'Functionality Execution' (CFE) contribute to the effort spent in the software development. They are derived mainly from the Functionality Execution (FE) description part and Logical Data Model (LDM) part of the Functional Requirements Specifications (FRS).

All the SCMFs of the CFE are measured. Their measurements form part of the Software Component's Feature Measurements (SCFMs) of the CFE, and are used for the calculations of the Software Component's Measurements (SCMs), Software Size and Effort Estimations (SSEEs), and Software Performance Quality Indicators (SPQIs).

4.1.5 Description of the Software Component's Measurable Features (SCMFs) of the Software's Measurable Component 'User Interface' (CUI)

User interface/screens are normally described as screen layout diagrams, their fields and input/output navigation links, and their text descriptions, in the User Interface (UI) description part of the Functional Requirements Specifications (FRS). Another important diagram, the interconnection diagram showing the connections of the input/output navigation links of the screens, helps to understand how the input/output links are interconnected and is useful for the verification that all the links are properly used. Also, it helps in design and testing.

Similar to the

a. class structure of the Functional Data;

b. functional operations and Functional Data used in the functional operations;

the screen structures consisting of the

a. screen layouts;

b. fields and input/output navigational links of the screens;

are a very important aspect to be considered for the effort spent in the software program development. The effort in the development regarding this is required for analyzing, designing, coding, and testing the screen structures; defining data structures for the screen fields; defining the linking of input/output navigational links from/to various screens/operations; various initializations of the screen fields at different stages of the operations; and so, the effort needs to be spent on their development and consequently, the effort required for the development needs to be estimated. Hence, the screens structures, their fields, and their input/output navigational links are all important to be taken into account for the measurement. They are all measured and form part of the measurements in the FSSM.

Corresponding to the aforementioned user screen features, there are 5 Software Component's Measurable Features (SCMFs) of the Software's Measurable Component 'User Interface' (CUI). All these 5 SCMFs of the CUI are important and are taken into account for the measurement in the FSSM. They are all measured and their measurements contribute to the component measurements, size and effort estimations, and performance indications in the FSSM. The information concerning 4 SCMFs of the CUI is normally available in the User Interface (UI) description part of the Functional Requirements Specifications (FRS). Concerning the remaining 1 SCMF of the CUI, the other parts of the FRS provide the information.

The description of the 5 Software Component's Measurable Features (SCMFs) which are considered in the FSSM for the measurement of the Software's Measurable Component 'User Interface' (CUI) follows.

4.1.5.1 Software Component's Measurable Feature 'User Screen' (FUS), 'User Screen Field' (FUF), 'User Screen Output Link' (FUO), and 'User Screen Input Link' (FUI) Description

All the user screens in the User Interface description part are considered as the Software Component's Measurable Feature 'User Screen' (FUS)

The screens contain the fields and navigational links. The fields are used to display the values of data or text in the screen, or for input of data from the screen. Also, there are the menu items in the screens which need to be considered.

All the fields of all the screens in the User Interface description part are considered as the Software Component's Measurable Feature 'User Screen Field' (FUF).

In the output display screens, the fields are used to display data or text. In the data input screens, the fields are used for the data input activity – some fields display the text information and others receive the input information. Also, the menu items to be selected form part of the screen fields.

All the output navigation links of all the user screens in the User Interface description part are considered as the Software Component's Measurable Feature 'User Screen Output Link' (FUO).

Output navigational links are used to navigate from the screen to other actions of the application, for example, to display another screen or execute other operations such as save data which was input from the screen, or exit the application.

All the input navigation links of all the user screens in the User Interface description part are considered as the Software Component's Measurable Feature 'User Screen Input Link' (FUI).

The input navigational links of the screen indicate from where the screen is entered to be displayed. It may be from the output navigational link of another screen, or some other part of the application.

All the FUSs, FUFs, FUOs, and FUIs are measured and form part of the measurements in the FSSM because they contribute to the effort spent in the software development, and the effort needs to be estimated. Their measurements contribute to the component measurements, size and effort estimations, and performance indications in the FSSM.

4.1.5.2 Software Component's Measurable Feature 'User Screen Missing' (FUM) Description

It may be possible that there are some missing screen items – user screens, screens' fields, screens' input navigation links, screens' output navigation links – in the User Interface description part, and these missing items are easily identifiable while performing the measurement.

All the apparent and obvious deficiencies in the screens or missing screen items – user screens, screens' fields, screens' input navigation links, screens' output navigation links – for all the screens described in the User Interface description part of the FRS are considered as the Software Component's Measurable Feature 'User Screen Missing' (FUM).

All the FUMs are measured and form part of the measurements in the FSSM. Their measurements contribute to the component measurements and performance indications in the FSSM.

The measurement of the Software Component's Measurable Feature 'User Screen Missing' (FUM) is not included in the size and effort estimation calculations. It is used to indicate the improvements required in the Functional Requirements Specifications (FRS).

4.1.6 Common Characteristics of the Software Component's Measurable Features (SCMFs) of the Software's Measurable Component 'User Interface' (CUI)

All the aforementioned 5 Software Component's Measurable Features (SCMFs) of the Software's Measurable Component 'User Interface' (CUI) contribute to the effort spent in the software development. They are derived mainly from the User Interface (UI) description part of the Functional Requirements Specifications (FRS).

All the SCMFs of the CUI are measured. Their measurements form part of the Software Component's Feature Measurements (SCFMs) of the CUI, and are used for the calculations of the Software Component's Measurements (SCMs), Software Size and Effort Estimations (SSEEs), and Software Performance Quality Indicators (SPQIs).

4.1.7 Description of the Software Component's Measurable Features (SCMFs) of the Software's Measurable Component 'Message Exchange' (CME)

Message Exchange description part of the Functional Requirements Specifications (FRS) normally describes the message structures with message identifiers, message fields, and other necessary details such as source of message and destination of message. The information needed about the messages for the FSSM is the message name/identifier and its fields.

Similar to the

a. data class structure;

b. functionality execution operations;

c. functional data used in the functional operations;

d. user interface/screens structure;

the message structure of the messages consisting of the message identifiers, message fields and other details, to be used in the application, is a very important aspect to be considered for the effort spent in the software program development. The effort in the development regarding this is required for analyzing, designing, coding, and testing the data structures for the messages in the programs; defining data structures for the message fields; various initializations of the data for the messages at different stages of operations; use of the message data for various operations and for processing in the software; and so, the effort needs to be spent on their development and consequently, the effort required for the development needs to be estimated. Hence, the messages and their fields are all important to be taken into account for measurement. They are all measured and form part of the measurements in the FSSM.

There are 3 Software Component's Measurable Features (SCMFs) of the Software's Measurable Component 'Message Exchange' (CME). All these 3 SCMFS of the CME are important and are taken into account for measurement in the FSSM. They are all measured and their measurements contribute to the component measurements, size and effort estimations, and performance indications in the FSSM. The information concerning 2 SCMFs of the CME is normally available in the Message Exchange (ME) description part of the Functional Requirements Specifications (FRS). Concerning the remaining 1 SCMF of the CME, the other parts of the FRS provide the information.

The description of the 3 Software Component's Measurable Features (SCMFs) which are considered in the FSSM for the measurement of the Software's Measurable Component 'Message Exchange' (CME) follows.

4.1.7.1 Software Component's Measurable Feature 'Notifying Message' (FNM) and 'Message Field' (FMF) Description

All the messages and all the fields of all the messages in the Message Exchange description part are considered as the Software Component's Measurable Feature 'Notifying Message' (FNM) and 'Message Field' (FMF), respectively.

All the FNMs and FMFs are measured and form part of the measurements in the FSSM because they contribute to the effort spent in the software development, and the effort needs to be estimated. Their measurements contribute to the component measurements, size and effort estimations, and performance indications in the FSSM.

4.1.7.2 Software Component's Measurable Feature 'Message Missing' (FMM) Description

It may be possible that there are some missing message items – messages and message fields – in the Message Exchange description part, and these missing items are easily identifiable while performing the measurement.

All the apparent and obvious deficiencies in messages or missing message items – messages and message fields – for all the messages described in the Message Exchange description part of the FRS are considered as the Software Component's Measurable Feature 'Message Missing' (FMM).

All the FMMs are measured and form part of the measurements in the FSSM. Their measurements contribute to the component measurements and performance indications in the FSSM.

The measurement of the Software Component's Measurable Feature 'Message Missing' (FMM) is not included in the size and effort estimation calculations. It is used to indicate the improvements required in the Functional Requirements Specifications (FRS).

4.1.8 Common Characteristics of the Software Component's Measurable Features (SCMFs) of the Software's Measurable Component 'Message Exchange' (CME)

All the aforementioned 3 Software Component's Measurable Features (SCMFs) of the Software's Measurable Component 'Message Exchange' (CME) contribute to the effort spent in the software development. They are derived mainly from the Message Exchange (ME) description part of the Functional Requirements Specifications (FRS).

All the SCMFs of the CME are measured. Their measurements form part of the Software Component's Feature Measurements (SCFMs) of the CME, and are used for the calculations of the Software Component's Measurements (SCMs), Software Size and Effort Estimations (SSEEs), and Software Performance Quality Indicators (SPQIs).

4.2 USAGE OF THE SOFTWARE COMPONENT'S MEASURABLE FEATURES (SCMFs)

The Software Component's Measurable Features (SCMFs) are the backbone of the Functional Size Measurement[1] in the FSSM. Thus, in total, the aforementioned 31 SCMFs of the 4 software's measurable components CFD, CFE, CUI, and CME (the Software's Measurable Component 'Functional Data', 'Functionality Execution', 'User Interface', and 'Message Exchange', respectively) are used for the complete software size measurements in the FSSM. Their measurements – Software Component's Feature Measurements (SCFMs) – are the basis for the calculations of the Software Component's Measurements (SCMs), Software Size and Effort Estimations (SSEEs), and Software Performance Quality Indicators (SPQIs) of both the types: Software Structural Indicators (SSIs)[5–7] and Software Operational Indicators (SOIs)[5–7].

4.3 SOFTWARE COMPONENT'S MEASURABLE FEATURES (SCMFs) PRESENCE AND QUANTITY

The absence, or presence and quantity of the different Software Component's Measurable Features (SCMFs) depend on the type of applications and thus, on the Functional Requirements Specifications (FRS) of the applications.

It may be possible that certain SCMFs are absent, or present in small quantity, but some others may be more voluminously present.

In fact, the varying sizes of the

a. Software Component's Measurable Features (SCMFs) measured by the Software Component's Feature Measurements (SCFMs);

b. Software's Measurable Component 'Functional Data' (CFD), 'Functionality Execution' (CFE), 'User Interface' (CUI), and 'Message Exchange' (CME) measured by the Software Component's Measurements (SCMs);

and thus, the total size of the software are dependent on this varying magnitude of the presence of various SCMFs, and so, the sizes – of the SCMFs, of the SMCs, and the total size – are determined based on this aspect of presence and quantity of SCMFs.

There is no upper limit of the presence and quantity of the SCMFs.

4.4 EXAMPLES

1. In the functional requirement "Class: Count; Attributes: identifier, description, DC, DA, DF, CM, DR, DW, DI, DO, FC, FL, FD, FR, FA, FE, MS, MR, MN, MF, US, UF, UO, UI, remark (there are a total of 25 attributes); Fields: each attribute has one field; Operations: 'enter data', 'calculate and display'" which forms part of data description in the Logical Data Model part of the FRS, all the following SCMFs (Software Component's Measurable Features) can be clearly identified:
   A. Software Component's Measurable Feature 'Data Class' (FDC) which is class Count;
   B. Software Component's Measurable Feature 'Data Attribute' (FDA) which are all the attributes: identifier, description, DC, DA, DF, CM, DR, DW, DI, DO, FC, FL, FD, FR, FA, FE, MS, MR, MN, MF, US, UF, UO, UI, remark;
   C. Software Component's Measurable Feature 'Data Field' (FDF) which are all the fields of all the attributes – one field for each attribute;
   D. Software Component's Measurable Feature 'Class Method' (FCM) which are all the class methods: 'enter data', 'calculate and display'.
   (*Note*: The aforementioned functional requirement is part of Chapter 14.)
2. In the functional requirement "After entering the data, either click 'Save' which saves the current entry: category, identifier, description, 22 counts; and continue to display the same, or click 'Next' that saves the current entry and prompts for new inputs, or click 'Calculate' which calculates the estimate.", all the following SCMFs (Software Component's Measurable Features) can be clearly identified:
   A. Software Component's Measurable Feature 'Data Input' (FDI) which is receiving input data when clicked on either 'Save', 'Next', or 'Calculate' buttons;

B. Software Component's Measurable Feature 'Function Decision Execution' (FFD) which is taking a decision if the 'Save' was clicked on or 'Next' or 'Calculate';
C. Software Component's Measurable Feature 'Data Write' (FDW) which is writing the data when clicked on 'Save' or 'Next';
D. Software Component's Measurable Feature 'Data Output' (FDO) which is displaying the screen for new inputs when 'Save' is clicked on;
E. Software Component's Measurable Feature 'Function Action Execution' (FFA) which are the actions of input data, taking decisions, writing data, and output data for display;
F. Software Component's Measurable Feature 'Memory Operations Functional Data' (FLM) for memory write data collection;
G. Software Component's Measurable Feature 'Input/Output Operations Functional Data' (FLI) for Data Collections handled in data input and output operations;
H. Software Component's Measurable Feature 'General Operations Functional Data' (FLG) for Data Collections handled in decision execution operations.

(*Note*: The aforementioned functional requirement is part of Chapter 14.)

3. In the functional requirement "Class: Count; Attributes: identifier, description, DC, DA, DF, CM, DR, DW, DI, DO, FC, FL, FD, FR, FA, FE, MS, MR, MN, MF, US, UF, UO, UI, remark (there are a total of 25 attributes); Fields: each attribute has one field; Operations: 'enter data', 'calculate and display'" which forms part of data description in the Logical Data Model part of the FRS, none of the following SCMFs (Software Component's Measurable Features) can be identified:

A. Software Component's Measurable Feature 'Data Write' (FDW) which is a memory data write operation;
B. Software Component's Measurable Feature 'User Screen' (FUS) which is the definition of a user screen;
C. Software Component's Measurable Feature 'Function Decision Execution' (FFD) which is a functional decision operation.

(*Note*: The aforementioned functional requirement is part of the Chapter 14.)

4. All the following are examples of the Software Component's Measurable Feature 'Message Missing' (FMM):

A. if a particular message is sent in the functionality description part of the Functional Requirements Specifications (FRS) but the message is not defined in the Message Exchange description part of the Functional Requirements Specifications (FRS);
B. if a message field is used in a message send operation in the functionality description part of the Functional Requirements Specifications (FRS) but the message field is not defined in the Message Exchange description part of the Functional Requirements Specifications (FRS).

5. All the following are examples of the Software Component's Measurable Feature 'Functionality Missing' (FFM):

A. if a particular message is defined in the Message Exchange description part of the Functional Requirements Specifications (FRS) but the message is not used in any message send or message receive operations in the functionality description part of the Functional Requirements Specifications (FRS);

B. if a screen with fields and input/output navigational links is defined in the User Interface description part of the Functional Requirements Specifications (FRS) but the screen is not used in any input/output operations in the functionality description part of the Functional Requirements Specifications (FRS);

C. if a screen output link is defined in the User Interface description part of the Functional Requirements Specifications (FRS) but no corresponding functionality when the link is clicked-on is defined in the functionality description part of the Functional Requirements Specifications (FRS).

4.5 CHAPTER SUMMARY

4.5.1 Software Component's Measurable Feature (SCMF): Summary

The 4 Software's Measurable Components (SMCs) which correspond to the 4 description parts of the Functional Requirements Specifications (FRS) – the Logical Data model, Functionality Execution, User Interface, and Message Exchange description parts – are the Software's Measurable Component 'Functional Data' (CFD), 'Functionality Execution' (CFE), 'User Interface' (CUI), and 'Message Exchange' (CME), respectively. They are composed of the Functional Data used by the application program, functional operations executed in the program for the required functionality, user interfaces/screens for the input/output communication, and messages for communication with the other programs/sub-programs, respectively.

All the 4 SMCs have their associated features known as the Software Component's Measurable Features (SCMFs). The SCMFs of the

a. CFD pertaining to the
- data classes, attributes, fields, and missing data items;

b. CFE pertaining to the
- memory read/write, input/output, message send/receive, computational, logical, decision, action, repeat, execution flow control, and error handling operations; data handled in the memory read/write, input/output, message send/receive, computational, logical, decision, repeat, and execution flow control operations; class methods; and missing functionality items;

c. CUI pertaining to the
- user screens, their fields, input/output links, and missing screen items;

d. CME pertaining to the
- messages, their fields and missing message items;

are all measured for comprehensive software measurement.

4.5.2 Usage, Presence, and Quantity of the Software Component's Measurable Features (SCMFs): Summary

The measurements of the Software Component's Measurable Features (SCMFs), that is, the Software Component's Features Measurements (SCFMs) are used for the complete software size measurements in the FSSM. The SCFMs are the basis for the calculations of the Software Component's Measurements (SCMs), Software Size and Effort Estimations

(SSEEs), and Software Performance Quality Indicators (SPQIs) of both the types Software Structural Indicators (SSIs)[5–7] and Software Operational Indicators (SOIs)[5–7].

The absence, or presence and quantity of the SCMFs depend on the type of applications and thus, on the functional requirements of the applications. There is no upper limit of the presence and quantity of the SCMFs.

EXERCISES

4.1 Which of the following SCMFs (Software Component's Measurable Features) is present in the functional requirement "Class: Count; Attributes: identifier, description, DC, DA, DF, CM, DR, DW, DI, DO, FC, FL, FD, FR, FA, FE, MS, MR, MN, MF, US, UF, UO, UI, remark (there are a total of 25 attributes); Fields: each attribute has one field; Operations: 'enter data', 'calculate and display'"?

A. Software Component's Measurable Feature 'Data Read' (FDR).

B. Software Component's Measurable Feature 'Data Input' (FDI).

C. Software Component's Measurable Feature 'Function Decision Execution' (FFD).

D. Software Component's Measurable Feature 'Data Class' (FDC).

E. Software Component's Measurable Feature 'User Screen Field' (FUF).

(*Note*: The aforementioned functional requirement is part of Chapter 14.)

4.2 Which of the following SCMFs (Software Component's Measurable Features) does the operation 'message send to other programs' signify?

A. Software Component's Measurable Feature 'Message Receive' (FMR).

B. Software Component's Measurable Feature 'Message Send' (FMS).

C. Software Component's Measurable Feature 'Data Output' (FDO).

4.3 Which of the following SCMFs (Software Component's Measurable Features) is not a measurable feature of the CFD (Software's Measurable Component 'Functional Data')?

A. Software Component's Measurable Feature 'Data Class' (FDC).

B. Software Component's Measurable Feature 'Data Attribute' (FDA).

C. Software Component's Measurable Feature 'Message Field' (FMF).

D. Software Component's Measurable Feature 'Data Field' (FDF).

4.4 Which of the following SCMFs (Software Component's Measurable Feature) does not signify a 'missing feature'?

A. Software Component's Measurable Feature 'Data Missing' (FDM).

B. Software Component's Measurable Feature 'User Screen Missing' (FUM).

C. Software Component's Measurable Feature 'Message Missing' (FMM).

D. Software Component's Measurable Feature 'Data Attribute' (FDA).

E. Software Component's Measurable Feature 'Functionality Missing' (FFM).

4.5 Which of the following SCMFs (Software Component's Measurable Features) is not present in the functional requirement "Class: Count; Attributes: identifier, description, DC, DA, DF, CM, DR, DW, DI, DO, FC, FL, FD, FR, FA, FE, MS, MR, MN, MF, US, UF, UO, UI, remark (there are a total of 25 attributes); Fields: each attribute has one field; Operations: 'enter data', 'calculate and display'" which forms part of data description in the Logical Data Model part of the FRS?

A. Software Component's Measurable Feature 'Data Class' (FDC) which is class: Count.

B. Software Component's Measurable Feature 'Data Attribute' (FDA) which are attributes: identifier, description, DC, DA, DF, CM, DR, DW, DI, DO, FC, FL, FD, FR, FA, FE, MS, MR, MN, MF, US, UF, UO, UI, remark.

C. Software Component's Measurable Feature 'Data Field' (FDF) which are the fields of the attributes: one field for each attribute.

D. Software Component's Measurable Feature 'User Screen' (FUS) which is the definition of a user screen.

E. Software Component's Measurable Feature 'Class Method' (FCM) which are: 'enter data', 'calculate and display'.

(*Note*: The aforementioned functional requirement is part of the Chapter 14.)

Part Three

FSSM: Measurements

Chapter 5

Software Component's Feature Points in the FSSM

The 4 Software's Measurable Components (SMCs) have their associated features known as the Software Component's Measurable Features (SCMFs). All the SCMFs are measured for comprehensive software measurement.

All the SCMFs are identified in the FRS (Functional Requirements Specifications), and the Software Component's Feature Points (SCFPs), that is, the Functional Size Unit (FSU), are assigned to them. The identification of the SCMFs and assigning the SCFPs (i.e., FSUs) is described in this chapter.

5.1 SOFTWARE COMPONENT'S FEATURE POINT (SCFP) DESCRIPTION

Measurement of the software size in the FSSM is done by measuring the size of the Software's Measurable Components (SMCs). These components are measured by the measurement of their individual Software Component's Measurable Features (SCMFs). The SCMFs for all the SMCs are measured in 3 steps. The first step is: assigning the Software Component's Feature Points (SCFPs), which are the Functional Size Units (FSUs) for the Software Component's Feature Measurements (SCFMs) and Software Component's Measurements (SCMs), to the SCMFs. Assigning the SCFPs (i.e., FSU) is done through analysis of the Functional Requirements Specifications (FRS) for identifying the SCMFs. For this, the following parts of the FRS are used:

1. Logical Data Model (LDM) description part;
2. Functionality Execution (FE) description part;
3. User Interface (UI) description part;
4. Message Exchange (ME) description part;

to extract the information about the Software Component's Feature Points (SCFPs) corresponding to the Software Component's Measurable Features (SCMFs) of the following Software's Measurable Components (SMCs), respectively:

1. Software's Measurable Component 'Functional Data' (CFD);
2. Software's Measurable Component 'Functional Execution' (CFE);

Functional Software Size Measurement Methodology with Effort Estimation and Performance Indication, First Edition. Jasveer Singh.

Companion website: http://booksupport.wiley.com

3. Software's Measurable Component 'User Interface '(CUI);
4. Software's Measurable Component 'Message Exchange' (CME).

At the beginning of the first step, the scope of the measurement of software is defined by determining the borderline of the software to be measured. Recalling what is mentioned about the scope and borderline definition in Section 2.1.4, borderline is defined where the communication from the software to be measured takes place for the following items:

1. communication with the Operating Systems functions;
2. communication with the permanent memory storage devices, for example, disks;
3. communication with the input/output devices, for example, keyboard and display;
4. communication with the other external application programs;
5. communication with the other sub-programs (modules) of the same application program.

Defining the borderline of the software to be measured ensures that all the SCMFs (Software Component's Measurable Features) related to the aforementioned communication that are identified through the analysis of the FRS (Functional Requirements Specifications), that is, memory read/write operations, input/output operations, and message send/receive operations, reside in the software to be measured and hence, they form part of the SCMFs (Software Component's Measurable Features) in the assignment process of SCFPs (Software Component's Feature Points) to various SCMFs.

SCFPs are calculated for all the features of all the SMCs (CFD, CFE, CUI, and CME) as described in the subsequent sections. For this, analysis of the Functional Requirements Specifications (FRS) is done by considering the functional requirements at the smallest granular level in order to enable the identification of the SCMFs (Software Component's Measurable Features) for all the SMCs (Software's Measurable Components) as indicated in Sections 3.1.1–3.1.4 about what needs to be checked in the Functional Requirements Specifications (FRS). These SCFPs for various Software Component's Measurable Features (SCMFs) of the 4 Software's Measurable Components (SCMs), in the second step of the measurements of the SCMFs, produce SCFP Counts (SCFPCs) for the concerned features. The SCFPCs, in the third step of the measurements of the SCMFs, are used further for arriving at the Software Component's Feature Measurements (SCFMs) (the second and third steps are described in Chapters 6 and 7, respectively). Ultimately, the SCFMs are used for the calculations of the SCMs (Software Component's Measurements), SSEEs (Software Size and Effort Estimations), and SPQIs (Software Performance Quality Indicators), as described in the subsequent chapters.

All the Software Component's Feature Points (SCFPs) corresponding to all the 31 Software Component's Measurable Features (SCMFs) of all the 4 Software's Measurable Components (SMCs) are shown in Figure 4 and their description follows.

5.1.1 Description of the Software Component's Feature Points (SCFPs) for the Software Component's Measurable Features (SCMFs) of the Software's Measurable Component 'Functional Data' (CFD)

The SCFPs for the SCMFs of the CFD are calculated from the Logical Data Model (LDM) normally available in the Functional Requirements Specifications (FRS). This is done for all the 4 SCMFs (Software Component's Measurable Features) of the CFD as described next.

5.1.1.1 Software Component's Feature Point for 'Data Class' (FPDC), 'Data Attribute' (FPDA), and 'Data Field' (FPDF) Description

For determining the Software Component's Feature Points for 'Data Class' (FPDCs), 'Data Attribute' (FPDAs), and 'Data Field' (FPDFs), all the Software Component's Measurable Features 'Data Class' (FDCs), 'Data Attribute' (FDAs), and 'Data Field' (FDFs) need to be identified, respectively, in the Functional Requirements Specifications (FRS) first.

Regarding the FDCs, all the data classes (also sometimes called data entity) and subclasses are identified in the Logical Data Model description part of the Functional Requirements Specifications (FRS), and 1 SCFP (i.e., FSU) is assigned to each identified data class and subclass.

Similarly, regarding the FDAs and FDFs, the attributes of all the data classes and subclasses; and fields of all the attributes of all the data classes and subclasses; are identified, respectively, in the Logical Data Model description part of the Functional Requirements Specifications (FRS). Then, 1 SCFP (i.e., FSU) is assigned to each identified data attribute of all the data classes and subclasses; and to each identified data field of all the data attributes of all the data classes and subclasses.

The SCFPs thus assigned to the identified data classes and subclasses; data attributes of all the data classes and subclasses; and data fields of all the attributes of all the data classes and subclasses; are known as the FPDCs (Software Component's Feature Points for 'Data Class'), FPDAs (Software Component's Feature Points for 'Data Attribute'), and FPDFs (Software Component's Feature Points for 'Data Fields'), respectively.

Hence, 1 FPDC signifies 1 data class or 1 data subclass. Similarly, 1 FPDA signifies 1 data attribute of the data class or subclass; and 1 FPDF signifies 1 data field of the attributes of the data class or subclass.

Thus, the FPDCs are computed for the total number of classes and subclasses in the Logical Data Model. Similarly, the FPDAs and FPDFs are computed for the total number of attributes of all the classes and subclasses; and fields of all the attributes of all the classes and subclasses; respectively, in the Logical Data Model.

5.1.1.2 Software Component's Feature Point for 'Data Missing' (FPDM) Description

For determining the Software Component's Feature Points for 'Data Missing' (FPDMs), all the Software Component's Measurable Features 'Data Missing' (FDMs) need to be identified in the Functional Requirements Specifications (FRS) first.

To do this, it is necessary to go through not only the class structure diagrams and their text descriptions in the Logical Data Model of the Functional Requirements Specifications (FRS), but also the other description parts which are the Functionality Execution description part, User Interface description part and Message Exchange description part, and then check and identify if any of the class, subclass, data attribute or data field is used in these parts but is missing in the Logical Data Model. This is found by observing if some details of data which are used in some Functionality Execution description, or in the screen structures, or in the message structures, and which should normally be present in the class structure described in the Logical Data Model but are absent in the class structures in the Logical

Data Model. Thus, if they are missing in the Logical Data Model, they form part of the apparently missing items of the CFD.

Then, 1 SCFP (i.e., FSU) is assigned to each of the following identified apparent and obvious missing CFD's features:

a. class;

b. subclass;

c. data attribute;

d. data field.

The SCFPs thus assigned to the identified missing CFD's features are known as the FPDMs (Software Component's Feature Points for 'Data Missing').

Hence, 1 FPDM signifies 1 missing data feature in the Logical Data Model.

Thus, the FPDMs are computed for the total number of apparent and obvious deficiencies or missing features for the aforementioned CFD's features in the Logical Data Model.

5.1.2 Description of the Software Component's Feature Points (SCFPs) for the Software Component's Measurable Features (SCMFs) of the Software's Measurable Component 'Functionality Execution' (CFE)

The SCFPs for the SCMFs of the CFE are calculated from the functionality description and Logical Data Model normally available in the Functional Requirements Specifications (FRS). This is done for all the 19 SCMFs (Software Component's Measurable Features) of the CFE, and their description follows.

5.1.2.1 Software Component's Feature Point for 'Data Read' (FPDR) and 'Data Write' (FPDW) Description

For determining the Software Component's Feature Points for 'Data Read' (FPDRs) and 'Data Write' (FPDWs), all the Software Component's Measurable Features 'Data Read' (FDRs) and 'Data Write' (FDWs) need to be identified, respectively, in the Functional Requirements Specifications (FRS) first.

Regarding the FDRs, all the memory data read operations from the non-volatile or permanent memory storage devices such as disks; and regarding the FDWs, all the memory data write operations to the non-volatile or permanent memory storage devices are identified in the functionality description part of the Functional Requirements Specifications (FRS).

Then, 1 SCFP (i.e., FSU) is assigned to each identified memory read operation for every Data Collection read from the memory, and to each identified memory write operation for every Data Collection written to the memory.

The SCFPs thus assigned to the identified memory read operations and write operations are known as the FPDRs (Software Component's Feature Points for 'Data Read') and FPDWs (Software Component's Feature Points for 'Data Write'), respectively.

Hence, 1 FPDR signifies 1 memory read operation, and 1 FPDW signifies 1 memory write operation.

Thus, the FPDRs/FPDWs are computed for the total number of memory read/write operations for all the Data Collections read/written from/to the memory, respectively, in the functionality.

5.1.2.2 Software Component's Feature Point for 'Data Input' (FPDI) and 'Data Output' (FPDO) Description

For determining the Software Component's Feature Points for 'Data Input' (FPDIs) and 'Data Output' (FPDOs), all the Software Component's Measurable Features 'Data Input' (FDIs) and 'Data Output' (FDOs) need to be identified, respectively, in the Functional Requirements Specifications (FRS) first.

Regarding the FDIs, all the data input operations from the input devices; and regarding the FDOs, all the data output operations to the output devices are identified in the functionality description part of the Functional Requirements Specifications (FRS).

Then, 1 SCFP (i.e., FSU) is assigned to each identified data input operation which receives the Data Collection(s) from the input devices, and to each identified data output operation which sends the Data Collection(s) to the output devices.

The SCFPs thus assigned to the identified data input operations and data output operations are known as the FPDIs (Software Component's Feature Points for 'Data Input') and FPDOs (Software Component's Feature Points for 'Data Output'), respectively.

Hence, 1 FPDI signifies 1 data input operation used for receiving the data from the input device, and 1 FPDO signifies 1 data output operation used for sending the data to the output device.

Thus, the FPDIs/FPDOs are computed for the total number of data input/output operations for all the Data Collections received/sent as input/output in all the data input/output operations from/to the input/output devices, respectively, in the functionality.

5.1.2.3 Software Component's Feature Point for 'Message Send' (FPMS) and 'Message Receive' (FPMR) Description

For determining the Software Component's Feature Points for 'Message Send' (FPMSs) and 'Message Receive' (FPMRs), all the Software Component's Measurable Features 'Message Send' (FMSs) and 'Message Receive' (FMRs) need to be identified, respectively, in the Functional Requirements Specifications (FRS) first.

Regarding the FMSs, all the message send operations used for sending the messages to the external application programs, or to the sub-programs (modules) of the same application program; and regarding the FMRs, all the message receive operations used for receiving the messages from the external application programs, or from the sub-programs (modules) of the same application program; are identified in the functionality description part of the Functional Requirements Specifications (FRS).

Then, 1 SCFP (i.e., FSU) is assigned to each identified message send operation used for sending the messages to the external application programs, or to the sub-programs (modules) of the same application program; and to each identified message receive operation used for receiving the messages from the external application programs, or from the sub-programs (modules) of the same application program.

The SCFPs thus assigned to the identified message send operations and message receive operations are known as the FPMSs (Software Component's Feature Points for 'Message Send') and FPMRs (Software Component's Feature Points for 'Message Receive'), respectively.

Hence, 1 FPMS signifies 1 message send operation and 1 FPMR signifies 1 message receive operation.

Thus, the FPMSs/FPMRs are computed for the total number of message send/receive operations used for sending/receiving the messages to/from the external application programs; or to/from the sub-programs (modules) of the same application program; respectively, in the functionality.

5.1.2.4 Software Component's Feature Point for 'Function Computational Operation' (FPFC), 'Function Logical Operation' (FPFL), and 'Function Error Handling' (FPFE) Description

For determining the Software Component's Feature Points for 'Function Computational Operation' (FPFCs), 'Function Logical Operation' (FPFLs), and 'Function Error Handling' (FPFEs), all the Software Component's Measurable Features 'Function Computational Operation' (FFCs), 'Function Logical Operation' (FFLs), and 'Function Error Handling' (FFEs) need to be identified, respectively, in the Functional Requirements Specifications (FRS) first.

Regarding the FFCs, all the computational operations – addition, subtraction, multiplication, division, power, log, and equals; regarding the FFLs, all the logical operations – AND, OR, NOT, and XOR; and regarding the FFEs, all the error handling operations; are identified in the functionality description part of the Functional Requirements Specifications (FRS).

Then, 1 SCFP (i.e., FSU) is assigned to each identified computational operation – addition, subtraction, multiplication, division, power, log, and equals; to each identified logical operation – AND, OR, NOT, and XOR; and to each identified error handling operation.

The SCFPs thus assigned to the identified computational operations, logical operations, and error handling operations are known as the FPFCs (Software Component's Feature Points for 'Function Computational Operation'), FPFLs (Software Component's Feature Points for 'Function Logical Operation'), and FPFEs (Software Component's Feature Points for 'Function Error Handling'), respectively.

Hence, 1 FPFC signifies 1 computational operation – addition, subtraction, multiplication, division, power, log, and equals. Similarly, 1 FPFL signifies 1 logical operation – AND, OR, NOT, and XOR; and 1 FPFE signifies 1 error handling operation.

Thus, the FPFCs are computed for the total number of computational operations – addition, subtraction, multiplication, division, power, log, and equals; FPFLs are computed for the total number of logical operations – AND, OR, NOT, and XOR; and FPFEs are computed for the total number of error handling operations in the functionality.

5.1.2.5 Software Component's Feature Point for 'Function Decision Execution' (FPFD), 'Function Repeat Execution' (FPFR), 'Function Action Execution' (FPFA), and 'Function Execution Flow Control' (FPFO) Description

For determining the Software Component's Feature Points for 'Function Decision Execution' (FPFDs), 'Function Repeat Execution' (FPFRs), 'Function Action Execution' (FPFAs), and 'Function Execution Flow Control' (FPFOs), all the Software Component's Measurable Features 'Function Decision Execution' (FFDs), 'Function Repeat Execution' (FFRs), 'Function Action Execution' (FFAs), and 'Function Execution Flow Control' (FFOs) need to be identified, respectively, in the Functional Requirements Specifications (FRS) first.

Regarding the FFDs, all the condition checking and decision-taking operations (e.g., if the condition is true, take the action) are identified in the functionality description part of the Functional Requirements Specifications (FRS), and 1 SCFP (i.e., FSU) is assigned to each identified condition checking and decision-taking operation.

Similarly, regarding the FFRs, FFAs, and FFOs, all the repeat operations for action(s); all the actions to be performed; and all the execution flow control operations to be performed; are identified, respectively, in the functionality description part of the Functional Requirements Specifications (FRS). Then, 1 SCFP (i.e., FSU) is assigned to each identified repeat operation for action(s); to each identified action to be performed; and to each identified execution flow control operation to be performed.

The SCFPs thus assigned to the identified decision execution operations, repeat execution operations, action execution operations, and execution flow control operations are known as the FPFDs (Software Component's Feature Points for 'Function Decision Execution'), FPFRs (Software Component's Feature Points for 'Function Repeat Execution'), FPFAs (Software Component's Feature Points for 'Function Action Execution'), and FPFOs (Software Component's Feature Points for 'Function Execution Flow Control'), respectively.

Hence, 1 FPFD signifies 1 condition checking and decision-taking operation (e.g., if the condition is true, take the action); 1 FPFR signifies 1 repeat operation for action(s); 1 FPFA signifies 1 action to be performed; and 1 FPFO signifies 1 execution flow control operation to be performed.

Thus, the FPFDs are computed for the total number of condition checking and decision-taking operations in the functionality. Similarly, the FPFRs, FPFAs, and FPFOs are computed for the total number of repeat operations for action(s); total number of the actions to be performed; and total number of execution flow control operations, respectively, in the functionality.

5.1.2.6 Software Component's Feature Point for 'Memory Operations Functional Data' (FPLM), 'Input/Output Operations Functional Data' (FPLI), 'Message Exchange Operations Functional Data' (FPLS), and 'General Operations Functional Data' (FPLG) Description

For determining the Software Component's Feature Points for 'Memory Operations Functional Data' (FPLMs), 'Input/Output Operations Functional Data' (FPLI), 'Message Exchange Operations Functional Data' (FPLS), and 'General Operations Functional Data' (FPLG), all the Software Component's Measurable Features 'Memory Operations Functional Data' (FLMs), 'Input/Output Operations Functional Data' (FLI), 'Message Exchange Operations Functional Data' (FLS), and 'General Operations Functional Data' (FLG) need to be identified, respectively, in the Functional Requirements Specifications (FRS) first.

Regarding the FLMs, all the Data Collections read/written from/to the memory are identified in all the FDRs (Software Component's Measurable Features 'Data Read') and FDWs (Software Component's Measurable Features 'Data Write') which are the memory data read and write operations for reading/writing the data from/to the non-volatile or permanent memory storage devices such as disks, in the functionality description part of the Functional Requirements Specifications (FRS).

Similarly, regarding the FLIs, all the Data Collections handled in the input/output operations used for receiving/sending the input/output data from/to the input/output devices in all the FDIs (Software Component's Measurable Features 'Data Input') and FDOs (Software Component's Measurable Features 'Data Output') which are the data input and output operations to receive/send the input/output data from/to the input/output devices such as keyboards, display, and instruments; regarding the FLSs, all the Data Collections handled in the message send/receive operations used for sending/receiving the messages to/from the external application programs in all the FMSs (Software Component's Measurable Features 'Message Send') and FMRs (Software Component's Measurable Features 'Message Receive') which are the message exchange operations to send/receive the messages to/from the external application programs; and regarding the FLG, all the Data Collections handled in the function computational, logical, decision execution, repeat execution, and execution flow control operations in all the FFCs (Software Component's Measurable Features 'Function Computational Operation'), FFLs (Software Component's Measurable Features 'Function Logical Operation'), FFDs (Software Component's Measurable Features 'Function Decision Execution'), FFRs (Software Component's Measurable Features 'Function Repeat Execution'), and FFOs (Software Component's Measurable Features 'Function Execution Flow Control'), respectively; are identified in the functionality description part of the Functional Requirements Specifications (FRS).

Then, 1 SCFP (i.e., FSU) is assigned to each identified read/written memory data collection handled in every memory read/write operation used for reading/writing the data from/to the memory; to each identified input/output data collection handled in every input/output operation used for receiving/sending the input/output data from/to the input/output devices; to each identified Data Collection handled in every message send/receive operation used for sending/receiving the messages to/from the external application programs or sub-programs (modules) of the same application program; and to each identified Data Collection handled in each of the following functional operations:

a. computational;

b. logical;

c. decision;

d. repeat;

e. execution flow control.

The SCFPs thus assigned to the identified read/written memory data collections handled in the memory read/write operations; to the identified Data Collections handled in the input/output operations; to the identified Data Collections handled in the message send/receive operations; and to the identified Data Collections handled in the general computational, logical, decision, repeat, and execution flow control operations; are known as the FPLMs (Software Component's Feature Points for 'Memory Operations Functional Data'), FPLIs (Software Component's Feature Points for 'Input/Output Operations Functional Data'), FPLSs (Software Component's Feature Points for 'Message Exchange Operations Functional Data'), and FPLGs (Software Component's Feature Points for 'General Operations Functional Data'), respectively.

Hence, 1 FPLM signifies 1 Data Collection handled in the memory read/write operation from/to the memory; 1 FPLI signifies 1 Data Collection handled in the input/output operation from/to the input/output devices; 1 FPLS signifies 1 Data Collection handled in the message send/receive operation to/from the external application programs or sub-programs (modules) of the same application program; and 1 FPLG signifies 1 Data Collection handled in the function computational, logical, decision execution, repeat execution, or execution flow control operations.

Thus, the FPLMs are computed for the total number of Data Collections handled in all the memory read/write operations from/to the memory in the entire functionality. Similarly, the FPLIs for the total number of Data Collections handled in all the input/output operations; the FPLIs for the total number of Data Collections handled in all the message exchange operations; and the FPLGs for the total number of data collections handled in all the function computational, logical, decision execution, repeat execution, and execution flow control operations; are computed for the entire functionality.

5.1.2.7 Software Component's Feature Point for 'Class Method' (FPCM) Description

For determining the Software Component's Feature Points for 'Class Method' (FPCMs), all the Software Component's Measurable Features 'Class Method' (FCMs) need to be identified in the Functional Requirements Specifications (FRS) first.

Regarding the FCMs, the methods (operations or procedures) of all the data classes and subclasses are identified in the Logical Data Model description part of the Functional Requirements Specifications (FRS). Then, 1 SCFP (i.e., FSU) is assigned to each identified method of all the data classes and subclasses.

The SCFPs thus assigned to the identified class methods of all the data classes and subclasses are known as the FPCMs (Software Component's Feature Points for 'Class Method').

Hence, 1 FPCM signifies 1 class method of the data class or subclass.

Thus, the FPCMs are computed for the total number of methods (operations or procedures) of all the classes and subclasses in the Logical Data Model.

5.1.2.8 Software Component's Feature Point for 'Functionality Missing' (FPFM) Description

For determining the Software Component's Feature Points for 'Functionality Missing' (FPFMs), all the Software Component's Measurable Features 'Functionality Missing' (FFMs) need to be identified in the Functional Requirements Specifications (FRS) first.

To do this, it is necessary to go through not only the Functionality Execution description part of the Functional Requirements Specifications (FRS), but also the other description parts which are the Logical Data Model containing the class structure diagrams and their text descriptions, User Interface description part containing the information about the user interfaces/screens, and Message Exchange description part containing the message structures for communication with the other programs or sub-programs of the same application; and then check and identify if any of the operations which are

- **a.** data read;
- **b.** data write;
- **c.** data input;
- **d.** data output;
- **e.** message send;
- **f.** message receive;
- **g.** computational;
- **h.** logical;
- **i.** decision execution;
- **j.** repeat execution;
- **k.** action execution;

l. execution flow control;

m. error handling;

or data handled which are functional data handled during the

a. memory read/write;

b. input/output;

c. message exchange;

d. general computational, logical, decision, repeat, and execution flow control;

operations which should normally be present in the functionality description, but are missing in the functionality description part; or class method which should normally be present in the Logical Data Model, but is missing in the Logical Data Model part. This is found by observing

a. if some classes, subclasses, attributes, or fields are defined in the Logical Data Model but are not used in any of the aforementioned functional operations;

b. or, if some screen structures, their fields or input/output navigational links are defined in the User Interface description part but are not used in any of the aforementioned functional operations;

c. or, if some message structures or their fields are defined in the Message Exchange description part but are not used in any of the aforementioned functional operations;

d. or, if some aforementioned functional operation is missing in the case where it should be present, for example, if in the case of a decision execution, if the condition is not true, it is evident that there should be an error indication in that particular case and some suitable operation(s) for error handling should be there but nothing has been described in the functionality regarding the error handling if the decision condition is not true, thus the error handling operation is considered to be missing;

e. or, if some data handled are missing in the case where they should be present;

f. or, if some class method is defined in the Logical Data Model part but is not used in the functionality.

Thus, these missing functionality items form part of the apparently missing items of the CFE.

Then, 1 SCFP (i.e., FSU) is assigned to each of the following identified apparent and obvious missing CFE's features:

a. data read;

b. data write;

c. data input;

d. data output;

e. message send;

f. message receive;

g. computational;

h. logical;

i. decision execution;

j. repeat execution;

k. action execution;

l. execution flow control;

m. error handling;

n. functional data handled during the memory read/write, input/output, message exchange, general computational, logical, decision, repeat, and execution flow control operations;

o. class method.

The SCFPs thus assigned to the identified missing CFE's features are known as the FPFMs (Software Component's Feature Points for 'Functionality Missing').

Hence, 1 FPFM signifies 1 missing functionality feature in the functionality description part.

Thus, the FPFMs are computed for the total number of apparent and obvious deficiencies or missing features for the aforementioned CFE's features in the functionality description part.

5.1.3 Description of the Software Component's Features Points (SCFPs) for the Software Component's Measurable Features (SCMFs) of the Software's Measurable Component 'User Interface' (CUI)

The SCFPs for the SCMFs of the CUI are calculated from the User Interface description normally available in the Functional Requirements Specifications (FRS). This is done for all the 5 SCMFs (Software Component's Measurable Features) of the CUI as described next.

5.1.3.1 Software Component's Feature Point for 'User Screen' (FPUS), 'User Screen Field' (FPUF), 'User Screen Output Link' (FPUO), and 'User Screen Input Link' (FPUI) Description

For determining the Software Component's Feature Points for 'User Screen' (FPUSs), 'User Screen Field' (FPUFs), 'User Screen Output Link' (FPUOs), and 'User Screen Input Link' (FPUIs), all the Software Component's Measurable Features 'User Screen' (FUSs), 'User Screen Field' (FUFs), 'User Screen Output Link' (FUOs), and 'User Screen Input Link' (FUIs) need to be identified, respectively, in the Functional Requirements Specifications (FRS) first.

For this, all the user screens, all the user screen fields of all the user screens, all the user screen output links of all the user screens and all the user screen input links of all the user screens are identified in the User Interface description part of the Functional Requirements Specifications (FRS).

Then, 1 SCFP (i.e., FSU) is assigned to each identified user screen; to each identified user screen field of all the user screens; to each identified user screen output link of all the user screens; and to each identified user screen input link of all the user screens.

The SCFPs thus assigned to the identified user screens; to the identified user screen fields of all the user screens; to the identified user screen output links of all the user screens; and to the identified user screen input links of all the user screens; are known as the FPUSs (Software Component's Feature Points for 'User Screen'), FPUFs (Software Component's Feature Points for 'User Screen Field'), FPUOs (Software Component's Feature Points for

'User Screen Output Link'), and FPUIs (Software Component's Feature Points for 'User Screen Input Link'), respectively.

Hence, 1 FPUS signifies 1 user screen; 1 FPUF signifies 1 user screen field of the user screen; 1 FPUO signifies 1 user screen output link of the user screen; and 1 FPUI signifies 1 user screen input link of the user screen.

Thus, the FPUSs, FPUFs, FPUOs, and FPUIs are computed for all the user screens; all the user screen fields of all the user screens; all the user screen output links of all the user screens; and all the user screen input links of all the user screens in the User Interface description part, respectively.

5.1.3.2 Software Component's Feature Point for 'User Screen Missing' (FPUM) Description

For determining the Software Component's Feature Points for 'User Screen Missing' (FPUMs), all the Software Component's Measurable Features 'User Screen Missing' (FUMs) need to be identified in the Functional Requirements Specifications (FRS) first.

To do this, it is necessary to go through not only the User Interface description part of the Functional Requirements Specifications (FRS), but also the other description parts which are the Functionality Execution description part, Message Exchange description part, and class structure diagrams and their text descriptions in the Logical Data Model part; and then check and identify if any of the following feature of the CUI:

a. user screen;
b. user screen field;
c. user screen output link;
d. user screen input link;

is missing in the User Interface description part. This is found by observing if some details of the user screens, their fields, output links or input links are used in some Functionality Execution description, or in the message structures, or in the Logical Data Model, and these screen details should normally be present in the User Interface described in the User Interface description part but they are absent in the User Interface described in the User Interface description part, they form part of the apparently missing items of the CUI.

Then, 1 SCFP (i.e., FSU) is assigned to each of the following identified apparent and obvious missing CUI's features:

a. user screen;
b. user screen field;
c. user screen output link;
d. user screen input link.

The SCFPs thus assigned to the identified missing CUI's features are known as the FPUMs (Software Component's Feature Points for 'User Screen Missing').

Hence, 1 FPUM signifies 1 missing user interface feature – screen or its field/input link/output link – in the User Interface description part.

Thus, the FPUMs are computed for the total number of apparent and obvious deficiencies or missing features for the aforementioned CUI's features in the User Interface description part.

5.1.4 Description of the Software Component's Feature Points (SCFPs) for the Software Component's Measurable Features (SCMFs) of the Software's Measurable Component 'Message Exchange' (CME)

The SCFPs for the SCMFs of the CME are calculated from the Message Exchange description normally available in the Functional Requirements Specifications (FRS). This is done for all the 3 SCMFs (Software Component's Measurable Features) of the CME as described next.

5.1.4.1 Software Component's Feature Point for 'Notifying Message' (FPNM) and 'Message Field' (FPMF) Description

For determining the Software Component's Feature Points for 'Notifying Message' (FPNMs) and 'Message Field' (FPMFs), all the Software Component's Measurable Features 'Notifying Message' (FNMs) and 'Message Field' (FMFs) need to be identified, respectively, in the Functional Requirements Specifications (FRS) first.

For this, all the messages used for communication with other application programs, or with the sub-programs (modules) of the same application program; and all the fields of all the messages used for communication with other application programs, or with the sub-programs (modules) of the same application program; are identified in the Message Exchange description part of the Functional Requirements Specifications (FRS).

Then, 1 SCFP (i.e., FSU) is assigned to each identified message used for communication and to each identified field of all the messages used for communication.

The SCFPs thus assigned to the identified messages and to the identified fields of all the messages are known as the FPNMs (Software Component's Feature Points for 'Notifying Message') and FPMFs (Software Component's Feature Points for 'Message Field'), respectively.

Hence, 1 FPNM signifies 1 message, and 1 FPMF signifies 1 field of the message.

Thus, the FPNMs and FPMFs are computed for the total number of messages and the fields of the messages, respectively, in the Message Exchange description part.

5.1.4.2 Software Component's Feature Point for 'Message Missing' (FPMM) Description

For determining the Software Component's Feature Points for 'Message Missing' (FPMMs), all the Software Component's Measurable Features 'Message Missing' (FMMs) need to be identified in the Functional Requirements Specifications (FRS) first.

To do this, it is necessary to go through not only the Message Exchange description part of the Functional Requirements Specifications (FRS), but also the other description parts which are the Functionality Execution description part, User Interface description part, and class structure diagrams and their text descriptions in the Logical Data Model part; and then check and identify if any of the following features of the CME:

a. message;

b. message field;

is missing in the Message Exchange description part. This is found by observing if some details of the messages or their fields are used in some Functionality Execution description, or in the User Interface description, or in the Logical Data Model, and these details should normally be present in the message structures described in the Message Exchange description part but are absent in the message structures described in the Message Exchange description part, they form part of the apparently missing items of the CME.

Then, 1 SCFP (i.e., FSU) is assigned to each of the following identified apparent and obvious missing CME's features:

a. message;

b. message field.

The SCFPs thus assigned to the identified missing CME's features are known as the FPMMs (Software Component's Feature Points for 'Message Missing').

Hence, 1 FPMM signifies 1 missing message feature in the Message Exchange description part.

Thus, the FPMMs are computed for the total number of apparent and obvious deficiencies or missing features for the aforementioned CME's features in the Message Exchange description part.

5.2 USAGE OF THE SOFTWARE COMPONENT'S FEATURE POINTS (SCFPs)

There are a total of 31 SCFPs (Software Component's Feature Points) corresponding to the 31 SCMFs (Software Component's Measurable Features) of the 4 SMCs (Software's Measurable Components). All the SCMFs are identified in the FRS, and the SCFPs are assigned to them for their measurements. All the assigned SCFPs are used, through the SCFPCs (Software Component's Feature Point Counts) and SCFMs (Software Component's Feature Measurements), for the calculations of the Software Component's Measurements (SCMs), Software Size and Effort Estimations (SSEEs), and Software Performance Quality Indicators (SPQIs) of both the types Software Structural Indicators (SSIs)[5–7] and Software Operational Indicators (SOIs)[5–7].

5.3 SOFTWARE COMPONENT'S FEATURE POINTS (SCFPs) PRESENCE AND QUANTITY

The presence of the different Software Component's Feature Points (SCFPs) and their quantity depends on the presence and quantity of the corresponding Software Component's Measurable Features (SCMFs) which in turn depends on the type of applications and thus, on the Functional Requirements Specifications (FRS) of the applications.

It may be possible that certain SCMFs are absent, or present in small quantity, but some others may be more voluminously present. According to this fact, the quantity of some SCFPs may be nil, for some others, it may be small number and for some others, it may be a big number.

In fact, the varying sizes of the Software Component's Measurable Features (SCMFs) measured by the Software Component's Feature Measurements (SCFMs); and of Software's Measurable Components (SMCs) – Software' s Measurable Component 'Functional Data' (CFD), 'Functionality Execution' (CFE), 'User Interface' (CUI), and 'Message Exchange' (CME) – measured by the Software Component's Measurements (SCMs); and thus, the total size of the software are dependent on the varying magnitude of the presence of various SCMFs, and consequently of the corresponding SCFPs, and are determined based on this.

There is no upper limit of the presence and quantity of the SCMFs and consequently the same is true for the SCFPs.

5.4 EXAMPLES

1. In the functional requirement "Class: Result; Attributes: data count, memory operations, computational operations, logical operations, decision execution operations, repeat execution operations, action execution operations, input/output operations, message exchange operations, error handling operations, class methods, code count, user interface count, message count, total software count, program lines, design effort, test effort, and total effort (there are a total of 19 attributes); Fields: each attribute has 1 field." which forms part of data description in the Logical Data Model part of the FRS, all the following SCFPs (Software Component's Features Points) will be assigned for the identifiable SCMFs:
   A. 1 SCFP for the Software Component's Feature Point for 'Data Class' (FPDC) which is for class Result. So, there will be 1 FPDC.
   B. 19 SCFPs for the Software Component's Feature Point for 'Data Attribute' (FPDA) which are for 19 attributes: data count, memory operations, computational operations, logical operations, decision execution operations, repeat execution operations, action execution operations, input/output operations, message exchange operations, error handling operations, class methods, code count, user interface count, message count, total software count, program lines, design effort, test effort, and total effort. So, there will be a total of 19 FPDAs – 1 FPDA for each attribute.
   C. 19 SCFPs for the Software Component's Feature Point for 'Data Field' (FPDF) which are the 19 fields of the attributes: 1 field for each attribute. So, there will be 19 FPDFs – 1 FPDF for each field.

   Thus, the total SCFPs assigned for the identifiable SCMFs are FPDC = 1, FPDAs = 19, FPDFs = 19.

   (*Note*: The aforementioned functional requirement is part of Chapter 14.)
2. In the functional requirement "The user enters the age of the student. The list of students above the input age is extracted from the student database and displayed." which forms part of the functionality description in the FRS, all the following SCFPs (Software Component's Features Points) will be assigned for the identifiable SCMFs:
   A. 3 SCFPs for the Software Component's Feature Point for 'Function Action Execution' (FPFA) which are for 3 actions performed: 1 action of receiving the input age data, 1 action for reading the student database, 1 action for data output to display the student's list above the input age. So, there will be 3 FPFAs.
   B. 1 SCFP for the Software Component's Feature Point for 'Data Input' (FPDI) which is for data input of age. So, there will be 1 FPDI.
   C. 1 SCFP for the Software Component's Feature Point for 'Data Read' (FPDR) which is for reading student data from the disk memory. So, there will be 1 FPDR.
   D. 1 SCFP for the Software Component's Feature Point for 'Data Output' (FPDO) for student data output for display. So, there will be 1 FPDO.

E. 2 SCFPs for the Software Component's Feature Point for 'Input/Output Operations Functional Data' (FPLI) which is for student data collection handling, handled in 2 functional operations, 1 for each of the following operations: 1 student data collection handling for data input from the input keyboard device; 1 student data collection handling for data output to the output display device. So, there will be 2 FPLIs.

F. 1 SCFP for the Software Component's Feature Point for 'Memory Operations Functional Data' (FPLM) which is for 1 Data Collection, that is, student data collection, handled in the memory data read functional operation. So, there will be 1 FPLM for 1 student data collection handled in data read from the memory.

Thus, the total SCFPs assigned for the identifiable SCMFs are FPFAs = 3, FPDI = 1, FPDR = 1, FPDO = 1, FPLIs = 2, FPLM = 1.

3. In the functional requirement "Entered user name is checked. If there is a non-alphabetical character in it, an error message is displayed." which forms part of the functionality description in the FRS, all the following SCFPs (Software Component's Features Points) will be assigned for the identifiable SCMFs:

A. 3 SCFPs for the Software Component's Feature Point for 'Function Action Execution' (FPFA) which are for 3 actions performed: 1 action of receiving user name, 1 action for decision for checking non-alphabetical character, 1 action for display of error message. So, there will be 3 FPFAs.

B. 1 SCFP for the Software Component's Feature Point for 'Data Input' (FPDI) which is for data input of user name. So, there will be 1 FPDI.

C. 1 SCFP for the Software Component's Feature Point for 'Function Decision Execution' (FPFD) which is for checking if there is a non-alphabetical character present in the user name. So, there will be 1 FPFD.

D. 1 SCFP for Software Component's Feature Point for 'Data Output' (FPDO) for display of error message. So, there will be 1 FPDO.

E. 1 SCFP for the Software Component's Feature Point for 'Function Error Handling' (FPFE) which is for error handling operation when non-alphabetical character is present. So, there will be 1 FPFE.

F. 2 SCFPs for the Software Component's Feature Point for 'Input/Output Operations Functional Data' (FPLI) which is for 2 Data Collections, that is, user data collection and error data collection, handled in 2 functional operations, 1 for each of the following operations: 1 user data collection handling for data input from the input keyboard device; 1 error data collection handling for error display data output operation to the output display device. So, there will be 2 FPLIs.

G. 1 SCFP for the Software Component's Feature Point for 'General Operations Functional Data' (FPLG) which is for 1 Data Collection, that is, alphabetical constant data, in 1 functional operation: 1 alphabetical constant data collection handling for decision operation. So, there will be 1 FPLG.

Thus, the total SCFPs assigned for the identifiable SCMFs are FPFAs = 3, FPDI = 1, FPFD = 1, FPDO = 1, FPFE = 1, FPLIs = 2, FPLG = 1.

4. In the functional requirement "Log-on screen displaying the fields user-id and password to log on." which forms part of the User Interface description in the FRS (see Figure 17), all the following SCFPs (Software Component's Features Points) will be assigned for the identifiable SCMFs:

A. 1 SCFP for the Software Component's Feature Point for 'User Screen' (FPUS) which is for the Log-on screen. So, there will be 1 FPUS.

B. 4 SCFPs for the Software Component's Feature Point for 'User Screen Field' (FPUF) which are 2 screen text fields displaying the texts – "user-id" and "password"; and 2 input fields for user-id and password. So, there will be 4 FPUFs.

C. 3 SCFPs for the Software Component's Feature Point for 'User Screen Missing' (FPUM) which are 2 output links – 1 for normal operation when user-id and password are entered, 1 for returning to the previous screen – and 1 input link from the previous screen from where this screen was arrived. So, there will be 3 FPUMs.

Thus, the total SCFPs assigned for the identifiable SCMFs are FPUS = 1, FPUFs = 4, FPUMs = 3.

(*Note*: The aforementioned functional requirement is part of the Chapter 14.)

5.5 CHAPTER SUMMARY

5.5.1 Software Component's Feature Point (SCFP): Summary

The Functional Requirements Specifications (FRS) contain 4 description parts – Logical Data Model, functionality, user screens and messages – on which the 4 Software's Measurable Components (SMCs) – Software's Measurable Component 'Functional Data' (CFD), 'Functionality Execution' (CFE), 'User Interface' (CUI), and 'Message Exchange' (CME) – are based, respectively.

The SMCs have Software Component's Measurable Features (SCMFs). For comprehensive measurement of the software, all the SCMFs (total 31) are measured by first identifying them in the FRS document, and then, by assigning the Software Component's Feature Points (SCFPs) to them. The SCFP is the Functional Size Unit (FSU) of the FSSM. Assignment of the SCFPs (i.e., FSU) to the 31 SCMFs produces 31 streams of the SCFPs, 1 stream for each SCMF, distinguished by the SCMF type. Thus the following SCFPs for

- data classes, attributes, fields, and missing data items for the CFD;
- memory read/write, input/output, message send/receive, computational, logical, decision, action, repeat, execution flow control, and error handling operations; data handled in the memory read/write, input/output, message send/receive, computational, logical, decision, repeat, and execution flow control operations; class methods; and missing functionality items for the CFE;
- user screens, their fields, input/output links, and missing screen items for the CUI;
- messages, their fields, and missing message items for the CME;

are obtained.

5.5.2 Usage, Presence, and Quantity of the Software Component's Feature Points (SCFPs): Summary

All the 31 SCFPs (Software Component's Feature Points) corresponding to the 31 SCMFs (Software Component's Measurable Features) of the 4 SMCs (Software's Measurable Components) are used for the calculations of the Software Component's Feature Measurements (SCFMs) which in turn are used for the calculations of the Software Component's Measurements (SCMs), Software Size and Effort Estimations (SSEEs), and Software Performance

Quality Indicators (SPQIs) of both the types Software Structural Indicators (SSIs)[5–7] and Software Operational Indicators (SOIs)[5–7].

The absence, or presence and quantity of the SCFPs depends on the absence, presence and quantity, respectively, of the SCMFs in the applications and thus, in the functional requirements of the applications. There is no upper limit of the presence and quantity of the SCMFs, and consequently, of the SCFPs.

EXERCISES

5.1 Which of the following SCFPs (Software Component's Feature Points) does not make part of the Software's Measurable Component 'Message Exchange' (CME)?

A. Software Component's Feature Point for 'Notifying Message' (FPNM).

B. Software Component's Feature Point for 'Message Send' (FPMS).

C. Software Component's Feature Point for 'Message Field' (FPMF).

D. Software Component's Feature Point for 'Message Missing' (FPMM).

5.2 In the functional requirement "Calculate User Interface Count = US + UF + UO + UI", how many Software Component's Feature Points for 'Function Computational Operation' (FPFC) are assigned?

A. 0, because there is no multiplication calculation.

B. 6, because there are 3 addition calculations.

C. 4, because there are 3 addition and 1 equals calculations.

(*Note*: The aforementioned functional requirement is part of the Chapter 14.)

5.3 In the functional requirement "Receive temperature from digital thermometer and display it", which of the following assigned Software Component's Feature Points (SCFPs) are correct?

A. There are 1 data input operation for receiving temperature, so 1 FPDI (Software Component's Feature Point for 'Data Input'); 1 data output operation for displaying temperature, so 1 FPDO (Software Component's Feature Point for 'Data Output'). Hence, there are 1 FPDI and 1 FPDO.

B. There are 1 data input operation for receiving temperature, so 1 FPDI (Software Component's Feature Point for 'Data Input'); 1 data output operation for displaying temperature, so 1 FPDO (Software Component's Feature Point for 'Data Output'); 1 user screen for displaying temperature, so 1 FPUS (Software Component's Feature Point for 'User Screen'). Hence, there are 1 FPDI, 1 FPDO, and 1 FPUS.

C. There are 2 actions – receiving temperature and displaying temperature – so 2 FPFAs (Software Component's Feature Point for 'Function Action Execution'); 1 data input operation for receiving temperature, so 1 FPDI (Software Component's Feature Point for 'Data Input'); 1 data output operation for displaying temperature, so 1 FPDO (Software Component's Feature Point for 'Data Output'); 3 Data Collections handled during input/output operations, so 3 FPLIs (Software Component's Feature Point for 'Input/Output Operations Functional Data'): 1 Data Collection 'temperature' in the input operation for receiving temperature; 1 Data Collection 'temperature' in the output operation for displaying temperature; 1 Data Collection 'temperature display screen' for displaying temperature. Hence, there are 2 FPFAs, 1 FPDI, 1 FPDO, and 3 FPLIs.

Chapter 6

Software Component's Feature Point Counts in the FSSM

For comprehensive measurement of the software, all the Software Component's Measurable Features (SCMFs) – a total of 31 – are measured by first identifying them in the FRS document and then, by assigning the Software Component's Feature Points (SCFPs), that is, the Functional Size Unit (FSU) of the FSSM, to them. Assignment of the SCFPs (i.e., FSU) to the 31 SCMFs produces 31 streams of the SCFPs, 1 stream for each SCMF, distinguished by the SCMF type.

The next step, which is the second step for the measurements of the SCMFs, is to calculate the Software Component's Feature Point Counts (SCFPCs) from the Software Component's Feature Points (SCFPs), and it is presented in this chapter (the first step for the measurements of the SCMFs has been presented in Chapter 5 and the third step is presented in Chapter 7).

6.1 SOFTWARE COMPONENT'S FEATURE POINT COUNT (SCFPC) DESCRIPTION

After having identified the Software Component's Measurable Features (SCMFs) of the SMCs (Software's Measurable Components) in the Functional Requirements Specifications (FRS), and having assigned the Software Component's Feature Points (SCFPs) to the SCMFs, the SCFPCs are calculated based on the SCFPs for all the features of all the SMCs (CFD, CFE, CUI and CME). The SCFPCs, thus calculated, are used further for calculating the SCFMs (Software Component's Feature Measurements) which in turn are used for the computations of the SCMs (Software Component's Measurements), SSEEs (Software Size and Effort Estimations), and SPQIs (Software Performance Quality Indicators). The calculations of the SCFPCs are described in this chapter.

All the Software Component's Feature Point Counts (SCFPCs) corresponding to all the Software Component's Feature Points (SCFPs) which in turn are corresponding to all the Software Component's Measurable Features (SCMFs) of the Software's Measurable Components (SMCs) are shown in Figure 4 and their description follows.

Functional Software Size Measurement Methodology with Effort Estimation and Performance Indication, First Edition. Jasveer Singh.

Companion website: http://booksupport.wiley.com

6.1.1 Description of the Software Component's Feature Point Counts (SCFPCs) for the Software Component's Measurable Features (SCMFs) of the Software's Measurable Component 'Functional Data' (CFD)

The SCFPCs for the CFD are calculated based on the SCFPs obtained from the Logical Data Model (LDM) description in the Functional Requirements Specifications (FRS) for all the SCMFs (Software Component's Measurable Features) of the CFD as described next.

6.1.1.1 Software Component's Feature Point Count for 'Data Class' (FCDC), 'Data Attribute' (FCDA), and 'Data Field' (FCDF) Description

All the Software Component's Feature Points for 'Data Class' (FPDCs), 'Data Attribute' (FPDAs), and 'Data Field' (FPDFs) which are produced by assigning the Software Component's Feature Points (SCFPs) to the Software Component's Measurable Features 'Data Class' (FDCs), 'Data Attribute' (FDAs), and 'Data Field' (FDFs), respectively, make part of the Software Component's Feature Point Count for 'Data Class' (FCDC), 'Data Attribute' (FCDAs), and 'Data Field' (FCDFs), respectively.

So, all the FPDCs obtained for all the classes and subclasses in the Logical Data Model are added together to produce the FCDC. Similarly, all the FPDAs obtained for all the attributes of all the classes and subclasses, and all the FPDFs obtained for all the fields of all the classes and subclasses, are added correspondingly to produce the FCDA and FCDF, respectively.

Thus, the FCDC signifies the total number of the classes and subclasses (data entity) in the Logical Data Model description part of the Functional Requirements Specifications (FRS). Similarly, FCDA and FCDF signify all the attributes of all the classes and subclasses; and all the fields of all the attributes of all the classes and subclasses; respectively, in the Logical Data Model description part of the Functional Requirements Specifications (FRS).

6.1.1.2 Software Component's Feature Point Count for 'Data Missing' (FCDM) Description

All the Software Component's Feature Points for 'Data Missing' (FPDMs) which are produced by assigning the Software Component's Feature Points (SCFPs) to the Software Component's Measurable Features 'Data Missing' (FDMs) make part of the Software Component's Feature Point Count for 'Data Missing' (FCDM).

So, all the FPDMs obtained for all the following apparent and obvious missing CFD's (Software's Measurable Component 'Functional Data') features:

- **a.** class;
- **b.** subclass;
- **c.** data attribute;
- **d.** data field;

in the Logical Data Model are added together to produce FCDM.

Thus, the FCDM is equal to the total number of apparent and obvious deficiencies or missing features for the aforementioned CFD's features in the Logical Data Model description part of the Functional Requirements Specifications (FRS).

6.1.2 Description of the Software Component's Feature Point Counts (SCFPCs) for the Software Component's Measurable Features (SCMFs) of the Software's Measurable Component 'Functionality Execution' (CFE)

The SCFPCs for the CFE are calculated based on the SCFPs obtained from the functionality description and Logical Data Model part in the Functional Requirements Specifications (FRS) for all the SCMFs (Software Component's Measurable Features) of the CFE as described next.

6.1.2.1 Software Component's Feature Point Count for 'Data Read' (FCDR) and 'Data Write' (FCDW) Description

All the Software Component's Feature Points for 'Data Read' (FPDRs) and 'Data Write' (FPDWs) which are produced by assigning the Software Component's Feature Points (SCFPs) to the Software Component's Measurable Features 'Data Read' (FDRs) and 'Data Write' (FDWs), respectively, make part of the Software Component's Feature Point Count for 'Data Read' (FCDR) and 'Data Write' (FCDW), respectively.

So, all the FPDRs/FPDWs obtained for all the memory data read/write operations, respectively, in the Functionality Execution are added correspondingly to produce the FCDR/FCDW, respectively.

Thus, the FCDR/FCDW signifies the total number of the memory data read/write operations, respectively, in the Functionality Execution description part of the Functional Requirements Specifications (FRS).

6.1.2.2 Software Component's Feature Point Count for 'Data Input' (FCDI) and 'Data Output' (FCDO) Description

All the Software Component's Feature Points for 'Data Input' (FPDIs) and 'Data Output' (FPDOs) which are produced by assigning the Software Component's Feature Points (SCFPs) to the Software Component's Measurable Features 'Data Input' (FDIs) and 'Data Output' (FDOs), respectively, make part of the Software Component's Feature Point Count for 'Data Input' (FCDI) and 'Data Output' (FCDO), respectively.

So, all the FPDIs/FPDOs obtained for all the data input/output operations used for receiving/sending the input/output data from/to all the input/output devices, respectively, in the Functionality Execution are added correspondingly to produce the FCDI/FCDO, respectively.

Thus, the FCDI/FCDO signifies the total number of the data input/output operations used for receiving/sending the input/output data from/to all the input/output devices, respectively, in the Functionality Execution description part of the Functional Requirements Specifications (FRS).

6.1.2.3 Software Component's Feature Point Count for 'Message Send' (FCMS) and 'Message Receive' (FCMR) Description

All the Software Component's Feature Points for 'Message Send' (FPMSs) and 'Message Receive' (FPMRs) which are produced by assigning the Software Component's Feature Points (SCFPs) to the Software Component's Measurable Features 'Message Send' (FMSs) and 'Message Receive' (FMRs), respectively, make part of the Software Component's Feature Point Count for 'Message Send' (FCMS) and 'Message Receive' (FCMR), respectively.

So, all the FPMSs/FPMRs obtained for all the message send/receive operations used for sending/receiving the messages to/from the other external application programs, respectively, or to/from the sub-programs (modules) of the same application program, respectively, in the Functionality Execution are added correspondingly to produce the FCMS/FCMR, respectively.

Thus, the FCMS/FCMR signifies the total number of the message send/receive operations used for sending/receiving the messages to/from the other external application programs, respectively, or to/from the sub-programs (modules) of the same application program, respectively, in the Functionality Execution description part of the Functional Requirements Specifications (FRS).

6.1.2.4 Software Component's Feature Point Count for 'Function Computational Operation' (FCFC), 'Function Logical Operation' (FCFL), and 'Function Error Handling' (FCFE) Description

All the Software Component's Feature Points for 'Function Computational Operation' (FPFCs), 'Function Logical Operation' (FPFLs), and 'Function Error Handling' (FPFEs) which are produced by assigning the Software Component's Feature Points (SCFPs) to the Software Component's Measurable Features 'Function Computational Operation' (FFCs), 'Function Logical Operation' (FFLs), and 'Function Error Handling' (FFEs), respectively, make part of the Software Component's Feature Point Count for 'Function Computational Operation' (FCFC), 'Function Logical Operation' (FCFL), and 'Function Error Handling' (FCFE), respectively.

So, all the FPFCs obtained for all the computational operations: addition, subtraction, multiplication, division, power, log, and equals; all the FPFLs obtained for all the logical operations: AND, OR, NOT, and XOR; and all the FPFEs obtained for all the error handling operations are added correspondingly to produce the FCFC, FCFL, and FCFE, respectively.

Thus, the FCFC, FCFL, and FCFE signify the total number of the computational operations: addition, subtraction, multiplication, division, power, log, and equals; total number of the logical operations: AND, OR, NOT, and XOR; and total number of the error handling operations; respectively, in the functionality description part of the Functional Requirements Specifications (FRS).

6.1.2.5 Software Component's Feature Point Count for 'Function Decision Execution' (FCFD), 'Function Repeat Execution' (FCFR), 'Function Action Execution' (FCFA), and 'Function Execution Flow Control' (FCFO) Description

All the Software Component's Feature Points for 'Function Decision Execution' (FPFDs), 'Function Repeat Execution' (FPFRs), 'Function Action Execution' (FPFAs), and 'Function Execution Flow Control' (FPFOs) which are produced by assigning the Software Component's Feature Points (SCFPs) to the Software Component's Measurable Features 'Function Decision Execution' (FFDs), 'Function Repeat Execution' (FFRs), 'Function Action Execution' (FFA), and 'Function Execution Flow Control' (FFO), respectively, make part of the Software Component's Feature Point Count for 'Function Decision Execution' (FCFD),

'Function Repeat Execution' (FCFR), 'Function Action Execution' (FCFA), and 'Function Execution Flow Control' (FCFO), respectively.

So, all the FPFDs, FPFRs, FPFAs, and FPFOs obtained for all the condition checking and decision-taking operations, all the repeat operations, all the actions to be performed, and all the execution flow control operations to be performed, respectively, in the functionality description are added correspondingly to produce the FCFD, FCFR, FCFA, and FCFO, respectively.

Thus, the FCFD, FCFR, FCFA, and FCFO signify the total number of condition checking and decision-taking operations (e.g., if the condition is true, take the action); total number of repeat operations; total number of actions to be performed; and total number of execution flow control operations; respectively, in the functionality description part of the Functional Requirements Specifications (FRS).

6.1.2.6 Software Component's Feature Point Count for 'Memory Operations Functional Data' (FCLM), Input/Output Operations Functional Data' (FCLI), 'Message Exchange Operations Functional Data' (FCLS), and 'General Operations Functional Data' (FCLG) Description

All the Software Component's Feature Points for 'Memory Operations Functional Data' (FPLMs), 'Input/Output Operations Functional Data' (FPLIs), 'Message Exchange Operations Functional Data' (FPLSs), and 'General Operations Functional Data' (FPLGs) which are produced by assigning the Software Component's Feature Points (SCFPs) to the Software Component's Measurable Features 'Memory Operations Functional Data' (FLMs), 'Input/Output Operations Functional Data' (FLIs), 'Message Exchange Operations Functional Data' (FLSs), and 'General Operations Functional Data' (FLGs), respectively, make part of the Software Component's Feature Point Count for 'Memory Operations Functional Data' (FCLM), 'Input/Output Operations Functional Data' (FCLI), 'Message Exchange Operations Functional Data' (FCLS), and 'General Operations Functional Data' (FCLG), respectively.

So, all the FPLMs, FPLIs, FPLSs, and FPLGs obtained for all the Data Collections read/written from/to the memory in the memory data read/write operations; all the Data Collections handled in the input/output operations used for receiving/sending the input/output data from/to the input/output devices; all the Data Collections handled in the messages sent/received to/from the external application programs or to/from the sub-programs (modules) of the same application program; all the Data Collections handled during the computational, logical, decision, repeat, and execution flow control operations; respectively, in the functionality execution are added correspondingly to produce the FCLM, FCLI, FCLS, and FCLG, respectively.

Thus, the FCLM, FCLI, FCLS, and FCLG signify the total number of Data Collections read/written from/to the memory in the memory data read/write operations; total number of Data Collections handled in the data input/output operations used for the data input/output from/to the input/output devices; total number of Data Collections handled in the messages sent/received to/from the external application programs or to/from the sub-programs (modules) of the same application program; and total number of Data Collections handled during the computational, logical, decision, repeat, and execution flow control functional operations; respectively, in the Functionality Execution description part of the Functional Requirements Specifications (FRS).

6.1.2.7 Software Component's Feature Point Count for 'Class Method' (FCCM) Description

All the Software Component's Feature Points for 'Class Method' (FPCMs) which are produced by assigning the Software Component's Feature Points (SCFPs) to the Software Component's Measurable Features 'Class Method' (FCMs) make part of the Software Component's Feature Point Count for 'Class Method' (FCCM).

So, all the FPCMs obtained for all the methods of all the classes and subclasses are added to produce the FCCM.

Thus, the FCCM signifies all the methods (operations or procedures) of all the classes and subclasses in the Logical Data Model description part of the Functional Requirements Specifications (FRS).

6.1.2.8 Software Component's Feature Point Count for 'Functionality Missing' (FCFM) Description

All the Software Component's Feature Points for 'Functionality Missing' (FPFMs) which are produced by assigning Software Component's Feature Points (SCFPs) to the Software Component's Measurable Features 'Functionality Missing' (FFMs) make part of the Software Component's Feature Point Count for 'Functionality Missing' (FCFM).

So, all the FPFMs obtained for all the following apparent and obvious missing CFE's (Software's Measurable Component 'Functionality Execution') features:

- **a.** data read;
- **b.** data write;
- **c.** data input;
- **d.** data output;
- **e.** message send;
- **f.** message receive;
- **g.** computational;
- **h.** logical;
- **i.** decision execution;
- **j.** repeat execution;
- **k.** action execution;
- **l.** execution flow control;
- **m.** error handling;
- **n.** functional data handled during the memory read/write, input/output, message exchange, general computational, logical, decision, repeat and execution flow control operations;

in the functionality description, and for the missing feature class methods in the Logical Data Model, are added together to produce the FCFM.

Thus, the FCFM is equal to the total number of apparent and obvious deficiencies or missing features for the aforementioned CFE's features in the functionality description part and Logical Data Model of the Functional Requirements Specifications (FRS).

6.1.3 Description of the Software Component's Feature Point Counts (SCFPCs) for the Software Component's Measurable Features (SCMFs) of the Software's Measurable Component 'User Interface' (CUI)

The SCFPCs for the CUI are calculated based on the SCFPs obtained from the User Interface description in the Functional Requirements Specifications (FRS) for all the SCMFs (Software Component's Measurable Features) of the CUI as described next.

6.1.3.1 Software Component's Feature Point Count for 'User Screen' (FCUS), 'User Screen Field' (FCUF), 'User Screen Output Link' (FCUO), and 'User Screen Input Link' (FCUI) Description

All the Software Component's Feature Points for 'User Screen' (FPUSs), 'User Screen Field' (FPUFs), 'User Screen Output Link' (FPUOs), and 'User Screen Input Link' (FPUIs) which are produced by assigning the Software Component's Feature Points (SCFPs) to the Software Component's Measurable Features 'User Screen' (FUSs), 'User Screen Field' (FUFs), 'User Screen Output Link' (FUOs), and 'User Screen Input Link' (FUIs), respectively, make part of the Software Component's Feature Point Count for 'User Screen' (FCUS), 'User Screen Field' (FCUF), 'User Screen Output Link' (FCUO), and 'User Screen Input Link' (FCUI), respectively.

So, all the FPUSs, FPUFs, FPUOs, and FPUIs obtained for all the user screens in the user interfaces/screens; all the fields of all the user screens; all the output navigational links of all the user screens; and all the input navigational links of all the user screens; respectively, in the User Interface description are added correspondingly to produce the FCUS, FCUF, FCUO, and FCUI, respectively.

Thus, the FCUS, FCUF, FCUO, and FCUI signify the total number of the user screens; total number of the fields of all the user screens; total number of the output navigational links of all the user screens; and total number of the input navigational links of all the user screens; respectively, in the User Interface description part of the Functional Requirements Specifications (FRS).

6.1.3.2 Software Component's Feature Point Count for 'User Screen Missing' (FCUM) Description

All the Software Component's Feature Points for 'User Screen Missing' (FPUMs) which are produced by assigning the Software Component's Feature Points (SCFPs) to the Software Component's Measurable Features 'User Screen Missing' (FUMs) make part of the Software Component's Feature Point Count for 'User Screen Missing' (FCUM).

So, all the FPUMs obtained for all the following apparent and obvious missing CUI's (Software's Measurable Component 'User Interface') features:

- **a.** user screen;
- **b.** user screen field;
- **c.** user screen output link;
- **d.** user screen input link;

in the User Interface description are added together to produce the FCUM.

Thus, the FCUM is equal to the total number of apparent and obvious deficiencies or missing features for the aforementioned CUI's features in the User Interface description part of the Functional Requirements Specifications (FRS).

6.1.4 Description of the Software Component's Feature Point Counts (SCFPCs) for the Software Component's Measurable Features (SCMFs) of the Software's Measurable Component 'Message Exchange' (CME)

The SCFPCs for the CME are calculated based on the SCFPs obtained from the Message Exchange description in the Functional Requirements Specifications (FRS) for all the SCMFs (Software Component's Measurable Features) of the CME as described next.

6.1.4.1 Software Component's Feature Point Count for 'Notifying Message' (FCNM) and 'Message Field' (FCMF) Description

All the Software Component's Feature Points for 'Notifying Message' (FPNMs) and 'Message Field' (FPMFs) which are produced by assigning the Software Component's Feature Points (SCFPs) to the Software Component's Measurable Features 'Notifying Message' (FNMs) and 'Message Field' (FMFs), respectively, make part of the Software Component's Feature Point Count for 'Notifying Message' (FCNM) and 'Message Field' (FCMF), respectively.

So, all the FPNMs and FPMFs obtained for all the messages and for all the fields of all the messages, respectively, in the Message Exchange description are added correspondingly to produce the FCNM and FCMF, respectively.

Thus, the FCNM and FCMF signify the total number of the messages and total number of the fields of all the messages, respectively, in the Message Exchange description part of the Functional Requirements Specifications (FRS).

6.1.4.2 Software Component's Feature Point Count for 'Message Missing' (FCMM) Description

All the Software Component's Feature Points for 'Message Missing' (FPMMs) which are produced by assigning the Software Component's Feature Points (SCFPs) to the Software Component's Measurable Features 'Message Missing' (FMMs) make part of the Software Component's Feature Point Count for 'Message Missing' (FCMM).

So, all the FPMMs obtained for all the apparent and obvious following missing CME's (Software's Measurable Component 'Message Exchange') features:

a. message;

b. message field;

in the Message Exchange description are added together to produce the FCFM.

Thus, the FCFM is equal to the total number of apparent and obvious deficiencies or missing features for the aforementioned CME's features in the Message Exchange description part of the Functional Requirements Specifications (FRS).

6.2 COUNTING GUIDELINES FLOWCHART FOR THE SOFTWARE COMPONENT'S MEASURABLE FEATURES (SCMFs) OF THE SOFTWARE'S MEASURABLE COMPONENT 'FUNCTIONALITY EXECUTION' (CFE)

Figures 14–16 present the flowchart of the counting guidelines for the Software Component's Measurable Features (SCMFs) of the Software's Measurable Component 'Functionality Execution' (CFE). Continuous and dotted type of lines with arrows are used in the flowchart to make the start/end point of the flow distinctly clear. This flowchart helps and guides about how to proceed for the counting of the Software Component's Measurable Features (SCMFs) of the Software's Measurable Component 'Functionality Execution' (CFE).

After the various Software Component's Feature Points (SCFPs) for different SCMFs of the CFE, that is, FPDRs, FPDWs, FPDIs, etc., have been created according to Figures 14–16, addition of corresponding SCFPs, that means adding together all the corresponding FPDRs, FPDWs, FPDIs, etc., respectively, produces corresponding Software Component's Feature Point Counts (SCFPCs), that is, FCDR, FCDW, FCDI, etc., respectively.

6.3 SOME SPECIFIC GUIDELINES FOR THE SOFTWARE COMPONENT'S FEATURE POINT (SCFP) COUNTING

The following are some guidelines to be applied for identifying the Software Component's Measurable Feature (SCMFs) and assigning Software Component's Feature Point (SCFP) to them for the Software Component's Feature Point Counts (SCFPCs) enumeration in some specific cases.

6.3.1 About User Screens

1. Both the 'input text/data fields' and 'output text/data fields' of the user screens are identified as the Software Component's Measurable Feature 'User Screen Field' (FUF) and so, 1 SCFP (Software Component's Feature Point) is assigned to each 'input text/data field' and each 'output text/data field' to obtain the FPUFs (Software Component's Feature Points for 'User Screen Field'), the sum of which produces the FCUF (Software Component's Feature Point Count for 'User Screen Field').

   Some more explanation about this follows. There are 2 types of fields in both the input and output screens: data fields where data is typed in the input screens and displayed in the output screens; and the text fields which carry information about the data contents of the input/output data fields. Both of them – text and data fields – are identified as separate FPUFs. The sum of FPUFs produces the FCUF (Software Component's Feature Point Count for 'User Screen Field').

2. 'Selection menu fields' of the user screens are identified as the Software Measurable Feature 'User Screen Field' (FUF) and so, 1 SCFP (Software Component's Feature Point) is assigned to each 'selection menu field' to obtain the FPUFs (Software Component's Feature Points for 'User Screen Field'), the sum of which produces the FCUF (Software Component's Feature Point Count for 'User Screen Field').

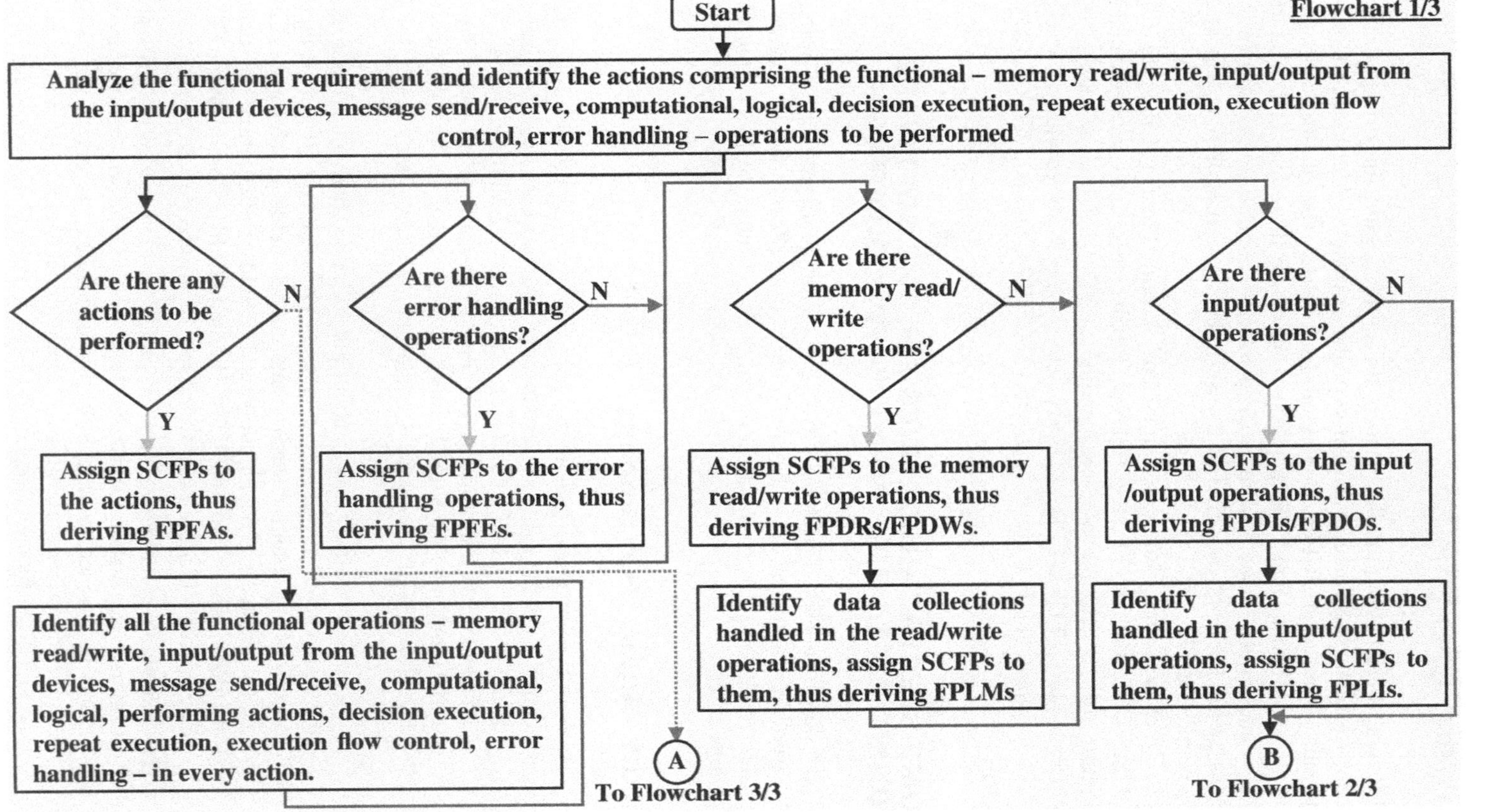

Figure 14 Counting guidelines flowchart (1/3) for the Software Component's Measurable Features (SCMFs) of the Software's Measurable Component 'Functionality Execution' (CFE).

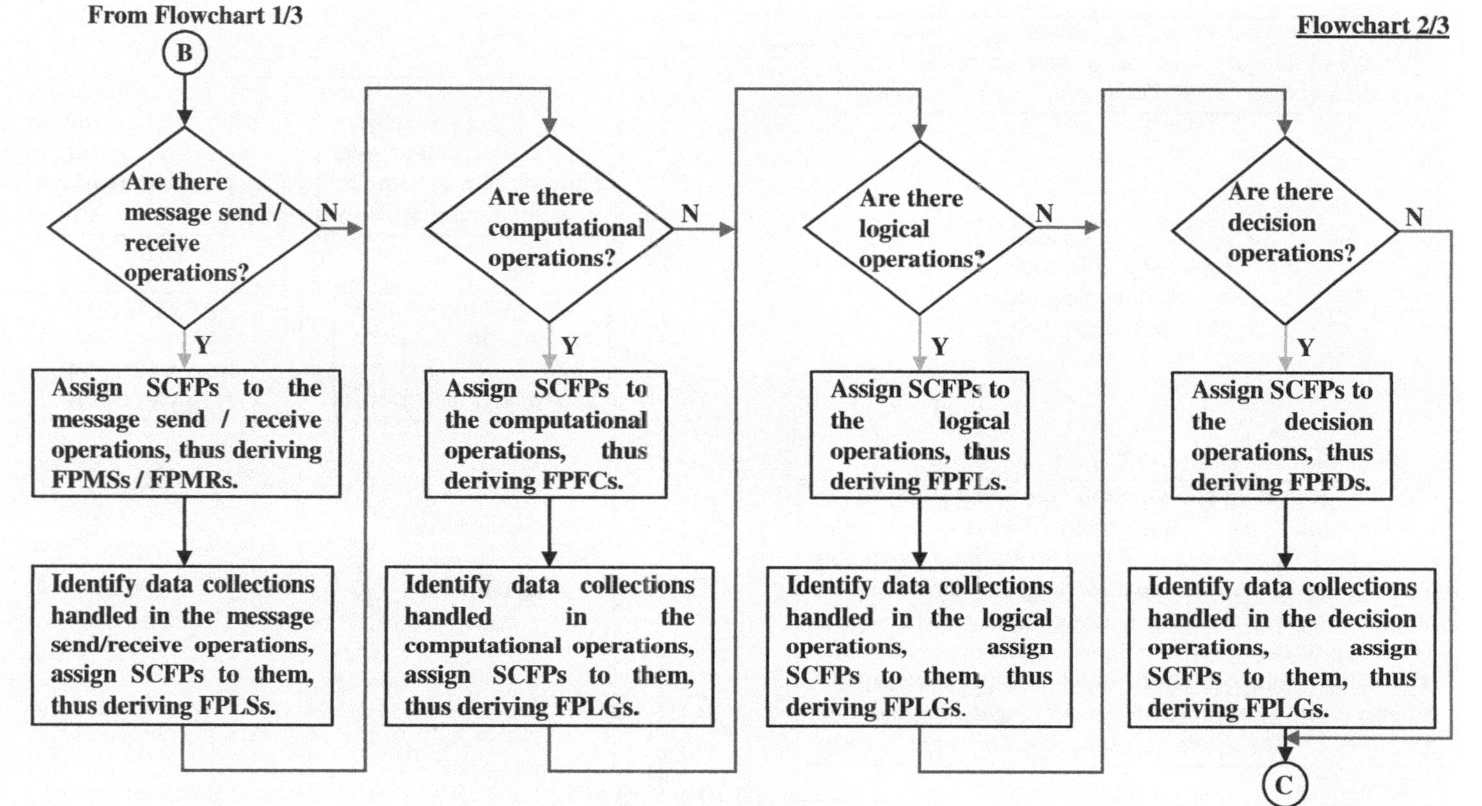

Figure 15 Counting guidelines flowchart (2/3) for the Software Component's Measurable Features (SCMFs) of the Software's Measurable Component 'Functionality Execution' (CFE).

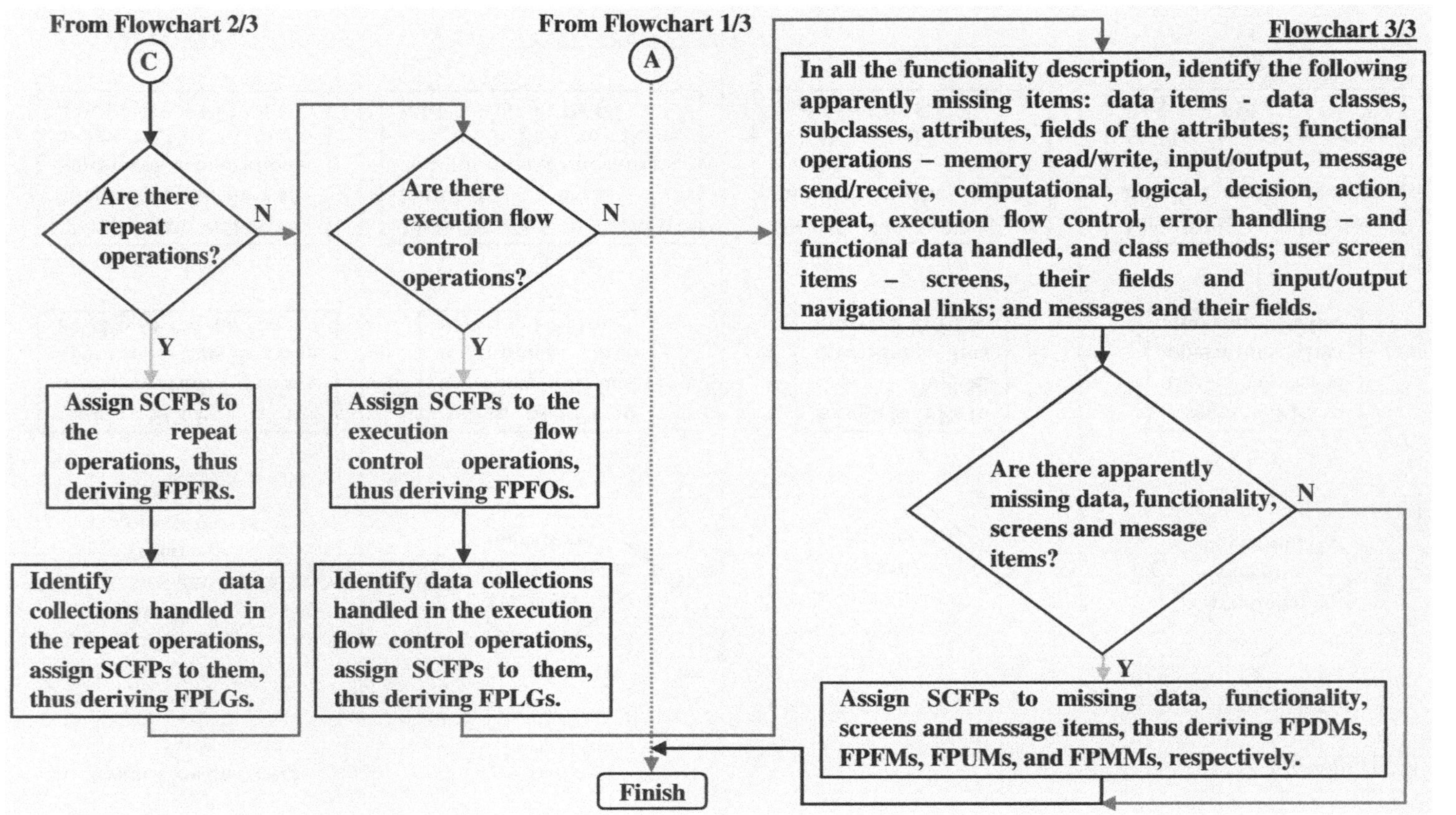

Figure 16 Counting guidelines flowchart (3/3) for the Software Component's Measurable Features (SCMFs) of the Software's Measurable Component 'Functionality Execution' (CFE).

6.3.2 About Data Manipulation Operations

Certain data manipulation operations are identified as the Software Component's Measurable Feature 'Data Read' (FDR) and Software Component's Measurable Feature 'Data Write' (FDW) as mentioned next.

6.3.2.1 About Software Component's Measurable Feature 'Data Read' (FDR)

Some functional requirements examples listed further ahead in this section do not mention an explicit memory data read operation but they contain memory data read operation implicitly and so, they are identified as the Software Component's Measurable Feature 'Data Read' (FDR). Thus, 1 SCFP (Software Component's Feature Point) is assigned to each such operation to obtain the FPDRs (Software Component's Feature Points for 'Data Read') the sum of which produces the FCDR (Software Component's Feature Point Count for 'Data Read').

The following are the examples of types of functions or operations mentioned as functional requirements in the Functional Requirements Specifications (FRS) that are equivalent to the memory data read operation:

1. get data;
2. select data;
3. find data;
4. access data;
5. display data – display contains 1 more operation after memory data read, that is, data output operation to the output display device;
6. verify data – verify contains some more operations after memory data read, that is, data verification which may involve some decision operations.

6.3.2.2 About Software Component's Measurable Feature 'Data Write' (FDW)

Some functional requirements examples listed further ahead in this section do not mention an explicit memory data write operation but they contain memory data write operation implicitly and so, they are identified as the Software Component's Measurable Feature 'Data Write' (FDW). Thus, 1 SCFP (Software Component's Feature Point) is assigned to each such operation to obtain the FPDWs (Software Component's Feature Points for 'Data Write') the sum of which produces the FCDW (Software Component's Feature Point Count for 'Data Write').

The following are the examples of types of functions or operations mentioned as functional requirements in the Functional Requirements Specifications (FRS) that are equivalent to the memory data write operation:

1. put data;
2. save data;
3. update data;
4. create data;

5. delete data;
6. insert data;
7. modify data.

6.3.3 About Decision Operations

Similar to the decision-taking functional requirement which is 'if' condition (e.g., if the condition is true, take some action) to which 1 SCFP is assigned and so it has 1 FPFD (Software Component's Feature Point for 'Function Decision Execution'), each 'else if' condition and each 'else' condition in decision-taking functional requirements is assigned 1 SCFP each, so each 'else if' has 1 FPFD and each 'else' has 1 FPFD. The sum of FPFDs produces the FCFD (Software Component's Feature Point Count for 'Function Decision Execution').

6.3.4 About Action Execution Operations

While identifying the actions performed and assigning SCFPs to the actions, care should be taken that if the actions are counted for a group of operations, all the individual operations in that group of operations should not be counted as actions, so avoiding double counting of the same operations as 2 actions.

6.4 SOFTWARE COMPONENT'S FEATURE POINT COUNTS (SCFPCs) FORMATION

All the SCFPs collected from the functional requirements descriptions in the Logical Data Model, functionality, user interfaces, and message specifications are consolidated and added respectively to give the corresponding SCFPCs as shown in Table 4.

6.5 USAGE OF THE SOFTWARE COMPONENT'S FEATURE POINT COUNTS (SCFPCs)

There are a total of 31 SCFPCs (Software Component's Feature Point Counts) corresponding to the 31 SCMFs (Software Component's Measurable Features) of the 4 SMCs (Software's Measurable Components). The SCFPCs are used for measuring the SCMFs which are all measured in the FSSM. The SCFPCs, obtained by summing up the corresponding SCFPs which are the result of the identification of the SCMFs in the functional requirements and the assignment of SCFPs to the SCMFs, are used for the calculations of the Software Component's Feature Measurements (SCFMs). The SCFMs are utilized for the calculations of the Software Component's Measurement (SCMs), Software Size and Effort Estimations (SSEEs), and Software Performance Quality Indicators (SPQIs) of both the types – Software Structural Indicators (SSIs)[5–7] and Software Operational Indicators (SOIs)[5–7].

Table 4 Software Component's Feature Points (SCFPs) Consolidation, Addition, and Conversion to the Software Component's Feature Point Counts (SCFPCs)

	Software Component's Feature Points (SCFPs) and Formation of their Corresponding Software Component's Feature Point Counts (SCFPCs)																													
SCFP→ Domain ↓	FPDC	FPDA	FPDF	FPCM	FPDM	FPDR	FPDW	FPDI	FPDO	FPFC	FPFL	FPFD	FPFR	FPFA	FPFO	FPFE	FPMS	FPMR	FPFM	FPLM	FPLI	FPLS	FPLG	FPNM	FPMF	FPMM	FPUS	FPUF	FPUO	FPUI	FPUM
LDM	X	X	X	X	X																										
FE						X	X	X	X	X	X	X	X	X	X	X	X	X	X	X	X	X	X								
UI																											X	X	X	X	X
ME																								X	X	X					
SCFPC →	X	X	X	X	X	X	X	X	X	X	X	X	X	X	X	X	X	X	X	X	X	X	X	X	X	X	X	X	X	X	X
	↑ FCDC	↑ FCDA	↑ FCDF	↑ FCCM	↑ FCDM	↑ FCDR	↑ FCDW	↑ FCDI	↑ FCDO	↑ FCFC	↑ FCFL	↑ FCFD	↑ FCFR	↑ FCFA	↑ FCFO	↑ FCFE	↑ FCMS	↑ FCMR	↑ FCFM	↑ FCLM	↑ FCLI	↑ FCLS	↑ FCLG	↑ FCNM	↑ FCMF	↑ FCMM	↑ FCUS	↑ FCUF	↑ FCUO	↑ FCUI	↑ FCUM

6.6 SOFTWARE COMPONENT'S FEATURE POINT COUNTS (SCFPCs) VALUE

The value zero, small or big of different Software Component's Feature Point Counts (SCFPCs) depends on the magnitude of presence of the corresponding Software Component's Feature Points (SCFPs). The quantity of the SCFPs in turn depends on the presence and quantity of the corresponding Software Component's Measurable Features (SCMFs). The presence and quantity of the SCMFs is dependent on the type of applications and their Functional Requirements Specifications (FRS).

It may be possible that certain SCMFs are absent, or present in small quantity, but some others may be more voluminously present. According to this fact, the quantity of some SCFPs may be nil, for some others it may be small number and for some others it may be a big number. Accordingly, the values of corresponding SCFPCs will be zero, small or big.

In fact, the varying sizes of the Software Component's Measurable Features (SCMFs) measured by the Software Component's Feature Measurements (SCFMs); and of Software's Measurable Components (SMCs) – Software's Measurable Component 'Functional Data' (CFD), 'Functionality Execution' (CFE), 'User Interface' (CUI), and 'Message Exchange' (CME) – measured by the Software Component's Measurements (SCMs); and thus, the total size of the software are dependent on this varying magnitude of the presence of various SCMFs. The absence or varying magnitudes of various SCMFs leads to the consequence of different quantities of the SCFPs, and that in turn results in different values of SCFPCs. Thus, the sizes of the SCMFs and SMCs, and the total size are determined based on these facts.

There is no upper limit of the presence and quantity of the SCMFs, so the same is true for the SCFPs as a result, and consequently, for the SCFPCs values also.

6.7 EXAMPLES

1. In the functional requirement "Class: Result; Attributes: data count, memory operations, computational operations, logical operations, decision execution operations, repeat execution operations, action execution operations, input/output operations, message exchange operations, error handling operations, class methods, code count, user interface count, message count, total software count, program lines, design effort, test effort, and total effort (there are a total of 19 attributes); Fields: each attribute has 1 field." which forms part of data description in the Logical Data Model part of the FRS, there are 1 FPDC, 19 FPDAs, and 19 FPDFs (see Section 5.4).

   Hence, there are the following SCFPCs (Software Component's Features Point Counts) in the functional requirement:

   FCDC = 1, FCDA = 19, and FCDF = 19.

   (*Note*: The aforementioned functional requirement is part of Chapter 14.)

2. In the functional requirement "The user enters the age of the student. The list of students above the input age is extracted from the student database and displayed." which forms part of the functionality description in the FRS, there are 3 FPFAs, 1 FPDI, 1 FPDR, 1 FPDO, 2 FPLIs, and 1 FPLM (see Section 5.4).

Hence, there are the following SCFPCs (Software Component's Features Point Counts) in the functional requirement:

FCFA = 3, FCDI = 1, FCDR = 1, FCDO = 1, FCLI = 2, and FCLM = 1.

3. In the functional requirement "Entered user name is checked. If there is a non-alphabetical character in it, an error message is displayed." which forms part of the functionality description in the FRS, there are 3 FPFAs, 1 FPDI, 1 FPFD, 1 FPDO, 1 FPFE, 2 FPLIs, and 1 FPLG (see Section 5.4).

   Hence, there are the following SCFPCs (Software Component's Features Point Counts) in the functional requirement:

   FCFA = 3, FCDI = 1, FCFD = 1, FCDO = 1, FCFE = 1, FCLI = 2, and FCLG = 1.

4. In the functional requirement "Log-on screen displaying the fields user-id and password to log on." which forms part of the User Interface description in the FRS (see Figure 17), there are 1 FPUS, 4 FPUFs, and 3 FPUMs (see Section 5.4).

   Hence, there are the following SCFPCs (Software Component's Features Point Counts) in the functional requirement:

   FCUS = 1, FCUF = 4, and FCUM = 3.

   (*Note*: The aforementioned functional requirement is part of Chapter 14.)

6.8 CHAPTER SUMMARY

6.8.1 Software Component's Feature Point Count (SCFPC): Summary

Software's main constituents are the 4 Software's Measurable Components (SMCs) which are the Software's Measurable Component 'Functional Data' (CFD), 'Functionality Execution' (CFE), 'User Interface' (CUI), and 'Message Exchange' (CME). The SMCs have the Software Component's Measurable Features (SCMFs). For the software size measurement, the respective 4, 19, 5, and 3 Software Component's Measurable Features (SCMFs) of the corresponding 4 SMCs are identified in the functional requirements.

Then, the Software Component's Feature Points (SCFPs) are assigned to these identified SCMFs. The SCFP is the Functional Size Unit (FSU) in the FSSM. This way, the corresponding SCFPs – for the 4 SCMFs of the CFD, 19 SCMFs of the CFE, 5 SCMFs of the CUI, and 3 SCMFs of the CME – are obtained.

Corresponding to the Software Component's Feature Points (SCFPs) for the respective Software Component's Measurable Features (SCMFs) of the Software Measurable Components (SMCs), there are the Software Component's Feature Point Counts (SCFPCs) which are obtained by the summation of the SCFPs for the respective SCMFs.

Thus, there are:

- 4 SCFPCs related to the data classes, attributes, fields, and missing data items for the CFD;

- 19 SCFPCs related to the memory read/write, input/output, message send/receive, computational, logical, decision, action, repeat, execution flow control, and error handling operations; data handled in the memory read/write, input/output, message send/receive, computational, logical, decision, repeat, and execution flow control operations; class methods; and missing functionality items for the CFE;
- 5 SCFPCs related to the user screens, their fields, input/output links, and missing screen items for the CUI;
- 3 SCFPCs related to the messages, their fields, and missing message items for the CME.

6.8.2 Usage and Value of the Software Component's Feature Point Counts (SCFPCs): Summary

All the 31 SCFPCs (Software Component's Feature Point Counts) corresponding to the 31 SCMFs (Software Component's Measurable Features) of the 4 SMCs (Software's Measurable Components) are used for the calculations of the Software Component's Feature Measurement (SCFMs) which in turn are used for the calculations of the Software Component's Measurement (SCMs), Software Size and Effort Estimations (SSEEs), and Software Performance Quality Indicators (SPQIs) of both the types – Software Structural Indicators (SSIs)[5–7] and Software Operational Indicators (SOIs)[5–7].

The values nil, small, or big of the SCFPCs depend on the absence, presence and quantity of the corresponding SCFPs which in turn depend on the absence, presence and quantity, respectively, of the corresponding SCMFs in the applications and thus, in the functional requirements of the applications. There is no upper limit of the presence and quantity of the SCMFs, and consequently, of the SCFPs and thus, of the values of the SCFPCs.

EXERCISES

6.1 The Software Component's Feature Point Count for 'Message Send' (FCMS) is equal to the sum of

A. all the Software Component's Feature Points for 'Message Send' (FPMSs).

B. all the Software Component's Feature Points for 'Message Send' (FPMSs) and all the Software Component's Feature Points for 'Notifying Message' (FPNMs).

C. all the Software Component's Feature Points for 'Message Send' (FPMSs) and all the Software Component's Feature Points for 'Message Receive' (FPMRs).

6.2 The Software Component's Feature Point Count for 'Data Class' (FCDC) signifies

A. the total number of the classes and subclasses in the class structure described in the Logical Data Model part of the Functional Requirements Specifications.

B. the total number of the classes, subclasses, and their attributes in the class structure described in the Logical Data Model part of the Functional Requirements Specifications.

C. the total number of the classes, subclasses, their attributes, and fields in their attributes in the class structure described in the Logical Data Model part of the Functional Requirements Specifications.

6.3 The Software Component's Feature Point Count for 'Message Send' (FCMS) signifies

A. the total number of the message send operations and message receive operations.

B. the total number of the message send operations.

C. the total number of the message send operations and number of the messages and their fields.

6.4 The Software Component's Feature Point Count for 'User Screen' (FCUS) signifies

A. the total number of the data output operations to display the screens.

B. the total number of the user screens and their fields.

C. the total number of the user screens.

Chapter 7

Software Component's Measurements through Software Component's Feature Measurements in the FSSM

The calculations for the Software Component's Measurements (SCMs) are based on the Software Component's Feature Measurements (SCFMs). The calculations for the SCFMs of the SCMFs (Software Component's Measurable Features) are performed by using the Software Component's Feature Point Counts (SCFPCs), the third step in the measurements of the SCMFs (as mentioned in Section 5.1, the calculations for the SCFMs of the SCMFs are performed in three steps. The descriptions of the first and second steps have been presented in Chapters 5 and 6, respectively). The description and formulae for the SCFMs, the third step, and SCMs are presented in this chapter.

7.1 SOFTWARE COMPONENT'S MEASUREMENT (SCM) AND SOFTWARE COMPONENT'S FEATURE MEASUREMENT (SCFM) DESCRIPTION

The Software Component's Measurements (SCMs) are the measurements of the Software's Measurable Components (SMCs) in terms of the Software Component's Feature Points (SCFPs) which are the Functional Size Units (FSUs) in the Functional Software Size Measurement Methodology with Effort Estimation and Performance Indication (FSSM). These measurements indicate the size and complexity of the 4 SMCs, their total size and the extent of the deficiencies in the Functional Requirements Specifications (FRS).

As described in the earlier chapters, firstly, 31 important and relevant Software Component's Measurable Features (SCMFs) of the 4 Software's Measurable Components (SMCs) – CFD, CFE, CUI, and CME – are considered to obtain the 31 Software Component's Feature Point Counts (SCFPCs) from the Logical Data Model, Functionality Execution, User Interface, and Message Exchange description parts which all are provided in the Functional Requirements Specifications (FRS). Then, these SCFPCs are used to calculate the 6

Functional Software Size Measurement Methodology with Effort Estimation and Performance Indication, First Edition. Jasveer Singh.

Companion website: http://booksupport.wiley.com

Software Component's Measurements (SCMs) through 28 Software Component's Feature Measurements (SCFMs) described next.

Figure 5 and Figure 6 show the summary overview diagrams of the SCFMs and SCMs. Figure 9 and Figure 10 show the summary diagrams of the SCFMs and SCMs. The aforementioned figures show the contents, and relationships and information flow in the contents of mainly the following constituents of the FSSM regarding the measurements: Software Component's Feature Measurements (SCFMs) and Software Component's Measurements (SCMs).

As shown in the aforementioned Figures 5, 6, 9, and 10, and in Figures 3 and 4, the Functional Requirements Specifications (FRS) which contain the descriptions of the

1. Functional Data (FD) in the Logical Data Model (LDM) part;
2. functionality in the Functionality Execution (FE) description part;
3. user interfaces/screens in the User Interface (UI) description part;
4. message communication in the Message Exchange (ME) description part;

are used to gather the information about the 31 Software Component's Feature Point Counts (SCFPCs) for the 31 Software Component's Measurable Features (SCMFs) of the 4 Software's Measurable Components (SMCs) – Software's Measurable Component 'Functional Data' (CFD), 'Functionality Execution' (CFE), 'User Interface' (CUI), and 'Message Exchange' (CME).

The complete information about the SCFPCs is derived from the Functional Requirements Specifications (FRS).

These SCFPCs are used to calculate the 28 Software Component's Feature Measurements (SCFMs) that are used further to obtain the 6 Software Component's Measurements (SCMs) by simple calculations.

The 6 SCMs (Software Component's Measurements) thus obtained provide the measurements about the 4 Software's Measurable Components (SMCs), total component's size, and requirements deficiency in terms of the Software Component's Feature Points (SCFPs) that are the Functional Size Units (FSUs) in the FSSM. The SCMs provide sufficient information about the size and complexity of the components, and about the total software size. The SCFMs and SCMs are used for deriving further information about the Software Size and Effort Estimations (SSEEs), and Software Performance Quality Indicators (SPQIs) of the two types – Software Structural Indicators (SSIs)[5–7], and Software Operational Indicators (SOIs)[5–7].

Description of the 6 SCMs and their underlying SCFMs follows.

7.1.1 Software Component 'Functional Data' Measurement (CFDM) Description

The CFDM (Software Component 'Functional Data' Measurement) indicates the Functional Data size and complexity.

The CFDM is based on 3 SCFMs which are calculated from 3 SCFPCs that are obtained from the Software Component's Feature Point (SCFP) counting of the classes, the subclasses, their attributes and their fields defined in the Logical Data Model.

The **CFDM** comprises the following Software Component's Feature Measurements (SCFMs):

1. **Data Class Entities (DCE)**: It is the measurement of the Software Component's Measurable Feature 'Data Class' (FDC), for all the data classes and subclasses defined in the Logical Data Model.
2. **Data Class Attribute Entities (DAE)**: It is the measurement of the Software Component's Measurable Feature 'Data Attribute' (FDA), for all the attributes of all the classes and subclasses.
3. **Data Class Field Entities (DFE)**: It is the measurement of the Software Component's Measurable Feature 'Data Field' (FDF), for all the fields of all the attributes of all the classes and subclasses.

The CFDM thus shows the enormity of the functional data used in the software application. This measurement helps to understand the requirement of the data expertise, for example, database experience, in the project development team that may be required for the execution of the project depending on the size and complexity indicated by the CFDM.

As explained in Section 1.3, the complexity of the software components is the level and degree of effort and time required for understanding, analyzing, designing, testing, and maintaining the components. As a general rule, the bigger the size of the component, the more the effort and time are required to understand, analyze, design, test, and maintain it; and the more the effort and time are required to understand, analyze, design, test, and maintain it, the more complex the component is.

7.1.2 Software Component 'Functionality Execution' Measurement (CFEM) Description

The CFEM (Software Component 'Functionality Execution' Measurement) indicates the functionality size and complexity, taking into account all the operations of the

1. software processing consisting of the computational, logical, decision execution, repeat execution, actions performed, and execution flow control;
2. memory transactions, that is, memory data read/write operations used for reading/writing the data from/to the non-volatile type of memory such as disk devices;
3. input/output device interactions used for receiving/sending the input/output data from/to the input/output devices;
4. message communications with the external application programs;
5. error handling;

and the amount of the functional data handling during the following functional operations:

1. memory data read/write;
2. input/output device interactions;
3. message send/receive used for sending/receiving the messages to/from the external application programs;
4. general operations which are of the type computational, logical, decision execution, repeat execution, and execution flow control;

as well as the class methods involved in the functionality.

The CFEM is based on 14 SCFMs which are calculated from 17 SCFPCs that are obtained from the Software Component's Feature Point (SCFP) counting of all the aforementioned operations, data handled in the operations and class methods.

The **CFEM** comprises two parts:

1. First, the **Functionality Execution Operations Measurement (FEOM)** which indicates the magnitude of the functional operations, and which is based on the following Software Component's Feature Measurements (SCFMs):
   a. **Memory Operations (MO)**: It is the measurement of the Software Component's Measurable Features 'Data Read' (FDR) and 'Data Write' (FDW), for all the memory read/write operations used for reading/writing the data from/to the memory devices.
   b. **Computational Operations (CO)**: It is the measurement of the Software Component's Measurable Feature 'Function Computational Operations' (FFC), for all the mathematical computational operations.
   c. **Logical Operations (LO)**: It is the measurement of the Software Component's Measurable Feature 'Logical Operations' (FFL), for all the logical operations of the type AND, OR, etc.
   d. **Decision Execution Operations (DEO)**: It is the measurement of the Software Component's Measurable Feature 'Decision Execution Operations' (FFD), for all the decision-taking operations, such as if, else if and else.
   e. **Repeat Execution Operations (REO)**: It is the measurement of the Software Component's Measurable Feature 'Repeat Execution Operations' (FFR), for all the repeat operations for actions or group of actions.
   f. **Action Execution Operations (AEO)**: It is the measurement of the Software Component's Measurable Feature 'Action Execution Operations' (FFA), for all the actions performing operations.
   g. **Execution Flow Control Operations (EFCO)**: It is the measurement of the Software Component's Measurable Feature 'Execution Flow Control Operations' (FFO), for all the operations which control the execution flow.
   h. **Error Handling Operations (EHO)**: It is the measurement of the Software Component's Measurable Feature 'Error Handling Operations' (FFE), for all the error handling operations.
   i. **Input/Output Operations (IOO)**: It is the measurement of the Software Component's Measurable Features 'Data Input' (FDI) and 'Data Output' (FDO), for all the input/output operations used for receiving/sending the input/output data from/to the input/output devices.
   j. **Message Exchange Operations (MEO)**: It is the measurement of the Software Component's Measurable Feature 'Message Send' (FMS) and 'Message Receive' (FMR), for all the message send/receive operations used for sending/receiving the messages to/from the other programs/sub-programs.

   as well as

   a. **Class Method Entities (CMDE)**: It is the measurement of the Software Component's Measurable Feature 'Class Method' (FCM), for all the class methods described in the Logical Data Model.

   For arriving at the Functionality Execution Operations Measurement (FEOM), an intermediate step is used to first evaluate the Functionality Execution Operations Dynamic Measurement (FEODM). The FEODM, which is the measurement of the dynamic functionality operations execution, indicates the dynamic run-time behavior of the software and is used for dynamic run-time operations performance calculations for the Software Performance Quality Indicators (SPQI) of the type Software Operational Indicators (SOIs)[5–7]. The value of the FEODM is calculated

by adding all the aforementioned operations values except the AEO and CMDE because only the software processing operations that are required to determine the dynamic run-time characteristics of the software are included in it.
Then, the value of FEOM is calculated by adding the values of the AEO and CMDE to the FEODM.

2. Second, the **Functionality Execution Data Manipulation Measurement (FEDM)** which indicates the magnitude of the functional data handled, and which is based on the following Software Component's Feature Measurements (SCFMs) (the types of functional operations during which the functional data are handled are indicated in the respective SCFMs that follow):
   a. **Memory Operations Functional Data Entities (MOFE)**: It is the measurement of the Software Component's Measurable Feature 'Memory Operations Functional Data' (FLM), for all the functional data handled during all the memory read/write operations.
   b. **Input/Output Operations Functional Data Entities (IOFE)**: It is the measurement of the Software Component's Measurable Feature 'Input/Output Operations Functional Data' (FLI), for all the functional data handled during all the input/output operations used for receiving/sending the input/output data from/to the input/output devices.
   c. **Message Exchange Operations Functional Data Entities (EOFE)**: It is the measurement of the Software Component's Measurable Feature 'Message Exchange Operations Functional Data' (FLS), for all the functional data handled during all the message send/receive operations for sending/receiving the messages to/from the other programs/sub-programs.
   d. **General Operations Functional Data Entities (GOFE)**: It is the measurement of the Software Component's Measurable Feature 'General Operations Functional Data' (FLG), for all the functional data handled during the following operations:
      i. computational:
      all the computational operations in the Functionality Execution, for example, addition, subtraction, multiplication, division, power, log, and equals;
      ii. logical:
      all the logical operations in the Functionality Execution, for example, AND, OR, NOT, and XOR;
      iii. decision execution:
      all the conditions checking and decision-taking (e.g., if the condition is true, take the action) operations in the Functionality Execution;
      iv. repeat execution:
      all the repeat operations in the Functionality Execution;
      v. execution flow control:
      all the execution flow control operations in the Functionality Execution.

The CFEM thus shows the enormity of the functionality in the software application in terms of the aforementioned various types of functional operations, functional data handled during the functional operations, and class methods. It helps thus to estimate the importance and requirement of the functionality design expertise in the development team for the project execution.

7.1.3 Software Component 'User Interface' Measurement (CUIM) Description

The CUIM (Software Component 'User Interface' Measurement) indicates the User Interface size and complexity.

The CUIM is based on 4 SCFMs which are calculated from 4 SCFPCs that are obtained from the Software Component's Feature Point (SCFP) counting of the user interfaces (screens), their fields and input/output navigation links interconnecting the user interfaces (screens).

The **CUIM** comprises the following Software Component's Feature Measurements (SCFMs):

1. **User Interface Screen Entities (UISE)**: It is the measurement of the Software Component's Measurable Feature 'User Screen' (FUS), for all the user interfaces/screens defined in the User Interface description part.
2. **User Interface Field Entities (UIFE)**: It is the measurement of the Software Component's Measurable Feature 'User Screen Field' (FUF), for all the fields of all the user interfaces/screens.
3. **User Interface Input Link Entities (UIIE)**: It is the measurement of the Software Component's Measurable Feature 'User Screen Input Link' (FUI), for all the input navigational links of all the user interfaces/screens.
4. **User Interface Output Link Entities (UIOE)**: It is the measurement of the Software Component's Measurable Feature 'User Screen Output Link' (FUO), for all the output navigational links of all the user interfaces/screens.

The CUIM thus shows the enormity of the size of the user interfaces in the software application. It helps to understand the requirement of the user interface expertise in the development team during the project execution for developing the user interface/screen structures and related aspects.

7.1.4 Software Component 'Message Exchange' Measurement (CMEM) Description

The CMEM (Software Component 'Message Exchange' Measurement) indicates the message structure size and complexity.

The CMEM is based on 2 SCFMs which are calculated from 2 SCFPCs that are obtained by the Software Component's Feature Point (SCFP) counting of the messages and their fields.

The **CMEM** comprises the following Software Component's Feature Measurements (SCFMs):

1. **Notifying Message Entities (NME)**: It is the measurement of the Software Component's Measurable Feature 'Notifying Messages' (FNM), for all the messages used for communication with the other programs.
2. **Message Field Entities (MFE)**: It is the measurement of the Software Component's Measurable Feature 'Message Field' (FMF), for all the fields of all the messages.

The CMEM thus shows the enormity of the size of the message exchange structures that are needed by the software application. It is helpful to understand the importance of the Message Exchange part design and hence, the expertise needed for message exchange structures design during the project execution.

7.1.5 Software Total Components Measurement (STCM) Description

The **STCM** (Software Total Components Measurement) indicates the total software size and complexity and is obtained by the addition of the measurements of all the 4 Software's Measurable Components (SMCs), that is, addition of the

1. **CFDM** (Software Component 'Functional Data' Measurement);
2. **CFEM** (Software Component 'Functionality Execution' Measurement);
3. **CUIM** (Software Component 'User Interface' Measurement);
4. **CMEM** (Software Component 'Message Exchange' Measurement).

The STCM shows the enormity, complexity, and size of the total software application.

7.1.6 Software Components Requirement Deficiency Measurement (CRDM) Description

The CRDM (Software Components Requirement Deficiency Measurement) indicates the apparently missing items, taking into account the apparent missing items in the following 4 Software's Measurable Components (SMCs):

1. CFD (Software's Measurable Component 'Functional Data');
2. CFE (Software's Measurable Component 'Functionality Execution');
3. CUI (Software's Measurable Component 'User Interface');
4. CME (Software's Measurable Component 'Message Exchange').

The CRDM is based on 4 SCFMs which are calculated from 4 SCFPCs that are obtained by the Software Component's Feature Point (SCFPs) counting of the apparently deficient (missing) items in all the aforementioned 4 SMCs (Software's Measurable Components).

The **CRDM** comprises the following Software Component's Feature Measurements (SCFMs):

1. **Functional Data Missing Entities (FDME)**: It is the measurement of the Software Component's Measurable Feature 'Data Missing' (FDM), for all the missing items in the Functional Data description.
2. **Functionality Execution Missing Entities (FEME)**: It is the measurement of the Software Component's Measurable Feature 'Function Missing' (FFM), for all the missing items in the Functionality Execution description.
3. **User Interface Missing Entities (UIME)**: It is the measurement of the Software Component's Measurable Feature 'User Screen Missing' (FUM), for all the missing items in the User Interface description.

4. **Message Exchange Missing Entities (MEME)**: It is the measurement of the Software Component's Measurable Feature 'Message Missing' (FMM), for all the missing items of the message structure in the Message Exchange description.

The CRDM thus shows the extent of improvements which may be needed to be done in the Functional Requirements Specifications (FRS), thus helping to improve the quality of the project at the early stages.

7.2 SOFTWARE COMPONENT'S MEASUREMENT (SCM) AND SOFTWARE COMPONENT'S FEATURE MEASUREMENT (SCFM) FORMULAE

From the 31 SCFPCs (Software Component's Feature Point Counts) obtained by adding the respective SCFPs (Software Component's Feature Points) derived by identifying and assigning the Functional Size Units (FSUs), that is, the SCFPs to the 31 SCMFs (Software Component's Measurable Features) of the 4 SMCs (Software's Measurable Components) available in the 4 description parts – the Logical Data Model (LDM), Functionality Execution (FE), User Interface (UI), and Message Exchange (ME) – of the Functional Requirements Specifications (FRS), calculations are made for the 28 Software Component's Feature Measurements (SCFMs). The SCFMs thus obtained are used for calculating the 6 Software Component's Measurements (SCMs), 4 Software Size and Effort Estimations (SSEEs), and 36 Software Performance Quality Indicators (SPQIs) of which 23 Software Structural Indicators (SSIs)[5–7], and 13 Software Operational Indicators (SOIs)[5–7].

Simple calculations formulae for the 6 SCMs based on the different SCFMs, and calculations formulae for the 28 SCFMs based on the different SCFPCs are described next.

7.2.1 Software Component 'Functional Data' Measurement (CFDM) Formulae

The Software Component 'Functional Data' Measurement (CFDM) signifies the size and complexity of the Software's Measurable Component 'Functional Data' (CFD).

Functional Data are described by the class structure.

Hence, the enormity and magnitude of the Functional Data are determined by taking into account the class structure of the Functional Data, that is, the number of classes and width of the classes.

The width of the classes is determined by the attributes of the classes and fields of the attributes.

Accordingly, the size of the Software's Measurable Component 'Functional Data' (CFD), measured by the Software Component 'Functional Data' Measurement (CFDM), is obtained by considering for the measurement all the following Software Component's Feature Measurements (SCFMs) of the functional data entities:

1. **Data Class Entities (DCE):**
   The Data Class Entities (DCE) is calculated from the
   a. Software Component's Feature Point Count for 'Data Class' (FCDC).
2. **Data Class Attribute Entities (DAE):**
   The Data Class Attribute Entities (DAE) is calculated from the
   a. Software Component's Feature Point Count for 'Data Attribute' (FCDA).

3. **Data Class Field Entities (DFE):**
   The Data Class Field Entities (DFE) is calculated from the
   a. Software Component's Feature Point Count for 'Data Field' (FCDF).

First, corresponding to the aforementioned data entities, the following calculations of the Software Component's Feature Measurements (SCFMs) are performed:

1. **Data Class Entities (DCE)** = FCDC;
2. **Data Class Attribute Entities (DAE)** = FCDA;
3. **Data Class Field Entities (DFE)** = FCDF.

Then, the CFDM is calculated by the following formula:

CFDM = Data Class Entities (DCE) + Data Class Attribute Entities (DAE) + Data Class Field Entities (DFE).

There is no upper limit for the CFDM.

7.2.2 Software Component 'Functionality Execution' Measurement (CFEM) Formulae

The Software Component 'Functionality Execution' Measurement (CFEM) signifies the size and complexity of the Software's Measurable Component 'Functionality Execution' (CFE).

Functionality Execution is described by the functionality execution operations and functionality execution data handling as well as by the class methods.

Hence, the enormity and magnitude of the Functionality Execution is determined by taking into account the functionality execution operations, functionality execution data handling and class methods.

Accordingly, the CFEM is divided in two parts – the Functionality Execution Operations Measurement (FEOM) and Functionality Execution Data Manipulation Measurement (FEDM). Their measurement formulae are described next.

7.2.2.1 Functionality Execution Operations Measurement (FEOM) Formulae

The first part of the CFEM (Software Component 'Functionality Execution' Measurement) is the FEOM (Functionality Execution Operations Measurement) which takes into account for the measurement all the following Software Component's Feature Measurements (SCFMs) of the functionality execution operations:

1. **Memory Operations (MO):**
   The Memory Operations (MO) is calculated by the addition of the following:
   a. Software Component's Feature Point Count for 'Data Read' (FCDR);
   b. Software Component's Feature Point Count for 'Data Write' (FCDW).
2. **Computational Operations (CO):**
   The Computational Operations (CO) is calculated from the
   a. Software Component's Feature Point Count for 'Function Computational Operation' (FCFC).

3. **Logical Operations (LO):**
   The Logical Operations (LO) is calculated from the
   a. Software Component's Feature Point Count for 'Function Logical Operation' (FCFL).
4. **Decision Execution Operations (DEO):**
   The Decision Execution Operations (DEO) is calculated from the
   a. Software Component's Feature Point Count for 'Function Decision Execution' (FCFD).
5. **Repeat Execution Operations (REO):**
   The Repeat Execution Operations (REO) is calculated from the
   a. Software Component's Feature Point Count for 'Function Repeat Execution (FCFR).
6. **Action Execution Operations (AEO):**
   The Action Execution Operations (AEO) is calculated from the
   Software Component's Feature Point Count for 'Function Action Execution (FCFA).
7. **Execution Flow Control Operations (EFCO):**
   The Execution Flow Control Operations (EFCO) is calculated from the
   a. Software Component's Feature Point Count for 'Function Execution Flow Control' (FCFO).
8. **Input/Output Operations (IOO):**
   The Input/Output Operations (IOO) is calculated by the addition of the following:
   a. Software Component's Feature Point Count for 'Data Input' (FCDI);
   b. Software Component's Feature Point Count for 'Data Output' (FCDO).
9. **Message Exchange Operations (MEO):**
   The Message Exchange Operations (MEO) is calculated by the addition of the following:
   a. Software Component's Feature Point Count for 'Message Send' (FCMS);
   b. Software Component's Feature Point Count for 'Message Receive' (FCMR).
10. **Error Handling Operations (EHO):**
    The Error Handling Operations (EHO) is calculated from the
    a. Software Component's Feature Point Count for 'Function Error Handling' (FCFE)

and the following Software Component's Feature Measurements (SCFMs) of the class methods:

1. **Class Method Entities (CMDE):**
   The Class Method Entities (CMDE) is calculated from the
   a. Software Component's Feature Point Count for 'Class Method' (FCCM).

The FEOM (Functionality Execution Operations Measurement) calculations are done as follows:

First, corresponding to the aforementioned functional operations and entities, the following calculations of the Software Component's Feature Measurements (SCFMs) are performed.

1. **Memory Operations (MO)** = FCDR + FCDW;
2. **Computational Operations (CO)** = FCFC;

3. **Logical Operations (LO)** = FCFL;
4. **Decision Execution Operations (DEO)** = FCFD;
5. **Repeat Execution Operations (REO)** = FCFR;
6. **Action Execution Operations (AEO)** = FCFA;
7. **Execution Flow Control Operations (EFCO)** = FCFO;
8. **Input/Output Operations (IOO)** = FCDI + FCDO;
9. **Message Exchange Operations (MEO)** = FCMS + FCMR;
10. **Error Handling Operations (EHO)** = FCFE;
11. **Class Method Entities (CMDE)** = FCCM.

Then, the Functionality Execution Operations Dynamic Measurement (FEODM) is calculated.

The FEODM is used for the calculations of the Software Performance Quality Indicators (SPQI) of the type Software Operational Indicators (SOIs)[5–7] to indicate the dynamic run-time behavioral performance of the software.

FEODM = Memory Operations (MO) + Computational Operations (CO) + Logical Operations (LO) + Decision Execution Operations (DEO) + Repeat Execution Operations (REO) + Execution Flow Control Operations (EFCO) + Input and Output Operations (IOO) + Message Exchange Operations (MEO).

Then, the FEOM (Functionality Execution Operations Measurement) is calculated by the following formula:

FEOM = FEODM + Action Execution Operations (AEO) + Class Method Entities (CMDE).

The AEO (Action Execution Operations) and CMDE (Class Method Entities) contribute for the static structure characteristics, and not for the run-time dynamic characteristics of the software. That is why they are included in the FEOM, but not in the FEODM because the FEODM is used to calculate the SPQIs (Software Performance Quality Indicators) of the type SOIs (Software Operational Indicators)[5–7] while the FEOM is used to calculate the SPQIs (Software Performance Quality Indicators) of the type SSIs (Software Structural Indicators)[5–7].

7.2.2.2 Functionality Execution Data Manipulation Measurement (FEDM) Formulae

The second part of the CFEM (Software Component 'Functionality Execution' Measurement) is the FEDM (Functionality Execution Data Manipulation Measurement) which takes into account for the measurement all the following Software Component's Feature Measurements (SCFMs) of the functional data handled during the indicated functionality execution operations:

1. **Memory Operations Functional Data Entities (MOFE):**
   The Memory Operations Functional Data Entities (MOFE) – data handled in the memory read/write operations – is calculated from the
   a. Software Component's Feature Point Count for 'Memory Operations Functional Data' (FCLM).

2. **Input/Output Operations Functional Data Entities (IOFE):**
   The Input/Output Operations Functional Data Entities (IOFE) – data handled in the input/output operations – is calculated from the
   a. Software Component's Feature Point Count for 'Input/Output Operations Functional Data' (FCLI).
3. **Message Exchange Operations Functional Data Entities (EOFE):**
   The Message Exchange Operations Functional Data Entities (EOFE) – data handled in the message send/receive operations – is calculated from the
   a. Software Component's Feature Point Count for 'Message Exchange Operations Functional Data' (FCLS).
4. **General Operations Functional Data Entities (GOFE):**
   The General Operations Functional Data Entities (GOFE) – data handled in the general computational, logical, decision, repeat, and execution flow control operations – is calculated from the
   a. Software Component's Feature Point Count for 'General Operations Functional Data' (FCLG).

The FEDM (Functionality Execution Data Manipulation Measurement) calculations are done as follows:

First, corresponding to the aforementioned functional data entities, the following calculations of the Software Component's Feature Measurements (SCFMs) are performed.

1. **Memory Operations Functional Data Entities (MOFE)** = FCLM;
2. **Input and Output Operations Functional Data Entities (IOFE)** = FCLI;
3. **Message Exchange Operations Functional Data Entities (EOFE)** = FCLS;
4. **General Operations Functional Data Entities (GOFE)** = FCLG.

Then, the FEDM (Functionality Execution Data Manipulation Measurement) is calculated by the following formula:

FEDM = Memory Operations Functional Data Entities (MOFE) + Input and Output Operations Functional Data Entities (IOFE) + Message Exchange Operations Functional Data Entities (EOFE) + General Operations Functional Data Entities (GOFE).

7.2.2.3 Software Component 'Functionality Execution' Measurement (CFEM) Determination Formulae

The CFEM (Software Component 'Functionality Execution' Measurement) which comprises the FEOM (Functionality Execution Operations Measurement) and FEDM (Functionality Execution Data Manipulation Measurement) is calculated by the following formula:

CFEM = FEOM + FEDM.

There is no upper limit for the CFEM.

7.2.3 Software Component 'User Interface' Measurement (CUIM) Formulae

The Software Component 'User Interface' Measurement (CUIM) signifies the size and complexity of the Software's Measurable Component 'User Interface' (CUI).

The User Interface is described by the user screens, their layouts, fields, output navigational links, and input navigational links defined in the User Interface description part.

Hence, the enormity and magnitude of the User Interface is determined by taking into account the user screens and spread of user screens.

The spread of the user screens is determined by their fields, output navigational links, and input navigational links.

Accordingly, the size of the Software's Measurable Component 'User Interface' (CUI), measured by the Software Component 'User Interface' Measurement (CUIM), is obtained by considering for the measurement all the following Software Component's Feature Measurements (SCFMs) of the user interface entities:

1. **User Interface Screen Entities (UISE):**
   The User Interface Screen Entities (UISE) is calculated from the
   a. Software Component's Feature Point Count for 'User Screen' (FCUS).
2. **User Interface Field Entities (UIFE):**
   The User Interface Field Entities (UIFE) is calculated from the
   a. Software Component's Feature Point Count for 'User Screen Field' (FCUF).
3. **User Interface Input Link Entities (UIIE):**
   The User Interface Input Link Entities (UIIE) is calculated from the
   a. Software Component's Feature Point Count for 'User Screen Input Link' (FCUI).
4. **User Interface Output Link Entities (UIOE):**
   The User Interface Output Link Entities (UIOE) is calculated from the
   a. Software Component's Feature Point Count for 'User Screen Output Link' (FCUO).

First, corresponding to the aforementioned user interface entities, the following calculations of the Software Component's Feature Measurements (SCFMs) are performed:

1. **User Interface Screen Entities (UISE)** = FCUS;
2. **User Interface Field Entities (UIFE)** = FCUF;
3. **User Interface Input Link Entities (UIIE)** = FCUI;
4. **User Interface Output Link Entities (UIOE)** = FCUO.

Then, the CUIM is calculated by the following formula:

CUIM = User Interface Screen Entities (UISE) + User Interface Field Entities (UIFE) + User Interface Input Link Entities (UIIE) + User Interface Output Link Entities (UIOE).

There is no upper limit for the CUIM.

7.2.4 Software Component 'Message Exchange' Measurement (CMEM) Formulae

The Software Component 'Message Exchange' Measurement (CMEM) signifies the size and complexity of the Software's Measurable Component 'Message Exchange' (CME).

Message Exchange is described by the message structures containing their fields in the Message Exchange description part.

Hence, the enormity and magnitude of the Message Exchange is determined by taking into account the messages and their fields.

Accordingly, the size of the Software's Measurable Component 'Message Exchange' (CME), measured by the Software Component 'Message Exchange' Measurement (CMEM), is obtained by considering for the measurement all the following Software Component's Feature Measurements (SCFMs) of the message exchange entities:

1. **Notifying Message Entities (NME):**
   The Notifying Message Entities (NME) is calculated from the
   a. Software Component's Feature Point Count for 'Notifying Message' (FCNM).
2. **Message Field Entities (MFE):**
   The Message Field Entities (MFE) is calculated from the
   a. Software Component's Feature Point Count for 'Message Field' (FCMF).

First, corresponding to the aforementioned message entities, the following calculations are performed:

1. **Notifying Message Entities (NME)** = FCNM;
2. **Message Field Entities (MFE)** = FCMF.

Then, the CMEM is calculated by the following formula:
CMEM = Notifying Message Entities (NME) + Message Field Entities (MFE).
There is no upper limit for the CMEM.

7.2.5 Software Total Components Measurement (STCM) Formulae

The Software Total Components Measurement (STCM) signifies the total size measurement of the software which takes into account the following measurements:

1. Software Component 'Functional Data' Measurement (CFDM);
2. Software Component 'Functionality Execution' Measurement (CFEM);
3. Software Component 'User Interface' Measurement (CUIM);
4. Software Component 'Message Exchange' Measurement (CMEM).

Thus, the STCM is calculated by the following formula:
STCM = CFDM + CFEM + CUIM + CMEM.
There is no upper limit for the STCM.

7.2.6 Software Components Requirement Deficiency Measurement (CRDM) Formulae

The Software Components Requirement Deficiency Measurement (CRDM) signifies the obvious missing and deficient items in the 4 Software's Measurable Components CFD, CFE, CUI, and CME.

Accordingly, the size of the Software Components Requirement Deficiency Measurement (CRDM) is obtained by considering for the measurement all the following Software Component's Feature Measurements (SCFMs) of the missing entities in the Functional Data, Functionality Execution, User Interface, and Message Exchange:

1. **Functional Data Missing Entities (FDME):**
   The Functional Data Missing Entities (FDME) is calculated from the
   a. Software Component's Feature Point Count for 'Data Missing' (FCDM).

2. **Functionality Execution Missing Entities (FEME):**
   The Functionality Execution Missing Entities (FEME) is calculated from the
   a. Software Component's Feature Point Count for 'Functionality Missing' (FCFM).
3. **User Interface Missing Entities (UIME):**
   The User Interface Missing Entities (UIME) is calculated from the
   a. Software Component's Feature Point Count for 'User Screen Missing' (FCUM).
4. **Message Exchange Missing Entities (MEME):**
   The Message Exchange Missing Entities (MEME) is calculated from the
   a. Software Component's Feature Point Count for 'Message Missing' (FCMM).

First, corresponding to the aforementioned missing entities, the following calculations of the Software Component's Feature Measurements (SCFMs) are performed:

1. **Functional Data Missing Entities (FDME)** = FCDM;
2. **Functionality Execution Missing Entities (FEME)** = FCFM;
3. **User Interface Missing Entities (UIME)** = FCUM;
4. **Message Exchange Missing Entities (MEME)** = FCMM.

Then, the CRDM is calculated by the following formula:

CRDM = Functional Data Missing Entities (FDME) + Functionality Execution Missing Entities (FEME) + User Interface Missing Entities (UIME) + Message Exchange Missing Entities (MEME).

There is no upper limit for the CRDM.

7.3 EXAMPLES

1. An application containing enormously diverse data of large widths that is characterized by many classes with many attributes and many fields, for example, telecom billing application, may have a big measurement size of the CFDM (Software Component 'Functional Data' Measurement);
2. An application containing enormously diverse data of large widths that is characterized by many classes with many attributes and many fields, as well as many input/output screens, such as datawarehouse application, may have a big measurement size of the CFDM (Software Component 'Functional Data' Measurement) and CUIM (Software Component 'User Interface' Measurement);
3. An application where large amount of simulations are done and big amount of data processing takes place, such as meteorological application, traffic analysis applications, Global Positioning System (GPS) applications, and radar applications, may have a big measurement size of the CFEM (Software Component 'Functionality Execution' Measurement);
4. An application in which a lot of message exchange takes place for communication with other external application programs or with the modules of the same application program, such as telecom call handling application, may have a big measurement size of the CMEM (Software Component 'Message Exchange' Measurement).

7.4 CHAPTER SUMMARY

7.4.1 Software Component's Measurement (SCM) and Software Component's Feature Measurement (SCFM): Summary

Measurement aspects – description and formulae – of the 4 Software's Measurable Components (SMCs) which are the Software's Measurable Component 'Functional Data' (CFD), 'Functionality Execution' (CFE), 'User Interface' (CUI), and 'Message Exchange' (CME) have been presented in this chapter.

There are 6 Software Component's Measurements (SCMs) which are summarized next, shown with the Software Component's Feature Measurements (SCFMs) used for their calculations:

1. The **CFDM** (Software Component 'Functional Data' Measurement) indicates the functional data size and complexity which is determined by taking into account the class structure of the functional data, that is, the number of classes and width of the classes.
   The CFDM is obtained by using the following SCFMs:
   a. Data Class Entities (DCE): DCE = FCDC;
   b. Data Class Attribute Entities (DAE): DAE = FCDA;
   c. Data Class Field Entities (DFE): DFE = FCDF.
   CFDM = DCE + DAE + DFE.
   There is no upper limit for the CFDM.
2. The **CFEM** (Software Component 'Functionality Execution' Measurement) indicates the functionality size and complexity in terms of the various types of functional operations, functional data handled during the functional operations, and class methods. The CFEM comprises two parts:
   a. The Functionality Execution Operations Measurement (FEOM) which indicates the magnitude of the functional operations and methods, and is obtained by using the following SCFMs:
      i. Memory Operations (MO): MO = FCDR + FCDW;
      ii. Computational Operations (CO): CO = FCFC;
      iii. Logical Operations (LO): LO = FCFL;
      iv. Decision Execution Operations (DEO): DEO = FCFD;
      v. Repeat Execution Operations (REO): REO = FCFR;
      vi. Action Execution Operations (AEO): AEO = FCFA;
      vii. Execution Flow Control Operations (EFCO): EFCO = FCFO;
      viii. Error Handling Operations (EHO): EHO = FCFE;
      ix. Input/Output Operations (IOO): IOO = FCDI + FCDO;
      x. Message Exchange Operations (MEO): MEO = FCMS + FCMR;
      xi. Class Method Entities (CMDE): CMDE = FCCM.
      The FEOM is calculated as follows:
      First the FEODM (Functionality Execution Operations Dynamic Measurement), which is the measurement of the dynamic functionality operations execution, is calculated as follows:
      FEODM = Memory Operations (MO) + Computational Operations (CO) + Logical Operations (LO) + Decision Execution Operations (DEO) + Repeat

Execution Operations (REO) + Execution Flow Control Operations (EFCO) + Input and Output Operations (IOO) + Message Exchange Operations (MEO). The FEODM is used for the calculations of the Software Performance Quality Indicators (SPQIs) of the type Software Operational Indicators (SOIs)[5–7]; Then, the FEOM is calculated as indicated next.
FEOM = FEODM + Action Execution Operations (AEO) + Class Method Entities (CMDE).

b. The Functionality Execution Data Manipulation Measurement (FEDM) which indicates the magnitude of the functional data handled during the functional operations, and is obtained by using the following SCFMs:
   i. Memory Operations Functional Data Entities (MOFE) handled during the memory read/write operations: MOFE = FCLM;
   ii. Input/Output Operations Functional Data Entities (IOFE) handled during the input/output operations: IOFE = FCLI;
   iii. Message Exchange Operations Functional Data Entities (EOFE) handled during the message send/receive operations: EOFE = FCLS;
   iv. General Operations Functional Data Entities (GOFE) handled during the
   - computational;
   - logical;
   - decision execution;
   - repeat execution;
   - execution flow control;

   operations: GOFE = FCLG.

   The FEDM is calculated as follows:
   FEDM = Memory Operations Functional Data Entities (MOFE) + Input and Output Operations Functional Data Entities (IOFE) + Message Exchange Operations Functional Data Entities (EOFE) + General Operations Functional Data Entities (GOFE).

The CFEM (Software Component 'Functionality Execution' Measurement) which comprises the FEOM (Functionality Execution Operations Measurement) and FEDM (Functionality Execution Data Manipulation Measurement) is calculated by the following formula:
CFEM = FEOM + FEDM.
There is no upper limit for the CFEM.

3. The **CUIM** (Software Component 'User Interface' Measurement) indicates the User Interface size and complexity which is determined by taking into account the user interfaces (screens), their size (input and output fields), and navigation links interconnecting the user interfaces (screens).
The CUIM is obtained by using the following SCFMs:
a. User Interface Screen Entities (UISE): UISE = FCUS;
b. User Interface Field Entities (UIFE): UIFE = FCUF;
c. User Interface Input Link Entities (UIIE): UIIE = FCUI;
d. User Interface Output Link Entities (UIOE): UIOE = FCUO.
CUIM = UISE + UIFE + UIIE + UIOE.
There is no upper limit for the CUIM.

4. The **CMEM** (Software Component 'Message Exchange' Measurement) indicates the message size and complexity and is determined by the number of messages and their fields;

The CMEM is obtained by using the following SCFMs:

a. Notifying Message Entities (NME): NME = FCNM;

b. Message Field Entities (MFE): MFE = FCMF.

CMEM = NME + MFE.

There is no upper limit for the CMEM.

5. The **STCM** (Software Total Components Measurement) indicates the total software size and complexity and is obtained by the addition of the measurements of all the 4 Software's Measurable Components (SMCs), that is, the addition of the

a. CFDM (Software Component 'Functional Data' Measurement);

b. CFEM (Software Component 'Functionality Execution' Measurement);

c. CUIM (Software Component 'User Interface' Measurement);

d. CMEM (Software Component 'Message Exchange' Measurement).

STCM = CFDM + CFEM + CUIM + CMEM.

There is no upper limit for the STCM.

6. The **CRDM** (Software Components Requirement Deficiency Measurement) indicates the apparently missing items in all the 4 SMCs (Software's Measurable Components), taking into account the apparent missing items in the following 4 Software's Measurable Components (SMCs):

a. CFD (Software's Measurable Component 'Functional Data');

b. CFE (Software's Measurable Component 'Functionality Execution');

c. CUI (Software's Measurable Component 'User Interface');

d. CME (Software's Measurable Component 'Message Exchange').

The CRDM is obtained by using the following SCFMs:

a. Functional Data Missing Entities (FDME): FDME = FCDM;

b. Functionality Execution Missing Entities (FEME): FEME = FCFM;

c. User Interface Missing Entities (UIME): UIME = FCUM;

d. Message Exchange Missing Entities (MEME): MEME = FCMM.

CRDM = FDME + FEME + UIME + MEME.

There is no upper limit for the CRDM.

EXERCISES

7.1 The Memory Operations Functional Data Entities (MOFE) is used to calculate which of the following measurements?

A. Functionality Execution Operations Measurement (FEOM).

B. Functionality Execution Data Manipulation Measurement (FEDM).

C. Software Components Requirement Deficiency Measurement (CRDM).

7.2 Which of the following measurements is not used for calculating the Software Total Components Measurement (STCM):

A. Software Component 'Functional Data' Measurement (CFDM).

B. Software Component 'Functionality Execution' Measurement (CFEM).

C. Software Component 'User Interface' Measurement (CUIM).

D. Software Component 'Message Exchange' Measurement (CMEM).

E. Software Components Requirement Deficiency Measurement (CRDM).

7.3 Which of the following Software Component's Feature Measurement (SCFM) is not used for calculating the Functionality Execution Operations Measurement (FEOM)?

A. Memory Operations (MO).

B. Input and Output Operations (IOO).

C. Message Exchange Operations (MEO).

D. Class Method Entities (CMDE).

E. Data Class Attribute Entities (DAE).

7.4 Which of the following Software Component's Feature Measurements (SCFMs) is not used for calculating the Software Components Requirement Deficiency Measurement (CRDM)?

A. Functional Data Missing Entities (FDME).

B. Functionality Execution Missing Entities (FEME).

C. User Interface Missing Entities (UIME).

D. Data Class Entities (DCE).

E. Message Exchange Missing Entities (MEME).

Part Four

FSSM: Estimations and Indications

Chapter 8

Software Size Determination and Effort Estimations in the FSSM

The calculations for the Software Size and Effort Estimations (SSEEs) are performed by using the Software Component's Feature Measurements (SCFMs) and Software Component's Measurements (SCMs). The description and formulae for the SSEEs are presented in this chapter.

8.1 SOFTWARE ANALYSIS – SIZE DETERMINATION AND EFFORT ESTIMATION, STATIC STRUCTURE, AND DYNAMIC CHARACTERISTICS IN THE FSSM

The software size determination, development effort estimation, and software performance characteristics related with the static structure and dynamic execution are an integral part in the FSSM. Their calculations are based on the measurements of the components and their features.

8.1.1 Software Size and Effort Estimations (SSEEs), Software Static Structural Analysis, and Software Dynamic (Run-time) Characteristics Analysis

Based on the Software Component's Feature Measurements (SCFMs) and Software Component's Measurements (SCMs), the following 3 types of analysis are performed for the software:

1. Software Size and Effort Estimations (SSEEs);
2. Software Static Structural Analysis through Software Structural Indicators (SSIs)[5–7];
3. Software Dynamic (Run-time) Characteristics Analysis through Software Operational Indicators (SOIs)[5–7].

The latter 2 categories are grouped together to form the Software Performance Quality Indicators (SPQIs).

Functional Software Size Measurement Methodology with Effort Estimation and Performance Indication, First Edition. Jasveer Singh.

Companion website: http://booksupport.wiley.com

The analysis details about the Software Size and Effort Estimations (SSEEs) are presented in this chapter and about the Software Performance Quality Indicators (SPQIs) are presented in the next chapter.

8.2 SOFTWARE SIZE AND EFFORT ESTIMATION (SSEE) DESCRIPTION

The SCFMs, which are used to calculate the Software Component's Measurements (SCMs), are also used, along with the SCMs, for the calculation of the 4 Software Size and Effort Estimations (SSEEs) about the software logical size and development effort.

First, the software logical size is calculated taking into account all the relevant SCFMs of the SMCs (CFD, CFE, CUI, and CME corresponding to the Functional Data, Functionality Execution, User Interface, and Message Exchange parts of the FRS, respectively).

Then, the 4 SCMs, that is, the CFDM, CFEM, CUIM, and CMEM, based on the average productivity, are used to calculate the analysis and design efforts for data and functionality; and the coding effort is calculated based on the software logical size and average productivity.

This way, the total effort required for analysis, design, and coding is obtained.

After that, the testing effort is calculated based on the total analysis, design, and coding efforts; and average productivity.

Finally, the total development effort required for analysis, design, coding, and testing of the software project is calculated. These estimations are described next.

Figure 6 shows the summary overview diagram and Figure 11 shows the summary diagram of the Software Size and Effort Estimations (SSEEs). Both the figures show the contents, and relationships and information flow in the contents of the following constituents of the FSSM: Software Component's Feature Measurements (SCFMs), Software Component's Measurements (SCMs), and Software Size and Effort Estimations (SSEEs).

As shown in Figures 6 and 11, and in Figures 3–5, there are 28 SCFMs which are obtained for the 4 SCMs by the following usual proceeding steps of the FSSM usage flow process:

- **a.** identification of the Software Component's Measurable Features (SCMFs) in the Logical Data Model (LDM), Functionality Execution (FE), User Interface (UI), and Message Exchange (ME) description parts of the FRS corresponding to the 4 Software's Measurable Components (SMCs) – CFD, CFE, CUI, and CME;
- **b.** assignment of the Software Component's Feature Points (SCFPs) to the identified SCMFs;
- **c.** summation of the corresponding SCFPs for the respective SCFPs corresponding to the SCMFs to produce the Software Component's Feature Point Counts (SCFPCs);
- **d.** calculations of the Software Component's Feature Measurements (SCFMs) by using the SCFPCs.

The SCFMs are used further to obtain the Software Component's Measurements (SCMs).

Both the SCFMs and SCMs are used to obtain the following 4 Software Size and Effort Estimations (SSEEs) by simple calculations:

1. Software Logical Size (SLS);
2. Software Analysis, Design, and Coding Effort (SADCE);

3. Software Testing Effort (STE);
4. Software Total Development Effort (STDE).

These size and effort estimations – the SLS, SADCE, STE, and STDE – form some of the important outputs of the FSSM and are presented next in this chapter.

8.2.1 Software Logical Size (SLS) Description

The Software Logical Size (SLS) is the logical size in approximate number of statements of the software that is developed to meet the functional requirements described in the Functional Requirements Specifications (FRS). It is a complex function of the feature measurements of the components composed of the

a. Functional Data (FD);
b. Functionality Execution (FE);
c. User Interface (UI);
d. Message Exchange (ME).

The SLS is calculated based on all the relevant SCFMs which have been used to obtain the software size measurements for the Functional Data, functionality, user interfaces, and messages. The SCFMs are used to derive the information about the program in an approximately modeled manner such that the program logical size approaches as near as the real program to be developed.

The software program is mainly constituted of different types of statements, mainly of 3 types, described next.

8.2.1.1 Software Data Statements (SDS) Description

The Software Data Statements (SDS) are the data declaration statements in the software program. They are mainly about the data structures that contain the information about the

a. classes, subclasses, their attributes, and fields of the attributes used in the various types of functional operations – memory read/write, input/output from/to the input/output devices, message communication, computational, logical, decision, repeat, execution flow control and error handling;
b. class methods;
c. input/output screens, their fields, and links used for the input/output operations related with the input/output devices;
d. message structures used for the communication with the external application programs or sub-programs (modules) of the same application program;
e. temporary data storage variables.

The data declaration statements are spread all over the program, that is, in the main program, the class methods, and various subroutines of the program.

8.2.1.2 Software Code Statements (SCDS) Description

The Software Code Statements (SCDS) are the statements which represent the code in the software programs. They perform various operations of the functionality. Mainly, they are required for the following types of functionality operations:

a. memory operations used for data read/write;

b. input/output operations used for receiving/sending the input/output data from/to the input/output devices;

c. message exchange operations (message send/receive) used for sending/receiving the messages to/from the external application programs or sub-programs (modules);

d. general functionality execution operations which are the following:
  i. computational;
  ii. logical;
  iii. decision execution;
  iv. repeat execution;
  v. action execution;
  vi. execution flow control;
  vii. error handling;

and the following types of functional data handling during the indicated functionality operations:

a. functional data handled in the memory read/write operations;

b. functional data handled in the input/output operations;

c. functional data handled in the message exchange operations;

d. functional data handled in the general functionality execution operations for the following types of general functional operations:
  i. computational;
  ii. logical;
  iii. decision execution;
  iv. repeat execution;
  v. execution flow control.

8.2.1.3 Software Comment Statements (SCS) Description

The Software Comment Statements (SCS) are the statements which are used as comments for explaining the significance of code and data statements in the software programs. They provide useful and helpful information about the data declaration statements and code statements. Meaningful comment statements are an essential part of the software program which help its understanding for the development and maintenance activities.

8.2.1.4 Software Logical Size (SLS) Determination Description

The Software Logical Size (SLS) is based on the data statements, code statements, and comments statements.

The values of the data statements and code statements are estimated based on 23 Software Component's Feature Measurements (SCFMs) which are calculated from the 26 Software Component's Measurable Feature Point Counts (SCFPCs). These 26 SCFPCs are obtained from the summation of the corresponding 26 Software Component's Feature Points (SCFPs), respectively. The 26 types of SCFPs are derived through the identification and assignment of the Software Component's Feature Points (SCFPs), that is, FSUs (Functional Size Units) to the corresponding 26 Software Component's Measurable Features (SCMFs) that are present in the 4 Software's Measurable Components (SMCs). The 4 SMCs are the

a. Software's Measurable Component 'Functional Data' (CFD);
b. Software's Measurable Component 'Functionality Execution' (CFE);
c. Software's Measurable Component 'User Interface' (CUI);
d. Software's Measurable Component 'Message Exchange' (CME);

corresponding to the 4 parts of the Functional Requirements Specifications (FRS) which are the

a. Logical Data Model (LDM) part for the Functional Data;
b. Functionality Execution (FE) description part for the functionality;
c. User Interface (UI) description part for the user interfaces/screens;
d. Message Exchange (ME) description part for the messages.

To summarize, FRS ⇒ 4 parts: LDM, FE, UI, and ME ⇒ correspondingly 4 SMCs: CFD, CFE, CUI, and CME ⇒ 26 SCMFs ⇒ 26 types of SCFPs by assigning FSUs ⇒ correspondingly 26 SCFPCs ⇒ 23 SCFMs ⇒ used for data statements and code statements of the SLS.

The value of comment statements is estimated based on the data statements and code statements.

Finally, the Software Logical Size (SLS) is calculated by adding together the Software Data Statements (SDS), Software Code Statements (SCDS), and Software Comment Statements (SCS).

8.2.2 Software Analysis, Design, and Coding Effort (SADCE) Description

The Software Analysis, Design, and Coding Effort (SADCE) is needed for the analysis, design, coding, and technical specifications documents preparation of the software.

The SADCE (Software Analysis, Design, and Coding Effort) is a function of the

a. Software Logical Size (SLS);
b. Software Component 'Functional Data' Measurement (CFDM);
c. Software Component 'Functionality Execution' Measurement (CFEM);
d. Software Component 'User Interface' Measurement (CUIM);
e. Software Component 'Message Exchange' Measurement (CMEM);
f. average effort required for analysing, designing and coding based on the average productivity.

The SADCE consists of three parts described next.

8.2.2.1 Software Data Analysis and Design Effort (SDADE) Description

The Software Data Analysis and Design Effort (SDADE) is the effort spent on analyzing the data and designing/defining the data structures (or data tables in database applications) to be used in the program. This is dependent on the size and complexity of the Software's Measurable Component 'Functional Data' (CFD), Software's Measurable Component 'User Interface' (CUI), and Software's Measurable Component 'Message Exchange' (CME), and thus on their respective three measurements: the Software Component 'Functional Data' Measurement (CFDM), Software Component 'User Interface' Measurement (CUIM), and Software Component 'Message Exchange' Measurement (CMEM). At the same time, it is calculated based on the average productivity for the data analysis and design activity. This effort forms part of the total software development effort and includes the effort for the technical documentation preparation part.

8.2.2.2 Software Functionality Analysis and Design Effort (SFADE) Description

The Software Functionality Analysis and Design Effort (SFADE) is the effort spent on analyzing the functionality and designing the software code structure. This is dependent on the size and complexity of the Software's Measurable Component 'Functionality Execution' (CFE) and thus, on its measurement: the Software Component 'Functionality Execution' Measurement (CFEM). At the same time, it is calculated based on the average productivity for the functionality analysis and design activity. This effort forms part of the total software development effort and includes the effort for the technical documentation preparation part.

8.2.2.3 Software Coding Effort (SCE) Description

The Software Coding Effort (SCE) is the effort spent on coding the software. This is dependent on the Software Logical Size (SLS). At the same time, it is calculated based on the average productivity for the coding activity. This effort forms part of the total software development effort and includes the effort for the technical documentation preparation part.

8.2.2.4 Software Analysis, Design, and Coding Effort (SADCE) Determination Description

All the aforementioned three parts for the effort calculation – the SDADE, SFADE, and SCE – are estimated from the Software Component's Measurements (SCMs) and Software Logical Size (SLS) based on the average normal effort needed to develop the programs including the technical documentation preparation effort.

The SADCE (Software Analysis, Design, and Coding Effort) is thus calculated from these three parts – the Software Data Analysis and Design Effort (SDADE), Software Functionality Analysis and Design Effort (SFADE), and Software Coding Effort (SCE).

8.2.3 Software Testing Effort (STE) Description

The Software Testing Effort (STE) which is needed for testing the software including the test specifications documents preparations is a function of the Software Analysis, Design, and Coding Effort (SADCE), and average productivity for the testing activity. The STE is calculated from the SADCE according to the approximations available in the software industry based on the experience about the testing activity effort.

8.2.4 Software Total Development Effort (STDE) Description

The Software Total Development Effort (STDE) is the total effort required for development: analysis, design, coding, and testing including the technical specification documents and test specifications documents preparation. This does not include the project management effort, nor the effort for deployment, nor for maintenance activities.

The STDE is thus obtained by the addition of the two following efforts:

1. Software Analysis, Design, and Coding Effort (SADCE);
2. Software Testing Effort (STE).

8.3 SOFTWARE SIZE AND EFFORT ESTIMATION (SSEE) FORMULAE

The formulae used for the calculations of the Software Size and Effort Estimations (SSEEs) are described next.

8.3.1 Software Logical Size (SLS) Formulae

The Software Logical Size (SLS) is a complex function of the Software Component's Feature Measurements (SCFMs) for the Software Component's Measurable Features (SCMFs) of the Software's Measurable Component 'Functional Data' (CFD), 'Functionality Execution' (CFE), 'User Interface' (CUI), and 'Message Exchange' (CME), and is calculated based on the SCFMs.

Software programs consist of mainly 3 constituents:

1. Data description and definition part where data declarations are made in which all the data structures related to the data classes, screens, messages, and temporary data, are defined;
2. Code for Functionality Execution which contains all the processing part of the functionality;
3. Comments which are interspersed in the data definitions and code parts.

So, first, the approximate logical size of these 3 parts – data statements, code statements, and comment statements – is calculated based on the 23 Software Component's Feature Measurements (SCFMs) calculated from the 26 Software Component's Feature Point Counts (SCFPCs) for the 4 Software's Measurable Components (SMCs). The formulae for these calculations use some practical approximations which give quite good results.

8.3.1.1 Software Data Statements (SDS) Formulae

The Software Data Statements (SDS) define the data structures of all the functional data used for various functional operations.

8.3.1.1.1 SCFMs and SCFPCs Used for SDS The SDS are calculated by taking into account the following relevant 10 Software Component's Feature Measurements (SCFMs) mentioned with their corresponding 10 Software Component's Feature Point Counts (SCFPCs):

1. The Software Component's Features Measurements (SCFMs) for the Software Component's Measurable Features (SCMFs) of the Software's Measurable Component 'Functional Data' (CFD):
   a. Data Class Entities (DCE) measured by the Software Component's Feature Point Count for 'Data Class' (FCDC);
   b. Data Class Attribute Entities (DAE) measured by the Software Component's Feature Point Count for 'Data Attribute' (FCDA);
   c. Data Class Field Entities (DFE) measured by the Software Component's Feature Point Count for 'Data Field' (FCDF).
2. The Software Component's Feature Measurements (SCFMs) for the Software Component's Measurable Features (SCMFs) of the Software's Measurable Component 'Functionality Execution' (CFE):
   a. Class Method Entities (CMDE) measured by the Software Component's Feature Point Count for 'Class Method' (FCCM).
3. The Software Component's Feature Measurements (SCFMs) for the Software Component's Measurable Features (SCMFs) of the Software's Measurable Component 'User Interface' (CUI):
   a. User Interface Screen Entities (UISE) measured by the Software Component's Feature Point Count for 'User Screen' (FCUS);
   b. User Interface Field Entities (UIFE) measured by the Software Component's Feature Point Count for 'User Screen Field' (FCUF);
   c. User Interface Input Link Entities (UIIE) measured by the Software Component's Feature Point Count for 'User Screen Input Link' (FCUI);
   d. User Interface Output Link Entities (UIOE) measured by the Software Component's Feature Point Count for 'User Screen Output Link' (FCUO).
4. The Software Component's Feature Measurements (SCFMs) for the Software Component's Measurable Features (SCMFs) of the Software's Measurable Component 'Message Exchange' (CME):
   a. Notifying Message Entities (NME) measured by the Software Component's Feature Point Count for 'Notifying Message' (FCNM);
   b. Message Field Entities (MFE) measured by the Software Component's Feature Point Count for 'Message Field' (FCMF).

8.3.1.1.2 SDS Calculation The Software Data Statements (SDS) are calculated by the following formula that is followed by its explanation:

SDS = 4 × DCE + 2 × DAE + 2 × CMDE + 2 × UISE + UIIE + UIOE + 2 × NME + DFE × (1 + 0.1 × CMDE) + UIFE × (1 + 0.1 × CMDE) + MFE × (1 + 0.1 × CMDE) + 0.1 × (DFE + UIFE + MFE).

The same formula in equivalent SCFPCs is

SDS = 4 × FCDC + 2 × FCDA + 2 × FCCM + 2 × FCUS + FCUI + FCUO + 2 × FCNM + FCDF × (1 + 0.1 × FCCM) + FCUF × (1 + 0.1 × FCCM) + FCMF × (1 + 0.1 × FCCM) + 0.1 × (FCDF + FCUF + FCMF).

8.3.1.1.3 SDS Calculation Explanation The following statements, listed along with their SCMFs and equivalent SCFPCs for calculation, are included in the SDS formulation:

1. 4 declaration statements for all the classes and subclasses each, that is, the Data Class Entities (DCE) measured by the Software Component's Feature Point Count for 'Data Class' (FCDC), in the main section of the program.
2. 2 declaration statements for all the class attributes each, that is, the Data Class Attribute Entities (DAE) measured by the Software Component's Feature Point Count for 'Data Attribute' (FCDA), in the main section of the program.
3. 1 declaration statement for all the class attribute fields each, that is, the Data Class Field Entities (DFE) measured by the Software Component's Feature Point Count for 'Data Field' (FCDF), in the main section of the program.
4. 2 declaration statements for all the class methods each, that is, the Class Method Entities (CMDE) measured by the Software Component's Feature Point Count for 'Class Method' (FCCM), in the main section of the program.
5. 2 declaration statements for all the user screens each, that is, the User Interface Screen Entities (UISE) measured by the Software Component's Feature Point Count for 'User Screen' (FCUS), in the main section of the program.
6. 1 declaration statement for all the user screen fields each, that is, the User Interface Field Entities (UIFE) measured by the Software Component's Feature Point Count for 'User Screen Field' (FCUF), in the main section of the program.
7. 1 declaration statement for all the user input navigational links each, that is, the User Interface Input Link Entities (UIIE) measured by the Software Component's Feature Point Count for 'User Screen Input Link' (FCUI), in the main section of the program.
8. 1 declaration statement for all the user output navigational links each, that is, the User Interface Output Link Entities (UIOE) measured by the Software Component's Feature Point Count for 'User Screen Output Link' (FCUO), in the main section of the program.
9. 2 declaration statements for all the messages each, that is, the Notifying Message Entities (NME) measured by the Software Component's Feature Point Count for 'Notifying Message' (FCNM), in the main section of the program.
10. 1 declaration statement for all the message fields each, that is, the Message Field Entities (MFE) measured by the Software Component's Feature Point Count for 'Message Field' (FCMF), in the main section of the program.
11. 10% of total data fields, that is, the Data Class Field Entities (DFE) measured by the Software Component's Feature Point Count for 'Data Field' (FCDF), as local declaration statements in all the class methods each, that is, the Class Method Entities (CMDE) measured by the Software Component's Feature Point Count for 'Class Method' (FCCM), of the program.
12. 10% of total user screen fields, that is, the User Interface Field Entities (UIFE) measured by the Software Component's Feature Point Count for 'User Screen Field' (FCUF), as local declaration statements in all the class methods each, that is, the Class Method Entities (CMDE) measured by the Software Component's Feature Point Count for 'Class Method' (FCCM), of the program.

13. 10% of total message fields, that is, the Message Field Entities (MFE) measured by the Software Component's Feature Point Count for 'Message Field' (FCMF), as local declaration statements in all the class methods each, that is, the Class Method Entities (CMDE) measured by the Software Component's Feature Point Count for 'Class Method' (FCCM), of the program.
14. 10% of total data fields, user screen fields and message fields, that is, the Data Class Field Entities (DFE), User Interface Field Entities (UIFE), and Message Field Entities (MFE), respectively, measured by the Software Component's Feature Point Count for 'Data Field' (FCDF), Software Component's Feature Point Count for 'User Screen Field' (FCUF), and Software Component's Feature Point Count for 'Message Field' (FCMF), respectively, as temporary variable definitions for the whole program including the main section and all the methods of the program.

8.3.1.2 Software Code Statements (SCDS) Formulae

The Software Code Statements (SCDS) define the code structure of all the functionality used for various functional operations and functional data handling.

8.3.1.2.1 SCFMs and SCFPCs Used for SCDS As the Software Code Statements (SCDS) are used for various functional operations, they are calculated by taking into account the following relevant 14 Software Component's Feature Measurements (SCFMs) mentioned with their corresponding 17 Software Component's Feature Point Counts (SCFPCs):

1. The Software Component's Feature Measurements (SCFMs) for the Software Component's Measurable Features (SCMFs) of the Software's Measurable Component 'Functionality Execution' (CFE):
   a. Memory Operations (MO) measured by the Software Component's Feature Point Count for 'Data Read' (FCDR) and 'Data Write' (FCDW);
   b. Input and Output Operations (IOO) measured by the Software Component's Feature Point Count for 'Data Input' (FCDI) and 'Data Output' (FCDO);
   c. Message Exchange Operations (MEO) measured by the Software Component's Feature Point Count for 'Message Send' (FCMS) and 'Message Receive' (FCMR);
   d. Computational Operations (CO) measured by the Software Component's Feature Point Count for 'Function Computational Operation' (FCFC);
   e. Logical Operations (LO) measured by the Software Component's Feature Point Count for 'Function Logical Operation' (FCFL);
   f. Decision Execution Operations (DEO) measured by the Software Component's Feature Point Count for 'Function Decision Execution' (FCFD);
   g. Repeat Execution Operations (REO) measured by the Software Component's Feature Point Count for 'Function Repeat Execution' (FCFR);
   h. Action Execution Operations (AEO) measured by the Software Component's Feature Point Count for 'Function Action Execution' (FCFA);
   i. Execution Flow Control Operations (EFCO) measured by the Software Component's Feature Point Count for 'Function Execution Flow Control' (FCFO);
   j. Memory Operations Functional Data Entities (MOFE) measured by the Software Component's Feature Point Count for 'Memory Operations Functional Data' (FCLM);

k. Input and Output Operations Functional Data Entities (IOFE) measured by the Software Component's Feature Point Count for 'Input/output Operations Functional Data' (FCLI);

l. Message Exchange Operations Functional Data Entities (EOFE) measured by the Software Component's Feature Point Count for 'Message Exchange Operations Functional Data' (FCLS);

m. General Operations Functional Data Entities (GOFE) measured by the Software Component's Feature Point Count for 'General Operations Functional Data' (FCLG);

n. Class Method Entities (CMDE) measured by the Software Component's Feature Point Count for 'Class Method' (FCCM).

8.3.1.2.2 SCDS Calculation The Software Code Statements (SCDS) are calculated by the following formula that is followed by its explanation:

$$\mathbf{SCDS} = 3 \times \text{CMDE} + 2 \times \text{DEO} + 2 \times \text{REO} + 2 \times \text{AEO} + 2 \times (1 + \text{CMDE}) + \text{EFCO} + \text{CO} + \text{LO} + 2 \times (\text{MO} + \text{IOO} + \text{MEO}) + \text{MOFE} + \text{IOFE} + \text{EOFE} + \text{GOFE}.$$

The same formula in equivalent SCFPCs is

$$\mathbf{SCDS} = 3 \times \text{FCCM} + 2 \times \text{FCFD} + 2 \times \text{FCFR} + 2 \times \text{FCFA} + 2 \times (1 + \text{FCCM}) + \text{FCFO} + \text{FCFC} + \text{FCFL} + 2 \times (\text{FCDR} + \text{FCDW} + \text{FCDI} + \text{FCDO} + \text{FCMS} + \text{FCMR}) + \text{FCLM} + \text{FCLI} + \text{FCLS} + \text{FCLG}.$$

8.3.1.2.3 SCDS Calculation Explanation The following statements, listed along with their SCMFs and equivalent SCFPC for calculation, are included in the SCDS formulation:

1. 3 statements for all the class methods each, that is, the Class Method Entities (CMDE) measured by the Software Component's Feature Point Count for 'Class Method' (FCCM), of the program.
2. 2 statements for each function decision operation, that is, the Decision Execution Entities (DEO) measured by the Software Component's Feature Point Count for 'Function Decision Execution' (FCFD), of the program (one statement for decision begin, that is, if statement, and one statement for decision end, i.e., if statement end).
3. 2 statements for each function repeat operation, that is, the Repeat Execution Entities (REO) measured by the Software Component's Feature Point Count for 'Function Repeat Execution' (FCFR) (one statement for repeat begin, i.e., repeat statement, and one statement for repeat end, i.e., repeat statement end).
4. 2 statements for each function action, that is, the Action Execution Entities (AEO) measured by the Software Component's Feature Point Count for 'Function Action Execution' (FCFA), of the program (one statement for do action begin, i.e., do statement, and one statement for do action end, i.e., do statement end).
5. 2 statements for the function action performed, that is, the Action Execution Entities (AEO) measured by the Software Component's Feature Point Count for 'Function Action Execution' (FCFA), for all the code in the main section of the program (i.e., do statement begin and do statement end for the main program begin and end).
6. 2 statements for the function action performed, that is, the Action Execution Entities (AEO) measured by the Software Component's Feature Point Count for 'Function

Action Execution' (FCFA), in all the methods each, that is, the Class Method Entities (CMDE) measured by the Software Component's Feature Point Count for 'Class Method' (FCCM), of the program (do statement begin and do statement end for the method begin and end).

7. 1 statement for each function execution flow control operation, that is, the Execution Flow Control Entities (EFCO) measured by the Software Component's Feature Point Count for 'Function Execution Flow Control (FCFO).
8. 1 statement for each computational operation, that is, the Computational Operations (CO) measured by the Software Component's Feature Point Count for 'Function Computational Operation' (FCFC).
9. 1 statement for each function logical operation, that is, the Logical Operations (LO) measured by the Software Component's Feature Point Count for 'Function Logical Operation' (FCFL), of the program.
10. 2 statements for each:
    a. data read and write operations, that is, the Memory Operations (MO) measured by the Software Component's Feature Point Count for 'Data Read' (FCDR) and 'Data Write' (FCDW);
    b. data input and output operations, that is, the Input and Output Operations (IOO) measured by the Software Component's Feature Point Count for 'Data Input' (FCDI) and 'Data Output' (FCDO);
    c. message send and receive operations, that is, the Message Exchange Operations (MEO) measured by the Software Component's Feature Point Count for 'Message Send' (FCMS) and 'Message Receive' (FCMR);

    of the program.
11. Initialization statements of all the data collections handled in accordance with 1 statement for each data collection handled in every
    a. data write and data read operation, that is, the Memory Operations Functional Data Entities (MOFE) measured by the Software Component's Feature Point Count for 'Memory Operations Functional Data' (FCLM);
    b. data output and data input operation, that is, the Input and Output Operations Functional Data Entities (IOFE) measured by the software Component's Feature Point Count for 'Input/Output Operations Functional Data' (FCLI);
    c. message send and message receive operation, that is, the Message Exchange Operations Functional Data Entities (EOFE) measured by the Software Component's Feature Point Count for 'Message Exchange Operations Functional Data' (FCLS);
    d. general – computational, logical, decision, repeat, and execution flow control – operation, that is, the General Operations Functional Data Entities (GOFE) measured by the Software Component's Feature Point Count for 'General Operations Functional Data' (FCLG).

8.3.1.3 Software Comment Statements (SCS) Formulae

The Software Comment Statements (SCS) are a help for understanding the data and code statements and form an essential addition to these two – data and code – statements. Their number is dependent on the quantity of the data and code statements.

8.3.1.3.1 SCS Calculation The Software Comment Statements (SCS) are thus calculated by the following formula:

SCS = 0.4 × (SDS + SCDS).

8.3.1.3.2 SCS Calculation Explanation Code statements are approximately 40% of the data and code statements.

8.3.1.4 Software Logical Size (SLS) Determination Formulae

From the aforementioned 3 parts – the SDS (Software Data Statements), SCDS (Software Code Statements), and SCS (Software Comment Statements) – the complete Software Logical Size (SLS) is calculated as follows:

SLS = SDS + SCDS + SCS.

8.3.2 Software Analysis, Design, and Coding Effort (SADCE) Formulae

The Software Analysis, Design, and Coding Effort (SADCE) is the effort required for the analysis, design, and coding of the software including the technical specifications documents preparation effort. It is a function of the Software Logical Size (SLS), Software Component 'Functional Data' Measurement (CFDM), Software Component 'User Interface' Measurement (CUIM), Software Component 'Message Exchange' Measurement (CMEM), and average productivity for the analysis, design, and coding activities.

The SADCE consists of the three parts described next.

8.3.2.1 Software Data Analysis and Design Effort (SDADE) Formulae

The Software Data Analysis and Design Effort (SDADE) is dependent on three measurements: the Software Component 'Functional Data' Measurement (CFDM), Software Component 'User Interface' Measurement (CUIM), and Software Component 'Message Exchange' Measurement (CMEM). It is calculated by using an average data analysis and design effort factor.

Software Data Analysis and Design Effort (SDADE) = ((CFDM + CUIM + CMEM) / 40) person days.

8.3.2.2 Software Functionality Analysis and Design Effort (SFADE) Formulae

The Software Functionality Analysis and Design Effort (SFADE) is dependent on one measurement: the Software Component 'Functionality Execution' Measurement (CFEM). It is calculated by using an average functionality analysis and design effort factor.

Software Functionality Analysis and Design Effort (SFADE) = (CFEM / 80) person days.

8.3.2.3 Software Coding Effort (SCE) Formulae

The Software Coding Effort (SCE) is derived from the Software Logical Size (SLS) by using an average coding effort factor.

Software Coding Effort (SCE) = (SLS / 80) person days.

8.3.2.4 Software Analysis, Design, and Coding Effort (SADCE) Determination Formulae

The total Software Analysis, Design, and Coding Effort (SADCE) is calculated from the aforementioned three efforts – the Software Data Analysis and Design Effort (SDADE), Software Functionality Analysis and Design Effort (SFADE), and Software Coding Effort (SCE) – as follows.

SADCE = (SDADE + SFADE + SCE) person days.

8.3.3 Software Testing Effort (STE) Formulae

The Software Testing Effort (STE) is the effort required for testing and test specifications documents preparation. It is a function of the Software Analysis, Design, and Coding Effort (SADCE) taking into account the average productivity for the testing activity.

The Software Testing Effort (STE) is calculated by the following formula:

STE = (1.2 × SADCE) person days.

8.3.4 Software Total Development Effort (STDE) Formulae

The Software Total Development Effort (STDE) is the total effort required for the development, that is, analysis, design, coding, and testing including technical specifications and test specifications documents preparation. It is obtained by the addition of the Software Analysis, Design, and Coding Effort (SADCE), and Software Testing Effort (STE):

STDE = (SADCE + STE) person days.

The STDE does not include the effort for project management, nor for deployment, nor for maintenance activities.

8.4 CHAPTER SUMMARY

8.4.1 Software Analysis – Size Determination and Effort Estimation, Static Structure, and Dynamic Characteristics in the FSSM: Summary

As a result of the analysis of the Software Component's Feature Measurements (SCFMs) and Software Component's Measurements (SCMs), the following are performed:

1. Software size determination;
2. Effort estimation;
3. Performance Indicators calculations which are related to the
   a. Software static structure;
   b. Software dynamic characteristics.

8.4.2 Software Size and Effort Estimation (SSEE): Summary

The Software Component's Feature Measurements (SCFMs) are used to calculate the Software Component's Measurements (SCMs), and the SCFMs along with the SCMs are used to calculate the following 4 Software Size and Effort Estimations (SSEEs):

1. Software Logical Size (SLS) is the approximate logical size of the software which is developed based on the functional requirements. It is the addition of the
   a. Software Data Statements (SDS) that are calculated from 10 Software Component's Feature Measurements (SCFMs) obtained from 10 SCFPCs of the corresponding 10 Software Component's Measurable Features (SCMFs) – 3 SCFPCs of the Software's Measurable Component 'Functional Data' (CFD); 1 SCFPC of the Software's Measurable Component 'Functionality Execution' (CFE); 4 SCFPCs of the Software's Measurable Component 'User Interface' (CUI); and 2 SCFPCs of the Software's Measurable Component 'Message Exchange' (CME):
   SDS = 4 × DCE + 2 × DAE + 2 × CMDE + 2 × UISE + UIIE + UIOE + 2 × NME + DFE × (1 + 0.1 × CMDE) + UIFE × (1 + 0.1 × CMDE) + MFE × (1 + 0.1 × CMDE) + 0.1 × (DFE + UIFE + MFE).
   The same formula in equivalent SCFPCs is
   SDS = 4 × FCDC + 2 × FCDA + 2 × FCCM + 2 × FCUS + FCUI + FCUO + 2 × FCNM + FCDF × (1 + 0.1 × FCCM) + FCUF × (1 + 0.1 × FCCM) + FCMF × (1 + 0.1 × FCCM) + 0.1 × (FCDF + FCUF + FCMF);
   b. Software Code Statements (SCDS) that are calculated from 14 Software Component's Feature Measurements (SCFMs) obtained from 17 SCFPCs of the corresponding 17 Software Component's Measurable Features (SCMFs) – 17 SCFPCs of the Software's Measurable Component 'Functionality Execution' (CFE):
   SCDS = 3 × CMDE + 2 × DEO + 2 × REO + 2 × AEO + 2 × (1 + CMDE) + EFCO + CO + LO + 2 × (MO + IOO + MEO) + MOFE + IOFE + EOFE + GOFE.
   The same formula in equivalent SCFPCs is
   SCDS = 3 × FCCM + 2 × FCFD + 2 × FCFR + 2 × FCFA+ 2 × (1 + FCCM) + FCFO + FCFC + FCFL + 2 × (FCDR + FCDW + FCDI + FCDO + FCMS + FCMR) + FCLM + FCLI + FCLS + FCLG;
   c. Software Comment Statements (SCS) that are calculated from the Software Data Statements (SDS) and Software Code Statements (SCDS):
   SCS = 0.4 × (SDS + SCDS);

   Hence, **SLS** = SDS + SCDS + SCS.
2. Software Analysis, Design, and Coding Effort (SADCE) needed to analyze, design, and code the software program including the technical documents preparation is the addition of the
   a. Software Data Analysis and Design Effort (SDADE) that is calculated from the Software Component 'Functional Data' Measurement (CFDM), Software Component 'User Interface' Measurement (CUIM), and Software Component 'Message Exchange' Measurement (CMEM) by taking into account the average productivity for the data analysis and design activity.
   SDADE = ((CFDM + CUIM + CMEM) / 40) person days.
   b. Software Functionality Analysis and Design Effort (SFADE) that is calculated from the Software Component 'Functionality Execution' Measurement (CFEM)

by taking into account the average productivity for the functionality analysis and design activity.
SFADE = (CFEM / 80) person days.

c. Software Coding Effort (SCE) that is calculated from the Software Logical Size (SLS) by taking into account the average productivity for the coding activity.
SCE = (SLS / 80) person days.

Hence, **SADCE** = (SDADE + SFADE + SCE) person days.

3. Software Testing Effort (STE) needed to test the software including the testing documents preparation is calculated based on the Software Analysis, Design, and Coding Effort (SADCE) by taking into account the average productivity for the testing activity.
Hence, **STE** = 1.2 × SADCE person days.

4. Software Total Development Effort (STDE) needed for analysis, design, coding, and testing the software is the addition of the Software Analysis, Design, and Coding Effort (SADCE), and Software Testing Effort (STE).
Hence, **STDE** = (SADCE + STE) person days.
The STDE includes the effort required for the technical and test documents preparation but does not include the effort for the project management, nor for deployment, nor for maintenance activities.

EXERCISES

8.1 The SCFM Logical Operations (LO), that is, the Software Component Feature Point Count for 'Logical Operation' (FCFL), is used for the calculation of which type of statements from the following in the Software Logical Size (SLS)?

A. Software Data Statements (SDS).

B. Software Code Statements (SCDS).

C. Software Comment Statements (SCS).

8.2 The SCFM Data Class Attribute Entities (DAE), that is, the Software Component Feature Point Count for 'Data Attribute' (FCFA), is used for the calculation of which type of statements from the following in the Software Logical Size (SLS)?

A. Software Data Statements (SDS).

B. Software Code Statements (SCDS).

C. Software Comment Statements (SCS).

8.3 The Software Component 'Functionality Execution' Measurement (CFEM) is used for the calculation of which type of effort from the following in the Software Analysis, Design, and Coding Effort (SADCE)?

A. Software Data Analysis and Design Effort (SDADE).

B. Software Functionality Analysis and Design Effort (SFADE).

C. Software Coding Effort (SCE).

8.4 The Software Logical Size (SLS) is used for the calculation of which item of the following?

A. Software Data Analysis and Design Effort (SDADE).

B. Software Component 'Functionality Execution' Measurement (CFEM).

C. Software Coding Effort (SCE).

Chapter 9

Software Performance Quality Indicators for Static Structure and Dynamic Characteristics in the FSSM

The calculations for the Software Performance Quality Indicators (SPQIs) of the two types – Software Structural Indicators (SSIs)[5–7] and Software Operational Indicators (SOIs)[5–7] – are performed from the Software Component's Feature Measurements (SCFMs) and from the Software Component's Measurements (SCMs). The description and formulae for the SPQIs are presented in this chapter.

9.1 SOFTWARE PERFORMANCE QUALITY INDICATOR (SPQI) DESCRIPTION

Consequent to the in-depth analysis of the Functional Requirements Specifications by using the 28 SCFMs (Software Component's Feature Measurements) obtained from 31 SCFPCs (Software Component's Feature Point Counts) for the corresponding 31 Software Component's Measurable Features (SCMFs) of the 4 Software's Measurable Components (SMCs), a number of specific Software Performance Quality Indicators (SPQIs) are generated based on the SCFMs and SCMs.

The SPQIs (Software Performance Quality Indicators) are indicators which present the performance quality aspects of the software and deficiency aspects of the functional requirements. They are divided into two categories: first, for indicating the static structural characteristics of the software and second, for indicating the dynamic run-time characteristics of the software. The indicators of these two categories are called the Software Structural Indicators (SSIs)[5–7] and Software Operational Indicators (SOIs)[5–7], respectively.

Figures 7 and 8 show the summary overview diagrams, and Figures 12 and 13 show the summary diagrams of the Software Performance Quality Indicators (SPQIs) – both the

Functional Software Size Measurement Methodology with Effort Estimation and Performance Indication, First Edition. Jasveer Singh.

Companion website: http://booksupport.wiley.com

Software Structural Indicators (SSIs)[5–7] and Software Operational Indicators (SOIs)[5–7]. These figures show the

a. contents of the SPQIs;

b. relationships along with information flow of the following constituents of the FSSM:

i. Software Component's Feature Measurements (SCFMs);
ii. Software Component's Measurements (SCMs);
in the contents of the SPQIs;

for both the Software Structural Indicators (SSIs)[5-7] and Software Operational Indicators (SOIs)[5-7].

As shown in Figures 7, 8, 12, and 13, and in Figures 3–5, by the usual proceeding steps of the FSSM usage flow process described earlier in Section 8.2, there are 28 SCFMs which are obtained for the 4 SCMs.

The SCFMs are the basis of calculations of the Software Component's Measurements (SCMs). The SCFMs and SCMs are used to obtain the Software Size and Effort Estimations (SSEEs) by simple calculations as described in Chapter 8.

The SCFMs and SCMs are also used to calculate the Software Performance Quality Indicators (SPQIs). The SPQIs give a conspicuous overview of the most important software characteristics – structural and operational. The SPQIs are thus divided into two groups: Software Structural Indicators (SSIs)[5–7] for software's structural aspects and Software Operational Indicators (SOIs)[5–7] for software's operational aspects. The following SPQIs are made available in the FSSM:

- 36 Software Performance Quality Indicators (SPQIs) of which
  - 23 are Software Structural Indicators (SSIs)[5–7];
  - 13 are Software Operational Indicators (SOIs)[5–7].

All the SPQIs are categorized in levels of Nil, Low, Medium, High, or Very High so that the areas which are below or above the desired level can accordingly be targeted for improvement, if required.

Description of these SPQIs – both SSIs and SOIs – follows.

9.1.1 Software Structural Indicators (SSIs) Description

There are 23 Software Structural Indicators (SSIs)[5–7] which are helpful in assessing the structure of the software from the point of view of its static content. They give the indication of the size and complexity of the Functional Data (FD), Functionality Execution (FE), User interface (UI), and Message Exchange (ME) parts which correspond to the Software's Measurable Component 'Functional Data' (CFD), 'Functionality Execution' (CFE), 'User Interface' (CUI), and 'Message Exchange' (CME), respectively; and further the proportion of various areas of functionality operations – memory read/write, input/output from/to the input/output devices, message exchange, computational, logical, decision, repeat, execution flow control, and error handling; the proportion of various functional data handling in the memory read/write, input/output from/to the input/output devices, message exchange, computational, logical, decision, repeat, and execution flow control operations; and deficiencies in the requirements.

The SSIs are assigned the values as Nil, Low, Medium, High, or Very High and are divided into the following 4 sub-categories:

1. 8 SSIs denoting the Software's Measurable Components (SMCs);
2. 10 SSIs denoting the Functionality Execution (FE) Operations;

3. 4 SSIs denoting the Functionality Execution (FE) Operations Data Handling;
4. 1 SSI denoting the deficiency in the Functional Requirements Specifications (FRS).

The SSIs of all the aforementioned sub-categories – related to the SMCs, FE operations, FE operations data handling, and FRS deficiency – in the FSSM are described next.

9.1.1.1 Description of the Software Structural Indicators (SSIs) Denoting the Software's Measurable Components (SMCs)

The Software Structural Indicators (SSIs)[5–7] in this category indicate the characteristics of the Software's Measurable Components which are the following:

1. Software's Measurable Component 'Functional Data' (CFD);
2. Software's Measurable Component 'Functionality Execution' (CFE);
3. Software's Measurable Component 'User Interface' (CUI);
4. Software's Measurable Component 'Message Exchange' (CME).

The characteristics indicated are related with the absolute size of the components, and they reflect the complexity of the components, and content proportion of the components in the static software structure as well.

9.1.1.1.1 Functional Data Complexity and Size (FDCS) Description The Functional Data Complexity and Size (FDCS) SSI provides an assessment about the enormity of the Software's Measurable Component 'Functional Data' (CFD) which is formed of total number of classes, subclasses, their attributes, and fields of the attributes.

The FDCS (Functional Data Complexity and Size) depends on the size of the Software's Measurable Component 'Functional Data' (CFD) for which the measurement is the Software Component 'Functional Data' Measurement (CFDM).

The FDCS is determined based on the CFDM – the bigger the CFDM, the more complex and the bigger the size of the Functional Data is in the software.

Depending on the value of the FDCS, the effort required for data design, that is, analyzing and defining the data structures in normal programming languages, or data tables in database programming languages, will vary. Also, the coding effort for data declarations and testing this part will vary accordingly.

9.1.1.1.2 Functionality Execution Complexity and Size (FECS) Description The Functionality Execution Complexity and Size (FECS) SSI provides an assessment about the enormity of the Software's Measurable Component 'Functionality Execution' (CFE) which is formed of the functional operations of the following types:

1. software processing consisting of the computational, logical, decision execution, repeat execution, actions performance, and execution flow control operations;
2. memory transactions, that is, memory data read/write operations from/to the non-volatile type of memory such as disk devices;
3. input/output device interactions;
4. communications with the external application programs;
5. error handling operations;

and at the same time, the functional data handling during the following functional operations:

1. memory data read/write;
2. input/output device interactions;
3. message communication to/from the external application programs;
4. general operations which are of the type computational, logical, decision execution, repeat execution, and execution flow control;

including the class methods involved in the functionality.

The FECS (Functionality Execution Complexity and Size) depends on the size of the Software's Measurable Component 'Functionality Execution' (CFE) for which the measurement is the Software Component 'Functionality Execution' Measurement (CFEM).

The FECS is determined based on the CFEM – the bigger the CFEM, the more complex and the bigger the size of the functionality is in the software.

Depending on the value of the FECS, the effort required for analyzing, designing, coding, and testing the functionality will vary.

9.1.1.1.3 User Interface Complexity and Size (UICS) Description The User Interface Complexity and Size (UICS) SSI provides an assessment about the enormity of the Software's Measurable Component 'User Interface' (CUI) which is formed of the user screens, their fields and input/output navigational links. The user screens are used for the input/output devices.

The UICS (User Interface Complexity and Size) depends on the size of the Software's Measurable Component 'User Interface' (CUI) for which the measurement is the Software Component 'User Interface' Measurement (CUIM).

The UICS is determined based on the CUIM – the bigger the CUIM, the more complex and the bigger the size of the User Interface part is in the software.

Depending on the value of the UICS, the effort required for analyzing and designing the input/output screen structures as well as the effort required for coding and testing them will vary.

9.1.1.1.4 Message Exchange Complexity and Size (MECS) Description The Message Exchange Complexity and Size (MECS) SSI provides an assessment about the enormity of the Software's Measurable Component 'Message Exchange' (CME) which is formed of the notifying messages and their fields used for external communication with either the external application programs or the sub-programs (modules) of the same application program.

The MECS (Message Exchange Complexity and Size) depends on the size of the Software's Measurable Component 'Message Exchange' (CME) for which the measurement is the Software Component 'Message Exchange' Measurement (CMEM).

The MECS is determined based on the CMEM – the bigger the CMEM, the more complex and the bigger the size of the Message Exchange part is in the software.

Depending on the value of the MECS, the effort required for analyzing and designing the message communication structures as well as for coding and testing them will vary.

9.1.1.1.5 Functional Data Component Proportion (FDCP) Description The Functional Data Component Proportion (FDCP) SSI indicates the static proportion of the Functional Data component in the total software.

The FDCP depends on the ratio of the size of the Software's Measurable Component 'Functional Data' (CFD) for which the measurement is the CFDM (Software Component 'Functional Data' Measurement) to the total software components size for which the measurement is the STCM (Software Total Components Measurement).

9.1.1.1.6 Functionality Execution Component Proportion (FECP) Description
The Functionality Execution Component Proportion (FECP) SSI indicates the static proportion of the Functionality Execution component in the total software.

The FECP depends on the ratio of the size of the Software's Measurable Component 'Functionality Execution' (CFE) for which the measurement is the CFEM (Software Component 'Functionality Execution' Measurement) to the total software components size for which the measurement is the STCM (Software Total Components Measurement).

9.1.1.1.7 User Interface Component Proportion (UICP) Description The User Interface Component Proportion (UICP) SSI indicates the static proportion of the User Interface component in the total software.

The UICP depends on the ratio of the size of the Software's Measurable Component 'User Interface' (CUI) for which the measurement is the CUIM (Software Component 'User Interface' Measurement) to the total software components size for which the measurement is the STCM (Software Total Components Measurement).

9.1.1.1.8 Message Exchange Component Proportion (MECP) Description The Message Exchange Component Proportion (MECP) SSI indicates the static proportion of the Message Exchange component in the total software.

The MECP depends on the ratio of the size of the Software's Measurable Component 'Message Exchange' (CME) for which the measurement is the CMEM (Software Component 'Message Exchange' Measurement) to the total software components size for which the measurement is the STCM (Software Total Components Measurement).

9.1.1.2 Description of the Software Structural Indicators (SSIs) Denoting the Functionality Execution (FE) Operations

Software Structural Indicators (SSIs)[5–7] in this category indicate the characteristics of the following Functionality Execution Operations of the Software's Measurable Component 'Functionality Execution' (CFE) in the static software structure:

- **a.** memory read/write operations used for the data reading/writing from/to the memory devices such as disks;
- **b.** computational operations for mathematical computations;
- **c.** logical operations such as AND, OR, NOT, and XOR;
- **d.** decision execution operations for checking the conditions and taking decisions for actions according to the conditions;
- **e.** repeat execution operations for repeating the actions;
- **f.** action performing operations;
- **g.** execution flow control operations for controlling the flow of execution of the software program;

h. data input/output operations used for receiving/sending the input/output data from/to the input/output devices for user communication;

i. message exchange operations used for sending/receiving the messages to/from the other programs/sub-programs;

j. error handling operations.

9.1.1.2.1 Memory Transaction Proportion (MTP) Description The Memory Transaction Proportion (MTP) SSI indicates the static proportion of the memory transactions – read/write operations – functionality, used for reading/writing the data from/to the non-volatile, permanent memory, for example, disk devices, in the total software.

The MTP depends on the ratio of the total memory read/write operations size which is measured by the MO (Memory Operations) to the total software components size which is measured by the STCM (Software Total Components Measurement).

9.1.1.2.2 Computational Operation Content Proportion (COCP) Description The Computational Operation Content Proportion (COCP) indicates the static proportion of the computational (mathematical calculations) operations part in the total software.

The COCP depends on the ratio of the total computational operations (mathematical calculations) size which is measured by the CO (Computational Operations) to the total software components size which is measured by the STCM (Software Total Components Measurement).

9.1.1.2.3 Logical Operation Content Proportion (LOCP) Description The Logical Operation Content Proportion (LOCP) SSI indicates the static proportion of the logical operations (AND, OR, etc.) part in the total software.

The LOCP depends on the ratio of the total logical operations (AND, OR, etc.) size which is measured by the LO (Logical Operations) to the total software components size which is measured by the STCM (Software Total Components Measurement).

9.1.1.2.4 Decision Execution Content Proportion (DECP) Description The Decision Execution Content Proportion (DECP) SSI indicates the static proportion of the decision operations part in the total software.

The DECP depends on the ratio of the total decisions execution operations size which is measured by the DEO (Decision Execution Operations) to the total software components size which is measured by the STCM (Software Total Components Measurement).

9.1.1.2.5 Repeat Execution Content Proportion (RECP) Description The Repeat Execution Content Proportion (RECP) indicates the static proportion of the repeat operations part in the total software.

The RECP depends on the ratio of the total repeat execution operations size which is measured by the REO (Repeat Execution Operations) to the total software components size which is measured by the STCM (Software Total Components Measurement).

9.1.1.2.6 Action Execution Content Proportion (AECP) Description The Action Execution Content Proportion (AECP) SSI indicates the static proportion of the different actions performance in the total software.

The AECP depends on the ratio of the total action execution operations size which is measured by the AEO (Action Execution Operations) to the total software components size which is measured by the STCM (Software Total Components Measurement).

9.1.1.2.7 Execution Flow Control Content Proportion (EFCCP) Description The Execution Flow Control Content Proportion (EFCCP) SSI indicates the static proportion of the execution flow control operations in the total software.

The EFCP depends on the ratio of the total execution flow control operations size which is measured by the EFCO (Execution Flow Control Operations) to the total software components size which is measured by the STCM (Software Total Components Measurement).

9.1.1.2.8 User Interaction Proportion (UIP) Description The User Interaction Proportion (UIP) SSI indicates the static proportion of the user interface related operations (input/output operations used for receiving/sending the input/output data from/to the input/output devices) part in the total software.

The UIP depends on the ratio of the total input/output operations size which is measured by the IOO (Input/Output Operations) to the total software components size which is measured by the STCM (Software Total Components Measurement).

9.1.1.2.9 External Communication Proportion (ECP) Description The External Communication Proportion (ECP) SSI indicates the static proportion of the message communication (message send/receive operations used for sending/receiving the messages to/from the external application programs or the sub-programs of the same application program) part in the total software.

The ECP depends on the ratio of the total message send/receive operations size which is measured by the MEO (Message Exchange Operations) to the total software components size which is measured by the STCM (Software Total Components Measurement).

9.1.1.2.10 Error Handling Proportion (EHP) Description The Error Handling Proportion (EHP) SSI indicates the static proportion of the error handling capability in the total software.

The EHP depends on the ratio of the total error handling operations size which is measured by the EHO (Error Handling Operations) to the total software components size which is measured by the STCM (Software Total Components Measurement).

9.1.1.3 Description of the Software Structural Indicators (SSIs) Denoting the Functionality Execution (FE) Operations Data Handling

Software Structural Indicators (SSIs)[5–7] in this category indicate the characteristics of the data handling in the following indicated Functionality Execution Operations of the Software's Measurable Component 'Functionality Execution' (CFE) in the static software structure, that is, the functional data handled during the

1. memory read/write operations used for reading/writing the data from/to the memory devices;
2. input/output operations used for receiving/sending the input/output data from/to the input/output devices;
3. message exchange operations used for sending/receiving the messages to/from the other programs;
4. general computational, logical, decision, repeat, and execution flow control operations.

9.1.1.3.1 Memory Operations Functional Data Proportion (MODP) Description The Memory Operations Functional Data Proportion (MODP) SSI indicates the static proportion of the functional data that is handled during the memory read/write operations in the total software.

The MOP depends on the ratio of the size of the total functional data handled during the memory read/write operations to the total software components size. The concerned measurements for this ratio are the MOFE (Memory Operations Functional Data Entities) and STCM (Software Total Components Measurement), respectively.

9.1.1.3.2 Input/Output Operations Functional Data Proportion (IODP) Description The Input/Output Operations Functional Data Proportion (IODP) SSI indicates the static proportion of the functional data that is handled during the input/output operations from/to the input/output devices in the total software.

The IODP depends on the ratio of the size of the total functional data handled during the user interactions in the input/output operations to the total software components size. The concerned measurements for this ratio are the IOFE (Input/Output Operations Functional Data Entities) and STCM (Software Total Components Measurement), respectively.

9.1.1.3.3 Message Exchange Operations Functional Data Proportion (EODP) Description The Message Exchange Operations Functional Data Proportion (EODP) SSI indicates the static proportion of the functional data that is handled during the message exchange operations (message send/receive) in the total software.

The EODP depends on the ratio of the size of the total functional data handled during the message send/receive operations to the total software components size. The concerned measurements for this ratio are the EOFE (Message Exchange Operations Functional Data Entities) and STCM (Software Total Components Measurement), respectively.

9.1.1.3.4 General Operations Functional Data Proportion (GODP) Description The General Operations Functional Data Proportion (GODP) SSI indicates the static proportion of the functional data that is handled during the general operations – computational, logical, decision, repeat, and execution flow control – in the total software.

The GODP depends on the ratio of the size of the total functional data handled during general functional operations – computational, logical, decision, repeat, and execution flow control – to the total software components size. The concerned measurements for this ratio are the GOFE (General Operations Functional Data Entities) and STCM (Software Total Components Measurement), respectively.

9.1.1.4 Description of the Software Structural Indicator (SSI) Denoting the Deficiency in the Functional Requirements Specifications (FRS)

Software Structural Indicator (SSI)[5–7] in this category indicates the extent of deficiencies in the Functional Requirements Specifications (FRS) related to the static software structure.

9.1.1.4.1 Requirements Deficiency Grade (RDG) Description The Requirements Deficiency Grade (RDG) SSI indicates the static proportion of the apparent deficient part in the Functional Requirements Specifications for the Functional Data, Functionality Execution, User Interface, and Message Exchange descriptions.

The RDG depends on the ratio of the size of the total observed deficiencies in the Functional Requirements Specifications which is measured by the CRDM (Software Components Requirement Deficiency Measurement) to the total software components size which is measured by the STCM (Software Total Components Measurement).

9.1.2 Software Operational Indicators (SOIs) (At Run-Time) Description

There are 13 SOIs which indicate the dynamic properties of the software at run-time. They are helpful in assessing the intensity of the data flows to/from the memory and external devices/programs, as well as the intensity of computations, logical operations, and other software operations – decision, repeat, and execution flow control.

The SOIs are assigned the values as Nil, Low, Medium, High, or Very High and are divided into the following 2 sub-categories:

1. 9 SOIs denoting the Functional Operations Execution;
2. 4 SOIs denoting the Functional Operations Data Handling.

The SOIs of both the sub-categories – denoting the Functional Operations Execution and Functional Operations Data Handling – in the FSSM are described next.

9.1.2.1 Description of the Software Operational Indicators (SOIs) Denoting the Functional Operations Execution

Software Operational Indicators (SOIs)[5–7] denoting the Functional Operations Execution indicate the run-time dynamic characteristics of the following functionality execution operations:

- **a.** memory read/write operations used for reading/writing the data from/to the memory devices such as disks;
- **b.** computational operations for mathematical computations;
- **c.** logical operations such as AND, OR, NOT, and XOR;
- **d.** decision execution operations for checking the conditions and taking decisions for actions according to the conditions;
- **e.** repeat execution operations for repeating the actions;
- **f.** execution flow control operations for controlling the flow of execution of the software program;
- **g.** data input/output operations used for receiving/sending the input/output data from/to the input/output devices for user communication;
- **h.** message exchange operations used for sending/receiving the messages to/from the other programs/sub-programs;
- **i.** error handling operations.

9.1.2.1.1 Memory Traffic Level (MTL) Description The Memory Traffic Level (MTL) SOI indicates the level of the memory traffic (read/write operations) to/from the non-volatile, permanent memory, for example, disk devices, at run-time in the entire functionality.

The MTL depends on the ratio of the total memory read/write operations which are measured by the MO (Memory Operations) to the total functionality executions operations considered for run-time dynamic behavior which are measured by the FEODM (Functionality Execution Operations Dynamic Measurement).

9.1.2.1.2 Computational Operations Level (COL) Description The Computational Operations Level (COL) SOI indicates the computational (mathematical calculations) level in the entire functionality at run-time.

The COL depends on the ratio of the total computational operations (mathematical calculations) which are measured by the CO (Computational Operations) to the total functionality executions operations considered for run-time dynamic behavior which are measured by the FEODM (Functionality Execution Operations Dynamic Measurement).

9.1.2.1.3 Logical Operations Level (LOL) Description The Logical Operations Level (LOL) SOI indicates the logical operations (AND, OR, etc.) level in the entire functionality at run-time.

The LOL depends on the ratio of the total logical operations (AND, OR, etc.) which are measured by the LO (Logical Operations) to the total functionality executions operations considered for run-time dynamic behavior which are measured by the FEODM (Functionality Execution Operations Dynamic Measurement).

9.1.2.1.4 Decision Execution Level (DEL) Description The Decision Execution Level (DEL) SOI indicates the level of the decisions execution in the entire functionality at run-time.

The DEL depends on the ratio of the total decisions execution operations which are measured by the DEO (Decision Execution Operations) to the total functionality executions operations considered for run-time dynamic behavior which are measured by the FEODM (Functionality Execution Operations Dynamic Measurement).

9.1.2.1.5 Repeat Execution Level (REL) Description The Repeat Execution Level (REL) SOI indicates the level of the repeat execution in the entire functionality at run-time.

The REL depends on the ratio of the total repeat execution operations which are measured by the REO (Repeat Execution Operations) to the total functionality executions operations considered for run-time dynamic behavior which are measured by the FEODM (Functionality Execution Operations Dynamic Measurement).

9.1.2.1.6 Execution Flow Control Level (EFCL) Description The Execution Flow Control Level (EFCL) SOI indicates the level of the execution flow control in the entire functionality at run-time.

The EFCL depends on the ratio of the total execution flow control operations which are measured by the EFCO (Execution Flow Control Operations) to the total functionality executions operations considered for run-time dynamic behavior which are measured by the FEODM (Functionality Execution Operations Dynamic Measurement).

9.1.2.1.7 User Interaction Level (UIL) Description The User Interaction Level (UIL) SOI indicates the level of the user interactions (input/output operations used for receiving/sending the input/output data from/to the input/output devices) in the entire functionality at run-time.

The UIL depends on the ratio of the total input/output operations which are measured by the IOO (Input/Output Operations) to the total functionality executions operations considered for run-time dynamic behavior which are measured by the FEODM (Functionality Execution Operations Dynamic Measurement).

9.1.2.1.8 External Communication Level (ECL) Description The External Communication Level (ECL) SOI indicates the level of the message exchange with external environment (message send/receive operations used for sending/receiving the messages to/from the external application programs or the sub-programs of the same application program) in the entire functionality at run-time.

The ECL depends on the ratio of the total message send/receive operations which are measured by the MEO (Message Exchange Operations) to the total functionality executions operations considered for run-time dynamic behavior which are measured by the FEODM (Functionality Execution Operations Dynamic Measurement).

9.1.2.1.9 Error Handling Capability (EHC) Description The Error Handling Capability (EHC) SOI indicates the level of the error handling operations execution in the entire functionality at run-time.

The EHC depends on the ratio of the total operations used for handling the error situations in the software which are measured by the EHO (Error Handling Operations) to the total functionality executions operations considered for run-time dynamic behavior which are measured by the FEODM (Functionality Execution Operations Dynamic Measurement).

9.1.2.2 Description of the Software Operational Indicators (SOIs) Denoting the Functional Operations Data Handling

Software Operational Indicators (SOIs)[5–7] denoting the Functional Operations Data Handling indicate the data handling characteristics of the functional operations at run-time. The data manipulations take place during the following operations:

a. memory read/write;

b. data input/output;

c. message exchange;

d. general functional which are the computational, logical, decision execution, repeat execution, and execution flow control operations.

9.1.2.2.1 Memory Traffic Functional Data Level (MTDL) Description The Memory Traffic Functional Data Level (MTDL) SOI indicates the level of the functional data handling for the memory traffic (read/write operations used for reading/writing the data from/to the permanent memory, e.g., disk devices) at run-time in the entire functionality.

The MTDL depends on the ratio of the total functional data handled during the memory read/write operations to the total functionality execution data manipulations. The concerned measurements for this ratio are the MOFE (Memory Operations Functional Data Entities) and FEDM (Functionality Execution Data Manipulation Measurement), respectively.

9.1.2.2.2 User Interaction Functional Data Level (UIDL) Description The User Interaction Functional Data Level (UIDL) SOI indicates the level of the functional data handling of the user interactions (input/output operations used for receiving/sending the input/output data from/to the input/output devices) in the entire functionality at run-time.

The UIDL depends on the ratio of the total functional data handled during the user interactions (input/output operations) to the total functionality execution data manipulations. The concerned measurements for this ratio are the IOFE (Input/Output Operations Functional Data Entities) and FEDM (Functionality Execution Data Manipulation Measurement), respectively.

9.1.2.2.3 External Communication Functional Data Level (ECDL) Description

The External Communication Functional Data Level (ECDL) SOI indicates the level of the functional data handling of the message exchanges (message send/receive operations) with the external application programs in the entire functionality at run-time.

The ECDL depends on the ratio of the total functional data handled during the message send/receive operations to the total functionality execution data manipulations. The concerned measurements for this ratio are the EOFE (Message Exchange Operations Functional Data Entities) and FEDM (Functionality Execution Data Manipulation Measurement), respectively.

9.1.2.2.4 General Operations Execution Functional Data Level (GODL) Description The General Operations Execution Functional Data Level (GODL) SOI indicates the level of the functional data handling of the general functional operations – computational, logical, decision, repeat, and execution flow control – in the entire functionality at run-time.

The GODL depends on the ratio of the total functional data handled during the general functional operations – computational, logical, decision, repeat, and execution flow control – to the total functionality execution data manipulations. The concerned measurements for this ratio are the GOFE (General Operations Functional Data Entities) and FEDM (Functionality Execution Data Manipulation Measurement), respectively.

9.2 SOFTWARE PERFORMANCE QUALITY INDICATOR (SPQI) CONSTRUCTION INFORMATION SOURCE

The calculations for all the Software Performance Quality Indicator (SPQIs) are based on the Software Component's Feature Measurements (SCFMs) and Software Component's Measurements (SCMs). The calculations for the SCMs are performed by using the Software Component's Feature Measurements (SCFMs). The SCFMs are calculated from the Software Component's Feature Point Counts (SCFPCs) which are obtained by applying the extensive and comprehensive counting of the Software Component's Feature Points for all the important and relevant Software Component's Measurable Features (31 SCMFs) of all the Software's Measurable Components (4 SMCs) which are available in the Functional Requirements Specifications (FRS) document consisting of the

- Logical Data Model;
- functionalities;
- user interfaces/screens;
- message exchanges.

So, all the information about the SPQIs is derived from the aforementioned 4 parts of the FRS.

Briefly, the procedure for deriving the information about the SPQIs is as follows:

1. First, all the Software Component's Measurable Features (SCMFs) – 31 types – are identified for the 4 Software's Measurable Components (SMCs) – the Software's Measurable Component 'Functional Data' (CFD), 'Functionality Execution' (CFE), 'User Interface' (CUI), and 'Message Exchange' (CME) – in the 4 parts of the Functional Requirements Specifications – Logical Data Model, Functionality Execution, User Interface, and Message Exchange description parts.
2. Then, the Software Component's Feature Points (SCFPs) which are the Functional Size Units (FSUs) are assigned to the SCMFs from which the 31 types of SCFPs for the 31 SCMFs are obtained, respectively.
3. Summing up the corresponding SCFPs for the 31 SCMFs produces the 31 Software Component's Feature Point Counts (SCFPCs), respectively.
4. These SCFPCs are used for the calculations of the 28 Software Component's Feature Measurements (SCFMs).
5. The SCFMs are used for the calculations of the Software Component's Measurements (SCMs).
6. The SCFMs and SCMs are used to calculate the Software Size and Effort Estimations (SSEEs), and Software Performance Quality Indicators (SPQIs).

9.3 SOFTWARE PERFORMANCE QUALITY INDICATOR (SPQI) FORMULAE

Software Performance Quality Indicators (SPQIs), which are 36 in number, are divided into 2 categories:

1. Software Structural Indicators (SSIs)[5–7].
   They are 23 in number.
2. Software Operational Indicators (SOIs)[5–7].
   They are 13 in number.

Both of these categories of SPQIs are calculated from the Software Component's Feature Measurements (SCFMs) and Software Component's Measurements (SCMs). All the SPQIs are categorized as Nil, Low, Medium, High, or Very High.

Formulae used to determine the SPQIs are presented next.

9.3.1 Formulae of the Software Component's Measurements (SCMs) Used in the Software Performance Quality Indicators (SPQIs)

All the 28 Software Component's Feature Measurements (SCFMs) and 6 Software Component's Measurements (SCMs) (see Chapter 7) are used in the Software Performance Quality Indicator (SPQI) calculations formulae. Summary of the SCM calculations is reproduced here for recollection.

9.3.1.1 Software Component 'Functional Data' Measurement (CFDM) Calculations

CFDM = DCE + DAE + DFE = FCDC + FCDA + FCDF.

9.3.1.2 Software Component 'Functionality Execution' Measurement (CFEM) Calculations

9.3.1.2.1 Functionality Execution Operations Measurement (FEOM) Calculations

Memory Operations (MO) = FCDR + FCDW.

Computational Operations (CO) = FCFC.

Logical Operations (LO) = FCFL.

Decision Execution Operations (DEO) = FCFD.

Repeat Execution Operations (REO) = FCFR.

Action Execution Operations (AEO) = FCFA.

Execution Flow Control Operations (EFCO) = FCFO.

Input and Output Operations (IOO) = FCDI + FCDO.

Message Exchange Operations (MEO) = FCMS + FCMR.

Error Handling Operations (EHO) = FCFE.

Class Method Entities (CMDE) = FCCM.

FEODM (Functionality Execution Operations Dynamic Measurement) = Memory Operations (MO) + Computational Operations (CO) + Logical Operations (LO) + Decision Execution Operations (DEO) + Repeat Execution Operations (REO) + Execution Flow Control Operations (EFCO) + Input and Output Operations (IOO) + Message Exchange Operations (MEO).

FEOM (Functionality Execution Operations Measurement) = FEODM + Action Execution Operations (AEO) + Class Method Entities (CMDE).

9.3.1.2.2 Functionality Execution Data Manipulation Measurement (FEDM) Calculations

Memory Operations Functional Data Entities (MOFE) = FCLM.

Input and Output Operations Functional Data Entities (IOFE) = FCLI.

Message Exchange Operations Functional Data Entities (EOFE) = FCLS.

General Operations Functional Data Entities (GOFE) = FCLG.

FEDM (Functionality Execution Data Manipulation Measurement) = Memory Operations Functional Data Entities (MOFE) + Input and Output Operations Functional Data Entities (IOFE) + Message Exchange Operations Functional Data Entities (EOFE) + General Operations Functional Data Entities (GOFE).

9.3.1.2.3 Software Component 'Functionality Execution' Measurement (CFEM) Determination Calculations

CFEM = FEOM + FEDM.

9.3.1.3 Software Component 'User Interface' Measurement (CUIM) Calculations

CUIM = UISE + UIFE + UIOE + UIIE = FCUS + FCUF + FCUO + FCUI.

9.3.1.4 Software Component 'Message Exchange' Measurement (CMEM) Calculations

CMEM = NME + MFE = FCNM + FCMF.

9.3.1.5 Software Total Components Measurement (STCM) Calculations

STCM = CFDM + CFEM + CUIM + CMEM.

9.3.1.6 Software Components Requirement Deficiency Measurement (CRDM) Calculations

CRDM = FDME + FEME + UIME + MEME = FCDM + FCFM + FCUM + FCMM.

9.3.2 Software Structural Indicators (SSIs) Formulae

Software Structural Indicators (SSIs)[5–7] calculations are done with the help of the aforementioned Software Component's Measurements (SCMs) and Software Component's Feature Measurements (SCFMs).

There are 4 categories of the Software Structural Indicators (SSIs)[5–7] – first, those denoting the Software's Measurable Components (SMCs); second, denoting the Functionality Execution (FE) Operations; third, denoting the Functionality Execution (FE) Operations Data Handling; and fourth, denoting the deficiencies in the Functional Requirements Specifications (FRS). Formulae for all the 4 categories are described next.

9.3.2.1 Formulae of the Software Structural Indicators (SSIs) Denoting the Software's Measurable Components (SMCs)

Calculations of the Software Structural Indicators (SSIs)[5–7] of this category are based on 2 types of measurements:

1. the following individual Software Component's Measurements (SCMs):
   a. Software Component 'Functional Data' Measurement (CFDM);
   b. Software Component 'Functionality Execution' Measurement (CFEM);
   c. Software Component 'User Interface' Measurement (CUIM);
   d. Software Component 'Message Exchange' Measurement (CMEM);
2. Software Total Components Measurement (STCM) which is obtained by the addition of the aforementioned individual Software Component's Measurements (SCMs).

9.3.2.1.1 Functional Data Complexity and Size (FDCS) Formulae The Functional Data Complexity and Size (FDCS) SSI is a function of the CFDM (Software Component 'Functional Data' Measurement).

The FDCS (Functional Data Complexity and Size) is evaluated directly based on the value of the CFDM.

The FDCS is assigned one of the values: Nil, Low, Medium, High, or Very High according to its status in the categories indicated in Table 5 which is presented and explained in Section 9.3.2.5.

Thus, the FDCS value (Nil, Low, Medium, High, or Very High) helps to identify and understand the significance of the enormity of the data part in the software static structure.

9.3.2.1.2 Functionality Execution Complexity and Size (FECS) Formulae The Functionality Execution Complexity and Size (FECS) SSI is a function of the CFEM (Software Component 'Functionality Execution' Measurement).

The FECS (Functionality Execution Complexity and Size) is evaluated directly based on the value of the CFEM.

The FECS is assigned one of the following values according to its status in the categories indicated next:

- **a.** Nil: when the CFEM (Software Component 'Functionality Execution' Measurement) is equal to zero;
- **b.** Low: when the CFEM (Software Component 'Functionality Execution' Measurement) is ((greater than 0) and (less than 201));
- **c.** Medium: when the CFEM (Software Component 'Functionality Execution' Measurement) is ((greater than or equal to 201) and (less than 1001));
- **d.** High: when the CFEM (Software Component 'Functionality Execution' Measurement) is ((greater than or equal to 1001) and (less than 2501));
- **e.** Very High: when the CFEM (Software Component 'Functionality Execution' Measurement) is (greater than or equal to 2501).

Thus, the FECS value (Nil, Low, Medium, High, or Very High) helps to identify and understand the significance of the enormity of the functionality operations and their data handling part in the software static structure.

9.3.2.1.3 User Interface Complexity and Size (UICS) Formulae The User Interface Complexity and Size (UICS) SSI is a function of the CUIM (Software Component 'User Interface' Measurement).

The UICS (User Interface Complexity and Size) is evaluated directly based on the value of the CUIM.

The UICS is assigned one of the values: Nil, Low, Medium, High, or Very High according to its status in the categories indicated in Table 5 which is presented and explained in Section 9.3.2.5.

Thus, the UICS value (Nil, Low, Medium, High, or Very High) helps to identify and understand the significance of the enormity of the User Interface part in the software static structure.

9.3.2.1.4 Message Exchange Complexity and Size (MECS) Formulae The Message Exchange Complexity and Size (MECS) SSI is a function of the CMEM (Software Component 'Message Exchange' Measurement).

The MECS (Message Exchange Complexity and Size) is evaluated directly based on the value of the CMEM.

The MECS is assigned one of the values: Nil, Low, Medium, High, or Very High according to its status in the categories indicated in Table 5 which is presented and explained in Section 9.3.2.5.

Thus, the MECS value (Nil, Low, Medium, High, or Very High) helps to identify and understand the significance of the enormity of the Message Exchange part in the software static structure.

9.3.2.1.5 Functional Data Component Proportion (FDCP) Formulae The Functional Data Component Proportion (FDCP) SSI is a function of the CFDM (Software Component 'Functional Data' Measurement) and STCM (Software Total Components Measurement).

The FDCP (Functional Data Component Proportion) is evaluated based on the percentage value of CFDM (Software Component 'Functional Data' Measurement) / STCM (Software Total Components Measurement).

The FDCP is assigned one of the values: Nil, Low, Medium, High, or Very High according to its status in the categories indicated in Table 7 which is presented and explained in Section 9.3.2.6.

Thus, the FDCP value (Nil, Low, Medium, High, or Very High) helps to identify and understand the significance of the enormity of the Functional Data component proportion in the software static structure.

9.3.2.1.6 Functionality Execution Component Proportion (FECP) Formulae The Functionality Execution Component Proportion (FECP) SSI is a function of the CFEM (Software Component 'Functionality Execution' Measurement) and STCM (Software Total Components Measurement).

The FECP (Functionality Execution Component Proportion) is evaluated based on the percentage value of CFEM (Software Component 'Functionality Execution' Measurement) / STCM (Software Total Components Measurement).

The FECP is assigned one of the values: Nil, Low, Medium, High, or Very High according to its status in the categories indicated in Table 7 which is presented and explained in Section 9.3.2.6.

Thus, the FECP value (Nil, Low, Medium, High, or Very High) helps to identify and understand the significance of the enormity of the Functionality Execution component proportion in the software static structure.

9.3.2.1.7 User Interface Component Proportion (UICP) Formulae The User Interface Component Proportion (UICP) SSI is a function of the CUIM (Software Component 'User Interface' Measurement) and STCM (Software Total Components Measurement).

The UICP (User Interface Component Proportion) is evaluated based on the percentage value of CUIM (Software Component 'User Interface' Measurement) / STCM (Software Total Components Measurement).

The UICP is assigned one of the values: Nil, Low, Medium, High, or Very High according to its status in the categories indicated in Table 7 which is presented and explained in Section 9.3.2.6.

Thus, the UICP value (Nil, Low, Medium, High, or Very High) helps to identify and understand the significance of the enormity of the User Interface component proportion in the software static structure.

9.3.2.1.8 Message Exchange Component Proportion (MECP) Formulae The Message Exchange Component Proportion (MECP) SSI is a function of the CMEM (Software Component 'Message Exchange' Measurement) and STCM (Software Total Components Measurement).

The MECP (Message Exchange Component Proportion) is evaluated based on the percentage value of CMEM (Software Component 'Message Exchange' Measurement) / STCM (Software Total Components Measurement).

The MECP is assigned one of the values: Nil, Low, Medium, High, or Very High according to its status in the categories indicated in Table 7 which is presented and explained in Section 9.3.2.6.

Thus, the MECP value (Nil, Low, Medium, High, or Very High) helps to identify and understand the significance of the enormity of the Message Exchange component proportion in the software static structure.

9.3.2.2 Formulae of the Software Structural Indicators (SSIs) Denoting the Functionality Execution (FE) Operations

Calculations of the Software Structural Indicators (SSIs)[5–7] of this category are based on 2 types of measurements:

1. the following Software Component's Feature Measurements (SCFMs) for the Functionality Execution (FE) Operations:
   a. Memory Operations (MO);
   b. Computational Operations (CO);
   c. Logical Operations (LO);
   d. Decision Execution Operations (DEO);
   e. Repeat Execution Operations (REO);
   f. Action Execution Operations (AEO);
   g. Execution Flow Control Operations (EFCO);
   h. Input/Output Operations (IOO);
   i. Message Exchange Operations (MEO);
   j. Error Handling Operations (EHO).
2. Software Total Components Measurement (STCM) which is obtained by the addition of the following individual Software Component's Measurements (SCMs):
   a. Software Component 'Functional Data' Measurement (CFDM);
   b. Software Component 'Functionality Execution' Measurement (CFEM);
   c. Software Component 'User Interface' Measurement (CUIM);
   d. Software Component 'Message Exchange' Measurement (CMEM).

9.3.2.2.1 Memory Transaction Proportion (MTP) Formulae The Memory Transaction Proportion (MTP) SSI is a function of partial CFEM (Software Component 'Functionality Execution' Measurement) and STCM (Software Total Components Measurement).

The MTP (Memory Transaction Proportion) is evaluated based on the percentage value of MO (Memory Operations) / STCM (Software Total Components Measurement).

The MTP is assigned one of the values: Nil, Low, Medium, High, or Very High according to its status in the categories indicated in Table 7 which is presented and explained in Section 9.3.2.6.

Thus, the MTP value (Nil, Low, Medium, High, or Very High) helps to identify and understand the significance of the enormity of the memory transaction proportion in the software static structure.

9.3.2.2.2 Computational Operation Content Proportion (COCP) Formulae The Computational Operation Content Proportion (COCP) SSI is a function of partial CFEM (Software Component 'Functionality Execution' Measurement) and STCM (Software Total Components Measurement).

The COCP (Computational Operation Content Proportion) is evaluated based on the percentage value of CO (Computational Operations) / STCM (Software Total Components Measurement).

The COCP is assigned one of the values: Nil, Low, Medium, High, or Very High according to its status in the categories indicated in Table 7 which is presented and explained in Section 9.3.2.6.

Thus, the COCP value (Nil, Low, Medium, High, or Very High) helps to identify and understand the significance of the enormity of the computational operations (mathematical calculations) proportion in the software static structure.

9.3.2.2.3 Logical Operation Content Proportion (LOCP) Formulae The Logical Operation Content Proportion (LOCP) SSI is a function of partial CFEM (Software Component 'Functionality Execution' Measurement) and STCM (Software Total Components Measurement).

The LOCP (Logical Operation Content Proportion) is evaluated based on the percentage value of LO (Logical Operations) / STCM (Software Total Components Measurement).

The LOCP is assigned one of the values: Nil, Low, Medium, High, or Very High according to its status in the categories indicated in Table 7 which is presented and explained in Section 9.3.2.6.

Thus, the LOCP value (Nil, Low, Medium, High, or Very High) helps to identify and understand the significance of the enormity of the logical operations (AND, OR, etc.) proportion in the software static structure.

9.3.2.2.4 Decision Execution Content Proportion (DECP) Formulae The Decision Execution Content Proportion (DECP) SSI is a function of partial CFEM (Software Component 'Functionality Execution' Measurement) and STCM (Software Total Components Measurement).

The DECP (Decision Execution Content Proportion) is evaluated based on the percentage value of DEO (Decision Execution Operations) / STCM (Software Total Components Measurement).

The DECP is assigned one of the values: Nil, Low, Medium, High, or Very High according to its status in the categories indicated in Table 7 which is presented and explained in Section 9.3.2.6.

Thus, the DECP value (Nil, Low, Medium, High, or Very High) helps to identify and understand the significance of the enormity of the decision execution operations proportion in the software static structure.

9.3.2.2.5 Repeat Execution Content Proportion (RECP) Formulae The Repeat Execution Content Proportion (RECP) SSI is a function of partial CFEM (Software

Component 'Functionality Execution' Measurement) and STCM (Software Total Components Measurement).

The RECP (Repeat Execution Content Proportion) is evaluated based on the percentage value of REO (Repeat Execution Operations) / STCM (Software Total Components Measurement).

The RECP is assigned one of values: Nil, Low, Medium, High, or Very High according to its status in the categories indicated in Table 7 which is presented and explained in Section 9.3.2.6.

Thus, the RECP value (Nil, Low, Medium, High, or Very High) helps to identify and understand the significance of the enormity of the repeat execution operations proportion in the software static structure.

9.3.2.2.6 Action Execution Content Proportion (AECP) Formulae The Action Execution Content Proportion (AECP) SSI is a function of partial CFEM (Software Component 'Functionality Execution' Measurement) and STCM (Software Total Components Measurement).

The AECP (Action Execution Content Proportion) is evaluated based on the percentage value of AEO (Action Execution Operations) / STCM (Software Total Components Measurement).

The AECP is assigned one of the values: Nil, Low, Medium, High, or Very High according to its status in the categories indicated in Table 7 which is presented and explained in Section 9.3.2.6.

Thus, the AECP value (Nil, Low, Medium, High, or Very High) helps to identify and understand the significance of the enormity of the action execution operations proportion in the software static structure.

9.3.2.2.7 Execution Flow Control Content Proportion (EFCCP) Formulae The Execution Flow Control Content Proportion (EFCCP) SSI is a function of partial CFEM (Software Component 'Functionality Execution' Measurement) and STCM (Software Total Components Measurement).

The EFCCP (Execution Flow Control Content Proportion) is evaluated based on the percentage value of EFCO (Execution Flow Control Operations) / STCM (Software Total Components Measurement).

The EFCCP is assigned one of the values: Nil, Low, Medium, High, or Very High according to its status in the categories indicated in Table 7 which is presented and explained in Section 9.3.2.6.

Thus, the EFCCP value (Nil, Low, Medium, High, or Very High) helps to identify and understand the significance of the enormity of the execution flow control operations proportion in the software static structure.

9.3.2.2.8 User Interaction Proportion (UIP) Formulae The User Interaction Proportion (UIP) SSI is a function of partial CFEM (Software Component 'Functionality Execution' Measurement) and STCM (Software Total Components Measurement).

The UIP (User Interaction Proportion) is evaluated based on the percentage value of IOO (Input and Output Operations) / STCM (Software Total Components Measurement).

The UIP is assigned one of the values: Nil, Low, Medium, High, or Very High according to its status in the categories indicated in Table 7 which is presented and explained in Section 9.3.2.6.

Thus, the UIP value (Nil, Low, Medium, High, or Very High) helps to identify and understand the significance of the enormity of the input/output operations proportion in the software static structure.

9.3.2.2.9 External Communication Proportion (ECP) Formulae The External Communication Proportion (ECP) SSI is a function of partial CFEM (Software Component 'Functionality Execution' Measurement) and STCM (Software Total Components Measurement).

The ECP (External Communication Proportion) is evaluated based on the percentage value of MEO (Message Exchange Operations) / STCM (Software Total Components Measurement).

The ECP is assigned one of the values: Nil, Low, Medium, High, or Very High according to its status in the categories indicated in Table 7 which is presented and explained in Section 9.3.2.6.

Thus, the ECP value (Nil, Low, Medium, High, or Very High) helps to identify and understand the significance of the enormity of the message exchange operations proportion in the software static structure.

9.3.2.2.10 Error Handling Proportion (EHP) Formulae The Error Handling Proportion (EHP) SSI is a function of the EHO (Error Handling Operations) and STCM (Software Total Components Measurement).

The EHP (Error Handling Proportion) is evaluated based on the percentage value of EHO (Error Handling Operations) / STCM (Software Total Components Measurement).

The EHP is assigned one of the values: Nil, Low, Medium, High, or Very High according to its status in the categories indicated in Table 7 which is presented and explained in Section 9.3.2.6.

Thus, the EHP value (Nil, Low, Medium, High, or Very High) helps to identify and understand the significance of the enormity of the error handling proportion in the software static structure.

9.3.2.3 Formulae of the Software Structural Indicators (SSIs) Denoting the Functionality Execution (FE) Operations Data Handling

Calculations of the Software Structural Indicators (SSIs)[5–7] of this category are based on 2 types of measurements:

1. constituents of the Functionality Execution Data Manipulation Measurements (FEDMs) which are the following Software Component's Feature Measurements (SCFMs):
   a. Memory Operations Functional Data Entities (MOFE);
   b. Input/Output Operations Functional Data Entities (IOFE);
   c. Message Exchange Operations Functional Data Entities (EOFE);
   d. General Operations Functional Data Entities (GOFE);
2. Software Total Components Measurement (STCM) which is obtained by the addition of the following individual Software Component's Measurements (SCMs):
   a. Software Component 'Functional Data' Measurement (CFDM);
   b. Software Component 'Functionality Execution' Measurement (CFEM);
   c. Software Component 'User Interface' Measurement (CUIM);
   d. Software Component 'Message Exchange' Measurement (CMEM).

9.3.2.3.1 Memory Operations Functional Data Proportion (MODP) Formulae

The Memory Operations Functional Data Proportion (MODP) SSI is a function of partial CFEM (Software Component 'Functionality Execution' Measurement) and STCM (Software Total Components Measurement).

The MODP (Memory Operations Functional Data Proportion) is evaluated based on the percentage value of MOFE (Memory Operations Functional Data Entities) / STCM (Software Total Components Measurement).

The MODP is assigned one of the values: Nil, Low, Medium, High, or Very High according to its status in the categories indicated in Table 7 which is presented and explained in Section 9.3.2.6.

Thus, the MODP value (Nil, Low, Medium, High, or Very High) helps to identify and understand the significance of the enormity of the memory operations functional data handling proportion in the software static structure.

9.3.2.3.2 Input/Output Operations Functional Data Proportion (IODP) Formulae

The Input/Output Operations Functional Data Proportion (IODP) SSI is a function of partial CFEM (Software Component 'Functionality Execution' Measurement) and STCM (Software Total Components Measurement).

The IODP (Input/Output Operations Functional Data Proportion) is evaluated based on the percentage value of IOFE (Input and Output Operations Functional Data Entities) / STCM (Software Total Components Measurement).

The IODP is assigned one of the values: Nil, Low, Medium, High, or Very High according to its status in the categories indicated in Table 7 which is presented and explained in Section 9.3.2.6.

Thus, the IODP value (Nil, Low, Medium, High, or Very High) helps to identify and understand the significance of the enormity of the input/output operations functional data handling proportion in the software static structure.

9.3.2.3.3 Message Exchange Operations Functional Data Proportion (EODP) Formulae

The Message Exchange Operations Functional Data Proportion (EODP) SSI is a function of partial CFEM (Software Component 'Functionality Execution' Measurement) and STCM (Software Total Components Measurement).

The EODP (Message Exchange Operations Functional Data Proportion) is evaluated based on the percentage value of EOFE (Message Exchange Operations Functional Data Entities) / STCM (Software Total Components Measurement).

The EODP is assigned one of the values: Nil, Low, Medium, High, or Very High according to its status in the categories indicated in Table 7 which is presented and explained in Section 9.3.2.6.

Thus, the EODP value (Nil, Low, Medium, High, or Very High) helps to identify and understand the significance of the enormity of the message exchange operations functional data handling proportion in the software static structure.

9.3.2.3.4 General Operations Functional Data Proportion (GODP) Formulae

The General Operations Functional Data Proportion (GODP) SSI is a function of partial CFEM (Software Component 'Functionality Execution' Measurement) and STCM (Software Total Components Measurement).

The GODP (General Operations Functional Data Proportion) is evaluated based on the percentage value of GOFE (General Operations Functional Data Entities) / STCM (Software Total Components Measurement).

The GODP is assigned one of the values: Nil, Low, Medium, High, or Very High according to its status in the categories indicated in Table 7 which is presented and explained in Section 9.3.2.6.

Thus, the GODP value (Nil, Low, Medium, High, or Very High) helps to identify and understand the significance of the enormity of the general operations – computational, logical, decision, repeat, and execution flow – functional data handling proportion in the software static structure.

9.3.2.4 Formulae of the Software Structural Indicator (SSI) Denoting the Deficiency in the Functional Requirements Specifications (FRS)

Calculations of the Software Structural Indicator (SSI)[5–7] of this category are based on 2 types of measurements:

1. Software Components Requirement Deficiency Measurement (CRDM);
2. Software Total Components Measurement (STCM) which is obtained by the addition of the following individual Software Component's Measurements (SCMs):
   a. Software Component 'Functional Data' Measurement (CFDM);
   b. Software Component 'Functionality Execution' Measurement (CFEM);
   c. Software Component 'User Interface' Measurement (CUIM);
   d. Software Component 'Message Exchange' Measurement (CMEM).

9.3.2.4.1 Requirements Deficiency Grade (RDG) Formulae The Requirements Deficiency Grade (RDG) SSI is a function of the CRDM (Software Components Requirement Deficiency Measurement) and STCM (Software Total Components Measurement).

The RDG (Requirements Deficiency Grade) is evaluated based on the percentage value of CRDM (Software Components Requirement Deficiency Measurement) / STCM (Software Total Components Measurement).

The RDG is assigned one of the values: Nil, Low, Medium, High, or Very High according to its status in the categories indicated in Table 7 which is presented and explained in Section 9.3.2.6.

Thus, the RDG value (Nil, Low, Medium, High, or Very High) helps to identify and understand the significance of the enormity of the requirements deficiency in the Functional Requirements Specifications (FRS) of the software static structure.

9.3.2.5 Software Structural Indicators (SSIs) Value Assignment Table I

Table 5 shows the value assignment of Nil, Low, Medium, High, or Very High for the mentioned Software Structural Indicators (SSIs)[5–7] along with the status category of their calculation formula. In this table, X needs to be substituted by the SSIs, the list of which follows in the table, and similarly, corresponding Y needs to be substituted by the formulae mentioned against the SSIs in the list.

An example of the use of Table 5 is presented in Table 6 where X and Y have been substituted by "User Interface Complexity and Size (UICS)" and "CUIM (Software

Table 5 The Software Structural Indicators (SSIs) Value Assignment I

Software Structural Indicators (SSIs)[5–7] Value Assignment I: SSI Value and Status Category of the Corresponding Calculation Formula	
SSI X Values	**Corresponding Calculation Formula Y Status Categories**
Nil Low Medium High Very High	When Y is equal to 0; When Y is ((greater than 0) and (less than 51)); When Y is ((greater than or equal to 51) and (less than 501)); When Y is ((greater than or equal to 501) and (less than 1001)); When Y is (greater than or equal to 1001).
X to be Substituted by	**Corresponding Y to be Substituted by**
Functional Data Complexity and Size (FDCS)	CFDM (Software Component 'Functional Data' Measurement)
User Interface Complexity and Size (UICS)	CUIM (Software Component 'User Interface' Measurement)
Message Exchange Complexity and Size (MECS)	CMEM (Software Component 'Message Exchange' Measurement)

Table 6 Example of the Software Structural Indicators (SSIs) Value Assignment

Software Structural Indicator (SSI)[5–7] Value	
User Interface Complexity and Size (UICS) Values	**CUIM (Software Component 'User Interface' Measurement) Status Categories**
Nil	When CUIM (Software Component 'User Interface' Measurement) is equal to 0;
Low	When CUIM (Software Component 'User Interface' Measurement) is ((greater than 0) and (less than 51));
Medium	When CUIM (Software Component 'User Interface' Measurement) is ((greater than or equal to 51) and (less than 501));
High	When CUIM (Software Component 'User Interface' Measurement) is ((greater than or equal to 501) and (less than 1001));
Very High	When CUIM (Software Component 'User Interface' Measurement) is (greater than or equal to 1001).

Component 'User Interface' Measurement)", respectively. This example is also applicable for the use of Tables 7 and 8 where X and Y can be selected and substituted similarly.

9.3.2.6 Software Structural Indicators (SSIs) Value Assignment Table II

Table 7 shows the value assignment of Nil, Low, Medium, High, or Very High for the mentioned Software Structural Indicators (SSIs)[5–7] along with the status category of their calculation formula. In this table, X needs to be substituted by the SSIs, the list of which follows in the table, and similarly, corresponding Y needs to be substituted by the formulae mentioned against the SSIs in the list.

Table 7 The Software Structural Indicators (SSIs) Value Assignment II

Software Structural Indicators (SSIs)[5–7] Value Assignment II: SSI Value and Status Category of the Corresponding Calculation Formula	
SSI X Values	**Corresponding Calculation Formula Y Status Categories**
Nil Low Medium High Very High	When Y is equal to 0; When Y is ((greater than 0) and (less than 21)); When Y is ((greater than or equal to 21) and (less than 41)); When Y is ((greater than or equal to 41) and (less than 71)); When Y is ((greater than or equal to 71) and (less than or equal to 100)).
X to be Substituted by	**Corresponding Y to be Substituted by**
Functional Data Component Proportion (FDCP)	(CFDM (Software Component 'Functional Data' Measurement) / STCM (Software Total Components Measurement)) × 100
Functionality Execution Component Proportion (FECP)	(CFEM (Software Component 'Functionality Execution' Measurement) / STCM (Software Total Components Measurement)) × 100
User Interface Component Proportion (UICP)	(CUIM (Software Component 'User Interface' Measurement) / STCM (Software Total Components Measurement)) × 100
Message Exchange Component Proportion (MECP)	(CMEM (Software Component 'Message Exchange' Measurement) / STCM (Software Total Components Measurement)) × 100
Memory Transaction Proportion (MTP)	(MO (Memory Operations) / STCM (Software Total Components Measurement)) × 100
Computational Operation Content Proportion (COCP)	(CO (Computational Operations) / STCM (Software Total Components Measurement)) × 100
Logical Operation Content Proportion (LOCP)	(LO (Logical Operations) / STCM (Software Total Components Measurement)) × 100
Decision Execution Content Proportion (DECP)	(DEO (Decision Execution Operations) / STCM (Software Total Components Measurement)) × 100
Repeat Execution Content Proportion (RECP)	(REO (Repeat Execution Operations) / STCM (Software Total Components Measurement)) × 100
Action Execution Content Proportion (AECP)	(AEO (Action Execution Operations) / STCM (Software Total Components Measurement)) × 100
Execution Flow Control Content Proportion (EFCCP)	(EFCO (Execution Flow Control Operations) / STCM (Software Total Components Measurement)) × 100
User Interaction Proportion (UIP)	(IOO (Input and Output Operations) / STCM (Software Total Components Measurement)) × 100
External Communication Proportion (ECP)	(MEO (Message Exchange Operations) / STCM (Software Total Components Measurement)) × 100
Error Handling Proportion (EHP)	(EHO (Error Handling Operations) / STCM (Software Total Components Measurement)) × 100
Memory Operations Functional Data Proportion (MODP)	(MOFE (Memory Operations Functional Data Entities) / STCM (Software Total Components Measurement)) × 100

Table 7 (*Continued*)

X to be substituted by	Corresponding Y to be substituted by
Input/Output Operations Functional Data Proportion (IODP)	(IOFE (Input and Output Operations Functional Data Entities) / STCM (Software Total Components Measurement)) × 100
Message Exchange Operations Functional Data Proportion (EODP)	(EOFE (Message Exchange Operations Functional Data Entities) / STCM (Software Total Components Measurement)) × 100
General Operations Functional Data Proportion (GODP)	(GOFE (General Operations Functional Data Entities) / STCM (Software Total Components Measurement)) × 100
Requirements Deficiency Grade (RDG)	(CRDM (Software Components Requirement Deficiency Measurement) / STCM (Software Total Components Measurement)) × 100

9.3.3 Software Operational Indicators (SOIs) Formulae

Software Operational Indicators (SOIs)[5–7] calculations are performed by using the Software Component's Feature Measurements (SCFMs) and Software Component's Measurements (SCMs).

There are two categories of the Software Operational Indicators (SOIs)[5–7] – firstly, those denoting the Functional Operations Execution and secondly, denoting the Functional Operations Data Handling. Formulae for both the categories are described next.

9.3.3.1 Formulae of the Software Operational Indicators (SOIs) Denoting the Functional Operations Execution

Calculations of the Software Operational Indicators (SOIs)[5–7] of this category are based on 2 types of measurements:

1. The following Software Component's Feature Measurements (SCFMs) for the Functionality Execution (FE) Operations:
   - **a.** Memory Operations (MO);
   - **b.** Computational Operations (CO);
   - **c.** Logical Operations (LO);
   - **d.** Decision Execution Operations (DEO);
   - **e.** Repeat Execution Operations (REO);
   - **f.** Execution Flow Control Operations (EFCO)
   - **g.** Input/Output Operations (IOO);
   - **h.** Message Exchange Operations (MEO);
   - **i.** Error Handling Operations (EHO);
2. Functionality Execution Operations Dynamic Measurement (FEODM) which is obtained by the addition of the following SCFMs for the Functionality Execution (FE) Operations:
   - **a.** Memory Operations (MO);
   - **b.** Computational Operations (CO);
   - **c.** Logical Operations (LO);
   - **d.** Decision Execution Operations (DEO);

e. Repeat Execution Operations (REO);
f. Execution Flow Control Operations (EFCO)
g. Input/Output Operations (IOO);
h. Message Exchange Operations (MEO).

9.3.3.1.1 Memory Traffic Level (MTL) Formulae The Memory Traffic Level (MTL) SOI is a function of the FEODM (Functionality Execution Operations Dynamic Measurement).

The MTL (Memory Traffic Level) is evaluated based on the percentage value of MO (Memory Operations) / FEODM (Functionality Execution Operations Dynamic Measurement).

The MTL is assigned one of the values: Nil, Low, Medium, High, or Very High according to its status in the categories indicated in Table 8 which is presented and explained in Section 9.3.3.3.

Thus, the MTL value (Nil, Low, Medium, High, or Very High) helps to identify and understand the significance of the enormity of the memory transactions (read/write operations) level in the software dynamic execution at run-time.

9.3.3.1.2 Computational Operations Level (COL) Formulae The Computational Operations Level (COL) SOI is a function of the FEODM (Functionality Execution Operations Dynamic Measurement).

The COL (Computational Operations Level) is evaluated based on the percentage value of CO (Computational Operations) / FEODM (Functionality Execution Operations Dynamic Measurement).

The COL is assigned one of the values: Nil, Low, Medium, High, or Very High according to its status in the categories indicated in Table 8 which is presented and explained in Section 9.3.3.3.

Thus, the COL value (Nil, Low, Medium, High, or Very High) helps to identify and understand the significance of the enormity of the computational operations (mathematical calculations) level in the software dynamic execution at run-time.

9.3.3.1.3 Logical Operations Level (LOL) Formulae The Logical Operations Level (LOL) SOI is a function of the FEODM (Functionality Execution Operations Dynamic Measurement).

The LOL (Logical Operations Level) is evaluated based on the percentage value of LO (Logical Operations) / FEODM (Functionality Execution Operations Dynamic Measurement).

The LOL is assigned one of the values: Nil, Low, Medium, High, or Very High according to its status in the categories indicated in Table 8 which is presented and explained in Section 9.3.3.3.

Thus, the LOL value (Nil, Low, Medium, High, or Very High) helps to identify and understand the significance of the enormity of the logical operations (AND, OR, etc.) level in the software dynamic execution at run-time.

9.3.3.1.4 Decision Execution Level (DEL) Formulae The Decision Execution Level (DEL) SOI is a function of the FEODM (Functionality Execution Operations Dynamic Measurement).

The DEL (Decision Execution Level) is evaluated based on the percentage value of DEO (Decision Execution Operations) / FEODM (Functionality Execution Operations Dynamic Measurement).

The DEL is assigned one of the values: Nil, Low, Medium, High, or Very High according to its status in the categories indicated in Table 8 which is presented and explained in Section 9.3.3.3.

Thus, the DEL value (Nil, Low, Medium, High, or Very High) helps to identify and understand the significance of the enormity of the decision execution operations level in the software dynamic execution at run-time.

9.3.3.1.5 Repeat Execution Level (REL) Formulae The Repeat Execution Level (REL) SOI is a function of the FEODM (Functionality Execution Operations Dynamic Measurement).

The REL (Repeat Execution Level) is evaluated based on the percentage value of REO (Repeat Execution Operations) / FEODM (Functionality Execution Operations Dynamic Measurement).

The REL is assigned one of the values: Nil, Low, Medium, High, or Very High according to its status in the categories indicated in Table 8 which is presented and explained in Section 9.3.3.3.

Thus, the REL value (Nil, Low, Medium, High, or Very High) helps to identify and understand the significance of the enormity of the repeat execution operations level in the software dynamic execution at run-time.

9.3.3.1.6 Execution Flow Control Level (EFCL) Formulae The Execution Flow Control Level (EFCL) SOI is a function of the FEODM (Functionality Execution Operations Dynamic Measurement).

The EFCL (Execution Flow Control Level) is evaluated based on the percentage value of EFCO (Execution Flow Control Operations) / FEODM (Functionality Execution Operations Dynamic Measurement).

The EFCL is assigned one of the values: Nil, Low, Medium, High, or Very High according to its status in the categories indicated in Table 8 which is presented and explained in Section 9.3.3.3.

Thus, the EFCL value (Nil, Low, Medium, High, or Very High) helps to identify and understand the significance of the enormity of the execution flow control operations level in the software dynamic execution at run-time.

9.3.3.1.7 User Interaction Level (UIL) Formulae The User Interaction Level (UIL) SOI is a function of the FEODM (Functionality Execution Operations Dynamic Measurement).

The UIL (User Interaction Level) is evaluated based on the percentage value of IOO (Input and Output Operations) / FEODM (Functionality Execution Operations Dynamic Measurement).

The UIL is assigned one of the values: Nil, Low, Medium, High, or Very High according to its status in the categories indicated in Table 8 which is presented and explained in Section 9.3.3.3.

Thus, the UIL value (Nil, Low, Medium, High, or Very High) helps to identify and understand the significance of the enormity of the input/output operations level in the software dynamic execution at run-time.

9.3.3.1.8 External Communication Level (ECL) Formulae The External Communication Level (ECL) SOI is a function of the FEODM (Functionality Execution Operations Dynamic Measurement).

The ECL (External Communication Level) is evaluated based on the percentage value of MEO (Message Exchange Operations) / FEODM (Functionality Execution Operations Dynamic Measurement).

The ECL is assigned one of the values: Nil, Low, Medium, High, or Very High according to its status in the categories indicated in Table 8 which is presented and explained in Section 9.3.3.3.

Thus, the ECL value (Nil, Low, Medium, High, or Very High) helps to identify and understand the significance of the enormity of the message exchange operations level in the software dynamic execution at run-time.

9.3.3.1.9 Error Handling Capability (EHC) Formulae The Error Handling Capability (EHC) SOI is a function of the EHO (Error Handling Operations) and FEODM (Functionality Execution Operations Dynamic Measurement).

The EHC (Error Handling Capability) is evaluated based on the percentage value of EHO (Error Handling Operations) / FEODM (Functionality Execution Operations Dynamic Measurement).

The EHC is assigned one of the values: Nil, Low, Medium, High, or Very High according to its status in the categories indicated in Table 8 which is presented and explained in Section 9.3.3.3.

Thus, the EHC value (Nil, Low, Medium, High, or Very High) helps to identify and understand the significance of the enormity of the error handling operations level in the software dynamic execution at run-time.

9.3.3.2 Formulae of the Software Operational Indicators (SOIs) Denoting the Functional Operations Data Handling

Calculations of the Software Operational Indicators (SOIs)[5–7] of this category are based on 2 types of measurements:

1. individual constituent measurements of the Functionality Execution Data Manipulation Measurement (FEDMs). These constituents are the
   a. Memory Operations Functional Data Entities (MOFE);
   b. Input/Output Operations Functional Data Entities (IOFE);
   c. Message Exchange Operations Functional Data Entities (EOFE);
   d. General Operations Functional Data Entities (GOFE).
2. Functionality Execution Data Manipulation Measurement (FEDM) which is obtained by the addition of its aforementioned individual constituents.

9.3.3.2.1 Memory Traffic Functional Data Level (MTDL) Formulae The Memory Traffic Functional Data Level (MTDL) SOI is a function of the FEDM (Functionality Execution Data Manipulation Measurement).

The MTDL (Memory Traffic Functional Data Level) is evaluated based on the percentage value of MOFE (Memory Operations Functional Data Entities) / FEDM (Functionality Execution Data Manipulation Measurement).

The MTDL is assigned one of the values: Nil, Low, Medium, High, or Very High according to its status in the categories indicated in Table 8 which is presented and explained in Section 9.3.3.3.

Thus, the MTDL value (Nil, Low, Medium, High, or Very High) helps to identify and understand the significance of the enormity of the memory traffic (read/write operations) functional data handling level in the software dynamic execution at run-time.

9.3.3.2.2 User Interaction Functional Data Level (UIDL) Formulae

The User Interaction Functional Data Level (UIDL) SOI is a function of the FEDM (Functionality Execution Data Manipulation Measurement).

The UIDL (User Interaction Functional Data Level) is evaluated based on the percentage value of IOFE (Input and Output Operations Functional Data Entities) / FEDM (Functionality Execution Data Manipulation Measurement).

The UIDL is assigned one of the values: Nil, Low, Medium, High, or Very High according to its status in the categories indicated in Table 8 which is presented and explained in Section 9.3.3.3.

Thus, the UIDL value (Nil, Low, Medium, High, or Very High) helps to identify and understand the significance of the enormity of the user interaction (input/output operations) functional data handling level in the software dynamic execution at run-time.

9.3.3.2.3 External Communication Functional Data Level (ECDL) Formulae

The External Communication Functional Data Level (ECDL) SOI is a function of the FEDM (Functionality Execution Data Manipulation Measurement).

The ECDL (External Communication Functional Data Level) is evaluated based on the percentage value of EOFE (Message Exchange Operations Functional Data Entities) / FEDM (Functionality Execution Data Manipulation Measurement).

The ECDL is assigned one of the values: Nil, Low, Medium, High, or Very High according to its status in the categories indicated in Table 8 which is presented and explained in Section 9.3.3.3.

Thus, the ECDL value (Nil, Low, Medium, High, or Very High) helps to identify and understand the significance of the enormity of the external communication (message send/receive operations) functional data handling level in the software dynamic execution at run-time.

9.3.3.2.4 General Operations Execution Functional Data Level (GODL) Formulae

The General Operations Execution Functional Data Level (GODL) SOI is a function of the FEDM (Functionality Execution Data Manipulation Measurement).

The GODL (General Operations Execution Functional Data Level) is evaluated based on the percentage value of GOFE (General Operations Functional Data Entities) / FEDM (Functionality Execution Data Manipulation Measurement).

The GODL is assigned one of the values: Nil, Low, Medium, High, or Very High according to its status in the categories indicated in Table 8 which is presented and explained in Section 9.3.3.3.

Thus, the GODL value (Nil, Low, Medium, High, or Very High) helps to identify and understand the significance of the enormity of the general operations (computational, logical, decision, repeat, and execution flow operations) functional data handling level in the software dynamic execution at run-time.

9.3.3.3 Software Operational Indicators (SOIs) Value Assignment Table

Table 8 shows the value assignment of Nil, Low, Medium, High, or Very High for the mentioned Software Operational Indicators (SOIs)[5–7] along with the status category of their calculation formula. In this table, X needs to be substituted by the SOIs, the list of which follows in the table, and similarly, corresponding Y needs to be substituted by the formulae mentioned against the SOIs in the list.

9.4 EXAMPLES

1. If the value of the SSI Requirements Deficiency Grade (RDG) is Medium, High, or Very High, it indicates all the following facts:
   - **A.** Functional Requirements Specifications (FRS) are not complete.
   - **B.** Significant improvements in the Functional Requirements Specifications (FRS) are required.
   - **C.** Software developed according to the Functional Requirements Specifications (FRS) without having done any improvements in the FRS may be of poor quality.
2. Nil or Low value of the SSI Error Handling Proportion (EHP) and SOI Error Handling Capability (EHC) indicate all the following facts:
   - **A.** Error cases and error handling measures have not been properly considered in the Functional Requirements Specifications (FRS).
   - **B.** Improvements in the error handling aspects should be considered and made in the Functional Requirements Specifications (FRS).
   - **C.** In the software developed according to the Functional Requirements Specifications (FRS) without having done any improvement in the FRS, the error handling aspects may be of poor quality.

9.5 CHAPTER SUMMARY

9.5.1 Software Performance Quality Indicator (SPQI): Summary

The Software Performance Quality Indicators (SPQIs) indicate the performance quality aspects of the software and functional requirements. They are of the following two types:

1. Software Structural Indicators (SSIs)[5–7];
2. Software Operational Indicators (SOIs)[5–7].

The Software Structural Indicators (SSIs)[5–7] provide the information about the software static structural aspects and Software Operational Indicators (SOIs)[5–7] provide the information about the software dynamic execution (run-time) aspects. Both of them are categorized as Nil, Low, Medium, High, or Very High. Their values are obtained based on the Software Component's Feature Measurements (SCFMs) and Software Component's Measurements (SCMs).

There are 23 Software Structural Indicators (SSIs)[5–7] divided in 4 sub-categories and 13 Software Operational Indicators (SOIs)[5–7] divided in 2 sub-categories summarized next.

Table 8 The Software Operational Indicators (SOIs) Value Assignment

Software Operational Indicators (SOIs)[5–7] Value Assignment: SOI Value and Status Category of the Corresponding Calculation Formula	
SOI X Values	**Corresponding Calculation Formula Y Status Categories**
Nil	When Y is equal to 0;
Low	When Y is ((greater than 0) and (less than 21));
Medium	When Y is ((greater than or equal to 21) and (less than 41));
High	When Y is ((greater than or equal to 41) and (less than 71));
Very High	When Y is ((greater than or equal to 71) and (less than or equal to 100)).
X to be Substituted by	**Corresponding Y to be Substituted by**
Memory Traffic Level (MTL)	(MO (Memory Operations) / FEODM (Functionality Execution Operations Dynamic Measurement)) × 100
Computational Operations Level (COL)	(CO (Computational Operations) / FEODM (Functionality Execution Operations Dynamic Measurement)) × 100
Logical Operations Level (LOL)	(LO (Logical Operations) / FEODM (Functionality Execution Operations Dynamic Measurement)) × 100
Decision Execution Level (DEL)	(DEO (Decision Execution Operations) / FEODM (Functionality Execution Operations Dynamic Measurement)) × 100
Repeat Execution Level (REL)	(REO (Repeat Execution Operations) / FEODM (Functionality Execution Operations Dynamic Measurement)) × 100
Execution Flow Control Level (EFCL)	(EFCO (Execution Flow Control Operations) / FEODM (Functionality Execution Operations Dynamic Measurement)) × 100
User Interaction Level (UIL)	(IOO (Input and Output Operations) / FEODM (Functionality Execution Operations Dynamic Measurement)) × 100
External Communication Level (ECL)	(MEO (Message Exchange Operations) / FEODM (Functionality Execution Operations Dynamic Measurement)) × 100
Error Handling Capability (EHC)	(EHO (Error Handling Operations) / FEODM (Functionality Execution Operations Dynamic Measurement)) × 100
Memory Traffic Functional Data Level (MTDL)	(MOFE (Memory Operations Functional Data Entities) / FEDM (Functionality Execution Data Manipulation Measurement)) × 100
User Interaction Functional Data Level (UIDL)	(IOFE (Input and Output Operations Functional Data Entities) / FEDM (Functionality Execution Data Manipulation Measurement)) × 100
External Communication Functional Data Level (ECDL)	(EOFE (Message Exchange Operations Functional Data Entities) / FEDM (Functionality Execution Data Manipulation Measurement)) × 100
General Operations Execution Functional Data Level (GODL)	(GOFE (General Operations Functional Data Entities) / FEDM (Functionality Execution Data Manipulation Measurement)) × 100

9.5.1.1 Software Structural Indicators (SSIs): Summary

9.5.1.1.1 Software Structural Indicators (SSIs) Denoting the Software's Measurable Components (SMCs): Summary

1. The **Functional Data Complexity and Size (FDCS)** provides the information about the Software's Measurable Component 'Functional Data' (CFD), that means the information about the class structure.
2. The **Functionality Execution Complexity and Size (FECS)** provides the information about the Software's Measurable Component 'Functionality Execution' (CFE), that means the information about the functionality operations and data handling during those operations.
3. The **User Interface Complexity and Size (UICS)** provides the information about the Software's Measurable Component 'User Interface' (CUI), that means the information about the user screens structure.
4. The **Message Exchange Complexity and Size (MECS)** provides the information about the Software's Measurable Component 'Message Exchange' (CME), that means the information about the message structure.
5. The **Functional Data Component Proportion (FDCP)** provides the information about the proportion of the Software's Measurable Component 'Functional Data' (CFD) in the software static structure.
6. The **Functionality Execution Component Proportion (FECP)** provides the information about the proportion of the Software's Measurable Component 'Functionality Execution' (CFE) in the software static structure.
7. The **User Interface Component Proportion (UICP)** provides the information about the proportion of the Software's Measurable Component 'User Interface' (CUI) in the software static structure.
8. The **Message Exchange Component Proportion (MECP)** provides the information about the proportion of the Software's Measurable Component 'Message Exchange' (CME) in the software static structure.

9.5.1.1.2 Software Structural Indicators (SSIs) Denoting the Functionality Execution (FE) Operations: Summary

1. The **Memory Transaction Proportion (MTP)** provides the information about the proportion of the memory read/write operations in the software static structure.
2. The **Computational Operation Content Proportion (COCP)** provides the information about the proportion of the computational operations (mathematical calculations) in the software static structure.
3. The **Logical Operation Content Proportion (LOCP)** provides the information about the proportion of the logical operations (AND, OR, etc.) in the software static structure.
4. The **Decision Execution Content Proportion (DECP)** provides the information about the proportion of the decision execution operations in the software static structure.
5. The **Repeat Execution Content Proportion (RECP)** provides the information about the proportion of the repeat execution operations in the software static structure.

6. The **Action Execution Content Proportion (AECP)** provides the information about the proportion of the action execution operations in the software static structure.
7. The **Execution Flow Control Content Proportion (EFCCP)** provides the information about the proportion of the execution flow control operations in the software static structure.
8. The **User Interaction Proportion (UIP)** provides the information about the proportion of the input/output operations used for receiving/sending the input/output data from/to the input/output devices in the software static structure.
9. The **External Communication Proportion (ECP)** provides the information about the proportion of the message send/receive operations used for sending/receiving the messages to/from the external application programs in the software static structure.
10. The **Error Handling Proportion (EHP)** provides the information about the proportion of the error handling operations in the software static structure.

9.5.1.1.3 Software Structural Indicators (SSIs) Denoting the Functionality Execution (FE) Operations Data Handling: Summary

1. The **Memory Operations Functional Data Proportion (MODP)** provides the information about the proportion of the memory read/write operations functional data handling in the software static structure.
2. The **Input/Output Operations Functional Data Proportion (IODP)** provides the information about the proportion of the input/output operations functional data handling in the software static structure.
3. The **Message Exchange Operations Functional Data Proportion (EODP)** provides the information about the proportion of the message exchange operations functional data handling in the software static structure.
4. The **General Operations Functional Data Proportion (GODP)** provides the information about the proportion of the general operations (computational, logical, decision, repeat, and execution flow control operations) functional data handling in the software static structure.

9.5.1.1.4 Software Structural Indicator (SSI) Denoting the Deficiency in the Functional Requirements Specifications (FRS): Summary

1. The **Requirements Deficiency Grade (RDG)** provides the information about the proportion of the deficiency in the functional requirements in the software static structure.

9.5.1.2 Software Operational Indicators(SOIs) (at Run-Time): Summary

9.5.1.2.1 Software Operational Indicators (SOIs) Denoting the Functional Operations Execution: Summary

1. The **Memory Traffic Level (MTL)** provides the run-time dynamic information about the extent of the memory read/write operations during the software execution.

2. The **Computational Operations Level (COL)** provides the run-time dynamic information about the extent of the computational operations (mathematical calculations) during the software execution.
3. The **Logical Operations Level (LOL)** provides the run-time dynamic information about the extent of the logical operations (AND, OR, etc.) during the software execution.
4. The **Decision Execution Level (DEL)** provides the run-time dynamic information about the extent of the decision execution operations during the software execution.
5. The **Repeat Execution Level (REL)** provides the run-time dynamic information about the extent of the repeat execution operations during the software execution.
6. The **Execution Flow Control Level (EFCL)** provides the run-time dynamic information about the extent of the execution flow control operations during the software execution.
7. The **User Interaction Level (UIL)** provides the run-time dynamic information about the extent of the input/output operations during the software execution.
8. The **External Communication Level (ECL)** provides the run-time dynamic information about the extent of the message send/receive operations during the software execution.
9. The **Error Handling Capability (EHC)** provides the run-time dynamic information about the extent of the error handling operations during the software execution.

9.5.1.2.2 Software Operational Indicators (SOIs) Denoting the Functional Operations Data Handling: Summary

1. The **Memory Traffic Functional Data Level (MTDL)** provides the run-time dynamic information about the extent of the data handling in the memory read/write operations during the software execution.
2. The **User Interaction Functional Data Level (UIDL)** provides the run-time dynamic information about the extent of the data handling in the input/output operations during the software execution.
3. The **External Communication Functional Data Level (ECDL)** provides the run-time dynamic information about the extent of the data handling in the message send/receive operations during the software execution.
4. The **General Operations Execution Functional Data Level (GODL)** provides the run-time dynamic information about the extent of the data handling in the general computational, logical, decision, repeat, and execution flow control operations during the software execution.

EXERCISES

9.1 Regarding the Memory Operations Functional Data Proportion (MODP), which of the following statements is correct?

A. It is a Software Performance Quality Indicator (SPQI) of the type Software Operational Indicator (SOI)[5–7]. It indicates the dynamic run-time level of the memory read/write operations in the software.

B. It is a Software Performance Quality Indicator (SPQI) of the type Software Structural Indicator (SSI)[5–7]. It indicates the proportion of the memory read/write operations functional data handling in the software static structure.

C. It is one of the Software Component's Measurable Features (SCMFs) of the Software's Measurable Component 'Functionality Execution' (CFE).

9.2 Regarding the Computational Operations Level (COL), which of the following statements is correct?

A. It is a Software Performance Quality Indicator (SPQI) of the type Software Structural Indicator (SSI)[5–7]. It provides the proportion of the computational operations (mathematical calculations) in the static software structure.

B. It is not a Software Performance Quality Indicator (SPQI).

C. It is a Software Performance Quality Indicator (SPQI) of the type Software Operational Indicator (SOI)[5–7]. It provides the run-time dynamic information about the extent of the computational operations (mathematical calculations) during the software execution.

9.3 Which of the following measurements is used as the base for the calculation of the Software Performance Quality Indicators (SPQIs) of the type Software Operational Indicator (SOI)[5–7] that belong to the sub-category SOIs denoting the Functional Operations Execution?

A. Functionality Execution Operations Dynamic Measurement (FEODM).

B. Functionality Execution Operations Measurement (FEOM).

C. Functionality Execution Data Manipulation Measurement (FEDM).

9.4 Which of the following measurements is used as the base for determining the values of the Software Performance Quality Indicators (SPQIs) of the type Software Operational Indicators (SOIs)[5–7] that belong to the sub-category SOIs denoting the Functional Operations Data Handling?

A. Functionality Execution Operations Dynamic Measurement (FEODM).

B. Functionality Execution Operations Measurement (FEOM).

C. Functionality Execution Data Manipulation Measurement (FEDM).

Part Five

FSSM: Summary Charts

Chapter 10

Summary Charts of the FSSM

In this chapter, the summary charts of the Functional Software Size Measurement Methodology with Effort Estimation and Performance Indication (FSSM) are presented.

These charts provide complementary summary information to the summary information presented in Figures 3–13.

10.1 SUMMARY CHARTS OF THE FSSM CONSTITUENTS

10.1.1 Software's Measurable Components (SMCs), Software Component's Measurable Features (SCMFs), Software Component's Feature Points (SCFPs), and Software Component's Feature Point Counts (SCFPCs) Summary Chart

Table 9 shows the summary chart of the Software's Measurable Components (SMCs), Software Component's Measurable Features (SCMFs), Software Component's Feature Points (SCFPs), and Software Component's Feature Point Counts (SCFPCs).

10.1.2 Software Component's Feature Measurements (SCFMs) Summary Chart

Table 10 presents the summary chart of the Software Component's Feature Measurements (SCFMs).

10.1.3 Software Component's Measurements (SCMs) Summary Chart

Table 11 presents the summary chart of the Software Component's Measurements (SCMs).

10.1.4 Software Size and Effort Estimations (SSEEs) Summary Chart

Table 12 presents the summary chart of the Software Size and Effort Estimations (SSEEs).

Functional Software Size Measurement Methodology with Effort Estimation and Performance Indication, First Edition. Jasveer Singh.

Companion website: http://booksupport.wiley.com

Table 9 The FSSM 1.0 Summary Part 1/5 Chart 1/1 for the SMCs, SCMFs, SCFPs, and SCFPCs

Functional Software Size Measurement Methodology with Effort Estimation and Performance Indication (FSSM 1.0) Summary Part 1/5 Chart 1/1			
Software's Measurable Components (SMCs), Software Component's Measurable Features SCMFs), Software Component's Feature Points (SCFPs), and Software Component Feature Point Counts (SCFPCs)			
SMCs	**SCMFs**	**SCFPs**	**SCFPCs**
'Functional Data' (CFD)	**'Data Class' (FDC)**	FPDC	FCDC
	'Data Attribute' (FDA)	FPDA	FCDA
	'Data Field' (FDF)	FPDF	FCDF
	'Data Missing' (FDM)	FPDM	FCDM
'Functionality Execution' (CFE)	**'Data Read' (FDR)**	FPDR	FCDR
	'Data Write' (FDW)	FPDW	FCDW
	'Memory Operations Functional Data' (FLM)	FPLM	FCLM
	'Data Input' (FDI)	FPDI	FCDI
	'Data Output' (FDO)	FPDO	FCDO
	'Input/Output Operations Functional Data' (FLI)	FPLI	FCLI
	'Message Send' (FMS)	FPMS	FCMS
	'Message Receive' (FMR)	FPMR	FCMR
	'Message Exchange Operations Functional Data' (FLS)	FPLS	FCLS
	'Function Computational Operation' (FFC)	FPFC	FCFC
	'Function Logical Operation' (FFL)	FPFL	FCFL
	'Function Decision Execution' (FFD)	FPFD	FCFD
	'Function Repeat Execution' (FFR)	FPFR	FCFR
	'Function Action Execution' (FFA)	FPFA	FCFA
	'Function Execution Flow Control' (FFO)	FPFO	FCFO
	'Function Error Handling' (FFE)	FPFE	FCFE
	'General Operations Functional Data' (FLG)	FPLG	FCLG
	'Class Method' (FCM)	FPCM	FCCM
	'Functionality Missing' (FFM)	FPFM	FCFM
'User Interface' (CUI)	**'User Screen' (FUS)**	FPUS	FCUS
	'User Screen Field' (FUF)	FPUF	FCUF
	'User Screen Output Link' (FUO)	FPUO	FCUO
	'User Screen Input Link' (FUI)	FPUI	FCUI
	'User Screen Missing' (FUM)	FPUM	FCUM
'Message Exchange' (CME)	**'Notifying Message' (FNM)**	FPNM	FCNM
	'Message Field' (FMF)	FPMF	FCMF
	'Message Missing' (FMM)	FPMM	FCMM

Table 10 The FSSM 1.0 Summary Part 2/5 Chart 1/1 for the SCFMs

<table>
<tr><th colspan="2">Functional Software Size Measurement Methodology with Effort Estimation and Performance Indication (FSSM 1.0) Summary Part 2/5 Chart 1/1</th></tr>
<tr><th colspan="2">Software Component's Feature Measurements (SCFMs) in terms of Software Component's Feature Points (SCFPs)</th></tr>
<tr><th>Software's Measurable Components (SMCs)</th><th>Software Component's Feature Measurements (SCFMs) and their Calculations from the Software Component's Feature Point Counts (SCFPCs)</th></tr>
<tr><td rowspan="4">'Functional Data' (CFD)</td><td>Data Class Entities (DCE) = FCDC</td></tr>
<tr><td>Data Class Attribute Entities (DAE) = FCDA</td></tr>
<tr><td>Data Class Field Entities (DFE) = FCDF</td></tr>
<tr><td>Functional Data Missing Entities (FDME) = FCDM</td></tr>
<tr><td rowspan="16">'Functionality Execution' (CFE)</td><td>Memory Operations (MO) = FCDR + FCDW</td></tr>
<tr><td>Computational Operations (CO) = FCFC</td></tr>
<tr><td>Logical Operations (LO) = FCFL</td></tr>
<tr><td>Decision Execution Operations (DEO) = FCFD</td></tr>
<tr><td>Repeat Execution Operations (REO) = FCFR</td></tr>
<tr><td>Action Execution Operations (AEO) = FCFA</td></tr>
<tr><td>Execution Flow Control Operations (EFCO) = FCFO</td></tr>
<tr><td>Input and Output Operations (IOO) = FCDI + FCDO</td></tr>
<tr><td>Message Exchange Operations (MEO) = FCMS + FCMR</td></tr>
<tr><td>Error Handling Operations (EHO) = FCFE</td></tr>
<tr><td>Class Method Entities (CMDE) = FCCM</td></tr>
<tr><td>Memory Operations Functional Data Entities (MOFE) = FCLM</td></tr>
<tr><td>Input and Output Operations Functional Data Entities (IOFE) = FCLI</td></tr>
<tr><td>Message Exchange Operations Functional Data Entities (EOFE) = FCLS</td></tr>
<tr><td>General Operations Functional Data Entities (GOFE) = FCLG</td></tr>
<tr><td>Functionality Execution Missing Entities (FEME) = FCFM</td></tr>
<tr><td rowspan="5">'User Interface' (CUI)</td><td>User Interface Screen Entities (UISE) = FCUS</td></tr>
<tr><td>User Interface Field Entities (UIFE) = FCUF</td></tr>
<tr><td>User Interface Input Link Entities (UIIE) = FCUI</td></tr>
<tr><td>User Interface Output Link Entities (UIOE) = FCUO</td></tr>
<tr><td>User Interface Missing Entities (UIME) = FCUM</td></tr>
<tr><td rowspan="3">'Message Exchange' (CME)</td><td>Notifying Message Entities (NME) = FCNM</td></tr>
<tr><td>Message Field Entities (MFE) = FCMF</td></tr>
<tr><td>Message Exchange Missing Entities (MEME) = FCMM</td></tr>
</table>

Table 11 The FSSM 1.0 Summary Part 3/5 Chart 1/1 for the SCMs

<table>
<tr><th colspan="2">Functional Software Size Measurement Methodology with Effort Estimation and Performance Indication (FSSM 1.0) Summary Part 3/5 Chart 1/1</th></tr>
<tr><th colspan="2">Software Component's Measurements (SCMs) in terms of Software Component's Feature Measurements (SCFMs)</th></tr>
<tr><th>Software Component's Measurements (SCMs)</th><th>Measurements Calculations from Software Component's Feature Measurements (SCFMs)</th></tr>
<tr><td>Software Component 'Functional Data' Measurement (CFDM)</td><td>CFDM = Data Class Entities (DCE) + Data Class Attribute Entities (DAE) + Data Class Field Entities (DFE)</td></tr>
<tr><td rowspan="4">Software Component 'Functionality Execution' Measurement (CFEM)
a. Functionality Execution Operations Dynamic Measurement (FEODM)
b. Functionality Execution Operations Measurement (FEOM)
c. Functionality Execution Data Manipulation Measurement (FEDM)</td><td>FEODM = Memory Operations (MO) + Computational Operations (CO) + Logical Operations (LO) + Decision Execution Operations (DEO) + Repeat Execution Operations (REO) + Execution Flow Control Operations (EFCO) + Input and Output Operations (IOO) + Message Exchange Operations (MEO)</td></tr>
<tr><td>FEOM = FEODM + Action Execution Operations (AEO) + Class Method Entities (CMDE)</td></tr>
<tr><td>FEDM = Memory Operations Functional Data Entities (MOFE) + Input and Output Operations Functional Data Entities (IOFE) + Message Exchange Operations Functional Data Entities (EOFE) + General Operations Functional Data Entities (GOFE)</td></tr>
<tr><td>CFEM = FEOM + FEDM</td></tr>
<tr><td>Software Component 'User Interface' Measurement (CUIM)</td><td>CUIM = User Interface Screen Entities (UISE) + User Interface Field Entities (UIFE) + User Interface Input Link Entities (UIIE) + User Interface Output Link Entities (UIOE)</td></tr>
<tr><td>Software Component 'Message Exchange' Measurement (CMEM)</td><td>CMEM = Notifying Message Entities (NME) + Message Field Entities (MFE)</td></tr>
<tr><td>Software Components Requirement Deficiency Measurement (CRDM)</td><td>CRDM = Functional Data Missing Entities (FDME) + Functionality Execution Missing Entities (FEME) + User Interface Missing Entities (UIME) + Message Exchange Missing Entities (MEME)</td></tr>
<tr><td>Software Total Components Measurement (STCM)</td><td>STCM = CFDM + CFEM + CUIM + CMEM</td></tr>
</table>

Table 12 The FSSM 1.0 Summary Part 4/5 Chart 1/1 for the SSEEs

Functional Software Size Measurement Methodology with Effort Estimation and Performance Indication (FSSM 1.0) Summary Part 4/5 Chart 1/1	
Software Size and Effort Estimations (SSEEs)	
Software Logical Size (SLS)	**Software Data Statements (SDS)** = 4 × DCE + 2 × DAE + 2 × CMDE + 2 × UISE + UIIE + UIOE + 2 × NME + DFE × (1 + 0.1 × CMDE) + UIFE × (1 + 0.1 × CMDE) + MFE × (1 + 0.1 × CMDE) + 0.1 × (DFE + UIFE + MFE) = 4 × FCDC + 2 × FCDA + 2 × FCCM + 2 × FCUS + FCUI + FCUO + 2 × FCNM + FCDF × (1 + 0.1 × FCCM) + FCUF × (1 + 0.1 × FCCM) + FCMF × (1 + 0.1 × FCCM) + 0.1 × (FCDF + FCUF + FCMF)
	Software Code Statements (SCDS) = 3 × CMDE + 2 × DEO + 2 × REO + 2 × AEO + 2 × (1 + CMDE) + EFCO + CO + LO + 2 × (MO + IOO + MEO) + MOFE + IOFE + EOFE + GOFE = 3 × FCCM + 2 × FCFD + 2 × FCFR + 2 × FCFA+ 2 × (1 + FCCM) + FCFO + FCFC + FCFL + 2 × (FCDR + FCDW + FCDI + FCDO + FCMS + FCMR) + FCLM + FCLI + FCLS + FCLG
	Software Comment Statements (SCS) = 0.4 × (SDS + SCDS)
	SLS = SDS + SCDS + SCS
Software Analysis, Design, and Coding Effort (SADCE) (including technical specifications documents)	**Software Data Analysis and Design Effort (SDADE)** (including technical specifications documents) = ((CFDM + CUIM + CMEM) / 40) person days
	Software Functionality Analysis and Design Effort (SFADE) (including technical specifications documents) = (CFEM / 80) person days
	Software Coding Effort (SCE) (including technical specifications documents) = (SLS / 80) person days
	SADCE = (SDADE + SFADE + SCE) person days
Software Testing Effort (STE) (including test specifications documents)	**STE** = (1.2 × SADCE) person days
Software Total Development Effort (STDE)	**STDE** = (SADCE + STE) person days

10.1.5 Software Performance Quality Indicators (SPQIs) Summary Chart

Tables 13 and 14 present the summary chart of the Software Performance Quality Indicators (SPQIs) – Software Structural Indicators (SSIs)[5–7] and Software Operational Indicators (SOIs)[5–7], respectively.

Table 13 The FSSM 1.0 Summary Part 5/5 Chart 1/2 for the SPQIs – SSIs

Functional Software Size Measurement Methodology with Effort Estimation and Performance Indication (FSSM 1.0) Summary Part 5/5 Chart 1/2	
Software Performance Quality Indicators (SPQIs)	
Software Structural Indicators (SSI)[5–7] categorized as Nil, Low, Medium, High, or Very High according to the calculated value	**Calculations**
1. SSIs denoting the Software's Measurable Components (SMCs):	
a. Functional Data Complexity and Size (FDCS)	CFDM
b. Functionality Complexity and Size (FECS)	CFEM
c. User Interface Complexity and Size (UICS)	CUIM
d. Message Exchange Complexity and Size (MECS)	CMEM
e. Functional Data Component Proportion (FDCP) %	CFDM/STCM
f. Functionality Execution Component Proportion (FECP) %	CFEM/STCM
g. User Interface Component Proportion (UICP) %	CUIM/STCM
h. Message Exchange Component Proportion (MECP) %	CMEM/STCM
2. SSIs denoting the Functionality Execution (FE) Operations:	
a. Memory Transaction Proportion (MTP) %	MO/STCM
b. Computational Operation Content Proportion (COCP) %	CO/STCM
c. Logical Operation Content Proportion (LOCP) %	LO/STCM
d. Decision Execution Content Proportion (DECP) %	DEO/STCM
e. Repeat Execution Content Proportion (RECP) %	REO/STCM
f. Action Execution Content Proportion (AECP) %	AEO/STCM
g. Execution Flow Control Content Proportion (EFCCP) %	EFCO/STCM
h. User Interaction Proportion (UIP) %	IOO/STCM
i. External Communication Proportion (ECP) %	MEO/STCM
j. Error Handling Proportion (EHP) %	EHO/STCM
3. SSIs denoting the Functionality Execution (FE) Operations Data Handling:	
a. Memory Operations Functional Data Proportion (MODP) %	MOFE/STCM
b. Input and Output Operations Functional Data Proportion (IODP) %	IOFE/STCM
c. Message Exchange Operations Functional Data Proportion (EODP) %	EOFE/STCM
d. General Operations Functional Data Proportion (GODP) %	GOFE/STCM
4. SSI denoting the deficiency in the Functional Requirements Specifications (FRS):	
a. Requirements Deficiency Grade (RDG) %	CRDM/STCM

10.1.6 Software Component's Measurable Feature (SCMF) Usage in the Other FSSM Constituents – Summary Chart

Tables 15–18 show the usage summary of the 31 Software Component's Measurable Features (SCMFs) of the 4 Software's Measurable Components (SMCs) in the different FSSM constituents, that is, in the 31 Software Component's Feature Points (SCFPs), 31 Software Component's Feature Point Counts (SCFPCs), 28 Software Component's Feature Measurements (SCFMs), 6 Software Component's Measurements (SCMs), 4 Software Size and Effort Estimations (SSEEs), and 36 Software Performance Quality Indicators (SPQIs) of both the types – Software Structural Indicators (SSIs)[5–7] which are 23 in number and Software Operational Indicators (SOIs)[5–7] which are 13 in number.

Table 14 The FSSM 1.0 Summary Part 5/5 Chart 2/2 for the SPQIs – SOIs

Functional Software Size Measurement Methodology with Effort Estimation and Performance Indication (FSSM 1.0) Summary Part 5/5 Chart 2/2	
Software Performance Quality Indicators (SPQIs)	
Software Operational Indicators (SOI)[5–7] categorized as Nil, Low, Medium, High, or Very High according to the calculated value	**Calculations**
1. SOIs denoting the Functional Operations Execution:	
a. Memory Traffic Level (MTL) %	MO/FEODM
b. Computational Operations Level (COL) %	CO/FEODM
c. Logical Operations Level (LOL) %	LO/FEODM
d. Decision Execution Level (DEL) %	DEO/FEODM
e. Repeat Execution Level (REL) %	REO/FEODM
f. Execution Flow Control Level (EFCL) %	EFCO/FEODM
g. User Interaction Level (UIL) %	IOO/FEODM
h. External Communication Level (ECL) %	MEO/FEODM
i. Error Handling Capability (EHC) %	EHO/FEODM
2. SOIs denoting the Functional Operations Data Handling:	
a. Memory Traffic Functional Data Level (MTDL) %	MOFE/FEDM
b. User Interaction Functional Data Level (UIDL) %	IOFE/FEDM
c. External Communication Functional Data Level (ECDL) %	EOFE/FEDM
d. General Operations Execution Functional Data Level (GODL) %	GOFE/FEDM

Table 15 The Software Component's Measurable Feature (SCMF) Usage in the Other FSSM Constituents – SCFPs, SCFPCs, and SCFMs – Summary (Part 1/4)

Functional Software Size Measurement Methodology with Effort Estimation and Performance Indication (FSSM 1.0) Usage of Constituents Part 1/4				
Software Component's Measurable Features (SCMFs) Usage Summary in the other FSSM Constituents – SCFPs, SCFPCs and SCFMs				
Software's Measurable Components (SMCs) and Software Component's Measurable Features (SCMFs) List		**The FSSM Constituents where the SCMF is used: Software Component's Feature Points (SCFPs), Software Component's Feature Point Counts (SCFPCs), and Software Component's Feature Measurements (SCFMs)**		
SMCs	**SCMFs**	**SCFPs**	**SCFPCs**	**SCFMs**
'Functional Data' (CFD)	**'Data Class' (FDC)**	FPDC	FCDC	Data Class Entities (DCE)
	'Data Attribute' (FDA)	FPDA	FCDA	Data Class Attribute Entities (DAE)
	'Data Field' (FDF)	FPDF	FCDF	Data Class Field Entities (DFE)
	'Data Missing' (FDM)	FPDM	FCDM	Functional Data Missing Entities (FDME)
'Functionality Execution' (CFE)	**'Data Read' (FDR)**	FPDR	FCDR	Memory Operations (MO)
	'Data Write' (FDW)	FPDW	FCDW	
	'Memory Operations Functional Data' (FLM)	FPLM	FCLM	Memory Operations Functional Data Entities (MOFE)
	'Data Input' (FDI)	FPDI	FCDI	Input/Output Operations (IOO)
	'Data Output' (FDO)	FPDO	FCDO	
	'Input/Output Operations Functional Data' (FLI)	FPLI	FCLI	Input/Output Operations Functional Data Entities (IOFE)
	'Message Send' (FMS)	FPMS	FCMS	Message Exchange Operations (MEO)
	'Message Receive' (FMR)	FPMR	FCMR	
	'Message Exchange Operations Functional Data' (FLS)	FPLS	FCLS	Message Exchange Operations Functional Data Entities (EOFE)
	'Function Computational Operation' (FFC)	FPFC	FCFC	Computational Operations (CO)
	'Function Logical Operation' (FFL)	FPFL	FCFL	Logical Operations (LO)
	'Function Decision Execution' (FFD)	FPFD	FCFD	Decision Execution Operations (DEO)
	'Function Repeat Execution' (FFR)	FPFR	FCFR	Repeat Execution Operations (REO)
	'Function Action Execution' (FFA)	FPFA	FCFA	Action Execution Operations (AEO)

Table 15 (*Continued*)

Functional Software Size Measurement Methodology with Effort Estimation and Performance Indication (FSSM 1.0) Usage of Constituents Part 1/4				
Software Component's Measurable Features (SCMFs) Usage Summary in the other FSSM Constituents – SCFPs, SCFPCs and SCFMs				
Software's Measurable Components (SMCs) and Software Component's Measurable Features (SCMFs) List		**The FSSM Constituents where the SCMF is used: Software Component's Feature Points (SCFPs), Software Component's Feature Point Counts (SCFPCs), and Software Component's Feature Measurements (SCFMs)**		
SMCs	**SCMFs**	**SCFPs**	**SCFPCs**	**SCFMs**
	'Function Execution Flow Control' (FFO)	FPFO	FCFO	Execution Flow Control Operations (EFCO)
	'Function Error Handling' (FFE)	FPFE	FCFE	Error Handling Operations (EHO)
	'General Operations Functional Data' (FLG)	FPLG	FCLG	General Operations Functional Data (GOFE)
	'Class Method' (FCM)	FPCM	FCCM	Class Method Entities (CMDE)
	'Functionality Missing' (FFM)	FPFM	FCFM	Functionality Execution Missing Entities (FEME)
'User Interface' (CUI)	**'User Screen' (FUS)**	FPUS	FCUS	User Interface Screen Entities (UISE)
	'User Screen Field' (FUF)	FPUF	FCUF	User Interface Field Entities (UIFE)
	'User Screen Output Link' (FUO)	FPUO	FCUO	User Interface Output Link Entities (UIOE)
	'User Screen Input Link' (FUI)	FPUI	FCUI	User Interface Input Link Entities (UIIE)
	'User Screen Missing' (FUM)	FPUM	FCUM	User Interface Missing Entities (UIME)
'Message Exchange' (CME)	**'Notifying Message' (FNM)**	FPNM	FCNM	Notifying Message Entities (NME)
	'Message Field' (FMF)	FPMF	FCMF	Message Field Entities (MFE)
	'Message Missing' (FMM)	FPMM	FCMM	Message Exchange Missing Entities (MEME)

Table 16 The Software Component's Measurable Feature (SCMF) Usage in the Other FSSM Constituents – SCFMs and SCMs – Summary (Part 2/4)

Functional Software Size Measurement Methodology with Effort Estimation and Performance Indication (FSSM 1.0) Usage of Constituents Part 2/4			
Software Component's Measurable Features (SCMFs) Usage Summary in the other FSSM Constituents – SCFMs and SCMs			
Software's Measurable Components (SMCs) and Software Component's Measurable Features (SCMFs) List		**The FSSM Constituents where the SCMF is used: Software Component's Feature Measurements (SCFMs) and Software Component's Measurements (SCMs)**	
SMCs	**SCMFs**	**SCFMs**	**SCMs**
'Functional Data' (CFD)	**'Data Class' (FDC)**	Data Class Entities (DCE)	CFDM, STCM
	'Data Attribute' (FDA)	Data Class Attribute Entities (DAE)	CFDM, STCM
	'Data Field' (FDF)	Data Class Field Entities (DFE)	CFDM, STCM
	'Data Missing' (FDM)	Functional Data Missing Entities (FDME)	CRDM, STCM
'Functionality Execution' (CFE)	**'Data Read' (FDR)**	Memory Operations (MO)	FEODM, FEOM, CFEM, STCM
	'Data Write' (FDW)		
	'Memory Operations Functional Data' (FLM)	Memory Operations Functional Data Entities (MOFE)	FEDM, CFEM, STCM
	'Data Input' (FDI)	Input/Output Operations (IOO)	FEODM, FEOM, CFEM, STCM
	'Data Output' (FDO)		
	'Input/Output Operations Functional Data' (FLI)	Input/Output Operations Functional Data Entities (IOFE)	FEDM, CFEM, STCM
	'Message Send' (FMS)	Message Exchange Operations (MEO)	FEODM, FEOM, CFEM, STCM
	'Message Receive' (FMR)		
	'Message Exchange Operations Functional Data' (FLS)	Message Exchange Operations Functional Data Entities (EOFE)	FEDM, CFEM, STCM
	'Function Computational Operation' (FFC)	Computational Operations (CO)	FEODM, FEOM, CFEM, STCM
	'Function Logical Operation' (FFL)	Logical Operations (LO)	FEODM, FEOM, CFEM, STCM
	'Function Decision Execution' (FFD)	Decision Execution Operations (DEO)	FEODM, FEOM, CFEM, STCM
	'Function Repeat Execution' (FFR)	Repeat Execution Operations (REO)	FEODM, FEOM, CFEM, STCM

Table 16 (*Continued*)

Functional Software Size Measurement Methodology with Effort Estimation and Performance Indication (FSSM 1.0) Usage of Constituents Part 2/4			
Software Component's Measurable Features (SCMFs) Usage Summary in the other FSSM Constituents – SCFMs and SCMs			
Software's Measurable Components (SMCs) and Software Component's Measurable Features (SCMFs) List		**The FSSM Constituents where the SCMF is used: Software Component's Feature Measurements (SCFMs) and Software Component's Measurements (SCMs)**	
SMCs	**SCMFs**	**SCFMs**	**SCMs**
	'Function Action Execution' (FFA)	Action Execution Operations (AEO)	FEOM, CFEM, STCM
	'Function Execution Flow Control' (FFO)	Execution Flow Control Operations (EFCO)	FEODM, FEOM, CFEM, STCM
	'Function Error Handling' (FFE)	Error Handling Operations (EHO)	
	'General Operations Functional Data' (FLG)	General Operations Functional Data (GOFE)	FEDM, CFEM, STCM
	'Class Method' (FCM)	Class Method Entities (CMDE)	CMDE, FEOM, CFEM, STCM
	'Functionality Missing' (FFM)	Functionality Execution Missing Entities (FEME)	CRDM, STCM
'User Interface' (CUI)	**'User Screen' (FUS)**	User Interface Screen Entities (UISE)	CUIM, STCM
	'User Screen Field' (FUF)	User Interface Field Entities (UIFE)	CUIM, STCM
	'User Screen Output Link' (FUO)	User Interface Output Link Entities (UIOE)	CUIM, STCM
	'User Screen Input Link' (FUI)	User Interface Input Link Entities (UIIE)	CUIM, STCM
	'User Screen Missing' (FUM)	User Interface Missing Entities (UIME)	CRDM, STCM
'Message Exchange' (CME)	**'Notifying Message' (FNM)**	Notifying Message Entities (NME)	CMEM, STCM
	'Message Field' (FMF)	Message Field Entities (MFE)	CMEM, STCM
	'Message Missing' (FMM)	Message Exchange Missing Entities (MEME)	CRDM, STCM

Table 17 The Software Component's Measurable Feature (SCMF) Usage in the Other FSSM Constituents – SCFMs and SSEEs – Summary (Part 3/4)

Functional Software Size Measurement Methodology with Effort Estimation and Performance Indication (FSSM) Usage of Constituents Part 3/4			
Software Component's Measurable Features (SCMFs) Usage Summary in the other FSSM Constituents – SCFMs and SSEEs			
Software's Measurable Components (SMCs) and Software Component's Measurable Features (SCMFs) List		**The FSSM Constituents where the SCMF is used: Software Component's Feature Measurements (SCFMs) and Software Size and Effort Estimations (SSEEs)**	
SMCs	**SCMFs**	**SCFMs**	**SSEEs**
'Functional Data' (CFD)	**'Data Class' (FDC)**	Data Class Entities (DCE)	SDS, SCS, SLS, SDADE, SCE, SADCE, STE, STDE
	'Data Attribute' (FDA)	Data Class Attribute Entities (DAE)	SDS, SCS, SLS, SDADE, SCE, SADCE, STE, STDE
	'Data Field' (FDF)	Data Class Field Entities (DFE)	SDS, SCS, SLS, SDADE, SCE, SADCE, STE, STDE
	'Data Missing' (FDM)	Functional Data Missing Entities (FDME)	
'Functionality Execution' (CFE)	**'Data Read' (FDR)**	Memory Operations (MO)	SCDS, SCS, SLS, SFADE, SCE, SADCE, STE, STDE
	'Data Write' (FDW)		
	'Memory Operations Functional Data' (FLM)	Memory Operations Functional Data Entities (MOFE)	SCDS, SCS, SLS, SFADE, SCE, SADCE, STE, STDE
	'Data Input' (FDI)	Input/Output Operations (IOO)	SCDS, SCS, SLS, SFADE, SCE, SADCE, STE, STDE
	'Data Output' (FDO)		
	'Input/Output Operations Functional Data' (FLI)	Input/Output Operations Functional Data Entities (IOFE)	SCDS, SCS, SLS, SFADE, SCE, SADCE, STE, STDE
	'Message Send' (FMS)	Message Exchange Operations (MEO)	SCDS, SCS, SLS, SFADE, SCE, SADCE, STE, STDE
	'Message Receive' (FMR)		
	'Message Exchange Operations Functional Data' (FLS)	Message Exchange Operations Functional Data Entities (EOFE)	SCDS, SCS, SLS, SFADE, SCE, SADCE, STE, STDE
	'Function Computational Operation' (FFC)	Computational Operations (CO)	SCDS, SCS, SLS, SFADE, SCE, SADCE, STE, STDE
	'Function Logical Operation' (FFL)	Logical Operations (LO)	SCDS, SCS, SLS, SFADE, SCE, SADCE, STE, STDE
	'Function Decision Execution' (FFD)	Decision Execution Operations (DEO)	SCDS, SCS, SLS, SFADE, SCE, SADCE, STE, STDE

Table 17 (*Continued*)

Functional Software Size Measurement Methodology with Effort Estimation and Performance Indication (FSSM) Usage of Constituents Part 3/4			
Software Component's Measurable Features (SCMFs) Usage Summary in the other FSSM Constituents – SCFMs and SSEEs			
Software's Measurable Components (SMCs) and Software Component's Measurable Features (SCMFs) List		**The FSSM Constituents where the SCMF is used: Software Component's Feature Measurements (SCFMs) and Software Size and Effort Estimations (SSEEs)**	
SMCs	**SCMFs**	**SCFMs**	**SSEEs**
	'Function Repeat Execution' (FFR)	Repeat Execution Operations (REO)	SCDS, SCS, SLS, SFADE, SCE, SADCE, STE, STDE
	'Function Action Execution' (FFA)	Action Execution Operations (AEO)	SCDS, SCS, SLS, SFADE, SCE, SADCE, STE, STDE
	'Function Execution Flow Control' (FFO)	Execution Flow Control Operations (EFCO)	SCDS, SCS, SLS, SFADE, SCE, SADCE, STE, STDE
	'Function Error Handling' (FFE)	Error Handling Opcrations (EHO)	
	'General Operations Functional Data' (FLG)	General Operations Functional Data (GOFE)	SCDS, SCS, SLS, SFADE, SCE, SADCE, STE, STDE
	'Class Method' (FCM)	Class Method Entities (CMDE)	SDS, SCDS, SCS, SLS, SFADE, SCE, SADCE, STE, STDE
	'Functionality Missing' (FFM)	Functionality Execution Missing Entities (FEME)	
'User Interface' (CUI)	**'User Screen' (FUS)**	User Interface Screen Entities (UISE)	SDS, SCS, SLS, SDADE, SCE, SADCE, STE, STDE
	'User Screen Field' (FUF)	User Interface Field Entities (UIFE)	SDS, SCS, SLS, SDADE, SCE, SADCE, STE, STDE
	'User Screen Output Link' (FUO)	User Interface Output Link Entities (UIOE)	SDS, SCS, SLS, SDADE, SCE, SADCE, STE, STDE
	'User Screen Input Link' (FUI)	User Interface Input Link Entities (UIIE)	SDS, SCS, SLS, SDADE, SCE, SADCE, STE, STDE
	'User Screen Missing' (FUM)	User Interface Missing Entities (UIME)	
'Message Exchange' (CME)	**'Notifying Message' (FNM)**	Notifying Message Entities (NME)	SDS, SCS, SLS, SDADE, SCE, SADCE, STE, STDE
	'Message Field' (FMF)	Message Field Entities (MFE)	SDS, SCS, SLS, SDADE, SCE, SADCE, STE, STDE
	'Message Missing' (FMM)	Message Exchange Missing Entities (MEME)	

Table 18 The Software Component's Measurable Feature (SCMF) Usage in the Other FSSM Constituents – SCFMs and SPQIs (SSIs and SOIs) – Summary (Part 4/4)

Functional Software Size Measurement Methodology with Effort Estimation and Performance Indication (FSSM) Usage of Constituents Part 4/4				
Software Component's Measurable Features (SCMFs) Usage Summary in the other FSSM Constituents – SCFMs and SPQIs (SSIs and SOIs)				
Software's Measurable Components (SMCs) and Software Component's Measurable Features (SCMFs) List		**The FSSM Constituents where the SCMF is used: Software Component's Feature Measurements (SCFMs) and Software Performance Quality Indicators (SPQIs) – Software Structural Indicators (SSIs)[5–7] and Software Operational Indicators (SOIs)[5–7]**		
SMCs	**SCMFs**	**SCFMs**	**SPQIs: SSIs main contribution**	**SPQIs: SOIs main contribution**
'Functional Data' (CFD)	**'Data Class' (FDC)**	Data Class Entities (DCE)	FDCS, FDCP	
	'Data Attribute' (FDA)	Data Class Attribute Entities (DAE)	FDCS, FDCP	
	'Data Field' (FDF)	Data Class Field Entities (DFE)	FDCS, FDCP	
	'Data Missing' (FDM)	Functional Data Missing Entities (FDME)	RDG	
'Functionality Execution' (CFE)	**'Data Read' (FDR)**	Memory Operations (MO)	FECS, FECP, MTP	MTL
	'Data Write' (FDW)		FECS, FECP, MTP	
	'Memory Operations Functional Data' (FLM)	Memory Operations Functional Data Entities (MOFE)	FECS, FECP, MODP	MTDL
	'Data Input' (FDI)	Input/Output Operations (IOO)	FECS, FECP, UIP	UIL
	'Data Output' (FDO)		FECS, FECP, UIP	
	'Input/Output Operations Functional Data' (FLI)	Input/Output Operations Functional Data Entities (IOFE)	FECS, FECP, IODP	UIDL
	'Message Send' (FMS)	Message Exchange Operations (MEO)	FECS, FECP, ECP	ECL
	'Message Receive' (FMR)		FECS, FECP, ECP	
	'Message Exchange Operations Functional Data' (FLS)	Message Exchange Operations Functional Data Entities (EOFE)	FECS, FECP, EODP	ECDL
	'Function Computational Operation' (FFC)	Computational Operations (CO)	FECS, FECP, COCP	COL
	'Function Logical Operation' (FFL)	Logical Operations (LO)	FECS, FECP, LOCP	LOL

Table 18 (*Continued*)

Functional Software Size Measurement Methodology with Effort Estimation and Performance Indication (FSSM) Usage of Constituents Part 4/4				
Software Component's Measurable Features (SCMFs) Usage Summary in the other FSSM Constituents – SCFMs and SPQIs (SSIs and SOIs)				
Software's Measurable Components (SMCs) and Software Component's Measurable Features (SCMFs) List		**The FSSM Constituents where the SCMF is used: Software Component's Feature Measurements (SCFMs) and Software Performance Quality Indicators (SPQIs) – Software Structural Indicators (SSIs)[5–7] and Software Operational Indicators (SOIs)[5–7]**		
SMCs	**SCMFs**	**SCFMs**	**SPQIs: SSIs main contribution**	**SPQIs: SOIs main contribution**
	'Function Decision Execution' (FFD)	Decision Execution Operations (DEO)	FECS, FECP, DECP	DEL
	'Function Repeat Execution' (FFR)	Repeat Execution Operations (REO)	FECS, FECP, RECP	REL
	'Function Action Execution' (FFA)	Action Execution Operations (AEO)	FECS, FECP, AECP	
	'Function Execution Flow Control' (FFO)	Execution Flow Control Operations (EFCO)	FECS, FECP, EFCCP	EFCL
	'Function Error Handling' (FFE)	Error Handling Operations (EHO)	ECP	EHC
	'General Operations Functional Data' (FLG)	General Operations Functional Data (GOFE)	FECS, FECP, GODP	GODL
	'Class Method' (FCM)	Class Method Entities (CMDE)	FECS, FECP	
	'Functionality Missing' (FFM)	Functionality Execution Missing Entities (FEME)	RDG	
'User Interface' (CUI)	**'User Screen' (FUS)**	User Interface Screen Entities (UISE)	UICS, UICP	
	'User Screen Field' (FUF)	User Interface Field Entities (UIFE)	UICS, UICP	
	'User Screen Output Link' (FUO)	User Interface Output Link Entities (UIOE)	UICS, UICP	
	'User Screen Input Link' (FUI)	User Interface Input Link Entities (UIIE)	UICS, UICP	
	'User Screen Missing' (FUM)	User Interface Missing Entities (UIME)	RDG	
'Message Exchange' (CME)	**'Notifying Message' (FNM)**	Notifying Message Entities (NME)	MECS, MECP	
	'Message Field' (FMF)	Message Field Entities (MFE)	MECS, MECP	
	'Message Missing' (FMM)	Message Exchange Missing Entities (MEME)	RDG	

10.2 CHAPTER SUMMARY

The following summary charts of the FSSM have been presented in this chapter:

1. Summary charts of all the constituents of the FSSM which are the
   a. Software's Measurable Components (SMCs);
   b. Software Component's Measurable Features (SCMFs);
   c. Software Component's Feature Points (SCFPs);
   d. Software Component's Feature Point Counts (SCFPCs);
   e. Software Component's Feature Measurements (SCFMs);
   f. Software Component's Measurements (SCMs);
   g. Software Size and Effort Estimations (SSEEs);
   h. Software Performance Quality Indicators (SPQIs).
2. Summary charts of the usage of the Software Component's Measurable Features (SCMFs) of the Software's Measurable Components (SMCs) in the following constituents of the FSSM:
   a. Software Component's Feature Points (SCFPs);
   b. Software Component's Feature Point Counts (SCFPCs);
   c. Software Component's Feature Measurements (SCFMs);
   d. Software Component's Measurements (SCMs);
   e. Software Size and Effort Estimations (SSEEs);
   f. Software Performance Quality Indicators (SPQIs).

Part Six

FSSM: Strengths

Chapter 11

Software Diagnostics Based on the Software Component's Feature Measurements and Software Performance Quality Indicators in the FSSM

How the Software Component's Feature Measurements (SCFMs) and Software Performance Quality Indicators (SPQIs) can be used as a help to diagnose the software and functional requirements is described in this chapter. The cases presented are for general help and should be used as general guidelines only because there may be some exceptions to the described cases in some particular software applications, so the diagnostics should not be very rigorously adhered to in those cases of exceptions.

11.1 BASIC DIAGNOSTICS ABOUT THE FUNCTIONAL REQUIREMENTS SPECIFICATIONS (FRS) AND SOFTWARE, BASED ON THE SOFTWARE COMPONENT'S FEATURE MEASUREMENTS (SCFMs)

A few basic diagnostic techniques to find out the condition and status of the Functional Requirements Specifications (FRS) and characteristics of the resulting software based on the FRS are presented next.

11.1.1 Software Component's Feature Measurements (SCFMs) Relationships; Cases, Criteria, Normal Conditions, Inferences, Cautions, and Exceptions

Some specific relationships amongst the Software Component's Feature Measurements (SCFMs) and resulting inferences consequent to these relationships are described here.

Functional Software Size Measurement Methodology with Effort Estimation and Performance Indication, First Edition. Jasveer Singh.

Companion website: http://booksupport.wiley.com

11.1.1.1 Relationship of the Data Class Entities (DCE) and Class Method Entities (CMDE)

11.1.1.1.1 Case: Data Classes Without Class Methods

11.1.1.1.1.1 Criteria DCE > 0 and (CMDE = 0 or CMDE < DCE).

11.1.1.1.1.2 Normal Conditions DCE should be > 0 and CMDE should be ≥DCE.

11.1.1.1.1.3 Inference for the Criteria The FRS may be incomplete or there may be an error in counting because there are classes but no methods are specified for all the classes.

11.1.1.1.1.4 Caution If DCE > 0 and CMDE ≥ DCE: Verify if all the defined data classes have their class methods defined. If not, there may be some classes for which the class methods need to be defined.

11.1.1.1.1.5 Exceptions In some applications, some classes may not have any methods. In that case, those classes should be deducted from the DCE while applying the criteria of Section 11.1.1.1.1.1.

11.1.1.2 Relationships of the Message Exchange Operations (MEO) and Notifying Message Entities (NME)

11.1.1.2.1 Case: Messages for External Communication Used but not Defined

11.1.1.2.1.1 Criteria MEO > 0 and NME = 0.

11.1.1.2.1.2 Normal Conditions If MEO > 0, then NME should be > 0.

11.1.1.2.1.3 Inference for the Criteria There are message send and/or receive operations in the functionality description in the FRS but the messages are not defined in the message part of the FRS. Hence, the FRS may be incomplete or there may be an error in counting.

11.1.1.2.1.4 Caution It should be verified that there are defined messages for all the message send/receive operations, and all the defined messages are used for message send/receive operations. If this is not the case, the FRS are not coherent. The FRS thus need to be corrected.

11.1.1.2.2 Case: Messages for External Communication Defined but not Used

11.1.1.2.2.1 Criteria (MEO > 0 and NME > 0) and NME > MEO.

11.1.1.2.2.2 Normal Conditions If MEO > 0 and NME > 0, then MEO should be ≥ NME.

11.1.1.2.2.3 Inference for the Criteria Messages are defined in the message part of the FRS, but they are not used for send/receive operations in the functionality description in the FRS. Hence, the FRS may be incomplete or there may be an error in counting.

11.1.1.2.2.4 Caution It should be verified that there are defined messages for all the message send/receive operations, and all the defined messages are used for message send/receive operations. If this is not the case, the FRS are not coherent. The FRS thus need to be corrected.

11.1.1.3 Relationships of the Input/Output Operations (IOO) and User Interface Screen Entities(UISE)

11.1.1.3.1 Case: User Screens for Input/Output Devices Used but not Defined

11.1.1.3.1.1 Criteria IOO > 0 and UISE = 0.

11.1.1.3.1.2 Normal Conditions If IOO > 0, then UISE should be > 0.

11.1.1.3.1.3 Inference for the Criteria There are data output and/or data input operations in the functionality description in the FRS but the user screens are not defined in the User Interface part of the FRS. Hence, the FRS may be incomplete or there may be an error in counting.

11.1.1.3.1.4 Caution It should be verified that there are defined user screens for all the data input/output operations, and all the defined user screens are used for data input/output operations. If this is not the case, the FRS are not coherent. The FRS thus need to be corrected.

11.1.1.3.2 Case: User Screens for Input/Output Interactions Defined but not Used

11.1.1.3.2.1 Criteria (IOO > 0 and UISE > 0) and UISE > IOO.

11.1.1.3.2.2 Normal Conditions If IOO > 0 and UISE > 0, then IOO should be ≥ UISE.

11.1.1.3.2.3 Inference for the Criteria User screens are defined in the User Interface part of the FRS, but they are not used for data input/output operations in the functionality description in the FRS. Hence, the FRS may be incomplete or there may be an error in counting.

11.1.1.3.2.4 Caution It should be verified that there are defined user screens for all the data input/output operations, and all the defined user screens are used for data input/output operations. If this is not the case, the FRS are not coherent. The FRS thus need to be corrected.

11.1.1.4 Relationship of the Error Handling Operations (EHO) and Action Execution Operations (AEO)

11.1.1.4.1 Case: Error Handling Missing or Insufficient

11.1.1.4.1.1 Criteria EHO = 0 or much less than AEO.

11.1.1.4.1.2 Normal Conditions EHO should be > 0 and AEO should be around 10–15% of AEO or more.

11.1.1.4.1.3 Inference for the Criteria Error handling operations are not properly specified in the FRS. They are either totally absent or very less in number. In both the cases, the software may run erroneously and errors may not be detected.

11.1.1.4.1.4 Caution The FRS should be improved with respect to taking into consideration the error handling operations and defining them suitably.

11.1.1.5 Status of the Functional Data Missing Entities (FDME), Functionality Execution Missing Entities (FEME), User Interface Missing Entities (UIME), and Message Exchange Missing Entities (MEME)

11.1.1.5.1 Case: Missing Features in the Functional Data, Functionality Execution, User Interface, and Message Exchange Parts of the FRS

11.1.1.5.1.1 Criteria Values of one or more of the FDME, FEME, UIME, or MEME are large (ideally they should all be zero).

11.1.1.5.1.2 Normal Conditions Values of the FDME, FEME, UIME, and MEME each should be either zero or as less as possible.

11.1.1.5.1.3 Inference for the Criteria The FRS may be incoherent and incomplete because there are many missing functional requirement descriptions for the Functional Data, Functionality Execution, User Interface, or Message Exchange component(s). That means, proper attention has not been paid from the point of view of coherence of the different parts of the FRS – Logical Data Model, Functionality Execution, User Interface, and Message Exchange. There are some details of either data, functionality, user screens, or messages in one or more parts of the FRS but the corresponding required details in the other parts of the FRS are not defined.

11.1.1.5.1.4 Caution The FRS should be improved with respect to the coherence of details in all the parts – Logical Data Model, Functionality Execution, User Interface, and Message Exchange – of the FRS. Also, the completeness of all the parts should be reviewed and improved.

11.1.1.6 Relationship of the Memory Operations Functional Data Entities (MOFE) and Memory Operations (MO)

11.1.1.6.1 Case: Functional Data Handling Incorrect in the Memory Operations

11.1.1.6.1.1 Criteria MOFE < MO or MOFE > MO.

11.1.1.6.1.2 Normal Conditions The MOFE should be equal to MO because each data read and data write operation reads and writes, respectively, one Data Collection each and so handles one Data Collection each.

11.1.1.6.1.3 Inference for the Criteria The FRS may be incomplete or there may be an error in counting because each data read and data write operation should handle one Data Collection each for reading and writing, respectively.

11.1.1.6.1.4 Caution It should be verified that all the data read and data write operations should handle one Data Collection each for reading and writing, respectively.

11.1.1.7 Relationship of the Input/Output Operations Functional Data Entities (IOFE) and Input/Output Operations (IOO)

11.1.1.7.1 Case: Functional Data Handling Incorrect in the Input/Output Operations

11.1.1.7.1.1 Criteria IOFE < IOO.

11.1.1.7.1.2 Normal Conditions The IOFE should be either equal to IOO or greater than IOO because each data input and data output operation receives and sends, respectively, one or more Data Collections each and so handles one or more Data Collections each.

11.1.1.7.1.3 Inference for the Criteria The FRS may be incomplete or there may be an error in counting because each data input and each data output operation should handle one or more Data Collections each for receiving and sending, respectively.

11.1.1.7.1.4 Caution It should be verified that all the data input and data output operations should handle one or more Data Collections each for receiving and sending, respectively.

11.1.1.8 Relationship of the Message Exchange Operations Functional Data Entities (EOFE) and Message Exchange Operations (MEO)

11.1.1.8.1 Case: Functional Data Handling Incorrect in the Message Send/Receive Operations

11.1.1.8.1.1 Criteria EOFE < MEO.

11.1.1.8.1.2 Normal Conditions The EOFE should be either equal to MEO or greater than MEO because each message send and receive operation handles one or more Data Collections each.

11.1.1.8.1.3 Inference for the Criteria The FRS may be incomplete or there may be an error in counting because each message send and receive operation should handle one or more Data Collections each.

11.1.1.8.1.4 Caution It should be verified that all the message send and receive operations should handle one or more Data Collections each.

11.1.1.9 Relationship of the Action Execution Operations (AEO), Memory Operations (MO), Input/Output Operations (IOO), Message Exchange Operations (MEO), Computational Operations (CO), Logical Operations (LO), Decision Execution Operations (DEO), Repeat Execution Operations (REO), and Execution Flow Control Operations (EFCO)

11.1.1.9.1 Case: More Actions Performed than the Described Operations

11.1.1.9.1.1 Criteria AEO > (MO + IOO + MEO + CO + LO + DEO + REO + EFCO).

11.1.1.9.1.2 Normal Conditions The AEO should be equal to or less than (MO + IOO + MEO + CO + LO + DEO + REO + EFCO) because the actions are either one operation or group of operations and so, the total number of actions cannot be more than the total number of operations (data read/write, data input/output, message send/receive, computational, logical, decision, repeat, and execution flow control).

11.1.1.9.1.3 Inference for the Criteria There may be an error in counting or the FRS may be incomplete because some actions are described without proper description of suitable operations (data read/write, data input/output, message send/receive, computational, logical, decision, repeat, and execution flow control) involved in them.

11.1.1.9.1.4 Caution It should be verified that action executions are counted properly and there are suitable operations (data read/write, data input/output, message send/receive, computational, logical, decision, repeat, and execution flow control) described for the actions. Regarding the counting of actions, if the actions are counted for a group of operations, all the individual operations in that group of operations should not be counted as actions, so avoiding double counting of the same operations as two actions (see Sections 4.1.3.5 and 6.3.4).

11.2 ADVANCED DIAGNOSTICS ABOUT THE SYSTEM ARCHITECTURE, FUNCTIONAL REQUIREMENTS SPECIFICATIONS (FRS), AND SOFTWARE, BASED ON THE SOFTWARE PERFORMANCE QUALITY INDICATORS (SPQIs)

Some more techniques to find out the condition and status of the Functional Requirements Specifications (FRS), the characteristics of the resulting software based on the FRS, and system architecture-oriented characteristics are presented next.

11.2.1 Software Performance Quality Indicators (SPQIs) Status: Cases, Criteria, and Inferences

11.2.1.1 Status of the SPQI-SSI Functional Data Complexity and Size (FDCS)

11.2.1.1.1 Case: High Functional Data Contents

11.2.1.1.1.1 Criteria The value of FDCS is High or Very High.

11.2.1.1.1.2 Inference for the Criteria Proper attention should be given for defining the software architecture regarding whether Data Base systems may be required to handle the data because there is big amount of data to be managed in the FRS. Also, database expertise may be required for designing the database systems.

11.2.1.2 Status of the SPQI-SSI Error Handling Proportion (EHP)

11.2.1.2.1 Case: Low Error Handling Contents

11.2.1.2.1.1 Criteria The value of EHP is Nil or Low.

11.2.1.2.1.2 Inference for the Criteria Error handling operations should be improved; otherwise, there is a risk of erroneous operation of software without the errors being detected, reported, and/or handled.

11.2.1.3 Status of the SPQI-SOI Memory Traffic Level (MTL)

11.2.1.3.1 Case: High Memory Traffic

11.2.1.3.1.1 Criteria The value of MTL is High or Very High.

11.2.1.3.1.2 Inference for the Criteria Memory (disk) reading and writing should be fast, and proper attention should be given to this aspect in the system architecture; otherwise, the software may run slow.

11.2.1.4 Status of the SPQI-SOI User Interaction Level (UIL)

11.2.1.4.1 Case: High User Interaction

11.2.1.4.1.1 Criteria The value of UIL is High or Very High.

11.2.1.4.1.2 Inference for the Criteria Input/output processing operations for the data from/to the input/output devices should be fast, and proper attention should be given to this aspect in the system architecture; otherwise, the software may run slow.

11.2.1.5 Status of the SPQI-SOI Computational Operations Level (COL)

11.2.1.5.1 Case: High Computational Operations

11.2.1.5.1.1 Criteria The value of COL is High or Very High.

11.2.1.5.1.2 Inference for the Criteria Proper attention should be given to the speed of processor(s) in the system hardware architecture; otherwise, the software may run slow.

11.2.1.6 Status of the SPQI-SOI Error Handling Capability (EHC)

11.2.1.6.1 Case: Low Error Handling Level

11.2.1.6.1.1 Criteria The value of EHC is Nil or Low.

11.2.1.6.1.2 Inference for the Criteria Error handling operations should be improved; otherwise, there is a risk of erroneous operation of software without the errors being detected, reported and/or handled.

11.3 CHAPTER SUMMARY

The importance of the Software Component's Feature Measurements (SCFMs) and Software Performance Quality Indicators (SPQIs) is demonstrated in the diagnostics of software. A few cases describe how the values of the SCFMs and SPQIs can help understand the status of the Functional Requirements Specifications (FRS) from the point of view of improvements needed in them, as well as the software architectural aspects from the point of view of attention needed for designing the software/hardware.

The relationships and status of the following SCFMs are considered:

- DCE and CMDE;
- MEO and NME;
- IOO and UISE;
- EHO and AEO;
- FDME, FEME, UIME, and MEME;
- MOFE and MO;
- IOFE and IOO;
- EOFE and MEO;
- AEO, MO, IOO, MEO, CO, LO, DEO, REO, and ECFO.

The status of the following SPQIs are considered:

- FDCS;
- EHP;
- MTL;
- UIL;
- COL;
- EHC.

Chapter 12

Convertibility and ISO/IEC Standards Compliance of the FSSM

12.1 CONVERTIBILITY OF THE FSSM TO OTHER FUNCTIONAL SIZE MEASUREMENT (FSM) METHODOLOGY COSMIC

The FSSM is fully convertible to the COSMIC[3] methodology with the consequence that if the results of the FSSM are converted to become the results of the COSMIC[3] methodology, all the advantages of the FSSM over the COSMIC[3] methodology as described in Chapter 13 are lost. The conversion process is described next in this chapter.

12.1.1 Equivalent Measurements of COSMIC in the FSSM

In the FSSM, 31 Software Component's Measurable Features (SCMFs) of the 4 Software's Measurable Components (SMCs) are measured. Out of these 31 SCMFs, there are 4 SCMFs the measurement of which are equivalent to the 4 measurements performed in the COSMIC[3] methodology. Table 19 shows these 4 measurements of the COSMIC[3] methodology and their equivalent SCMFs, SCFMs, and SCFPCs in the FSSM.

12.1.2 Conversion of the FSSM to COSMIC

In order to convert the counts of the FSSM to the counts of COSMIC[3], the following Software Component's Feature Point Counts (SCFPCs) need to be taken from the FSSM:

1. Software Component's Feature Point Count for 'Data Input' (FCDI);
2. Software Component's Feature Point Count for 'Data Output' (FCDO);
3. Software Component's Feature Point Count for 'Data Read' (FCDR);
4. Software Component's Feature Point Count for 'Data Write' (FCDW);

and they need to be substituted for the following corresponding counts of COSMIC[3], respectively:

1. Entry[3];
2. Exit[3];

Functional Software Size Measurement Methodology with Effort Estimation and Performance Indication, First Edition. Jasveer Singh.

Companion website: http://booksupport.wiley.com

Table 19 Equivalent Measurements of the COSMIC Methodology in the FSSM

<table>
<tr><th colspan="4">COSMIC[3] Measurements and their equivalent FSSM SCMFs, SCFMs and SCFPCs</th></tr>
<tr><th>COSMIC measurements</th><th>Equivalent FSSM Software Component's Measurable Features (SCMFs)</th><th>The FSSM Software Component's Feature Measurements (SCFMs)</th><th>The FSSM Software Component's Feature Point Counts (SCFPCs)</th></tr>
<tr><td>Entry[3]</td><td>Software Component's Measurable Feature 'Data Input' (FDI)</td><td rowspan="2">IOO</td><td>FCDI</td></tr>
<tr><td>Exit[3]</td><td>Software Component's Measurable Feature 'Data Output' (FDO)</td><td>FCDO</td></tr>
<tr><td>Read[3]</td><td>Software Component's Measurable Feature 'Data Read' (FDR)</td><td rowspan="2">MO</td><td>FCDR</td></tr>
<tr><td>Write[3]</td><td>Software Component's Measurable Feature 'Data Write' (FDW)</td><td>FCDW</td></tr>
</table>

3. Read[3];
4. Write[3].

Thus, the following needs to be done to convert the FSSM counts to the COSMIC[3] counts:

1. Entry[3] = FCDI;
2. Exit[3] = FCDO;
3. Read[3] = FCDR;
4. Write[3] = FCDW.

Then, the addition of the aforementioned counts will give the equivalent result of COSMIC in COSMIC Function Points (CFP)[3]:
COSMIC CFP[3] = FCDI + FCDO + FCDR + FCDW.

12.2 ISO/IEC STANDARDS COMPLIANCE OF THE FSSM

The FSSM is fully compliant with the ISO/IEC 14143-1[1] standards. The compliance details are presented next.

12.2.1 ISO/IEC 14143-1 Compliance Details

Table 20 shows the details and explanations of the full compliance of the FSSM with the ISO/IEC 14143-1[1] standards. This table is adapted from the "ISO/IEC 14143-2:2011(E), B.2.3 Part 3 – Cross-reference between provisions of ISO/IEC 14143-1:2007 and evaluation questions"[2].

Table 20 ISO/IEC 14143-1 compliance table for the FSSM. Adapted from ISO/IEC 14143-2:2011(E), B.2.3 Part 3 – Cross-reference between provisions of ISO/IEC 14143-1:2007 and evaluation questions. Reproduced with permission of NBN.

The FSSM Compliance with the ISO/IEC 14143-1[1] Details					
Sl. No.	**ISO/IEC 14143-1:2007[1]**		**Compliance Requirement Description**	**Compliance**	**Compliance Explanation about the FSSM**
	Section	**Provision**			
1.	5.1.1 FSM[1] Method Characteristics	5.1.1.1 (a)	Use of Functional User Requirements (FUR)[1]	Fully compliant	In the FSSM, it is mandatory to use the Functional User Requirements (FUR)[1] which are usually called the Functional Requirements Specifications (FRS). The FRS describing the **a.** Logical Data Model (LDM); **b.** Functionality Execution (FE); **c.** User Interfaces (UI); **d.** Message Exchanges (ME); from the user point of view are used to get all the measurement information about the 4 Software's Measurable Components (SMCs), that is, BFCs[1]. The SMCs are the **a.** CFD (Software's Measurable Component 'Functional Data'); **b.** CFE (Software's Measurable Component 'Functionality Execution'); **c.** CUI (Software's Measurable Component 'User Interface'); **d.** CME (Software's Measurable Component 'Message Exchange'); in the FSSM (see Chapters 1–4).
		5.1.1.1 (b)	Use of Functional User Requirements (FUR)[1] as soon as they are defined and available	Fully compliant	Functional User Requirements (FUR)[1], that is, the Functional Requirements Specifications (FRS), can be used in the FSSM for assessment as soon as they are defined and available (see Section 2.1.2).

(*continued*)

Table 20 (*Continued*)

The FSSM Compliance with the ISO/IEC 14143-1[1] Details					
Sl. No.	**ISO/IEC 14143-1:2007[1]**		**Compliance Requirement Description**	**Compliance**	**Compliance Explanation about the FSSM**
	Section	**Provision**			
		5.1.1.1 (c)	Functional Size[1] derived through the assessment of Base Functional Components (BFCs)[1]	Fully compliant	There are 4 Base Functional Components (BFCs)[1] in the FSSM that are called the Software's Measurable Components (SMCs). They are the **a.** CFD (Software's Measurable Component 'Functional Data'); **b.** CFE (Software's Measurable Component 'Functionality Execution'); **c.** CUI (Software's Measurable Component 'User Interface'); **d.** CME (Software's Measurable Component 'Message Exchange'). The functional size is fully derived through the assessment of these 4 SMCs, that is, the BFCs[1] (see Chapters 3 and 7).
		5.1.1.2	Independence of the measurement method from particular software development methods or technologies	Fully compliant	The FSSM is fully independent of any particular software development method or technology (see Section 2.1.5).
2.	5.1.2 Base Functional Component[1] Characteristics	5.1.2 (a)	BFC[1] expresses only Functional User Requirements (FUR)	Fully compliant	BFCs[1], that is, all the 4 SMCs (Software's Measurable Components) of the FSSM express only the Functional User Requirements (FUR)[1], that is, the Functional Requirements Specifications (FRS) (see Chapter 3).
		5.1.2 (b)	BFC[1] classified as one, and only one BFC Type[1]	Fully compliant	Each of the BFCs[1], that is, the SMCs (Software's Measurable Components) in the FSSM is distinct BFC[1] and all the BFC Types[1] which are called the Software Component's Measurable Features (SCMFs) in the FSSM are distinct BFC Types[1]. Each SMC can be classified as one, and only one BFC Type[1] (see Chapters 3 and 4).

3.	5.1.3 Functional Size[1] Characteristics	5.1.3 (a)	Functional Size[1] not derived from the effort required to develop the software	Fully compliant	Functional Size[1] is derived from the Functional User Requirements (FUR)[1], that is, the Functional Requirements Specifications (FRS), in the FSSM, not from the effort required to develop the software (see Chapters 3–7).
		5.1.3 (b)	Functional Size[1] not derived from the effort required to support the software	Fully compliant	Functional Size[1] is derived from the Functional User Requirements (FUR)[1], that is, the Functional Requirements Specifications (FRS), in the FSSM, not from the effort required to support the software (see Chapters 3–7).
		5.1.3 (c)	Functional Size[1] independent of the methods used to develop the software	Fully compliant	Functional Size[1] is derived from the Functional User Requirements (FUR)[1], that is, the Functional Requirements Specifications (FRS), in the FSSM and is independent of the methods used to develop the software (see Chapters 3–7).
		5.1.3 (d)	Functional Size[1] independent of the methods used to support the software	Fully compliant	Functional Size[1] is derived from the Functional User Requirements (FUR)[1], that is, the Functional Requirements Specifications (FRS), in the FSSM and is independent of the methods used to support the software (see Chapters 3–7).
		5.1.3 (e)	Functional Size[1] independent of the physical components of the software	Fully compliant	Functional Size[1] is derived from the Functional User Requirements (FUR)[1], that is, the Functional Requirements Specifications (FRS), in the FSSM and is independent of the physical components of the software (see Chapters 3–7).
		5.1.3 (f)	Functional Size[1] independent of the technological components of the software	Fully compliant	Functional Size[1] is derived from the Functional User Requirements (FUR)[1], that is, the Functional Requirements Specifications (FRS), in the FSSM and is independent of the technological components of the software (see Chapters 3–7).

(*continued*)

Table 20 (*Continued*)

The FSSM Compliance with the ISO/IEC 14143-1[1] Details					
Sl. No.	**ISO/IEC 14143-1:2007[1]**		**Compliance Requirement Description**	**Compliance**	**Compliance Explanation about the FSSM**
	Section	Provision			
4.	5.2.1 FSM[1] Method Requirements	5.2.1.1 (a)	Attributes of the BFCs[1]	Fully compliant	There are 4 BFCs[1] which are defined as the SMCs (Software's Measurable Components) in the FSSM. Each SMC has definite attributes which are defined as the Software Component's Measurable Features (SCMFs) which are the BFC Types[1]. Thus, the • SMC CFD (Software's Measurable Component 'Functional Data') has 4 SCMFs; • SMC CFE (Software's Measurable Component 'Functionality Execution') has 19 SCMFs; • SMC CUI (Software's Measurable Component 'User Interface') has 5 SCMFs; • SMC CME (Software's Measurable Component 'Message Exchange') has 3 SCMFs; (see Chapters 3 and 4).
		5.2.1.1 (b)	Rules used to assess the BFCs[1]	Fully compliant	All the rules to assess the BFCs[1], that is, the SMCs, in the FSSM are described in the book (see Chapters 3–7).
		5.2.1.1 (c)	Units of Functional Size[2]	Fully compliant	Unit of the Functional Size[2] is defined as the Software Component's Feature Point (SCFP), that is, the Functional Size Unit (FSU), in the FSSM (see Chapters 5–7).
		5.2.1.1 (d)	Functional Domain[1]	Fully compliant	The type of applications for which the FSSM is applicable is described in the book (see Section 2.1.3).
		5.2.1.2 (a)	Information necessary	Fully compliant	The kind of information necessary to use the FSSM is described in the book (see Section 2.1.3, its sub-sections, and Chapter 3).
		5.2.1.2 (b)	Guidelines for documentation	Fully compliant	The procedure for the use of the FSSM and documentation is described in the book (see Chapter 14).
		5.2.1.2 (c)	Purposes of use	Fully compliant	The purpose of the use of the FSSM is described in the book (see Sections "Prelude", "About the Book", and 2.1.1).
		5.2.1.2 (d)	Convertibility to other sizing methods	Fully compliant	The FSSM is fully convertible to the COSMIC[3] methodology, it is described in the book (see Sections 2.1.9 and 12.1).

5.	5.2.2 Base Functional Component[1] assessment requirements	5.2.2 (a)	BFC Types[1] Definition	Fully compliant	All the BFC Types[1], that is, the SCMFs (Software Component's Measurable Features), in the FSSM are fully defined and described in the book (see Chapter 4).
		5.2.2 (b)	Functional User Requirements (FUR)[1] identification	Fully compliant	Which Functional User Requirements (FUR)[1], that is, the Functional Requirements Specifications (FRS), are required to be used in the FSSM is described in the book (see Chapters 3 and 4).
		5.2.2 (c)	BFCs[1] identification	Fully compliant	The BFCs[1], that is, the SMCs (Software's Measurable Components), identification in the FSSM from the Functional User Requirements (FUR)[1], that is, the Functional Requirements Specifications (FRS), is described in the book (see Chapters 3 and 4).
		5.2.2 (d)	BFCs[1] classification into BFC Types[1]	Fully compliant	The BFCs[1], that is, the SMCs (Software's Measurable Components), classification into the BFC Types[1], that is, the SCMFs (Software Component's Measurable Features), in the FSSM is described in the book (see Chapters 3 and 4).
		5.2.2 (e)	BFC Type[1] numeric value	Fully compliant	The procedure to assign numeric value to the BFC Type[1], that is, the SCMFs (Software Component's Measurable Features), is described in the book (see Chapters 5, 6, and 14).
		5.2.2 (f)	BFC Type[1] and boundary[1] relationship	Fully compliant	The BFC Type[1], that is, the SCMFs (Software Component's Measurable Features), and boundary[1], that is, the borderline, relationship is described in the book (see Section 2.1.4 and Chapters 3–5).
		5.2.2 (g)	BFC Type[1] inter-relationships	Fully compliant	The BFC Type[1], that is, the SCMFs (Software Component's Measurable Features), inter-relationship is described in the book (see Chapters 3 and 4).
6.	5.2.3 Designation of Functional Size[1]	5.2.3 (a)	Units	Fully compliant	Functional Size Unit (FSU) in the FSSM is the Software Component's Feature Point (SCFP) (see Sections 1.4, 2.3, and Chapter 5).
		5.2.3 (b)	Name	Fully compliant	The name of the methodology is FSSM (see Section 2.1.10). The current version number is 1.0. Hence the current full name is FSSM 1.0.
		5.2.3 (c)	Local customization	Fully compliant	Local customization is with suffix cx, where x = 1, 2, 3, etc. (see Section 2.1.10).

(continued)

Table 20 (*Continued*)

The FSSM Compliance with the ISO/IEC 14143-1[1] Details					
Sl. No.	**ISO/IEC 14143-1:2007[1]**		**Compliance Requirement Description**	**Compliance**	**Compliance Explanation about the FSSM**
	Section	Provision			
7.	6. Process for applying an FSM[1] Method	6 (a)	Activity scope determination	Fully compliant	Scope is determined in the FSSM before starting the measurement (see Sections 2.1.4, 2.3, and 5.1).
		6 (b)	Activity functional user requirements[1] identification	Fully compliant	Functional user requirements[1] are identified in the FSSM in the Logical Data Model, Functionality Execution, User Interface, and Message Exchange parts of the Functional Requirements Specifications (FRS) (see Chapters 3–5).
		6 (c)	Activity BFCs[1] identification	Fully compliant	The BFCs[1], that is, the SMCs (Software's Measurable Components) are identified in the FSSM in the 4 parts of the Functional Requirements Specifications – Logical Data Model, Functionality Execution, User Interface, and Message Exchange (see Chapters 3–5).
		6 (d)	Activity BFC Types[1] classification	Fully compliant	Classification of the BFC Types[1] is the activity of identifying the Software Component's Measurable Features (SCMFs) in the FSSM (see Chapters 3–5).
		6 (e)	Activity assigning functional size units	Fully compliant	Assigning functional size unit activity in the FSSM is done by assigning the Software Component's Feature Point (SCFP), that is, Functional Size Unit (FSU), to the Software Component's Measurable Features (SCMFs) (see Chapters 5 and 6).
		6 (f)	Activity calculating functional size[1]	Fully compliant	Functional size[1] is calculated in the FSSM by measuring the size of the Software Component's Measurable Features (SCMFs) to obtain the Software Component's Feature Measurements (SCFMs), and then the Software Component's Measurements (SCMs) are obtained through the SCFMs, and finally the total software functional size is obtained from the SCMs (see Chapters 5–7).
8.	7. FSM[1] Method Labelling Conventions	7 (a)	Name	Fully compliant	The name of the methodology is FSSM (see Section 2.1.10). The current version number is 1.0. Hence the current full name is FSSM 1.0.
		7 (b)	Version number	Fully compliant	The current version number is 1.0 (see Section 2.1.10). Hence the current full name is FSSM 1.0.

12.3 CHAPTER SUMMARY

12.3.1 Convertibility of the FSSM to Other Functional Size Measurement (FSM) Methodology COSMIC: Summary

The FSSM counts can be converted to COSMIC[3] counts by substituting the values of the Software Component's Feature Point Count for 'Data Input' (FCDI), Software Component's Feature Point Count for 'Data Output' (FCDO), Software Component's Feature Point Count for 'Data Read' (FCDR), and Software Component's Feature Point Count for 'Data Write' (FCDW) of the FSSM for Entry[3], Exit[3], Read[3], and Write[3] counts of COSMIC[3], respectively. Then, addition of these counts will give the equivalent COSMIC[3] result in CFPs (COSMIC Function Points)[3].

12.3.2 ISO/IEC Standards Compliance of the FSSM: Summary

The FSSM is fully compliant with the ISO/IEC 14143-1[1] standards. All the requirements of the ISO/IEC 14143-1[1] standards which are the

1. FSM[1] Method Characteristics;
2. Base Functional Component[1] Characteristics;
3. Functional Size[1] Characteristics;
4. FSM[1] Method Requirements;
5. Base Functional Component[1] assessment requirement;
6. Designation of Functional Size[1];
7. Process for applying an FSM[1] Method;
8. FSM[1] Method Labelling Conventions;

as listed in the table "B.2.3 Part 3 – cross-reference between provisions of ISO/IEC 14143-1:2007 and evaluation questions"[2] of the ISO/IEC 14143-2:2011 (E)[2], are fully supported by FSSM for full compliance with the standards. All the compliance details and explanations are provided in this chapter.

Chapter 13

Significant Strengths of the FSSM

The FSSM possesses some significant strengths – capabilities and advantages – which are worth considering in favor of its usage. Capabilities of the FSSM in comparison to some of the popular methodologies and advantages of the FSSM over those methodologies are described next.

13.1 COVERAGE CAPABILITIES OF THE FSSM IN COMPARISON WITH SOME EXISTING SOFTWARE SIZE MEASUREMENT METHODOLOGIES

13.1.1 Measurement Coverage Introduction

It is clear from the description in the earlier chapters that there are 4 Software's Measurable Components (SMCs) that have 31 Software Component's Measurable Features (SCMFs), and they all are important for a complete and comprehensive software measurement and are measured in the FSSM.

The 4 Software's Measurable Components (SMCs) derived from the 4 description parts – the Logical Data Model (LDM), the Functionality Execution (FE), the User Interface (UI), and the Message Exchange (ME) – of the Functional Requirements Specifications (FRS) are the following:

1. Software's Measurable Component 'Functional Data' (CFD);
2. Software's Measurable Component 'Functionality Execution' (CFE);
3. Software's Measurable Component 'User Interface' (CUI);
4. Software's Measurable Component 'Message Exchange' (CME).

There are the following 31 respective Software Component's Measurable Features (SCMFs) for the aforementioned 4 SCMs:

1. 4 Software Component's Measurable Features (SCMFs) for the Software's Measurable Component 'Functional Data' (CFD):
   a. Software Component's Measurable Feature 'Data Class' (FDC);
   b. Software Component's Measurable Feature 'Data Attribute' (FDA);
   c. Software Component's Measurable Feature 'Data Field' (FDF);
   d. Software Component's Measurable Feature 'Data Missing' (FDM);

Functional Software Size Measurement Methodology with Effort Estimation and Performance Indication, First Edition. Jasveer Singh.

Companion website: http://booksupport.wiley.com

2. 19 Software Component's Measurable Features (SCMFs) for the Software's Measurable Component 'Functionality Execution' (CFE):
   a. Software Component's Measurable Feature 'Data Read' (FDR);
   b. Software Component's Measurable Feature 'Data Write' (FDW);
   c. Software Component's Measurable Feature 'Memory Operations Functional Data' (FLM);
   d. Software Component's Measurable Feature 'Data Input' (FDI);
   e. Software Component's Measurable Feature 'Data Output' (FDO);
   f. Software Component's Measurable Feature 'Input/Output Operations Functional Data' (FLI);
   g. Software Component's Measurable Feature 'Message Send' (FMS);
   h. Software Component's Measurable Feature 'Message Receive' (FMR);
   i. Software Component's Measurable Feature 'Message Exchange Operations Functional Data' (FLS);
   j. Software Component's Measurable Feature 'Function Computational Operation' (FFC);
   k. Software Component's Measurable Feature 'Function Logical Operation' (FFL);
   l. Software Component's Measurable Feature 'Function Decision Execution' (FFD);
   m. Software Component's Measurable Feature 'Function Repeat Execution' (FFR);
   n. Software Component's Measurable Feature 'Function Action Execution' (FFA);
   o. Software Component's Measurable Feature 'Function Execution Flow Control' (FFO);
   p. Software Component's Measurable Feature 'Function Error Handling' (FFE);
   q. Software Component's Measurable Feature 'General Operations Functional Data' (FLG);
   r. Software Component's Measurable Feature 'Class Method' (FCM);
   s. Software Component's Measurable Feature 'Functionality Missing' (FFM);
3. 5 Software Component's Measurable Features (SCMFs) for the Software's Measurable Component 'User Interface' (CUI):
   a. Software Component's Measurable Feature 'User Screen' (FUS);
   b. Software Component's Measurable Feature 'User Screen Field' (FUF);
   c. Software Component's Measurable Feature 'User Screen Output Link' (FUO);
   d. Software Component's Measurable Feature 'User Screen Input Link' (FUI);
   e. Software Component's Measurable Feature 'User Screen Missing' (FUM);
4. 3 Software Component's Measurable Features (SCMFs) for the Software's Measurable Component 'Message Exchange' (CME):
   a. Software Component's Measurable Feature 'Notifying Message' (FNM);
   b. Software Component's Measurable Feature 'Message Field' (FMF);
   c. Software Component's Measurable Feature 'Message Missing' (FMM).

All the aforementioned 31 SCMFs of the 4 SCMs are measured in the FSSM.

We will now see which components and which of their features are covered by some of the existing, popular software measurement methodologies in order to understand the strengths and main capabilities of the FSSM regarding software size measurement. In the brief description of the two methodologies, COSMIC (Common Software Measurement International Consortium)[3] and IFPUG (The International Function Point Users Group)[4], that follows, the presentation viewpoint is based on the basic measurement reference structure of the FSSM to see what is measured in these two methodologies with respect to the FSSM.

13.1.2 The FSSM Coverage in Comparison with the Existing Software Size Measurement Methodologies Coverage

13.1.2.1 The FSSM Coverage in Comparison with the COSMIC (Common Software Measurement International Consortium) Coverage

In the COSMIC[3] methodology, Functional User Requirements (FUR)[1] are analyzed and CFPs (COSMIC Function Points)[3] are assigned to the following 4 types of data movement operations in the FUR:

1. Entry[3]: This is the data movement from outside into the software.
2. Exit[3]: This is the data movement from the software to the outside world.
3. Read[3]: This is the data movement from the persistent storage (e.g., disk storage) to the software.
4. Write[3]: This is the data movement from the software to the persistent storage (e.g., disk storage).

These 4 data movements are equivalent to the 4 SCMFs (Software Component's Measurable Features) of the component CFE (Software's Measurable Component 'Functionality Execution') in the FSSM. These 4 SCMFs, respectively, are the

1. Software Component's Measurable Feature 'Data Input' (FDI);
2. Software Component's Measurable Feature 'Data Output' (FDO);
3. Software Component's Measurable Feature 'Data Read' (FDR);
4. Software Component's Measurable Feature 'Data Write' (FDW).

Hence, we can see that in comparison to the FSSM where 31 SCMFs of the 4 SMCs – 4 SCMFs of the CFD (Software's Measurable Component 'Functional Data'), 19 SCMFs of the CFE (Software's Measurable Component 'Functionality Execution'), 5 SCMFs of the CUI (Software's Measurable Component 'User Interface'), and 3 SCMFs of the CME (Software's Measurable Component 'Message Exchange') – are taken into consideration for measurement, only the equivalent 4 SCMFs of 1 SCM, that is, the CFE (Software's Measurable Component 'Functionality Execution') are measured in the COSMIC[3] methodology. Thus the size obtained with the COSMIC[3] methodology is only of the 4 SCMFs, and as these 4 SCMFs do not have any fixed size proportion relationship with the other remaining 27 SCMFs in various applications, the size of the complete software cannot be determined and known accurately and reliably because the remaining size of the 27 SCMFs is not measured at all. The size obtained by the FSSM covering the 31 SCMFs is comprehensive and complete in comparison to the COSMIC[3] methodology.

Table 21 shows the 31 SCMFs (Software Component's Measurable Features) of the 4 SMCs (Software's Measurable Components) which the FSSM takes into consideration for

Table 21 The Software's Measurable Components (SMCs) and Software Component's Measurable Features (SCMF) Coverage Capability Comparison of the FSSM, COSMIC, and IFPUG

Software's Measurable Components (SMCs) and Software Component's Measurable Features (SCMFs) Covered in the FSSM, COSMIC[3], and IFPUG[4]				
Software's Measurable Component (SMC)	**Software Component's Measurable Feature (SCMF)**	**FSSM Coverage**	**COSMIC[3] Coverage**	**IFPUG[4] Coverage**
1. Software's Measurable Component 'Functional Data' (CFD)	a. 'Data Class' (FDC)	✓		
	b. 'Data Attribute' (FDA)	✓		✓
	c. 'Data Field' (FDF)	✓		✓
	d. 'Data Missing' (FDM)	✓		
2. Software's Measurable Component 'Functionality Execution' (CFE)	a. 'Data Read' (FDR)	✓	✓	
	b. 'Data Write' (FDW)	✓	✓	
	c. 'Memory Operations Functional Data' (FLM)	✓		
	d. 'Data Input' (FDI)	✓	✓	✓
	e. 'Data Output' (FDO)	✓	✓	✓
	f. 'Input/Output Operations Functional Data' (FLI)	✓		
	g. 'Message Send' (FMS)	✓		✓
	h. 'Message Receive' (FMR)	✓		
	i. 'Message Exchange Operations Functional Data' (FLS)	✓		
	j. 'Function Computational Operation' (FFC)	✓		
	k. 'Function Logical Operation' (FFL)	✓		
	l. 'Function Decision Execution' (FFD)	✓		
	m. 'Function Repeat Execution' (FFR)	✓		
	n. 'Function Action Execution' (FFA)	✓		
	o. 'Function Execution Flow Control' (FFO)	✓		
	p. 'Function Error Handling' (FFE)	✓		
	q. 'General Operations Functional Data' (FLG)	✓		
	r. 'Class Method' (FCM)	✓		
	s. 'Functionality Missing' (FFM)	✓		
3. Software's Measurable Component 'User Interface' (CUI)	a. 'User Screen (FUS)	✓		
	b. 'User Screen Field' (FUF)	✓		
	c. 'User Screen Output Link' (FUO)	✓		
	d. 'User Screen Input Link' (FUI)	✓		
	e. 'User Screen Missing' (FUM)	✓		
4. Software's Measurable Component 'Message Exchange' (CME)	a. 'Notifying Message' (FNM)	✓		
	b. 'Message Field' (FMF)	✓		
	c. 'Message Missing' (FMM)	✓		

the software size measurement as compared to the 4 SCMFs of 1 SMC for the COSMIC[3] methodology.

13.1.2.2 The FSSM Coverage in Comparison with the IFPUG (The International Function Point Users Group) Coverage

In the IFPUG[4] methodology, Functional User Requirements (FUR)[1] are analyzed, and first, unadjusted FPs (Functions Points)[4] are calculated by assigning the Function Points (FPs)[4] to the following 5 types of data and transaction functions types according to a set of complex rules in association with the characteristics of the data involved:

1. Internal Logical File (ILF)[4];
2. External Interface File (EIF)[4];
3. External Input (EI)[4];
4. External Output (EO)[4];
5. External Inquiry (EQ)[4].

These 5 data and transaction function types are roughly equivalent to the following 5 SCMFs (Software Component's Measurable Features) of the components CFD (Software's Measurable Component 'Functional Data') and CFE (Software's Measurable Component 'Functionality Execution') in the FSSM:

1. SCMFs of the Software's Measurable Component 'Functional Data' (CFD):
   a. Software Component's Measurable Feature 'Data Attribute' (FDA);
   b. Software Component's Measurable Feature 'Data Field' (FDF);
2. SCMFs of the Software's Measurable Component 'Functionality Execution' (CFE):
   a. Software Component's Measurable Feature 'Data Input' (FDI);
   b. Software Component's Measurable Feature 'Data Output' (FDO);
   c. Software Component's Measurable Feature 'Message Send' (FMS).

Afterwards, based on adjustment multiplication factors, the FPs[4] are adjusted.

Hence, we can see that in comparison to the FSSM where 31 SCMFs of the 4 SMCs – 4 SCMFs of the CFD (Software's Measurable Component 'Functional Data'), 19 SCMFs of the CFE (Software's Measurable Component 'Functionality Execution'), 5 SCMFs of the CUI (Software's Measurable Component 'User Interface'), and 3 SCMFs of the CME (Software's Measurable Component 'Message Exchange') – are taken into consideration for measurement, only the equivalent 5 SCMFs of the 2 SMCs, that is, the CFD (Software's Measurable Component 'Functional Data') and CFE (Software's Measurable Component 'Functionality Execution') are measured in the IFPUG[4] methodology. Thus the size obtained with the IFPUG[4] methodology is based on only 5 SCMFs, and as these 5 SCMFs do not have any fixed size proportion relationship with the other remaining 26 SCMFs, the size of the complete software cannot be determined and known because the remaining size of 26 SCMFs is not measured at all. The size obtained by the FSSM covering the 31 SCMFs is comprehensive and complete in comparison to the IFPUG[4] methodology.

Table 21 shows the 31 SCMFs (Software Component's Measurable Features) of the 4 SMCs (Software's Measurable Component) which the FSSM takes into consideration for the software size measurement as compared to the 5 SCMFs of the 2 SMCs for the IFPUG[4].

13.2 ADVANTAGES OF THE FSSM OVER THE CURRENTLY AVAILABLE METHODOLOGIES

The FSSM is simple, very elaborate, and is applied in a straightforward manner.

Some of the existing software size measurement methodologies such as COSMIC and IFPUG are indeed widely used; however, the FSSM unlike COSMIC and IFPUG pays more attention to many more essential aspects of the software constituents to ensure that a comprehensive and complete software measurement result is obtained.

13.2.1 Conspicuous, Significant Advantages over the Existing Methodologies

The FSSM has significant advantages over the existing methodologies. Some of the major, conspicuous advantages, which are due to the special characteristics of the FSSM are mentioned next.

1. It is simple, elaborate, and applied in a straightforward manner;
2. It covers all the major, important, and relevant constituents/components – data, functionality, user interfaces/screens, and message exchanges – of the software;
3. It measures all the relevant and important features of all the software components – data, functionality, user interfaces/screens, and message communication; hence it is quite elaborate and does a measurement of the totality of the software;

   The features covered for the size measurement are

   a. for the data – the class structures;
   b. for the functionality:
      i. the following operations: memory read/write, input/output, message communication, computational, logical, decision, repeat, action, execution flow, and error handling;
      ii. the data handled during the following operations: memory read/write, input/output, message communication, computational, logical, decision, repeat, and execution flow;
      iii. the class methods;
   c. for the user interfaces – the screen structures;
   d. for the message communication – the message structures;
4. It is possible to judge about the complexity and size of all the components of the software, that is, the Functional Data, Functionality Execution, User Interface, and Message Exchange. It is done by the Software Component's Feature Measurements (SCFMs) and Software Component's Measurements (SCMs) about the size of the 4 software components and total software:
   a. size and complexity of data with respect to the amount of classes, class attributes, and fields of the attributes. This helps to assess the enormity of the effort needed for the data related development work;
   b. size and complexity of the User Interface with respect to the enormity of the screens, their layout in terms of fields, and their input/output links from/to the other screens/operations. This helps to assess the enormity of the effort needed for the user interface related development work;

c. size and complexity of the Message Exchange with respect to the quantity of messages and enormity of their fields. This helps to assess the enormity of the effort needed for the message exchange related development work;

d. code complexity and its size regarding the following functionality execution operations:

  i. memory data read/write used for reading/writing from/to the memory devices;
  ii. data input/output used for receiving/sending the input/output data from/to the input/output devices;
  iii. message exchange used for sending/receiving the messages to/from the other programs;
  iv. computational for mathematical calculations;
  v. logical for AND, OR type of logical functions;
  vi. decision actions;
  vii. repeat actions;
  viii. actions performed;
  ix. execution flow control actions;
  x. error handling actions;

as well as regarding the functional data handling magnitude of the following operations:

  i. memory data read/write;
  ii. data input/output;
  iii. message exchange;
  iv. computational;
  v. logical;
  vi. decision;
  vii. repeat;
  viii. execution flow control;

and regarding the

  i. class methods;

This helps to assess the enormity of the effort needed for the functionality related development work;

5. Based on the knowledge of the complexity and size of the components obtained from the results, it is possible to see where more attention needs to be paid in the design, both in the software and hardware aspects. For example, regarding software: whether data design needs more attention and/or code design; regarding hardware: whether the computational part needs more attention and/or the input/output operations processing part;

6. It provides a realistic software development effort estimation and thus, there is no need to use any assumptive multiplication factors according to the past statistics of efforts spent on the projects in different domains of applications categorized according to the types and complexity of the applications. It is done by the Software Size and Effort Estimations (SSEEs) which provide the following estimations:

a. software logical size in number of logical statements;
b. software analysis, design, and coding effort;
c. software testing effort;
d. software total development effort;

7. It provides software performance quality indicators for software's static structure analysis and for software's dynamic run-time characteristics determination and understanding. It is done by the Software Performance Quality Indicators (SPQIs) of two types – Software Structural Indicators (SSIs)[5–7] and Software Operational Indicators (SOIs)[5–7]:
   a. software structure indication regarding the sizes and content proportion of the
      i. Functional Data;
      ii. Functionality Execution;
      iii. User Interface;
      iv. Message Exchange for communication with other programs;

      and regarding the content proportion of the
      i. memory transactions and their functional data handling;
      ii. user interactions and their functional data handling;
      iii. external message communications and their functional data handling;
      iv. computational operations;
      v. logical operations;
      vi. decision operations;
      vii. repeat operations;
      viii. execution flow control operations;
      ix. actions performed operations;
      x. functional data handling of the computational, logical, decision, repeat, and execution flow control operations;
      xi. error handling operations;
      xii. requirements deficiencies;
   b. dynamic characteristics of the software regarding the dynamic run-time levels of the
      i. memory transactions and their functional data handling;
      ii. user interactions and their functional data handling;
      iii. external message communications and their functional data handling;
      iv. computational operations;
      v. logical operations;
      vi. decision operations;
      vii. repeat operations;
      viii. execution flow control operations;
      ix. functional data handling of the computational, logical, decision, repeat, and execution flow control operations;
      x. error handling operations;
8. It is possible to see if the Functional Requirements Specifications are deficient and have missing items with respect to the Functional Data; Functionality Execution and its data handling; user interfaces/screens; and message communication. It is done by the Software Component's Measurements (SCMs) and Software Performance Quality Indicators (SPQIs);
9. The status of the error handling part can be judged. It is done by the Software Performance Quality Indicators (SPQIs);
10. No complex procedures for counting are required. Rules for counting are simple;
11. Software diagnostic is possible based on the Software Component's Feature Measurements (SCFMs) and Software Component's Measurements (SCMs);

12. Automation to obtain the results from the Software Component's Feature Point Counts (SCFPCs) can be done very easily;
13. It is fully ISO/IEC 14143-1[1] compliant;
14. It is convertible to the COSMIC[3] methodology.

13.2.2 Specific Advantages over Specific Methodologies

Some specific advantages over the COSMIC and IFPUG methodologies are mentioned next.

13.2.2.1 Specific Advantages over COSMIC (Common Software Measurement International Consortium)

In the COSMIC[3] methodology, only the following 4 Software Component's Measurable Feature (SCMFs) of 1 Software's Measurable Component (SMC) – Software's Measurable Component 'Functionality Execution' (CFE) – are considered for measurement out of the 31 SCMFs of the 4 SMCs used in the FSSM:

1. Software Component's Measurable Feature 'Data Read' (FDR);
2. Software Component's Measurable Feature 'Data Write' (FDW);
3. Software Component's Measurable Feature 'Data Input' (FDI);
4. Software Component's Measurable Feature 'Data Output' (FDO).

Hence, based on these 4 measurements in the COSMIC[3] methodology, only the size of the

a. data read[3] and write[3] operations used for reading/writing the data from/to the memory devices;
b. data entry[3] and exit[3] operations used for receiving/sending the input/output data to/from the input/output devices;

can be determined.

Since this part of the software – data read[3]/write[3] operations and data entry[3]/exit[3] operations – has no fixed proportion relationship with the other remaining parts of the software – remaining Functionality Execution complexity and size composed of the operations which are of the type computational, logical, decision operations, repeat, execution flow control, error handling, and message exchange; data complexity and size; user interface complexity and size; message communication complexity and size – it means that with the available measurements from the COSMIC[3] methodology, the following essential aspects of the software cannot be determined while their determination is done by the FSSM:

1. Size and complexity of data with respect to the amount of classes, class attributes, and fields of the attributes:
   It is not possible by the COSMIC[3] methodology to determine whether major effort may be needed for data analysis and design in the software development, but it is possible to judge this in the FSSM by the Software Component's Feature Measurements (SCFMs), Software Component's Measurements (SCMs), and Software Performance Quality Indicators (SPQIs).

2. Size and complexity of the user interfaces with respect to the enormity of the screens, their layout in terms of fields, and their input/output links from/to the other screens/operations:
   This aspect is determined by the Software Component's Feature Measurements (SCFMs), Software Component's Measurements (SCMs), and Software Performance Quality Indicators (SPQIs) in the FSSM.
3. Size and complexity of the message exchanges with respect to the quantity of messages and enormity of their fields:
   This aspect is determined by the Software Component's Feature Measurements (SCFMs), Software Component's Measurements (SCMs), and Software Performance Quality Indicators (SPQIs) in the FSSM.
4. Indication of the code complexity and its size regarding the other functionality execution operations which are not covered by the COSMIC[3] methodology:
   They are the following type of operations:
   a. computational;
   b. logical;
   c. decision;
   d. repeat;
   e. actions performed;
   f. execution flow control;
   g. error handling;
   h. message exchange.
   This indication is provided by the Software Component's Feature Measurements (SCFMs), Software Component's Measurements (SCMs), and Software Performance Quality Indicators (SPQIs) in the FSSM.
5. Indication of the functional data handling magnitude in the functionality execution operations:
   They are the data handled during the following operations:
   a. memory read/write;
   b. input/output;
   c. message exchange;
   d. computational;
   e. logical;
   f. decision;
   g. repeat;
   h. execution flow control.
   This indication is provided by the Software Component's Feature Measurements (SCFMs), Software Component's Measurements (SCMs), and Software Performance Quality Indicators (SPQIs) in the FSSM.
6. Indication of the enormity of the class methods:
   This indication is provided by the Software Component's Feature Measurements (SCFMs) in the FSSM.
7. Software development effort estimation:
   This estimation with the following information
   a. software logical size in number of logical statements;
   b. software analysis, design, and coding effort;
   c. software testing effort;
   d. software total development effort;
   is obtained by the Software Size and Effort Estimations (SSEEs) in the FSSM.

8. Deficiency items in the requirements, to be used to improve the Functional Requirements Specifications (FRS):
   This is obtained by the Software Component's Measurements (SCMs) in the FSSM regarding the missing items in the Functional Data; Functionality Execution and its data handling; user interfaces/screens; and message communication.
9. Static software structure indication:
   This indication is regarding the sizes and content proportion of the
   a. Functional Data;
   b. Functionality Execution;
   c. user interfaces/screens;
   d. messages for communication with other programs;
   and regarding the content proportion of the
   a. memory transactions and their functional data handling;
   b. user interactions and their functional data handling;
   c. external message communications and their functional data handling;
   d. computational operations;
   e. logical operations;
   f. decision operations;
   g. repeat operations;
   h. actions performed operations;
   i. execution flow control operations;
   j. functional data handling of the computational, logical, decision, repeat, and execution flow control operations;
   k. error handling operations;
   l. requirements deficiencies.
   This is done by the Software Structural Indicators (SSIs)[5–7] in the FSSM.
10. Indication of the dynamic characteristics of the software:
   This indication is regarding the dynamic run-time levels of the
   a. memory transactions and their functional data handling;
   b. user interactions and their functional data handling;
   c. external message communications and their functional data handling;
   d. computational operations;
   e. logical operations;
   f. decision operations;
   g. repeat operations;
   h. execution flow control operations;
   i. functional data handling of the computational, logical, decision, repeat, and execution flow control operations;
   j. error handling operations.
   This is done in the FSSM by the Software Operational Indicators (SOIs)[5–7].

All the aforementioned aspects are not possible to be determined in the COSMIC[3] methodology (see also two relevant examples mentioned in Section 1.3, list item number 7).

13.2.2.2 Specific Advantages over IFPUG (the International Function Point Users Group)

In the IFPUG[4] methodology, a very complex way of counting is performed based on multiple types of decisions which need to be taken for counting. Basically, rough equivalent of only 5 Software Component's Measurable Feature (SCMFs) of the 2 Software's Measurable Components (SMCs) – Software's Measurable Component 'Functional Data' (CFD) and 'Functionality Execution' (CFE) – are considered for measurement in the IFPUG[4] methodology out of the 31 SCMFs of the 4 SMCs used in the FSSM. The equivalent SCMFs of the FSSM which are used in the IFPUG[4] methodology are the following:

1. Software Component's Measurable Feature 'Data Input' (FDI);
2. Software Component's Measurable Feature 'Data Output' (FDO);
3. Software Component's Measurable Feature 'Message Send' (FMS);
4. Software Component's Measurable Feature 'Data Attribute' (FDA);
5. Software Component's Measurable Feature 'Data Field' (FDF).

Hence, based on these 5 measurements in the IFPUG, only the size of the

a. data input and output operations used for receiving/sending the input/output data to/from the input/output devices;
b. message communication of message send operations used for sending the messages to the other programs;
c. limited amount of data size and complexity;

can be determined.

Since this part of the software – data input/output operations, message send operations, data attribute, and data fields – has no fixed proportion relationship with the other remaining parts of the software – remaining Functionality Execution complexity and size composed of the operations which are of the type computational, logical, decision, repeat, execution flow control, error handling, message receive, data read/write; complete data complexity and size; user interface complexity and size; message complexity and size – it means that with the available measurements from the IFPUG[4] methodology, the following essential aspects of the software cannot be determined by this methodology while their determination is done by the FSSM:

1. Size and complexity of data with respect to the amount of classes, class attributes, and fields of the attributes. So, it is not possible to determine whether major effort may be needed for data analysis and design in the software development.
2. Size and complexity of the user interfaces with respect to the enormity of the screens, their layout in terms of fields, and their input/output links from/to the other screens/operations.
3. Size and complexity of the message exchanges with respect to the quantity of messages and enormity of their fields.
4. Indication of the code complexity and its size regarding the other functionality execution operations which are not covered by the IFPUG methodology; they are the following types of operations:
   a. computational;
   b. logical;
   c. decision;
   d. repeat;
   e. actions performed;
   f. execution flow control
   g. error handling;

   h. message receive;
   i. memory read/write.
5. Indication of the functional data handling magnitude of the following operations:
   a. computational;
   b. logical;
   c. decision;
   d. repeat;
   e. execution flow control;
   f. input/output;
   g. message send/receive;
   h. memory read/write.
6. Indication of the enormity of the class methods.
7. Software development effort estimation with the following information:
   a. software logical size in number of logical statements;
   b. software analysis, design and coding effort;
   c. software testing effort;
   d. software total development effort.
8. Deficiency items in the requirements, to be used to improve the Functional Requirements Specifications (FRS), regarding the missing items in the Functional Data; Functionality Execution and its data handling; user interfaces/screens; and message communication.
9. Static software structure indication regarding the sizes and content proportion of the
   a. Functional Data;
   b. Functionality Execution;
   c. user interfaces/screens;
   d. messages for communication with other programs;
   and regarding the content proportion of the
   a. memory transactions and their functional data handling;
   b. user interactions and their functional data handling;
   c. external message communications and their functional data handling;
   d. computational operations;
   e. logical operations;
   f. decision operations;
   g. repeat operations;
   h. actions performed operations;
   i. execution flow control operations;
   j. functional data handling of the computational, logical, decision, repeat, and execution flow control operations;
   k. error handling operations;
   l. requirements deficiencies.
10. Indication of the dynamic characteristics of the software regarding the dynamic runtime levels of the
   a. memory transactions and their functional data handling;
   b. user interactions and their functional data handling;
   c. external message communications and their functional data handling;
   d. computational operations;
   e. logical operations;

f. decision operations;
g. repeat operations;
h. execution flow control operations;
i. functional data handling of the computational, logical, decision, repeat, and execution flow control operations;
j. error handling operations.

All the aforementioned aspects are determined by the SCFMs, SCMs, SSEEs, and SPQIs – SSIs and SOIs – in the FSSM, but their determination in the IFPUG[4] methodology is not possible to be done.

13.3 EXAMPLES

1. The results from the FSSM clearly state the sizes of different components, so it is possible to judge the extents of effort which will be required for the development of different parts of the software. The results from the other methodologies, for example, COSMIC[3] do not reveal these facts. This will become clear by considering the following cases:

   A. In COSMIC[3], if the data size is big, that is, there are many classes with many attributes and fields of the attributes; and there are low number of data read/write operations for each of the data entity, it has the same output result as in the case of small data size, that is, very less number of classes with small number of attributes and fields of the attributes; and high number of data read/write operations for each of the data entity. Consider the following:

   If an application has 20 data classes (or entities) with their average 5 attributes each and average 4 fields each of every attribute; and there are 2 memory read/write operations in the functionality for each data class, there are 40 memory read/write operations. In this case, the COSMIC[3] count for these data movements (Read[3] and Write[3]) will be 40. In another application, if there are 2 data classes with their average 2 attributes and 1 field each of every attribute; and there are 20 memory read/write operations in the functionality for each data class, there are 40 memory read/write operations. In this case, the COSMIC[3] count for the data movements (Read[3] and Write[3]) is also 40.

   Now, the data size and complexity in the first case is much more than in the second case because the number of total data items to be handled in the software are 20 (classes) × (1 (class) + 5 (attributes) + (5 (attributes) × 4 (fields))) = 20 × (1 + 5 + (5 × 4)) = 20 × 26 = 520 in the first case, and 2 (classes) × (1 (class) + 2 (attributes) + (2 (attributes) × 1 (field))) = 2 × (1 + 2 + (2 × 1)) = 2 × 5 = 10 in the second case.

   So, the effort required for data design in the first case will be much more than in the second case, but the COSMIC[3] count in both the cases is the same because the size and complexity of data are not taken into account in COSMIC[3].

   It shows that the size of data and its complexity can be many times more in one application than another resulting in much more design effort in one application than the other but if the number of data read and write operations in both is the same, the COSMIC[3] count will be the same because there is no differentiation due to the size and complexity of the data.

Moreover, this is only a tiny part of the software; the other parts and their features which are all considered in the FSSM are not considered in COSMIC[3] and in other methodologies.

B. In COSMIC[3], if the screen component size is big, that is, there are many screens with many input/output fields and many input/output navigational links; and there are low number of data input/output operations for receiving/sending the input/output data from/to the input/output devices for each of the screen, it has the same output result as in the case of small screen component size, that is, very less number of screens with small number of input/output fields and small number of input/output navigational links; and high number of data input/output operations for receiving/sending the input/output data from/to the input/output devices for each of the screen. Consider the following:

If an application has 20 user screens with their average 5 input and output fields each and average 4 input and output links each; and there are 2 data input/output operations for each screen, there are 40 data input/output operations. In this case, the COSMIC[3] count for these data movements (Entry[3] and Exit[3]) will be 40. In another application, if there are 2 user screens with their average 2 input and output fields each and 1 input and output link each; and there are 20 data input/output operations for each screen, there are 40 data input/output operations. In this case, the COSMIC[3] count for the data movements (Entry[3] and Exit[3]) is also 40.

Now, the screens size and complexity in the first case is much more than the second case, because the number of total screen items to be handled in the software are 20 (screens) × (1 (screen) + 5 (input fields) + 5 (output fields) + 4 (input links) + 4 (output links)) $= 20 \times (1 + 5 + 5 + 4 + 4) = 20 \times 19 = 380$ in the first case, and 2 (screens) × (1 (screen) + 2 (input fields) + 2 (output fields) + 1 (input link) + 1 (output link)) $= 2 \times (1 + 2 + 2 + 1 + 1) = 2 \times 7 = 14$ in the second case.

So, the effort required for the design related with the screens structures in the first case will be much more than the second case, but the COSMIC[3] count in both the cases is the same because the size and complexity of user interface component are not taken into account in COSMIC[3].

It shows that the number of screens and their complexity can be many times more in one application than another resulting in much more design effort in one application than the other but if the number of entries and exits in both is the same, the COSMIC[3] count will be the same because there is no differentiation due to the size and complexity of the screens.

Moreover, this is only a tiny part of the software; the other parts and their features which are all considered in the FSSM are not considered in COSMIC[3] and in other methodologies.

In the FSSM, the output results of the measurements of the components, that is, the Software Component's Measurements (SCMs), and Software Performance Quality Indicators (SPQIs) clearly reveal all the facts. Also, the effort estimations from the Software Size and Effort Estimations (SSEEs) are quite accurate.

As COSMIC[3] and other methodologies consider only a subset of the total software constituents for counting, the size obtained by these counts is only a subset of the size. Hence, the estimations do not take into account the complete size, only partial size is considered in these methodologies.

In this respect, the FSSM considers the complete software, all the constituents, and all the features of all the constituents of the software; hence, it offers an excellent approach of software size measurement.

13.4 CHAPTER SUMMARY

In comparison to the FSSM where 31 SCMFs (Software Component's Measurable Features) of the 4 SMCs (Software's Measurable Components) – 4 SCMFs of the CFD (Software's Measurable Component 'Functional Data'), 19 SCMFs of the CFE (Software's Measurable Component 'Functionality Execution'), 5 SCMFs of the CUI (Software's Measurable Component 'User Interface'), and 3 SCMFs of the CME (Software's Measurable Component 'Message Exchange') – are taken into consideration for measurement:

a. only equivalent 4 SCMFs (Software Component's Measurable Features) of 1 SMC (Software's Measurable Component), that is, the CFE (Software's Measurable Component 'Functionality Execution') are measured in the COSMIC[3] methodology;

b. only equivalent 5 SCMFs (Software Component's Measurable Features) of the 2 SMCs (Software's Measurable Components), that is, the CFD (Software's Measurable Component 'Functional Data'), and CFE (Software's Measurable Component 'Functionality Execution') are measured in the IFPUG[4] methodology.

Hence, the FSSM provides more elaborate, comprehensive, and complete measurement in comparison to the COSMIC[3] and IFPUG[4] methodologies, and is, therefore, more reliable and accurate.

Additionally, the FSSM provides the 6 Software Component's Measurements (SCMs) of the 4 Software's Measurable Component's (SMCs) through 28 Software Component's Feature Measurements (SCFMs) for judging the size and complexity of the software components; 4 Software Size and Effort Estimations (SSEEs) for the software development effort estimation; and 36 Software Performance Quality Indicators for assessing the performance of the software by 2 types of indicators – the Software Structural Indicators (SSIs)[5–7] for software static structure and Software Operational Indicators (SOIs)[5–7] for the software dynamic characteristics.

From the FSSM, the following results are obtained which no other existing methodology provides.

1. Size and complexity of data with respect to the amount of classes, class attributes, and fields of the attributes. This helps to assess the enormity of the effort needed for the data related development work.
2. Size and complexity of the user interfaces with respect to the enormity of the screens, their layout in terms of fields, and their input/output links from/to the other screens/operations. This helps to assess the enormity of the effort needed for the User Interface related development work.
3. Size and complexity of the message exchanges with respect to the quantity of messages and enormity of their fields. This helps to assess the enormity of the effort needed for the Message Exchange related development work.
4. Code complexity and its size regarding the following type of functionality execution operations:

a. memory data read/write used for reading/writing data from/to the memory devices;
b. data input/output used for receiving/sending the input/output data from/to the input/output devices;
c. message exchange used for sending/receiving the messages to the other programs;
d. computational;
e. logical;
f. decision;
g. repeat;
h. actions performed;
i. execution flow control;
j. error handling;

as well as regarding the functional data handling magnitude of the following operations:

a. memory read/write;
b. input/output;
c. message exchange;
d. computational;
e. logical;
f. decision;
g. repeat;
h. execution flow control;

and regarding the

a. class methods.

This helps to assess the enormity of the effort needed for the functionality related development work.

5. Deficiency items in the requirements, to be used to improve the Functional Requirements Specifications (FRS), regarding the missing items in the Functional Data, Functionality Execution and its data handling, user interfaces/screens, and message communication.

6. Software development effort estimation in the form of the following estimations:
a. software logical size in number of logical statements;
b. software analysis, design, and coding effort;
c. software testing effort;
d. software total development effort.

7. Software static structure indication regarding the sizes and content proportion of the
a. Functional Data;
b. Functionality Execution;
c. user interfaces/screens;
d. messages for communication with other programs;

and regarding the content proportion of the

a. memory transactions and their functional data handling;
b. user interactions and their functional data handling;
c. external message communications and their functional data handling;
d. computational operations;
e. logical operations;
f. decision operations;

g. repeat operations;
h. execution flow control operations;
i. actions performed operations;
j. functional data handling of the computational, logical, decision, repeat, and execution flow control operations;
k. error handling operations;
l. requirements deficiencies.

8. Dynamic characteristics of the software regarding the dynamic run-time levels of the
a. memory transactions and their functional data handling;
b. user interactions and their functional data handling;
c. external message communications and their functional data handling;
d. computational operations;
e. logical operations;
f. decision operations;
g. repeat operations;
h. execution flow control operations;
i. functional data handling of the computational, logical, decision, repeat, and execution flow control operations;
j. error handling operations.

Part Seven

FSSM: Usage – Example

Chapter 14

Example for Using the FSSM

This chapter presents a worked-out example with its functional requirements, counting table, explanation of the counting, and output results, for demonstrating the usage and presentation of the output results of the FSSM.

14.1 MINI-FSSM APPLICATION SOFTWARE DEVELOPMENT (ASD) INTRODUCTION

The usage of the FSSM is shown with the help of an example for a software application which is similar to the FSSM itself; that means the example application is the application software development for a functional software size measurement methodology. The FSSM is applied to determine the functional size of the software, effort estimation, and performance indications for this example.

The example software application is of functional software size measurement, effort estimation, and performance indication by using a simplified, limited, and mini-version of the FSSM, called Mini-FSSM Application Software Development (ASD). The example mini-FSSM includes the details of the

1. Functional Requirement Specifications;
2. Software Component's Feature Points (SCFPs) and Software Component's Feature Point Counts (SCFPCs) to demonstrate how the SCFPs are determined to compute the SCFPCs;
3. results which are the
   a. Software Component's Feature Measurements (SCFMs);
   b. Software Component's Measurements (SCMs);
   c. Software Size and Effort Estimations (SSEEs);
   d. Software Performance Quality Indicators (SPQIs) of the types: Software Structural Indicators (SSIs)[5–7] and Software Operational Indicators (SOIs)[5–7].

All the aforementioned details are presented in descriptive, tabular, and graphical forms.

Although the Mini-FSSM example is based on the real FSSM, there may be many differences in the two for many aspects. The differences have no influence on the real FSSM in any way; they are there only in the example which is used for illustrating the use of the real FSSM.

Functional Software Size Measurement Methodology with Effort Estimation and Performance Indication, First Edition. Jasveer Singh.

Companion website: http://booksupport.wiley.com

14.2 FUNCTIONAL REQUIREMENTS SPECIFICATIONS (FRS) OF THE EXAMPLE – 'MINI-FSSM APPLICATION SOFTWARE DEVELOPMENT'

14.2.1 Brief Description of the Mini-FSSM Application Software Development (ASD)

Mini-FSSM application is a small version of the real FSSM described in this book. In the mini-FSSM application, there is a class Count which has several attributes. The attributes are taken in the application as input from a screen. These inputs are saved and various calculations are made on them, and the results are displayed. To manage this, a few screens (both input and output) are used. Concise descriptions of the functional data, functionality, and screens are presented next. Functional Requirements Specifications (FRS) are grouped under separate requirement identifiers.

14.2.2 Mini-FSSM Logical Data Model (LDM) Contents

The textual description of the class structure which is required in the example 'Mini-FSSM ASD' is presented next under the requirement identifiers LD1 through LD3.

14.2.2.1 LD1

These data come as input data from the screen. The data are saved and calculations are made using these data.

Class: Count.

Attributes: identifier, description, DC, DA, DF, CM, DR, DW, DI, DO, FC, FL, FD, FR, FA, FE, MS, MR, MN, MF, US, UF, UO, UI, remark (there are a total of 25 attributes).

Fields: each attribute has one field.

Methods: 'enter data', 'calculate and display' (there are a total of 2 methods).

14.2.2.2 LD2

These are the result data which are the outcome of the calculations made on the saved input data.

Class: Result.

Attributes: data count, memory operations, computational operations, logical operations, decision execution operations, repeat execution operations, action execution operations, input/output operations, message exchange operations, error operations, class methods, code count, user interface count, message count, total software count, program lines, design effort, test effort, and total effort (there are a total of 19 attributes).

Fields: each attribute has one field.

14.2.2.3 LD3

This is another set of result data which is the outcome of the calculations made on the saved input data.

Class: KSI (Key Software Indicator)[5–7].

Attributes: memory traffic level, computational level, logical operations level, decision execution level, repeat execution level, action execution level, user interaction level, external communication level, error handling capability, data complexity and size, code complexity and size, data operation and transaction proportion, decision content proportion, repeat content proportion, action content proportion, user interaction proportion, external communication proportion, and error handling proportion (there are a total of 18 attributes).

Fields: each attribute has one field.

14.2.3 Mini-FSSM Functionality Execution (FE) Contents

The functionality description of the example 'Mini-FSSM ASD' is presented next under the requirement identifiers FS1 through FS43.

14.2.3.1 FS1

On SCCM web site (see Section 14.2.4.1) Initial screen, click on the SCCM link. (*Note*: SCCM web site does not exist, it is a fictitious site).

14.2.3.2 FS2

On Log-on screen (see Section 14.2.4.2), type user-id and password to log on. This opens the application window where application environment screen (see Section 14.2.4.3) is shown.

14.2.3.3 FS3

User clicks on the application icon and application starts running.

14.2.3.4 FS4

Application opens a window Option screen (see Section 14.2.4.4) and asks if it is a new count estimate or continue working from an old estimate file. If user clicks on 'New', it is a new estimate, open a new window New Entry screen (see Section 14.2.4.5) for new entry data.

14.2.3.5 FS5

In New Entry screen, enter identifier (any text, maximum 20 char), description (any text, maximum 2000 char), and any of the 22 counts – DC, DA, DF, CM, DR, DW, DI, DO, FC, FL, FD, FR, FA, FE, MN, MF, MS, MR, US, UF, UO, and UI (integer only).

14.2.3.6 FS6

In the received count data, if text limit is crossed or count is not integer, display errors with the received values and get new values. Repeat until error-free values are received.

14.2.3.7 FS7

After entering the data, either click 'Save' which saves the current entry – category, identifier, description, 22 counts, and continue to display the same, or click 'Next' which saves the current entry and prompts for new inputs, or click ‘Calculate’ which saves the entry and calculates the estimate. Before saving in all the 3 cases, check the error condition in FS6.

14.2.3.8 FS8

If ‘Calculate’ is clicked, calculate, save, and display the following results – total counts, results, and KSIs (see Sections 14.2.4.6–14.2.4.8). Calculations for total counts, results, and KSIs are handled in other requirements that follow.

14.2.3.9 FS8.1

Calculate total counts: read all the stored counts from the memory and add all the 22 counts – DC, DA, DF, CM, DR, DW, DI, DO, FC, FL, FD, FR, FA, FE, MN, MF, MS, MR, US, UF, UO, and UI – respectively.

14.2.3.10 FS9

Results calculations:

Calculate Data Count = DC+DA+DF.

14.2.3.11 FS10

Code Count:

- **a.** Memory Operations = DR + DW;
- **b.** Computational Operations = FC.;
- **c.** Logical Operations = FL;
- **d.** Decision Execution Operations = FD;
- **e.** Repeat Execution Operations = FR;
- **f.** Action Execution Operations = FA;
- **g.** Input and Output Operations = DI + DO;
- **h.** Message Exchange Operations = MS + MR;
- **i.** Error Operations = FE;
- **j.** Class Methods = CM.

14.2.3.12 FS11

Calculate Total Code Count = Memory Operations + Computational Operations + Logical Operations + Decision Execution Operations + Repeat Execution Operations + Action Execution Operations + Input and Output Operations + Message Exchange Operations + Error Operations + Class Methods.

14.2.3.13 FS12

Calculate User Interface Count = US + UF + UO + UI.

14.2.3.14 FS13

Calculate Message Count = MN + MF.

14.2.3.15 FS14

Calculate Total Software Count = Data Count + Code Count + User Interface Count + Message Count.

14.2.3.16 FS15

Number of program lines: a complex function of data, code, user interface, and message counts.

14.2.3.17 FS16

Calculate Data Lines = $4 \times DC + 2 \times DA + 2 \times US + 2 \times MN + DF \times (1 + 0.1 \times CM) + UF \times (1 + 0.1 \times CM) + MF \times (1 + 0.1 \times CM)$.

14.2.3.18 FS17

Calculate Code Lines = $5 \times CM + 2 \times FD + 2 \times FR + 2 \times FA + FC + FL + FE + DR + DW + DI + DO + 10 \times US + UO + UI + 5 \times MN + MS + MR + 0.05 \times DF \times (DW + DO) + 0.05 \times UF \times UO + 0.05 \times MF \times MS$.

14.2.3.19 FS18

Calculate Comment Lines = $0.4 \times$ (code lines).

14.2.3.20 FS19

Calculate Total Program Lines = Data Lines + Code Lines + Comment Lines.

14.2.3.21 FS20

Design Effort (technical specifications documents + coding): a function of number of program lines.

14.2.3.22 FS21

Calculate Data Design = ((Data Count) / 20) person days.

14.2.3.23 FS22

Calculate Code Design = ((Total Program Lines) / 40) person days.

14.2.3.24 FS23

Calculate Design Effort = Data Design + Code Design.

14.2.3.25 FS24

Calculate Testing Effort (test specifications documents + testing): a function of design effort = 1.2 × Design Effort.

14.2.3.26 FS25

Calculate Total Effort = Design Effort + Testing Effort.

14.2.3.27 FS26

KSIs:

An indication of Low, Medium, High, and Very High is given.
Software Operational Indicators[5–7]:
Memory Traffic Level – a function of code count:

a. Low: Memory Operations / Total Code Count % 1–5;

b. Medium: Memory Operations / Total Code Count % 6–25;

c. High: Memory Operations / Total Code Count % 26–50;

d. Very High: Memory Operations / Total Code Count % 51–100.

14.2.3.28 FS27

Computational Level – a function of code count:

a. Low: Computational Operations / Total Code Count % 1–5;

b. Medium: Computational Operations / Total Code Count % 6–25;

c. High: Computational Operations / Total Code Count % 26–50;

d. Very High: Computational Operations / Total Code Count % 51–100.

14.2.3.29 FS28

Logical Operations Level – a function of code count:

a. Low: Logical Operations / Total Code Count % 1–5;

b. Medium: Logical Operations / Total Code Count % 6–25;

c. High: Logical Operations / Total Code Count % 26–50;

d. Very High: Logical Operations / Total Code Count % 51–100.

14.2.3.30 FS29

Decision Execution Level – a function of code count:

a. Low: Decision Execution Operations / Total Code Count % 1–5;

b. Medium: Decision Execution Operations / Total Code Count % 6–25;

c. High: Decision Execution Operations / Total Code Count % 26–50;

d. Very High: Decision Execution Operations / Total Code Count % 51–100.

14.2.3.31 FS30

Repeat Execution Level – a function of code count:

a. Low: Repeat Execution Operations / Total Code Count % 1–5;
b. Medium: Repeat Execution Operations / Total Code Count % 6–25;
c. High: Repeat Execution Operations / Total Code Count % 26–50;
d. Very High: Repeat Execution Operations / Total Code Count % 51–100.

14.2.3.32 FS31

Action Execution Level – a function of code count:

a. Low: Action Execution Operations / Total Code Count % 1–5;
b. Medium: Action Execution Operations / Total Code Count % 6–25;
c. High: Action Execution Operations / Total Code Count % 26–50;
d. Very High: Action Execution Operations/Total Code Count % 51–100.

14.2.3.33 FS32

User Interaction Level – a function of code count:

a. Low: Input and Output Operations / Total Code Count % 1–5;
b. Medium: Input and Output Operations / Total Code Count % 6–25;
c. High: Input and Output Operations / Total Code Count % 26–50;
d. Very High: Input and Output Operations / Total Code Count % 51–100.

14.2.3.34 FS33

External Communication Level – a function of code count:

a. Low: Message Exchange Operations / Total Code Count % 1–5;
b. Medium: Message Exchange Operations / Total Code Count % 6–25;
c. High: Message Exchange Operations / Total Code Count % 26–50;
d. Very High: Message Exchange Operations / Total Code Count % 51–100.

14.2.3.35 FS34

Error Handling Capability – a function of code count:

a. Low: Error Operations / Total Code Count % 1–5;
b. Medium: Error Operations / Total Code Count % 6–20;
c. High: Error Operations / Total Code Count % 21–40;
d. Very High: Error Operations / Total Code Count % 41–100.

14.2.3.36 FS35

Software Structural Indicators[5–7]:

Data Complexity and Size – a function of software count:

a. Low: Data Count 1–50;
b. Medium: Data Count 51–500;
c. High: Data Count 501–1000;
d. Very High: Data Count above 1000.

14.2.3.37 FS36

Code Complexity and Size – a function of software count:

a. Low: Total Code Count 1–200;
b. Medium: Total Code Count 201–1000;
c. High: Total Code Count 1001–2500;
d. Very High: Total Code Count above 2500.

14.2.3.38 FS37

Data Operation and Transaction Proportion – a function of software count:

a. Low: (Data Count + Memory Operations + Computational Operations + Logical Operations) / Total Software Count % 1–5;
b. Medium: (Data Count + Memory Operations + Computational Operations + Logical Operations) / Total Software Count % 6–20;
c. High: (Data Count + Memory Operations + Computational Operations + Logical Operations) / Total Software Count % 21–40;
d. Very High: (Data Count + Memory Operations + Computational Operations + Logical Operations) / Total Software Count % 41–100.

14.2.3.39 FS38

Decision Execution Content Proportion – a function of software count:

a. Low: Decision Execution Operations / Total Software Count % 1–5;
b. Medium: Decision Execution Operations / Total Software Count % 6–20;
c. High: Decision Execution Operations / Total Software Count % 21–40;
d. Very High: Decision Execution Operations / Total Software Count % 41–100.

14.2.3.40 FS39

Repeat Execution Content Proportion – a function of software count:

a. Low: Repeat Execution Operations / Total Software Count % 1–5;
b. Medium: Repeat Execution Operations / Total Software Count % 6–20;
c. High: Repeat Execution Operations / Total Software Count % 21–40;
d. Very High: Repeat Execution Operations / Total Software Count % 41–100.

14.2.3.41 FS40

Action Execution Content Proportion – a function of software count:

a. Low: Action Execution Operations / Total Software Count % 1–5;
b. Medium: Action Execution Operations / Total Software Count % 6–20;
c. High: Action Execution Operations / Total Software Count % 21–40;
d. Very High: Action Execution Operations / Total Software Count % 41–100.

14.2.3.42 FS41

User Interaction Proportion – a function of software count:

a. Low: (User Interface Count + Input and Output Operations) / Total Software Count % 1–5;
b. Medium: (User Interface Count + Input and Output Operations) / Total Software Count % 6–20;
c. High: (User Interface Count + Input and Output Operations) / Total Software Count % 21–40;
d. Very High: (User Interface Count + Input and Output Operations) / Total Software Count % 41–100.

14.2.3.43 FS42

External Communication Proportion – a function of software count:

a. Low: (Message Count + Message Exchange Operations) / Total Software Count % 1–5;
b. Medium: (Message Count + Message Exchange Operations) / Total Software Count % 6–20;
c. High: (Message Count + Message Exchange Operations) / Total Software Count % 21–40;
d. Very High: (Message Count + Message Exchange Operations) / Total Software Count % 41–100.

14.2.3.44 FS43

Error Handling Proportion – a function of software count:

a. Low: (Error Operations) / Total Software Count % 1–5;
b. Medium: (Error Operations) / Total Software Count % 6–20;
c. High: (Error Operations) / Total Software Count % 21–40;
d. Very High: (Error Operations) / Total Software Count % 41–100.

14.2.4 Mini-FSSM User Interface (UI) Contents

Following is the User Interface description of the example 'Mini-FSSM ASD' under the requirement identifiers UI1 through UI8. After the description, the layout of some of the screens is presented.

14.2.4.1 UI1

Initial screen: SCCM web site screen displaying SCCM summary text and SCCM link on clicking which the Log-on screen is presented. (*Note*: SCCM web site does not exist, it is a fictitious site).

14.2.4.2 UI2

Log-on screen displaying the fields user-id and password to log on. See Figure 17 for the layout of the screen.

14.2.4.3 UI3

Application environment screen displays the application icon.

14.2.4.4 UI4

Option screen to ask if "a new count estimate is required", or "continue working from an old estimate file".

14.2.4.5 UI5

New Entry screen where the following inputs can be typed:

Select category from menu items LDM, FS, UI, and ME.

Can enter identifier (any text, maximum 20 char), description (any text, maximum 2000 char), any of the 22 counts – DC, DA, DF, CM, DR, DW, DI, DO, FC, FL, FD, FR, FA, FE, MN, MF, MS, MR, US, UF, UO, UI (integer only), remark.

Output link: 'Save', 'Calculate', or 'Next.'

See Figure 18 for the layout of the screen.

14.2.4.6 UI6

Total Counts screen (part of Calculate and Display screen).

Output link: 'Exit'.

See Figure 19 for the layout of the screen.

14.2.4.7 UI7

Results screen (part of Calculate and Display screen).

Output link: 'Exit'.

See Figure 20 for the layout of the screen.

14.2.4.8 UI8

KSI screen (part of Calculate and Display screen).

Output link: 'Exit'.

See Figure 21 for the layout of the screen.

14.2.4.9 Screens Layout

14.2.4.9.1 UI2 Log-on Screen Figure 17 shows the Log-on screen layout.

14.2.4.9.2 UI5 New Entry Screen Figure 18 shows the New Entry screen layout.

14.2.4.9.3 UI6 Total Counts Screen There are 3 parts in the Calculate and Display screen: Total Counts, Results, and KSIs. Display the results in the form shown next.

Table 22 shows the information to be displayed in the Total Counts screen. In the right-most column, the numbers will be the total counts. Figure 19 shows the Total Counts screen layout.

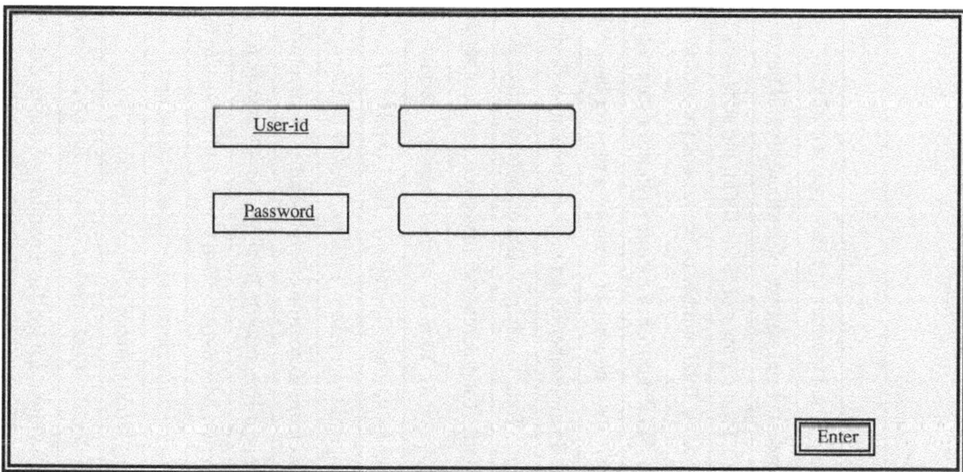

Figure 17 Example mini-FSSM Log-on screen layout.

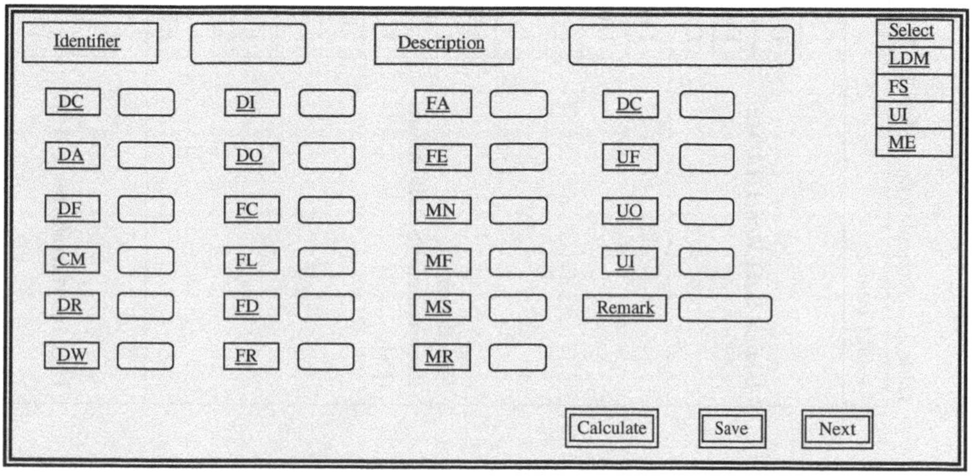

Figure 18 Example mini-FSSM New Entry screen layout.

Table 22 Example Mini-FSSM Total Counts Screen Contents

Total Counts		
Logical Data Model (LDM):	DC (Data Classes): Total number of classes (data entity)	5
	DA (Data Attributes): Total number of attributes for all the classes (data entity)	25
	DF (Data Fields): Total number of fields for all the attributes	100
	CM (Class Methods): Total number of operations (procedures) for all the classes (data entity)	20
Functional Requirements/Specifications (FS):	DR (Data Read): Total number of memory reads for data collections	50
	DW (Data Write): Total number of memory writes for data collections	50
	DI (Data Input): Total number of data inputs from input devices for data collections	60
	DO (Data Output): Total number of data outputs to output devices for data collections	60
	MS (Message Sent): Total number of messages sent to other programs	20
	MR (Message Received): Total number of messages received from other programs	15
	FC (Function Computational Operation): Total number of computational operations	50
	FL (Function Logical Operation): Total number of logical operations – AND, OR, NOT, XOR	30
	FD (Function Decision Execution): Total number of conditions checking and taking decisions	20
	FR (Function Repeat Execution): Total number of repeats for action(s)	10
	FA (Function Action Execution): Total number of actions to be performed	41
	FE (Function Error): Total number of errors to be treated	30
User Interfaces/Screens (UI):	US (User Screen): Total number of user screens	10
	UF (User Screen Field): Total number of fields for all the screens	35
	UO (User Screen Output Link): Total number of output links for all the user screens	50
	UI (User Screen Input Link): Total number of input links for all the user screens	50
Message Exchange (ME):	MN (Notifying Message): Total number of messages	10
	MF (Message Field): Total number of fields for all the messages	30

Total Counts		Exit
Logical Data Model (LDM)	DC (Data Classes): Total number of classes (data entity)	
	DA (Data Attributes): Total number of attributes for all the classes (data entity)	
	DF (Data Fields): Total number of fields for all the attributes	
	CM (Class Methods): Total number of operations (procedures) for all the classes (data entity)	
Functional Requirements/ Specifications (FS)	DR (Data Read): Total number of memory reads for data collections	
	DW (Data Write): Total number of memory writes for data collections	
	DI (Data Input): Total number of data inputs from input devices for data collections	
	DO (Data Output): Total number of data outputs to output devices for data collections	
	MS (Message Sent): Total number of messages sent to other programs	
	MR (Message Received): Total number of messages received from other programs	
	FC (Function Computational operation): Total number of computational operations	
	FL (Function Logical operation): Total number of logical operations – AND, OR, NOT, XOR	
	FD (Function Decision execution): Total number of conditions checking and taking decisions	
	FR (Function Repeat execution): Total number of repeats for action(s)	
	FA (Function Action execution): Total number of actions to be performed	
	FE (Function Error): Total number of errors to be treated	
User Interfaces/ Screens (UI)	US (User Screen): Total number of user screens	
	UF (User screen Field): Total number of fields for all the screens	
	UO (User screen Output link): Total number of output links for all the user screens	
	UI (User screen Input link): Total number of input links for all the user screens	
Message Exchange (ME)	MN (Message Number): Total number of messages	
	MF (Message Field): Total number of fields for all the messages	

Figure 19 Example mini-FSSM Total Counts screen layout.

Table 23 Example Mini-FSSM Results Screen Contents. Adapted from Software Comprehensive Count with Quality Indicators (SCCQI), Jasveer Singh, UKSMA/COSMIC Conference 2012, SMEF 2012, NESMA Autumn Meeting 2012.

Software Comprehensive Count Method (SCCM) Calculations			
Software Count:		**Effort:**	
Data Count	**130**		
Code Count			
Memory Operations	100		
Computational Operations	120		
Logical Operations	35		
Decision Execution Operations	50		
Repeat Execution Operations	30		
Action Execution Operations	20		
Input and Output Operations	10		
Message Exchange Operations	41	**Number of Program Lines**	**2739**
Error Operations	30		
Class Methods	20	**Design Effort (tech spec+coding) person days**	**75**
Total Code Count	**456**		
User Interface Count	**145**	**Testing Effort (test spec+testing) person days**	**90**
Message Count	**40**		
Total Software Count	**771**	**Total Effort (design+testing) person days**	**165**

14.2.4.9.4 UI7 Results Screen Table 23 shows the information to be displayed in the Results screen. The numbers in the table will be coming from the output of the program. Figure 20 shows the Results screen layout.

14.2.4.9.5 UI8 KSI Screen Table 24 shows the information to be displayed in the KSI screen. The results Low, Medium, and High will be coming from the output of the program. Figure 21 shows the KSI screen layout.

14.2.5 Mini-FSSM Message Exchange (ME) Contents

There are no messages to be used.

14.3 SOFTWARE COMPONENT'S FEATURE POINT (SCFP) COUNTING EXPLANATION FOR THE EXAMPLE MINI-FSSM ASD

For the Mini-FSSM ASD example for which the Functional Requirements Specifications (FRS) are presented in Section 14.2, the counting details are presented in this section.

Software Component's Feature Points (SCFPs) counting with the explanation for all the functional requirements of the Mini-FSSM ASD example is presented next. To provide the explanations about the counting for the Functional Requirements Specifications of

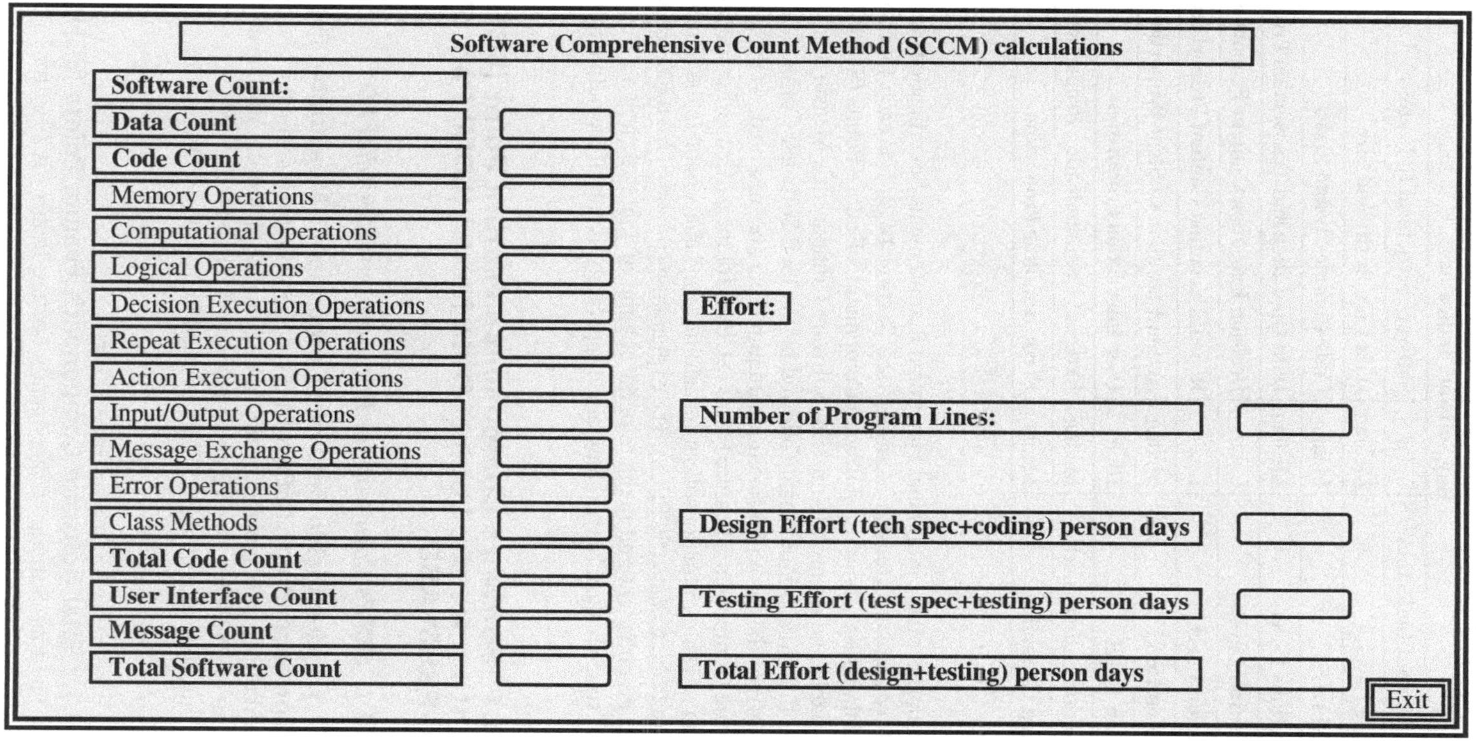

Figure 20 Example mini-FSSM Results screen layout[5–7]. Adapted from Software Comprehensive Count with Quality Indicators (SCCQI), Jasveer Singh, UKSMA/COSMIC Conference 2012[5], SMEF 2012[6], NESMA Autumn Meeting 2012[7].

Table 24 Example Mini-FSSM KSI Screen Contents. Adapted from Software Comprehensive Count with Quality Indicators (SCCQI), Jasveer Singh, UKSMA/COSMIC Conference 2012, SMEF 2012, NESMA Autumn Meeting 2012.

Key Software Indicators[5–7]			
Software Operational Indicators[5–7]		**Software Structural Indicators[5–7]**	
Memory Traffic Level	Medium	**Data Complexity and Size**	Medium
Computational Level	Medium	**Code Complexity and Size**	Medium
Logical Operations Level	Medium	**Data Operation and Transaction Proportion**	High
Decision Execution Level	Low	**Decision Execution Content Proportion**	Low
Repeat Execution Level	Low	**Repeat Execution Content Proportion**	Low
Action Execution Level	Medium	**Action Execution Content Proportion**	Low
User interaction Level	High	**User Interaction Proportion**	High
External Communication Level	Medium	**External Communication Proportion**	Medium
Error Handling Capability	Medium	**Error Handling Proportion**	Low

the example, all the individual Functional Requirements Specifications are considered indicated by their requirement identifier (see Section 14.2). For each functional requirement, the explanations about the Software Component's Feature Points (SCFPs) counting for the identifiable and apparently missing Software Component's Measurable Features (SCMFs) in that functional requirement followed by the total Software Component's Feature Points (SCFPs) for the particular functional requirement are presented. At the same time, the total Software Component's Feature Points (SCFPs) for the particular functional requirement are entered in Table 25 for consolidation, addition, and conversion to the Software Component's Feature Point Counts (SCFPCs). The explanations provided for the functional requirements should be either entered in the remarks column of Table 25 (it is not done here because of lack of space in the table) or maintained separately as part of the output results of the FSSM.

14.3.1 Software Component's Feature Point (SCFP) Counting for the Logical Data Model (LDM) Part of the Mini-FSSM ASD

14.3.1.1 SCFPs Counting for Requirement Identifier LD1

14.3.1.1.1 Identifiable Software Component's Measurable Features (SCMFs) and Corresponding SCFPs for LD1 There are 1 class which is class Count (1 FPDC), 25 attributes of the class (25 FPDAs), 25 fields of the 25 attributes – 1 field for each attribute – (25 FPDFs), and 2 class methods (2 FPCMs).

Thus, the identifiable SCFPs are: FPDC = 1, FPDAs = 25, FPDFs = 25, and FPCMs = 2.

14.3.1.1.2 Total Software Component's Feature Points (SCFPs) Counted for LD1 The total Software Component's Feature Points (SCFPs) for LD1 are: FPDC = 1, FPDAs = 25, FPDFs = 25, and FPCMs = 2.

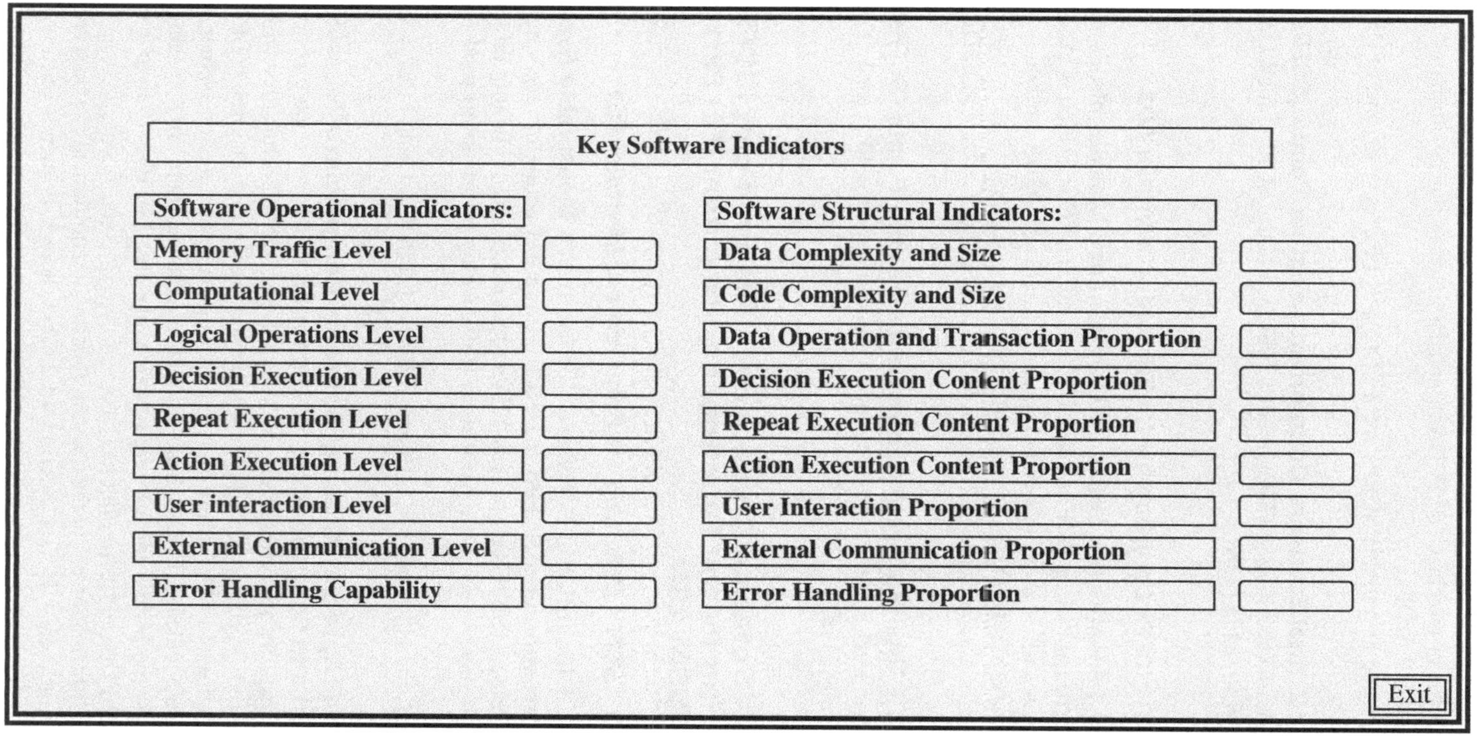

Key Software Indicators

Software Operational Indicators:		Software Structural Indicators:	
Memory Traffic Level		Data Complexity and Size	
Computational Level		Code Complexity and Size	
Logical Operations Level		Data Operation and Transaction Proportion	
Decision Execution Level		Decision Execution Content Proportion	
Repeat Execution Level		Repeat Execution Content Proportion	
Action Execution Level		Action Execution Content Proportion	
User interaction Level		User Interaction Proportion	
External Communication Level		External Communication Proportion	
Error Handling Capability		Error Handling Proportion	

Exit

Figure 21 Example mini-FSSM KSI screen layout[5–7]. Adapted from Software Comprehensive Count with Quality Indicators (SCCQI), Jasveer Singh, UKSMA/COSMIC Conference 2012[5], SMEF 2012[6], NESMA Autumn Meeting 2012[7].

14.3.1.2 SCFPs Counting for Requirement Identifier LD2

14.3.1.2.1 Identifiable Software Component's Measurable Features (SCMFs) and Corresponding SCFPs for LD2 There are 1 class which is class Result (1 FPDC), 19 attributes of the class (19 FPDAs), and 19 fields of the 19 attributes – 1 field for each attribute – (19 FPDFs).

Thus, the identifiable SCFPs are: FPDC = 1, FPDAs = 19, and FPDFs = 19.

14.3.1.2.2 Total Software Component's Feature Points (SCFPs) Counted for LD2 The total Software Component's Feature Points (SCFPs) for LD2 are: FPDC = 1, FPDAs = 19, and FPDFs = 19.

14.3.1.3 SCFPs Counting for Requirement Identifier LD3

14.3.1.3.1 Identifiable Software Component's Measurable Features (SCMFs) and Corresponding SCFPs for LD3 There are 1 class which is class KSI (1 FPDC), 18 attributes of the class (18 FPDAs), and 18 fields of the 18 attributes – 1 field for each attribute – (18 FPDFs).

Thus, the identifiable SCFPs are: FPDC = 1, FPDAs = 18, and FPDFs = 18.

14.3.1.3.2 Total Software Component's Feature Points (SCFPs) Counted for LD3 The total Software Component's Feature Points (SCFPs) for LD3 are: FPDC = 1, FPDAs = 18, and FPDFs = 18.

14.3.2 Software Component's Feature Point (SCFP) Counting for the Functionality Execution (FE) Part of the Mini-FSSM ASD

14.3.2.1 SCFPs Counting for Requirement Identifier FS1

14.3.2.1.1 Identifiable Software Component's Measurable Features (SCMFs) and Corresponding SCFPs for FS1 There is 1 action of receiving the input clicking performed (1 FPFA). There is 1 data input operation of clicking on the link (1 FPDI) for which there is one Data Collection (for clicking information) used for the data input (1 FPLI).

Thus, the identifiable SCFPs are: FPFA = 1, FPDI = 1, and FPLI = 1.

14.3.2.1.2 Apparent Missing Software Component's Measurable Features (SCMFs) and Corresponding SCFPs for FS1 There is one function missing which is displaying the Log-on screen (on clicking on the SCCM link) for which the following are required: 1 action of data output for displaying the Log-on screen (1 FPFA), 1 data output operation (1 FPDO) for displaying the Log-on screen, and one screen information data collection handled (1 FPLI); these are missing. Hence, there are 3 missing function items.

Thus, the SCFPs for missing functionality are: 3 FPFMs (due to 1 missing FPFA, 1 missing FPDO, and 1 missing FPLI).

The information about the missing functional requirement can be seen in the user interface requirement UI1 (see Section 14.2.4.1) where it is mentioned that on clicking the SCCM link, the Log-on screen is presented. Since this functionality is not described in the functionality description, it is a case of the Software Component's Measurable Feature 'Functionality Missing' (FPFM).

14.3.2.1.3 Total Software Component's Feature Points (SCFPs) Counted for FS1 The total Software Component's Feature Points (SCFPs) for FS1 are: FPDI = 1, FPFA = 1, FPLI = 1, and FPFMs = 3.

14.3.2.2 SCFPs Counting for Requirement Identifier FS2

14.3.2.2.1 Identifiable Software Component's Measurable Features (SCMFs) and Corresponding SCFPs for FS2 There are 2 actions performed: receiving the user-id information and opening the application environment screen (2 FPFAs). There is 1 data input operation with user-id information (1 FPDI) and 1 data output operation to open a new application environment screen (1 FPDO).

There is 1 Data Collection (user) used for data input operation (1 FPLI) and 1 Data Collection (screen information data) used for application environment screen output (1 FPLI).

Thus, the identifiable SCFPs are: FPFAs = 2, FPDI = 1, FPDO = 1, and FPLIs = 2.

14.3.2.2.2 Apparent Missing Software Component's Measurable Features (SCMFs) and Corresponding SCFPs for FS2 There are a few functions missing which are: checking if the user-id and password are OK; if OK, then open the application window; otherwise, display error message and display the Log-on screen. So, there are the following missing items: two decision operations – one 'if', one 'else' which is the error case (2 FPFDs); one Data Collection (input 'clicking' information) for one 'if' decision operation (1 FPLG); one error operation for error message display (1 FPFE); two actions performed – one to check for decision and the other for error display (2 FPFAs); one data output operation for displaying the Log-on screen (1 FPDO); one Data Collection (screen information) for data output operation (1 FPLI).

Hence, the SCFPs because of these missing function items are: 8 FPFMs (due to 2 missing FPFDs, 1 missing FPLG, 1 missing FPFE, 2 missing FPFAs, 1 missing FPDO, and 1 missing FPLI).

Also, there is 1 class 'user' missing in the LDM. This class should have minimum 1 attribute 'user-id' with minimum 2 fields 'user-id' and 'password'. Also, it should have at least 3 class methods, namely, 'create user', 'update user', and 'delete user'.

So, there are 7 data features missing, hence the SCFPs for these missing data features are: 7 FPDMs (due to 1 missing class – 1 FPDC, 1 missing attribute – 1 FPDA, 2 missing fields – 2 FPDFs, 3 missing class methods – 3 FPCMs).

Thus, the total SCFPs for missing items are: FPFMs = 8 and FPDMs = 7.

14.3.2.2.3 Total Software Component's Feature Points (SCFPs) Counted for FS2 The total Software Component's Feature Points (SCFPs) for FS2 are: FPFA = 2, FPDI = 1, FPDO = 1, FPLI = 2, FPFM = 8, and FPDM = 7.

14.3.2.3 SCFPs Counting for Requirement Identifier FS3

14.3.2.3.1 Identifiable Software Component's Measurable Features (SCMFs) and Corresponding SCFPs for FS3 There are 1 action of receiving the clicking operation (FPFA = 1) and 1 data input operation of clicking on the application icon (FPDI = 1). There is 1 Data Collection (for clicking information) used for data input (FPLI = 1).

So, the identifiable SCFPs are: FPFA = 1, FPDI = 1, and FPLI = 1.

14.3.2.3.2 Total Software Component's Feature Points (SCFPs) Counted for FS3 The total Software Component's Feature Points (SCFPs) for FS3 are: FPFA = 1, FPDI = 1, and FPLI = 1.

14.3.2.4 SCFPs Counting for Requirement Identifier FS4

14.3.2.4.1 Identifiable Software Component's Measurable Features (SCMFs) and Corresponding SCFPs for FS4 First, there is one action being taken (1 FPFA) to display the Option screen (1 FPDO) for which there is one Data Collection for screen information used (1 FPLI). Then, there is one action of receiving the clicking input (1 FPFA) from the user for which 1 data input operation (1 FPDI) is there. For the clicking input, there is one Data Collection of clicking data used (1 FPLI). After the clicking input, there are 2 decisions (2 FPFDs) whether new count or old file. For decisions, there is 1 Data Collection for clicking information used (1 FPLG). For 2 decisions, 2 actions are to be taken but only one action for new entry is defined (1 FPFA) and the other action for old files is not defined (SCFPs for missing items are considered separately). For the action new entry, 1 screen New Entry is opened (1 FPDO). For this screen, there is 1 screen Data Collection used (1 FPLI).

Hence, the total identifiable SCFPs are: FPFAs = 3, FPDOs = 2, FPDI = 1, FPFDs = 2, FPLIs = 3, and FPLG = 1.

14.3.2.4.2 Apparent Missing Software Component's Measurable Features (SCMFs) and Corresponding SCFPs for FS4 There is one action (1 FPFA) missing which is 1 data output operation for opening another screen for old file (1 FPDO). For this, one screen information data collection will be used (1 FPLI). So the missing SCFPs are: 1 FPFA, 1 FPDO, and 1 FPLI.

Hence, the SCFPs for missing functionality are: 3 FPFMs (due to 1 missing FPFA, 1 missing FPDO, and 1 missing FPLI).

14.3.2.4.3 Total Software Component's Feature Points (SCFPs) Counted for FS4 The total Software Component's Feature Points (SCFPs) for FS4 are: FPFA = 3, FPDO = 2, FPDI = 1, FPFD = 2, FPLI = 3, FPLG = 1, and FPFM = 3.

14.3.2.5 SCFPs Counting for Requirement Identifier FS5

14.3.2.5.1 Identifiable Software Component's Measurable Features (SCMFs) and Corresponding SCFPs for FS5 Here, only data are being entered on the screen, so no Software Component's Feature Point (SCFP) counting occurs. Actions are taken in the other requirement identifiers (see Sections 14.3.2.6–14.3.2.8 where counting is mentioned for these identifiers).

14.3.2.6 SCFPs Counting for Requirement Identifier FS6

14.3.2.6.1 Identifiable Software Component's Measurable Features (SCMFs) and Corresponding SCFPs for FS6 There is one group of actions to check the error conditions (1 FPFA). There are 25 decisions (25 FPFDs) for which there are 25 logical operations (25 FPFLs) to check the error conditions and based on the result, 25 actions to be taken (25 FPFAs). There are 25 error operations (25 FPFEs) to handle 25 error messages. For error message display, there is 1 memory data read for reading the error message data (1 FPDR) and 1 data output operation for error display (1 FPDO) with the received values.

For 25 decisions, 1 Data Collection (class Count) is used (1 FPLG). For 25 logical operations, 1 Data Collection (class Count) and another Data Collection of constant limits are being used (2 FPLGs). For memory data read, there is 1 Data Collection (error message data) handled (1 FPLM) and there are 2 Data Collections handled for data output operation – error message data (1 FPLI) to display the error message and count data which were received and are to be displayed (1 FPLI).

After displaying the error messages, there is 1 data input operation for receiving the new data (1 FPDI) and 1 repeat operation (1 FPFR). There is 1 Data Collection handled (count) for the input operation (1 FPLI) and 1 Data Collection for the repeat operation (received count data) (1 FPLG).

Hence, the identifiable SCFPs are: FPFAs = 26, FPFDs = 25, FPFLs = 25, FPFEs = 25, FPDR = 1, FPDI = 1, FPDO = 1, FPFR = 1, FPLGs = 4, FPLM = 1, and FPLIs = 3.

14.3.2.6.2 Total Software Component's Feature Points (SCFPs) Counted for FS6 The total Software Component's Feature Points (SCFPs) for FS6 are: FPFAs = 26, FPFDs = 25, FPFLs = 25, FPFEs = 25, FPDR = 1, FPDI = 1, FPDO = 1, FPFR = 1, FPLGs = 4, FPLM = 1, and FPLIs = 3.

14.3.2.7 SCFPs Counting for Requirement Identifier FS7

14.3.2.7.1 Identifiable Software Component's Measurable Features (SCMFs) and Corresponding SCFPs for FS7 There is one action of receiving the input of clicking information (1 FPFA). In this action which is 1 data input operation (1 FPDI), the clicking information about whether 'Save', 'Next', or 'Calculate', so 1 Data Collection (click information) is received (1 FPLI), and count data input, so another Data Collection, is received (1 FPLI).

After this, there is 1 action of taking decisions to see which clicking information is received (1 FPFA). There are 3 decisions to check if 'Save', 'Next', or 'Calculate' (3 FPFDs), and 1 action for each decision, so 3 actions performed (3 FPFAs). There is one Data Collection (clicking information) handled in the 3 decision operations (1 FPLG).

Then, for 'Save', error conditions of FS6 are checked, so it is an execution flow control operation (1 FPFO). The Data Collection handled in the execution flow control operation is the count data (1 FPLG). Then, there is 1 memory data write operation (1 FPDW) with the Data Collection handled being count data (1 FPLM). After that, there is 1 data output to display the screen for 'Save' (1 FPDO) with the Data Collections handled being screen information data (1 FPLI) and count data (1 FPLI).

For 'Next', error conditions of FS6 are checked, so it is an execution flow control operation (1 FPFO). The Data Collection handled in the execution flow control operation is the count data (1 FPLG). Then, there is 1 memory data write operation (1 FPDW) with the Data Collection handled being count data (1 FPLM). After that, there is 1 data output to display the screen for New Entry (1 FPDO) with the Data Collection handled being screen information data (1 FPLI).

For 'Calculate', error conditions of FS6 are checked, so it is an execution flow control operation (1 FPFO). The Data Collection handled in the execution flow control operation is the count data (1 FPLG). Then, there is 1 memory data write operation (1 FPDW) with the Data Collection handled being count data (1 FPLM).

Hence, the identifiable SCFPs are: FPFAs = 5, FPDI = 1, FPFDs = 3, FPFOs = 3, FPDWs = 3, FPDOs = 2, FPLIs = 5, FPLGs = 4, and FPLMs = 3.

14.3.2.7.2 Total Software Component's Feature Points (SCFPs) Counted for FS7 The total Software Component's Feature Points (SCFPs) for FS7 are: FPFAs = 5, FPDI = 1, FPFDs = 3, FPFOs = 3, FPDWs = 3, FPDOs = 2, FPLIs = 5, FPLGs = 4, and FPLMs = 3.

14.3.2.8 SCFPs Counting for Requirement Identifier FS8

14.3.2.8.1 Identifiable Software Component's Measurable Features (SCMFs) and Corresponding SCFPs for FS8 Software component's feature point counting for calculations of total counts, results, and KSIs is done in the function identifiers that follow. Here, counting is considered for only the save and display part of total counts, results, and KSIs:

a. 3 groups of actions are performed, one for each of the total counts, results, and KSIs. The group of actions are execution flow control for calculations; memory write; and display screens – Total Counts, Results, and KSIs (3 FPFAs).
So, FPFAs = 3.

b. 3 execution flow control operations for the calculations of total counts, results, and KSIs (3 FPFOs);
Data handled in the aforementioned execution flow control operations – Data Collections total counts, results, and KSIs, one in each execution flow control operation, respectively (3 FPLGs).
So, FPFOs = 3, FPLGs = 3.

c. 3 data writes for total counts, results, and KSIs after calculations (3 FPDWs);
Data handled for the aforementioned data write operations: 3 Data Collections (classes Count, Result, and KSI) for 3 data writes (3 FPLMs), 1 Data Collection in each operation.
So, FPDWs = 3, FPLMs = 3.

d. 3 data outputs for display (3 FPDOs);
Data handled for the aforementioned data output operations: 3 screen Data Collections for 3 display screens (3 FPLIs), 3 Data Collections (classes Count, Result, and KSI) for screen data to be displayed (3 FPLIs).
So, FPDO = 3 and FPLI = 6.

Hence, the total identifiable SCFPs are: FPFAs = 3, FPFOs = 3, FPDWs = 3, FPDOs = 3, FPLGs = 3, FPLMs = 3, and FPLIs = 6.

14.3.2.8.2 Total Software Component's Feature Points (SCFPs) Counted for FS8 The total Software Component's Feature Points (SCFPs) for FS8 are: FPFAs = 3, FPFOs = 3, FPDWs = 3, FPDOs = 3, FPLGs = 3, FPLMs = 3, and FPLIs = 6.

14.3.2.9 SCFPs Counting for Requirement Identifier FS8.1

14.3.2.9.1 Identifiable Software Component's Measurable Features (SCMFs) and Corresponding SCFPs for FS8.1 Here, counting is considered for the calculation of total counts:

Addition of all the 22 counts which form the result count: this has 1 action (1 FPFA) for the following group of operations: repeat (1 FPFR), read memory to get the Data Collection count (1 FPDR), and add the 22 respective counts – for this, 22 additions and 22 equals operations (FPFCs = 44).

Data handled for the aforementioned operations: 1 Data Collection for repeat (1 FPLG), reading 1 Data Collection (class Count) for 1 data read (1 FPLM), and 1 Data Collection (class Count) for addition (1 FPLG).

So, FPFA = 1, FPFR = 1, FPDR = 1, FPFCs = 44, FPLM = 1, and FPLGs = 2.

Hence, the total identifiable SCFPs are: FPFA = 1, FPFR = 1, FPDR = 1, FPFCs = 44, FPLM = 1, and FPLGs = 2.

14.3.2.9.2 Total Software Component's Feature Points (SCFPs) Counted for FS8.1 The total Software Component's Feature Points (SCFPs) for FS8.1 are: FPFA = 1, FPFR = 1, FPDR = 1, FPFCs = 44, FPLM = 1, and FPLGs = 2.

14.3.2.10 SCFPs Counting for Requirement Identifier FS9

14.3.2.10.1 Identifiable Software Component's Measurable Features (SCMFs) and Corresponding SCFPs for FS9 There are: 1 action for calculations (1 FPFA) and 3 computational operations – 2 additions and 1 equals (3 FPFCs). Data handled in the computations are 2 Data Collections (class Count and class Result) (2 FPLGs).

So, the total identifiable SCFPs are: FPFA= 1, FPFCs = 3, and FPLGs = 2.

14.3.2.10.2 Total Software Component's Feature Points (SCFPs) Counted for FS9 The total Software Component's Feature Points (SCFPs) for FS9 are: FPFA= 1, FPFCs = 3, and FPLGs = 2.

14.3.2.11 SCFPs Counting for Requirement Identifier FS10

14.3.2.11.1 Identifiable Software Component's Measurable Features (SCMFs) and Corresponding SCFPs for FS10 There is 1 action (1 FPFA) for the group of operations which are: 3 computational operations for additions (3 FPFCs) and 10 equals operations (10 FPFCs). There are 2 Data Collections (class Count and class Result) handled in this action group operations (2 FPLGs).

So, the identifiable SCFPs are: FPFA = 1, FPFCs = 13, and FPLGs = 2.

14.3.2.11.2 Total Software Component's Feature Points (SCFPs) Counted for FS10 The total Software Component's Feature Points (SCFPs) for FS10 are: FPFA = 1, FPFCs = 13, and FPLGs = 2.

14.3.2.12 SCFPs Counting for Requirement Identifier FS11

14.3.2.12.1 Identifiable Software Component's Measurable Features (SCMFs) and Corresponding SCFPs for FS11 There is 1 action (FPFA = 1) for the group of operations which are: 10 computational operations (10 FPFCs) – 9 additions and 1 equals operation. There is 1 Data Collection (class Result) handled (1 FPLG).

So, the identifiable SCFPs are: FPFA = 1, FPFCs = 10, and FPLG = 1.

14.3.2.12.2 Total Software Component's Feature Points Counted for FS11 The total Software Component's Feature Points (SCFPs) for FS11 are: FPFA = 1, FPFCs = 10, and FPLG = 1.

14.3.2.13 SCFPs Counting for Requirement Identifier FS12

14.3.2.13.1 Identifiable Software Component's Measurable Features (SCMFs) and Corresponding SCFPs for FS12 There is 1 action (FPFA = 1) for the group of operations which are: 4 computational operations (4 FPFCs) – 3 additions and 1 equals operation. There are 2 Data Collections (class Count and class Result) handled in the computational operations (2 FPLGs).

So, the identifiable SCFPs are: FPFA = 1, FPFCs = 4, and FPLGs = 2.

14.3.2.13.2 Total Software Component's Feature Points Counted for FS12 The total Software Component's Feature Points (SCFPs) for FS12 are: FPFA = 1, FPFCs = 4, and FPLGs = 2.

14.3.2.14 SCFPs Counting for Requirement Identifier FS13

14.3.2.14.1 Identifiable Software Component's Measurable Features (SCMFs) and Corresponding SCFPs for FS13 There is 1 action (FPFA = 1) for the group of operations which are: 2 computational operations (2 FPFCs) – 1 addition and 1 equals operation. There are 2 Data Collections (class Count and class Result) handled in the computational operations (2 FPLGs).

So, the identifiable SCFPs are: FPFA = 1, FPFCs = 2, and FPLGs = 2.

14.3.2.14.2 Total Software Component's Feature Points (SCFPs) Counted for FS13 The total Software Component's Feature Points (SCFPs) for FS13 are: FPFA = 1, FPFCs = 2, and FPLGs = 2.

14.3.2.15 SCFPs Counting for Requirement Identifier FS14

14.3.2.15.1 Identifiable Software Component's Measurable Features (SCMFs) and Corresponding SCFPs for FS14 There is 1 action (FPFA = 1) for the group of operations which are: 4 computational operations (4 FPFCs) – 3 additions and 1 equals operation. There is 1 Data Collection (class Result) handled in the computational operations (1 FPLG).

So, the identifiable SCFPs are: FPFA = 1, FPFCs = 4, and FPLG = 1.

14.3.2.15.2 Total Software Component's Feature Points (SCFPs) Counted for FS14 The total Software Component's Feature Points (SCFPs) for FS14 are: FPFA = 1, FPFCs = 4, and FPLG = 1.

14.3.2.16 SCFPs Counting for Requirement Identifier FS15

14.3.2.16.1 Identifiable Software Component's Measurable Features (SCMFs) and Corresponding SCFPs for FS15 This is just information, so no Software Component's Feature Point (SCFP) counting is required here.

14.3.2.17 SCFPs Counting for Requirement Identifier FS16

14.3.2.17.1 Identifiable Software Component's Measurable Features (SCMFs) and Corresponding SCFPs for FS16 There is 1 action (FPFA = 1) for the group of operations which are: 20 computational operations (20 FPFCs) – 10 multiplications, 9 additions, and 1 equals operations. There are 2 Data Collections (class Count and class Result) handled (2 FPLGs) in the computational operations.

So, the identifiable SCFPs are: FPFA = 1, FPFCs = 20, and FPLGs = 2.

14.3.2.17.2 Apparent Missing Software Component's Measurable Features (SCMFs) and Corresponding SCFPs for FS16 Here, we see a result 'Data Lines' which should be part of the class Result, but it is not available in the definition of the class Result (see Section 14.2.2.2). So, there is one field 'Data Lines' (1 FPDF) missing in the class Result in the LDM (1 FPDM).

Therefore, the missing SCFPs are: FPDM = 1 (due to 1 missing FPDF).

14.3.2.17.3 Total Software Component's Feature Points (SCFPs) Counted for FS16 The total Software Component's Feature Points (SCFPs) for FS16 are: FPFA = 1, FPFCs = 20, FPLGs = 2, and FPDM = 1.

14.3.2.18 SCFPs Counting for Requirement Identifier FS17

14.3.2.18.1 Identifiable Software Component's Measurable Features (SCMFs) and Corresponding SCFPs for FS17 There is 1 action (FPFA = 1) for the group of operations which are: 33 computational operations (20 FPFCs) – 12 multiplications, 20 additions, and 1 equals operations. There are 2 Data Collections (class Count and class Result) handled (2 FPLGs) in the computational operations.

So, the identifiable SCFPs are: FPFA = 1, FPFCs = 33, and FPLGs = 2.

14.3.2.18.2 Apparent Missing Software Component's Measurable Features (SCMFs) and Corresponding SCFPs for FS17 Here, we see a result 'Code Lines' which should be part of the class Result, but it is not available in the definition of the class Result (see Section 14.2.2.2). So, there is one field 'Code Lines' missing in the class Result in the LDM (1 FPDM).

Therefore, the missing SCFPs are: FPDM = 1 (due to 1 missing FPDF).

14.3.2.18.3 Total Software Component's Feature Points Counted for FS17 The total Software Component's Feature Points (SCFPs) for FS17 are: FPFA = 1, FPFCs = 33, FPLGs = 2, and FPDM = 1.

14.3.2.19 SCFPs Counting for Requirement Identifier FS18

14.3.2.19.1 Identifiable Software Component's Measurable Features (SCMFs) and Corresponding SCFPs for FS18 There is 1 action (FPFA = 1) for 2 computational operations (2 FPFCs) – 1 multiplication and 1 equals operation. There is 1 Data Collection (class Result) handled (1 FPLG) in the computational operations.

So, the identifiable SCFPs are: FPFA = 1, FPFCs = 2, and FPLG = 1.

14.3.2.19.2 Apparent Missing Software Component's Measurable Features (SCMFs) and Corresponding SCFPs for FS18 Here, we see a result 'Comment Lines' which should be part of the class Result, but it is not available in the definition of the class Result (see Section 14.2.2.2). So, there is one field 'Comment Lines' missing in the class Result in the LDM (1 FPDM).

Therefore, the missing SCFPs are: FPDM = 1 (due to 1 missing FPDF).

14.3.2.19.3 Total Software Component's Feature Points (SCFPs) Counted for FS18 The total Software Component's Feature Points (SCFPs) for FS18 are: FPFA = 1, FPFCs = 2, FPLG = 1, and FPDM = 1.

14.3.2.20 SCFPs Counting for Requirement Identifier FS19

14.3.2.20.1 Identifiable Software Component's Measurable Features (SCMFs) and Corresponding SCFPs for FS19 There is 1 action (FPFA = 1) for 3 computational operations (3 FPFCs) – 2 additions and 1 equals operation. There is 1 Data Collection (class Result) handled (1 FPLG) in the computational operations.

So, the identifiable SCFPs are: FPFA = 1, FPFCs = 3, and FPLG = 1.

14.3.2.20.2 Total Software Component's Feature Points (SCFPs) Counted for FS19 The total Software Component's Feature Points (SCFPs) for FS19 are: FPFA = 1, FPFCs = 3, and FPLG = 1.

14.3.2.21 SCFPs Counting for Requirement Identifier FS20

14.3.2.21.1 Identifiable Software Component's Measurable Features (SCMFs) and Corresponding SCFPs for FS20 This is just information, so no Software Component's Feature Point (SCFP) counting is required here.

14.3.2.22 SCFPs Counting for Requirement Identifier FS21

14.3.2.22.1 Identifiable Software Component's Measurable Features (SCMFs) and Corresponding SCFPs for FS21 There is 1 action (FPFA = 1) for 2 computational operations (2 FPFCs) – 1 division and 1 equals operation. There is 1 Data Collection (class Result) handled (1 FPLG) in the computational operations.

So, the identifiable SCFPs are: FPFA = 1, FPFCs = 2, and FPLG = 1.

14.3.2.22.2 Apparent Missing Software Component's Measurable Features (SCMFs) and Corresponding SCFPs for FS21 Here, we see a result 'Data Design' which should be part of the class Result, but it is not available in the definition of the class Result (see Section 14.2.2.2). So, there is one field 'Data Design' missing in the class Result in the LDM (1 FPDM).

Therefore, the missing SCFPs are: FPDM = 1 (due to 1 missing FPDF).

14.3.2.22.3 Total Software Component's Feature Points (SCFPs) Counted for FS21 The total Software Component's Feature Points (SCFPs) for FS21 are: FPFA = 1, FPFCs = 2, FPLG = 1, and FPDM = 1.

14.3.2.23 SCFPs Counting for Requirement Identifier FS22

14.3.2.23.1 Identifiable Software Component's Measurable Features (SCMFs) and Corresponding SCFPs for FS22 There is 1 action (FPFA = 1) for 2 computational operations (2 FPFCs) – 1 division and 1 equals operation. There is 1 Data Collection (class Result) handled (1 FPLG) in the computational operations.

So, the identifiable SCFPs are: FPFA = 1, FPFCs = 2, and FPLG = 1.

14.3.2.23.2 Apparent Missing Software Component's Measurable Features (SCMFs) and Corresponding SCFPs for FS22 Here, we see a result 'Code Design' which should be part of the class Result, but it is not available in the definition of the class Result (see Section 14.2.2.2). So, there is one field 'Code Design' missing in the class Result in the LDM (1 FPDM).

Therefore, the missing SCFPs are: FPDM = 1 (due to 1 missing FPDF).

14.3.2.23.3 Total Software Component's Feature Points Counted for FS22 The total Software Component's Feature Points (SCFPs) for FS22 are: FPFA = 1, FPFCs = 2, FPLG = 1, and FPDM = 1.

14.3.2.24 SCFPs Counting for Requirement Identifier FS23

14.3.2.24.1 Identifiable Software Component's Measurable Features (SCMFs) and Corresponding SCFPs for FS23 There is 1 action (FPFA = 1) for 2 computational operations (2 FPFCs) – 1 addition and 1 equals operation. There is 1 Data Collection (class Result) handled (1 FPLG) in the computational operations.

So, the identifiable SCFPs are: FPFA = 1, FPFCs = 2, and FPLG = 1.

14.3.2.24.2 Total Software Component's Feature Points (SCFPs) Counted for FS23 The total Software Component's Feature Points (SCFPs) for FS23 are: FPFA = 1, FPFCs = 2, and FPLG = 1.

14.3.2.25 SCFPs Counting for Requirement Identifier FS24

14.3.2.25.1 Identifiable Software Component's Measurable Features (SCMFs) and Corresponding SCFPs for FS24 There is 1 action (FPFA = 1) for 2 computational operations (2 FPFCs) – 1 multiplication and 1 equals operation. There is 1 Data Collection (class Result) handled (1 FPLG) in the computational operations.

So, the identifiable SCFPs are: FPFA = 1, FPFCs = 2, and FPLG = 1.

14.3.2.25.2 Total Software Component's Feature Points Counted for FS24 The total Software Component's Feature Points (SCFPs) for FS24 are: FPFA = 1, FPFCs = 2, and FPLG = 1.

14.3.2.26 SCFPs Counting for Requirement Identifier FS25

14.3.2.26.1 Identifiable Software Component's Measurable Features (SCMFs) and Corresponding SCFPs for FS25 There is 1 action (FPFA = 1) for 2 computational operations (2 FPFCs) – 1 addition and 1 equals operation. There is 1 Data Collection (class Result) handled (1 FPLG) in the computational operations.

So, the identifiable SCFPs are: FPFA = 1, FPFCs = 2, and FPLG = 1.

14.3.2.26.2 Total Software Component's Feature Points Counted for FS25 The total Software Component's Feature Points (SCFPs) for FS25 are: FPFA = 1, FPFCs = 2, and FPLG = 1.

14.3.2.27 SCFPs Counting for Requirement Identifier FS26

14.3.2.27.1 Identifiable Software Component's Measurable Features (SCMFs) and Corresponding SCFPs for FS26 There is 1 action (1 FPFA) to do the following:

- 3 computations to calculate the intermediate % of the Memory Traffic Level: 1 division, 1 multiplication, and 1 equals (3 FPFCs);
  Data handling of 3 Data Collections (class Result, class KSI, and constants) in the computations (3 FPLGs);
- 4 decisions to check the limits (4 FPFDs);
  Data handling of 2 Data Collections (class KSI and constants) in the decisions (2 FPLGs);
- 4 logical AND operations in 4 decisions for lower and upper limits (4 FPFLs);
  Data handling of 1 data collection (constants) in the logical operations (1 FPLG);
- 4 actions as a result of 4 decisions to assign a value to the Memory Traffic Level (4 FPFAs);
- 4 computational operations – equals – for assigning a value to the Memory Traffic Level (4 FPFCs);
  Data handling of 2 Data Collections (class KSI and constants) in the computations (2 FPLGs).

Hence, the total identifiable SCFPs are: FPFAs = 5, FPFCs = 7, FPFDs = 4, FPFLs = 4, and FPLGs = 8.

14.3.2.27.2 Total Software Component's Feature Points (SCFPs) Counted for FS26 The total Software Component's Feature Points (SCFPs) for FS26 are: FPFAs = 5, FPFCs = 7, FPFDs = 4, FPFLs = 4, and FPLGs = 8.

14.3.2.28 SCFPs Counting for Requirement Identifier FS27

14.3.2.28.1 Identifiable Software Component's Measurable Features (SCMFs) and Corresponding SCFPs for FS27 There is 1 action (1 FPFA) to do the following:

- 3 computations to calculate the intermediate % of the Computational Level: 1 division, 1 multiplication, and 1 equals (3 FPFCs);
  Data handling of 3 Data Collections (class Result, class KSI, and constants) in the computations (3 FPLGs);
- 4 decisions to check the limits (4 FPFDs);
  Data handling of 2 Data Collections (class KSI and constants) in the decisions (2 FPLGs);
- 4 logical AND operations in 4 decisions for lower and upper limits (4 FPFLs);
  Data handling of 1 data collection (constants) in the logical operations (1 FPLG);
- 4 actions as a result of 4 decisions to assign a value to the Computational Level (4 FPFAs);

- 4 computational operations – equals – for assigning a value to the Computational Level (4 FPFCs);
  Data handling of 2 Data Collections (class KSI and constants) in the computations (2 FPLGs).

Hence, the total identifiable SCFPs are: FPFAs = 5, FPFCs = 7, FPFDs = 4, FPFLs = 4, and FPLGs = 8.

14.3.2.28.2 Total Software Component's Feature Points (SCFPs) Counted for FS27 The total Software Component's Feature Points (SCFPs) for FS27 are: FPFAs = 5, FPFCs = 7, FPFDs = 4, FPFLs = 4, and FPLGs = 8.

14.3.2.29 SCFPs Counting for Requirement Identifier FS28

14.3.2.29.1 Identifiable Software Component's Measurable Features (SCMFs) and Corresponding SCFPs for FS28 There is 1 action (1 FPFA) to do the following:

- 3 computations to calculate the intermediate % of the Logical Operations Level: 1 division, 1 multiplication, and 1 equals (3 FPFCs);
  Data handling of 3 Data Collections (class Result, class KSI, and constants) in the computations (3 FPLGs);
- 4 decisions to check the limits (4 FPFDs);
  Data handling of 2 Data Collections (class KSI and constants) in the decisions (2 FPLGs);
- 4 logical AND operations in 4 decisions for lower and upper limits (4 FPFLs);
  Data handling of 1 Data Collection (constants) in the logical operations (1 FPLG);
- 4 actions as a result of 4 decisions to assign a value to the Logical Operations Level (4 FPFAs);
- 4 computational operations – equals – for assigning a value to the Logical Operations Level (4 FPFCs);
  Data handling of 2 Data Collections (class KSI and constants) in the computations (2 FPLGs).

Hence, the total identifiable SCFPs are: FPFAs = 5, FPFCs = 7, FPFDs = 4, FPFLs = 4, and FPLGs = 8.

14.3.2.29.2 Total Software Component's Feature Points (SCFPs) Counted for FS28 The total Software Component's Feature Points (SCFPs) for FS28 are: FPFAs = 5, FPFCs = 7, FPFDs = 4, FPFLs = 4, and FPLGs = 8.

14.3.2.30 SCFPs Counting for Requirement Identifier FS29

14.3.2.30.1 Identifiable Software Component's Measurable Features (SCMFs) and Corresponding SCFPs for FS29 There is 1 action (1 FPFA) to do the following:

- 3 computations to calculate the intermediate % of the Decision Execution Level: 1 division, 1 multiplication, and 1 equals (3 FPFCs);
  Data handling of 3 Data Collections (class Result, class KSI, and constants) in the computations (3 FPLGs);

- 4 decisions to check the limits (4 FPFDs);
  Data handling of 2 Data Collections (class KSI and constants) in the decisions (2 FPLGs);
- 4 logical AND operations in 4 decisions for lower and upper limits (4 FPFLs);
  Data handling of 1 Data Collection (constants) in the logical operations (1 FPLG);
- 4 actions as a result of 4 decisions to assign a value to the Decision Execution Level (4 FPFAs);
- 4 computational operations – equals – for assigning a value to the Decision Execution Level (4 FPFCs);
  Data handling of 2 Data Collections (class KSI and constants) in the computations (2 FPLGs).

Hence, the total identifiable SCFPs are: FPFAs = 5, FPFCs = 7, FPFDs = 4, FPFLs = 4, and FPLGs = 8.

14.3.2.30.2 Total Software Component's Feature Points (SCFPs) Counted for FS29 The total Software Component's Feature Points (SCFPs) for FS29 are: FPFAs = 5, FPFCs = 7, FPFDs = 4, FPFLs = 4, and FPLGs = 8.

14.3.2.31 SCFPs Counting for Requirement Identifier FS30

14.3.2.31.1 Identifiable Software Component's Measurable Features (SCMFs) and Corresponding SCFPs for FS30 There is 1 action (1 FPFA) to do the following:

- 3 computations to calculate the intermediate % of the Repeat Execution Level: 1 division, 1 multiplication, and 1 equals (3 FPFCs);
  Data handling of 3 Data Collections (class Result, class KSI, and constants) in the computations (3 FPLGs);
- 4 decisions to check the limits (4 FPFDs);
  Data handling of 2 Data Collections (class KSI and constants) in the decisions (2 FPLGs);
- 4 logical AND operations in 4 decisions for lower and upper limits (4 FPFLs);
  Data handling of 1 Data Collection (constants) in the logical operations (1 FPLG);
- 4 actions as a result of 4 decisions to assign a value to the Repeat Execution Level (4 FPFAs);
- 4 computational operations – equals – for assigning a value to the Repeat Execution Level (4 FPFCs);
  Data handling of 2 Data Collections (class KSI and constants) in the computations (2 FPLGs).

Hence, the total identifiable SCFPs are: FPFAs = 5, FPFCs = 7, FPFDs = 4, FPFLs = 4, and FPLGs = 8.

14.3.2.31.2 Total Software Component's Feature Points (SCFPs) Counted for FS30 The total Software Component's Feature Points (SCFPs) for FS30 are: FPFAs = 5, FPFCs = 7, FPFDs = 4, FPFLs = 4, and FPLGs = 8.

14.3.2.32 SCFPs Counting for Requirement Identifier FS31

14.3.2.32.1 Identifiable Software Component's Measurable Features (SCMFs) and Corresponding SCFPs for FS31 There is 1 action (1 FPFA) to do the following:

- 3 computations to calculate the intermediate % of Action Execution Level: 1 division, 1 multiplication, and 1 equals (3 FPFCs);
  Data handling of 3 Data Collections (class Result, class KSI, and constants) in computations (3 FPLGs);
- 4 decisions to check the limits (4 FPFDs);
  Data handling of 2 Data Collections (class KSI and constants) in decisions (2 FPLGs);
- 4 logical AND operations in 4 decisions for lower and upper limits (4 FPFLs);
  Data handling of 1 Data Collection (constants) in logical operations (1 FPLG);
- 4 actions as a result of 4 decisions to assign a value to Action Execution Level (4 FPFAs);
- 4 computational operations – equals – for assigning a value to Action Execution Level (4 FPFCs);
  Data handling of 2 Data Collections (class KSI and constants) in computations (2 FPLGs).

Hence, the total identifiable SCFPs are: FPFAs = 5, FPFCs = 7, FPFDs = 4, FPFLs = 4, and FPLGs = 8.

14.3.2.32.2 Total Software Component's Feature Points (SCFPs) Counted for FS31 The total Software Component's Feature Points (SCFPs) for FS31 are: FPFAs = 5, FPFCs = 7, FPFDs = 4, FPFLs = 4, and FPLGs = 8.

14.3.2.33 SCFPs Counting for Requirement Identifier FS32

14.3.2.33.1 Identifiable Software Component's Measurable Features (SCMFs) and Corresponding SCFPs for FS32 There is 1 action (1 FPFA) to do the following:

- 3 computations to calculate the intermediate % of the User Interaction Level: 1 division, 1 multiplication, and 1 equals (3 FPFCs);
  Data handling of 3 Data Collections (class Result, class KSI, and constants) in the computations (3 FPLGs);
- 4 decisions to check the limits (4 FPFDs);
  Data handling of 2 Data Collections (class KSI and constants) in the decisions (2 FPLGs);
- 4 logical AND operations in 4 decisions for lower and upper limits (4 FPFLs);
  Data handling of 1 Data Collection (constants) in the logical operations (1 FPLG);
- 4 actions as a result of 4 decisions to assign a value to the User Interaction Level (4 FPFAs);
- 4 computational operations – equals – for assigning a value to the User Interaction Level (4 FPFCs);

Data handling of 2 Data Collections (class KSI and constants) in the computations (2 FPLGs).

Hence, the total identifiable SCFPs are: FPFAs = 5, FPFCs = 7, FPFDs = 4, FPFLs = 4, and FPLGs = 8.

14.3.2.33.2 Total Software Component's Feature Points (SCFPs) Counted for FS32 The total Software Component's Feature Points (SCFPs) for FS32 are: FPFAs = 5, FPFCs = 7, FPFDs = 4, FPFLs = 4, and FPLGs = 8.

14.3.2.34 SCFPs Counting for Requirement Identifier FS33

14.3.2.34.1 Identifiable Software Component's Measurable Features (SCMFs) and Corresponding SCFPs for FS33 There is 1 action (1 FPFA) to do the following:

- 3 computations to calculate the intermediate % of the External Communication Level: 1 division, 1 multiplication, and 1 equals (3 FPFCs);
  Data handling of 3 Data Collections (class Result, class KSI, and constants) in the computations (3 FPLGs);
- 4 decisions to check the limits (4 FPFDs);
  Data handling of 2 Data Collections (class KSI and constants) in the decisions (2 FPLGs);
- 4 logical AND operations in 4 decisions for lower and upper limits (4 FPFLs);
  Data handling of 1 Data Collection (constants) in the logical operations (1 FPLG);
- 4 actions as a result of 4 decisions to assign a value to the External Communication Level (4 FPFAs);
- 4 computational operations – equals – for assigning a value to the External Communication Level (4 FPFCs);
  Data handling of 2 Data Collections (class KSI and constants) in the computations (2 FPLGs).

Hence, the total identifiable SCFPs are: FPFAs = 5, FPFCs = 7, FPFDs = 4, FPFLs = 4, and FPLGs = 8.

14.3.2.34.2 Total Software Component's Feature Points (SCFPs) Counted for FS33 The total Software Component's Feature Points (SCFPs) for FS33 are: FPFAs = 5, FPFCs = 7, FPFDs = 4, FPFLs = 4, and FPLGs = 8.

14.3.2.35 SCFPs Counting for Requirement Identifier FS34

14.3.2.35.1 Identifiable Software Component's Measurable Features (SCMFs) and Corresponding SCFPs for FS34 There is 1 action (1 FPFA) to do the following:

- 3 computations to calculate the intermediate % of the Error Handling Capability: 1 division, 1 multiplication, and 1 equals (3 FPFCs);
  Data handling of 3 Data Collections (class Result, class KSI, and constants) in the computations (3 FPLGs);
- 4 decisions to check the limits (4 FPFDs);
  Data handling of 2 Data Collection (class KSI and constants) in the decisions (2 FPLGs);

- 4 logical AND operations in 4 decisions for lower and upper limits (4 FPFLs);
  Data handling of 1 Data Collection (constants) in the logical operations (1 FPLG);
- 4 actions as a result of 4 decisions to assign a value to the Error Handling Capability (4 FPFAs);
- 4 computational operations – equals – for assigning a value to the Error Handling Capability (4 FPFCs);
  Data handling of 2 Data Collections (class KSI and constants) in the computations (2 FPLGs).

Hence, the total identifiable SCFPs are: FPFAs = 5, FPFCs = 7, FPFDs = 4, FPFLs = 4, and FPLGs = 8.

14.3.2.35.2 Total Software Component's Feature Points (SCFPs) Counted for FS34 The total Software Component's Feature Points (SCFPs) for FS34 are: FPFAs = 5, FPFCs = 7, FPFDs = 4, FPFLs = 4, and FPLGs = 8.

14.3.2.36 SCFPs Counting for Requirement Identifier FS35

14.3.2.36.1 Identifiable Software Component's Measurable Features (SCMFs) and Corresponding SCFPs for FS35 There is 1 action (1 FPFA) to do the following:

- 4 decisions to check the limits (4 FPFDs);
  Data handling of 2 Data Collections (class Results, constants) in the decisions (2 FPLGs);
- 3 logical AND operations in 3 decisions for lower and upper limits (3 FPFLs);
  Data handling of 1 Data Collection (constants) in the logical operations (1 FPLG);
- 4 actions as a result of 4 decisions to assign a value to the Data Complexity and Size (4 FPFAs);
- 4 computational operations – equals – for assigning a value to the Data Complexity and Size (4 FPFCs);
  Data handling of 2 Data Collections (class KSI and constants) in the computations (2 FPLGs).

Hence, the total identifiable SCFPs are: FPFAs = 5, FPFCs = 4, FPFDs = 4, FPFLs = 3, and FPLGs = 5.

14.3.2.36.2 Total Software Component's Feature Points (SCFPs) Counted for FS35 The total Software Component's Feature Points (SCFPs) for FS35 are: FPFAs = 5, FPFCs = 4, FPFDs = 4, FPFLs = 3, and FPLGs = 5.

14.3.2.37 SCFPs Counting for Requirement Identifier FS36

14.3.2.37.1 Identifiable Software Component's Measurable Features (SCMFs) and Corresponding SCFPs for FS36 There is 1 action (1 FPFA) to do the following:

- 4 decisions to check the limits (4 FPFDs);
  Data handling of 2 Data Collections (class Results, constants) in the decisions (2 FPLGs);

- 3 logical AND operations in 4 decisions for lower and upper limits (3 FPFLs);
  Data handling of 1 Data Collection (constants) in the logical operations (1 FPLG);
- 4 actions as a result of 4 decisions to assign a value to the Code Complexity and Size (4 FPFAs);
- 4 computational operations – equals – for assigning a value to the Code Complexity and Size (4 FPFCs);
  Data handling of 2 Data Collections (class KSI and constants) in computations (2 FPLGs).

Hence, the total identifiable SCFPs are: FPFAs = 5, FPFCs = 4, FPFDs = 4, FPFLs = 3, and FPLGs = 5.

14.3.2.37.2 Total Software Component's Feature Points (SCFPs) Counted for FS36 The total Software Component's Feature Points (SCFPs) for FS36 are: FPFAs = 5, FPFCs = 4, FPFDs = 4, FPFLs = 3, and FPLGs = 5.

14.3.2.38 SCFPs Counting for Requirement Identifier FS37

14.3.2.38.1 Identifiable Software Component's Measurable Features (SCMFs) and Corresponding SCFPs for FS37 There is 1 action (1 FPFA) to do the following:

- 6 computations to calculate the intermediate % of Data Operation and Transaction Proportion: 3 additions, 1 division, 1 multiplication, and 1 equals (6 FPFCs);
  Data handling of 3 Data Collections (class Result, class KSI, and constants) in the computations (3 FPLGs);
- 4 decisions to check the limits (4 FPFDs);
  Data handling of 2 Data Collections (class KSI and constants) in the decisions (2 FPLGs);
- 4 logical AND operations in 4 decisions for lower and upper limits (4 FPFLs);
  Data handling of 1 Data Collection (constants) in the logical operations (1 FPLG);
- 4 actions as a result of 4 decisions to assign a value to the Data Operation and Transaction Proportion (4 FPFAs);
- 4 computational operations – equals – for assigning a value to the Data Operation and Transaction Proportion (4 FPFCs);
  Data handling of 2 Data Collections (class KSI and constants) in the computations (2 FPLGs).

Hence, the total identifiable SCFPs are: FPFAs = 5, FPFCs = 10, FPFDs = 4, FPFLs = 4, and FPLGs = 8.

14.3.2.38.2 Total Software Component's Feature Points (SCFPs) Counted for FS37 The total Software Component's Feature Points (SCFPs) for FS37 are: FPFAs = 5, FPFCs = 10, FPFDs = 4, FPFLs = 4, and FPLGs = 8.

14.3.2.39 SCFPs Counting for Requirement Identifier FS38

14.3.2.39.1 Identifiable Software Component's Measurable Features (SCMFs) and Corresponding SCFPs for FS38 There is 1 action (1 FPFA) to do the following:

- 3 computations to calculate the intermediate % of the Decision Execution Content Proportion: 1 division, 1 multiplication, and 1 equals (3 FPFCs);
  Data handling of 3 Data Collections (class Result, class KSI, and constants) in computations (3 FPLGs);
- 4 decisions to check the limits (4 FPFDs);
  Data handling of 2 Data Collections (class KSI and constants) in the decisions (2 FPLGs);
- 4 logical AND operations in 4 decisions for lower and upper limits (4 FPFLs);
  Data handling of 1 Data Collection (constants) in the logical operations (1 FPLG);
- 4 actions as a result of 4 decisions to assign a value to the Decision Execution Content Proportion (4 FPFAs);
- 4 computational operations – equals – for assigning a value to the Decision Execution Content Proportion (4 FPFCs);
  Data handling of 2 Data Collections (class KSI and constants) in the computations (2 FPLGs).

Hence, the total identifiable SCFPs are: FPFAs = 5, FPFCs = 7, FPFDs = 4, FPFLs = 4, and FPLGs = 8.

14.3.2.39.2 Total Software Component's Feature Points (SCFPs) Counted for FS38 The total Software Component's Feature Points (SCFPs) for FS38 are: FPFAs = 5, FPFCs = 7, FPFDs = 4, FPFLs = 4, and FPLGs = 8.

14.3.2.40 SCFPs Counting for Requirement Identifier FS39

14.3.2.40.1 Identifiable Software Component's Measurable Features (SCMFs) and Corresponding SCFPs for FS39 There is 1 action (1 FPFA) to do the following:

- 3 computations to calculate the intermediate % of the Repeat Execution Content Proportion: 1 division, 1 multiplication, and 1 equals (3 FPFCs);
  Data handling of 3 Data Collections (class Result, class KSI, and constants) in the computations (3 FPLGs);
- 4 decisions to check the limits (4 FPFDs);
  Data handling of 2 Data Collections (class KSI and constants) in the decisions (2 FPLGs);
- 4 logical AND operations in 4 decisions for lower and upper limits (4 FPFLs);
  Data handling of 1 Data Collection (constants) in the logical operations (1 FPLG);
- 4 actions as a result of 4 decisions to assign a value to the Repeat Execution Content Proportion (4 FPFAs);
- 4 computational operations – equals – for assigning a value to the Repeat Execution Content Proportion (4 FPFCs);

Data handling of 2 Data Collections (class KSI and constants) in the computations (2 FPLGs).

Hence, the total identifiable SCFPs are: FPFAs = 5, FPFCs = 7, FPFDs = 4, FPFLs = 4, and FPLGs = 8.

14.3.2.40.2 Total Software Component's Feature Points (SCFPs) Counted for FS39 The total Software Component's Feature Points (SCFPs) for FS39 are: FPFAs = 5, FPFCs = 7, FPFDs = 4, FPFLs = 4, and FPLGs = 8.

14.3.2.41 SCFPs Counting for Requirement Identifier FS40

14.3.2.41.1 Identifiable Software Component's Measurable Features (SCMFs) and Corresponding SCFPs for FS40 There is 1 action (1 FPFA) to do the following:

- 3 computations to calculate the intermediate % of the Action Execution Content Proportion: 1 division, 1 multiplication, and 1 equals (3 FPFCs);
  Data handling of 3 Data Collections (class Result, class KSI, and constants) in the computations (3 FPLGs);
- 4 decisions to check the limits (4 FPFDs);
  Data handling of 2 Data Collections (class KSI and constants) in the decisions (2 FPLGs);
- 4 logical AND operations in 4 decisions for lower and upper limits (4 FPFLs);
  Data handling of 1 Data Collection (constants) in the logical operations (1 FPLG);
- 4 actions as a result of 4 decisions to assign a value to the Action Execution Content Proportion (4 FPFAs);
- 4 computational operations – equals – for assigning a value to the Action Execution Content Proportion (4 FPFCs);
  Data handling of 2 Data Collections (class KSI and constants) in the computations (2 FPLGs).

Hence, the total identifiable SCFPs are: FPFAs = 5, FPFCs = 7, FPFDs = 4, FPFLs = 4, and FPLGs = 8.

14.3.2.41.2 Total Software Component's Feature Points (SCFPs) Counted for FS40 The total Software Component's Feature Points (SCFPs) for FS40 are: FPFAs = 5, FPFCs = 7, FPFDs = 4, FPFLs = 4, and FPLGs = 8.

14.3.2.42 SCFPs Counting for Requirement Identifier FS41

14.3.2.42.1 Identifiable Software Component's Measurable Features (SCMFs) and Corresponding SCFPs for FS41 There is 1 action (1 FPFA) to do the following:

- 4 computations to calculate the intermediate % of the User Interaction Proportion: 1 addition, 1 division, 1 multiplication, and 1 equals (4 FPFCs);
  Data handling of 3 Data Collections (class Result, class KSI, and constants) in the computations (3 FPLGs);
- 4 decisions to check the limits (4 FPFDs);

Data handling of 2 Data Collections (class KSI and constants) in the decisions (2 FPLGs);

- 4 logical AND operations in 4 decisions for lower and upper limits (4 FPFLs);
  Data handling of 1 Data Collection (constants) in the logical operations (1 FPLG);
- 4 actions as a result of 4 decisions to assign a value to the User Interaction Proportion (4 FPFAs);
- 4 computational operations – equals – for assigning a value to the User Interaction Proportion (4 FPFCs);
  Data handling of 2 Data Collections (class KSI and constants) in the computations (2 FPLGs).

Hence, the total identifiable SCFPs are: FPFAs = 5, FPFCs = 8, FPFDs = 4, FPFLs = 4, and FPLGs = 8.

14.3.2.42.2 Total Software Component's Feature Points (SCFPs) Counted for FS41 The total Software Component's Feature Points (SCFPs) for FS41 are: FPFAs = 5, FPFCs = 8, FPFDs = 4, FPFLs = 4, and FPLGs = 8.

14.3.2.43 SCFPs Counting for Requirement Identifier FS42

14.3.2.43.1 Identifiable Software Component's Measurable Features (SCMFs) and Corresponding SCFPs for FS42 There is 1 action (1 FPFA) to do the following:

- 4 computations to calculate the intermediate % of the External Communication Proportion: 1 addition, 1 division, 1 multiplication, and 1 equals (4 FPFCs);
  Data handling of 3 Data Collections (class Result, class KSI, and constants) in the computations (3 FPLGs);
- 4 decisions to check the limits (4 FPFDs);
  Data handling of 2 Data Collections (class KSI and constants) in the decisions (2 FPLGs);
- 4 logical AND operations in 4 decisions for lower and upper limits (4 FPFLs);
  Data handling of 1 Data Collection (constants) in the logical operations (1 FPLG);
- 4 actions as a result of 4 decisions to assign a value to the External Communication Proportion (4 FPFAs);
- 4 computational operations – equals – for assigning a value to the External Communication Proportion (4 FPFCs);
  Data handling of 2 Data Collections (class KSI and constants) in the computations (2 FPLGs).

Hence, the total identifiable SCFPs are: FPFAs = 5, FPFCs = 8, FPFDs = 4, FPFLs = 4, and FPLGs = 8.

14.3.2.43.2 Total Software Component's Feature Points (SCFPs) Counted for FS42 The total Software Component's Feature Points (SCFPs) for FS42 are: FPFAs = 5, FPFCs = 8, FPFDs = 4, FPFLs = 4, and FPLGs = 8.

14.3.2.44 SCFPs Counting for Requirement Identifier FS43

14.3.2.44.1 Identifiable Software Component's Measurable Features (SCMFs) and Corresponding SCFPs for FS43 There is 1 action (1 FPFA) to do the following:

- 3 computations to calculate the intermediate % of the Error Handling Proportion: 1 division, 1 multiplication, and 1 equals (3 FPFCs);
  Data handling of 3 Data Collections (class Result, class KSI, and constants) in the computations (3 FPLGs);
- 4 decisions to check the limits (4 FPFDs);
  Data handling of 2 Data Collections (class KSI and constants) in the decisions (2 FPLGs);
- 4 logical AND operations in 4 decisions for lower and upper limits (4 FPFLs);
  Data handling of 1 Data Collection (constants) in the logical operations (1 FPLG);
- 4 actions as a result of 4 decisions to assign a value to the Error Handling Proportion (4 FPFAs);
- 4 computational operations – equals – for assigning a value to the Error Handling Proportion (4 FPFCs);
  Data handling of 2 Data Collections (class KSI and constants) in the computations (2 FPLGs).

Hence, the total identifiable SCFPs are: FPFAs = 5, FPFCs = 7, FPFDs = 4, FPFLs = 4, and FPLGs = 8.

14.3.2.44.2 Total Software Component's Feature Points (SCFPs) Counted for FS43 The total Software Component's Feature Points (SCFPs) for FS43 are: FPFAs = 5, FPFCs = 7, FPFDs = 4, FPFLs = 4, and FPLGs = 8.

14.3.3 Software Component's Feature Point (SCFP) Counting for the User Interface (UI) Part of the Mini-FSSM ASD

14.3.3.1 SCFPs Counting for Requirement Identifier UI1

14.3.3.1.1 Identifiable Software Component's Measurable Features (SCMFs) and Corresponding SCFPs for UI1 There are 1 screen (1 FPUS), 2 text display fields – summary text and SCCM link (URL) (2 FPUFs), and one output link which is the SCCM link (1 FPUO).

So, the identifiable SCFPs are: FPUS = 1, FPUFs = 2, and FPUO = 1.

14.3.3.1.2 Apparent Missing Software Component's Measurable Features (SCMFs) and Corresponding SCFPs for UI1 After going through the functionality description and other screens descriptions/layouts, it is clear that there are 7 missing input links which are not mentioned:

- 1 from the Log-on screen – 'Exit' (1 FPUI);
- 1 from the application environment screen – 'Log-out' (1 FPUI);
- 1 from the Option screen – 'Log-out' (1 FPUI);

- 1 from the New Entry screen – 'Log-out' (1 FPUI);
- 1 from the Total Count screen – 'Exit' (1 FPUI);
- 1 from the Results screen – 'Exit' (1 FPUI);
- 1 from the KSI screen – 'Exit' (1 FPUI).

Hence, the SCFPs for missing user interface items are: 7 FPUMs (due to 7 missing FPUIs).

14.3.3.1.3 Total Software Component's Feature Points (SCFPs) Counted for UI1 The total Software Component's Feature Points (SCFPs) for UI1 are: FPUS = 1, FPUFs = 2, FPUO = 1, and FPUMs = 7.

14.3.3.2 SCFPs Counting for Requirement Identifier UI2

14.3.3.2.1 Identifiable Software Component's Measurable Features (SCMFs) and Corresponding SCFPs for UI2 There are 1 screen (1 FPUS), 2 text display fields for user-id and password text display (2 FPUFs), 2 input fields for user-id and password input (2 FPUFs), one text display field for the text of the output link 'Enter' display (1 FPUF), and one output link to the application environment screen – 'Enter' (1 FPUO).

So, the identifiable SCFPs are: FPUS = 1, FPUFs = 5, and FPUO = 1.

14.3.3.2.2 Apparent Missing Software Component's Measurable Features (SCMFs) and Corresponding SCFPs for UI2 After going through the functionality description and other screens descriptions/layouts, it is clear that there is 1 missing output link ('Exit') to the Initial screen (1 FPUO); and one missing input link from the Initial screen (1 FPUI), see Section 14.2.4.1 where this input link is described. There should be a text field for the missing output link ('Exit'), so 1 screen field is missing (1FPUF).

Also, there is no functionality description about the output link 'Exit', that is, 1 decision operation to check if the 'Exit' was clicked on (1 FPFD).

Hence, the total SCFPs for missing user interface items and related functionality are: FPUMs = 3 (due to 1 missing FPUO, 1 missing FPUF, and 1 missing FPUI) and FPFM = 1 (due to 1 missing FPFD).

14.3.3.2.3 Total Software Component's Feature Points (SCFPs) Counted for UI2 The total Software Component's Feature Points (SCFPs) for UI2 are: FPUS = 1, FPUFs = 5, FPUO = 1, FPUMs = 3, and FPFM = 1.

14.3.3.3 SCFPs Counting for Requirement Identifier UI3

14.3.3.3.1 Identifiable Software Component's Measurable Features (SCMFs) and Corresponding SCFPs for UI3 There are 1 screen (1 FPUS) and 1 field – application icon (1 FPUF).

So, the identifiable SCFPs are: FPUS = 1 and FPUF = 1.

14.3.3.3.2 Apparent Missing Software Component's Measurable Features (SCMFs) and Corresponding SCFPs for UI3 There are the following missing items: one output link (by clicking on the application icon) to the Option screen (1 FPUO), one output link – 'Log-out' to the Initial screen (1 FPUO) and one input link from the Log-on screen (1 FPUI); also, the text field (1 FPUF) for the missing output link ('Log-out') is missing; they form part of the user interface missing items, hence FPUMs. The missing links description for 2 links can be found in the functionality description: for the output link to the Option screen, see Sections 14.2.3.3 and 14.2.3.4; for the input link from the Log-on screen, see Section 14.2.3.2. For the third missing output link 'Log-out', there is no functionality description, that is, 1 decision operation to check if 'Log-out' was clicked on (1 FPFD), so there is a missing functional feature item which is part of FPFMs.

Hence, the total SCFPs for missing items are: FPUMs = 4 (due to 2 missing FPUOs, 1 missing FPUF, and 1 missing FPUI) and FPFM = 1 (due to 1 missing FPFD).

14.3.3.3.3 Total Software Component's Feature Points (SCFPs) Counted for UI3 The total Software Component's Feature Points (SCFPs) for UI3 are: FPUS = 1, FPUF = 1, FPUMs = 4, and FPFM = 1.

14.3.3.4 SCFPs Counting for Requirement Identifier UI4

14.3.3.4.1 Identifiable Software Component's Measurable Features (SCMFs) and Corresponding SCFPs for UI4 There are 1 screen (1 FPUS) and 2 fields for displaying text – new estimate or old files (2 FPUFs).

So, the identifiable SCFPs are: FPUS = 1 and FPUFs = 2.

14.3.3.4.2 Apparent Missing Software Component's Measurable Features (SCMFs) and Corresponding SCFPs for UI4 There are some missing items: 2 output links for new estimate or old file (2 FPUOs) and 1 input link from the Application screen (1 FPUI). Also, there is one output link – 'Log-out' – missing to the Initial screen (1 FPUO), 1 text field to display the output link ('Log-out') is missing (1 FPUF), and there is no functionality description for the output link – 'Log-out', that is, decision operation for checking the 'Log-out' clicking information (1 FPFD). For the description of the missing input link from the Application screen, see Sections 14.2.3.3 and 14.2.3.4. For the missing output link for new estimate, see the description in Section 14.2.3.4.

Hence, the SCFPs for the missing items are: 5 FPUMs (due to 3 missing FPUOs, 1 missing FPUF, and 1 missing FPUI) and 1 FPFM (due to 1 missing FPFD).

14.3.3.4.3 Total Software Component's Feature Points (SCFPs) Counted for UI4 The total Software Component's Feature Points (SCFPs) for UI4 are: FPUS = 1, FPUFs = 2, FPUMs = 5, and FPFM = 1.

14.3.3.5 SCFPs Counting for Requirement Identifier UI5

14.3.3.5.1 Identifiable Software Component's Measurable Features (SCMFs) and Corresponding SCFPs for UI5 There are 1 screen (1 FPUS) and 54 fields (54 FPUFs) which are

a. 25 text display fields to display the text for 25 items which are identifier; description; 22 counts – DC, DA, DF, CM, DR, DW, DI, DO, FC, FL, FD, FR, FA, FE, MN, MF, MS, MR, US, UF, UO, UI (integer only); and remark (25 FPUFs);

b. 25 input fields for 25 input items which are identifier; description; 22 counts – DC, DA, DF, CM, DR, DW, DI, DO, FC, FL, FD, FR, FA, FE, MN, MF, MS, MR, US, UF, UO, UI (integer only); and remark (25 FPUFs);

c. 1 select menu item with 4 fields for menu item selection of LDM, FS, UI, and ME (4 FPUFs);
d. 3 text display fields to display the text for 3 output links 'Save', 'Calculate', and 'Next' (3 FPUFs).

There are 3 output links for 'Save', 'Calculate', and 'Next' (3 FPUOs).
Thus, the identifiable SCFPs are: FPUS = 1, FPUFs = 57, and FPUOs = 3.

14.3.3.5.2 Apparent Missing Software Component's Measurable Features (SCMFs) and Corresponding SCFPs for UI5 There are the following missing items:

- one input link from the Option screen is missing (1 FPUI), see Section 14.2.3.4;
- one output link – 'Log-out' – to the Initial screen is missing (1 FPUO);
- text field to display the text for output link ('Log-out') is missing (1 FPUF);
- one field for displaying errors is missing, see Section 14.2.3.6 (1 FPUF);
- functionality description for the output link – 'Log-out', that is, decision operation for checking the 'Log-out' clicking information (1 FPFD).

So, the SCFPs for the missing items are: FPUMs = 4 (due to 1 missing FPUI, 1 missing FPUO, 1 missing FPUF, and 1 missing FPUF) and FPFM = 1 (due to 1 missing FPFD).

14.3.3.5.3 Total Software Component's Feature Points (SCFPs) Counted for UI5 The total Software Component's Feature Points (SCFPs) for UI5 are: FPUS = 1, FPUFs = 57, FPUOs = 3, FPUMs = 4, and FPFM = 1.

14.3.3.6 SCFPs Counting for Requirement Identifier UI6

14.3.3.6.1 Identifiable Software Component's Measurable Features (SCMFs) and Corresponding SCFPs for UI6 There are 1 screen (1 FPUS) and 50 fields (50 FPUFs) which are

a. 22 output fields for the result counts (22 FPUFs);
b. 27 text display fields to display the text (27 FPUFs);
c. 1 text field for the text of the output link 'Exit' to be displayed (1 FPUF).

There is 1 output link – 'Exit' – to go to the Initial screen (1 FPUO).
So, the identifiable SCFPs are: FPUS = 1, FPUFs = 50, and FPUO = 1.

14.3.3.6.2 Apparent Missing Software Component's Measurable Features (SCMFs) and Corresponding SCFPs for UI6 There is 1 input link missing from the New Entry screen (1 FPUI), see Sections 14.2.3.7 and 14.2.3.8 and 1 input link from the Results screen ('Previous') is missing (1 FPUI). Also, there is 1 output link – 'Next' – to the Results screen missing (1 FPUO). The text field to display the output link text ('Next') is missing (1 FPUF). At the same time, the description of functionality for receiving the input for the output link 'Next', that is, decision operation to check if the output link 'Next' is clicked on, is missing (1 FPFD).

So, the SCFPs for the missing items are: FPUMs = 4 (due to 2 missing FPUIs, 1 missing FPUO, and 1 missing FPUF) and FPFM = 1 (due to 1 missing FPFD).

14.3.3.6.3 Total Software Component's Feature Points (SCFPs) Counted for UI6 The total Software Component's Feature Points (SCFPs) for UI6 are: FPUS = 1, FPUF = 50, FPUO = 1, FPUM = 4, and FPFM = 1.

14.3.3.7 SCFPs Counting for Requirement Identifier UI7

14.3.3.7.1 Identifiable Software Component's Measurable Features (SCMFs) and Corresponding SCFPs for UI7 There are 1 screen (1 FPUS) and 44 fields which are

- **a.** 20 output fields for the result numbers (20 FPUFs);
- **b.** 23 text display fields to display the text (23 FPUFs);
- **c.** 1 text field for the text of the output link 'Exit' to be displayed (1 FPUF).

There is 1 output link – 'Exit' – to go to the Initial screen (1 FPUO).
So, the identifiable SCFPs are: FPUS = 1, FPUFs = 44, and FPUO = 1.

14.3.3.7.2 Apparent Missing Software Component's Measurable Features (SCMFs) and Corresponding SCFPs for UI7 There is 1 input link missing from the Total Counts screen (1 FPUI), see Section 14.2.3.8. There is 1 input link missing from the KSI screen (1 FPUI). Also, there is 1 output link – 'Next' – to go to the KSI screen missing (1 FPUO) and 1 output link – 'Previous' – to go to the Total Counts screen is missing (1 FPUO). Also, the 2 text fields for the 2 output links ('Next', 'Previous') are missing (2 FPUFs).

At the same time, the description of the functionality for decisions to check if the output link 'Next' or 'Previous' is clicked on is missing (2 FPFDs).

So, the SCFPs for the missing items are: FPUMs = 6 (due to 2 missing FPUIs, 2 missing FPUOs, and 2 missing FPUFs) and FPFMs = 2 (due to 2 missing FPFDs).

14.3.3.7.3 Total Software Component's Feature Points (SCFPs) Counted for UI7 The total Software Component's Feature Points (SCFPs) for UI7 are: FPUS = 1, FPUFs = 44, FPUO = 1, FPUMs = 6, and FPFMs = 2.

14.3.3.8 SCFPs Counting for Requirement Identifier UI8

14.3.3.8.1 Identifiable Software Component's Measurable Features (SCMFs) and Corresponding SCFPs for UI8 There are 1 screen (1 FPUS) and 40 fields (40 FPUFs) which are

- **a.** 18 output fields for the results texts (18 FPUFs);
- **b.** 21 text display fields to display the text (21 FPUFs);
- **c.** 1 text field for the text of the output link 'Exit' to be displayed (1 FPUF).

There is 1 output link – 'Exit' – to go to the Initial screen (1 FPUO).
So, the identifiable SCFPs are: FPUS = 1, FPUFs = 40, and FPUO = 1.

14.3.3.8.2 Apparent Missing Software Component's Measurable Features (SCMFs) and Corresponding SCFPs for UI8 There is 1 input link missing from the Results screen (1 FPUI), see Section 14.2.3.8. Also, there is 1 output link – 'Previous' –

to go to the Total Counts screen missing (1 FPUO), and the text field to display the output link ('Previous') is missing (1 FPUF).

At the same time, the description of the functionality for decision to check if the output link 'Previous' is clicked on is missing (1 FPFD).

So, the SCFPs for the missing items are: FPUMs = 3 (due to 1 missing FPUI, 1 missing FPUO, and 1 missing FPUF) and FPFM = 1 (due to 1 missing FPFD).

14.3.3.8.3 Total Software Component's Feature Points (SCFPs) Counted for UI8 The total Software Component's Feature Points (SCFPs) for UI8 are: FPUS = 1, FPUFs = 40, FPUO = 1, FPUMs = 3, and FPFM = 1.

14.4 SOFTWARE COMPONENT'S FEATURE POINT (SCFP) COUNTING AND SOFTWARE COMPONENT'S FEATURE POINT COUNT (SCFPC) FORMATION TABLE FOR THE EXAMPLE MINI-FSSM ASD

Table 25 shows the Software Component's Feature Points (SCFPs) derived and counted from the Functional Requirements Specifications of the Mini-FSSM ASD example (see Section 14.2), and their consolidation, addition, and conversion to the Software Component's Feature Point Counts (SCFPCs). The counting method, counts, and explanations for the example have been presented in Section 14.3. As mentioned earlier, the explanations for the counting presented in that section should be either entered in the remarks column of Table 25 (it is not done here because of lack of space in the table) or maintained separately as part of the output results of the FSSM.

14.5 FSSM RESULTS TABLES FOR THE SOFTWARE EXAMPLE MINI-FSSM APPLICATION SOFTWARE DEVELOPMENT

All the results – calculations and final – for the mini-FSSM example follow.

14.5.1 Software Component's Feature Points (SCFPs) Consolidation, Addition, and Conversion to the Software Component's Feature Point Counts (SCFPCs) Table

Table 26 shows how the SCFPs for different SCMFs of the SMCs are collected and added together to convert to the SCFPCs for the mini-FSSM example.

14.5.2 Results for the Mini-FSSM Example – Software Component's Feature Point Counts (SCFPCs) Table

Table 27 shows the final SCFPCs status for all the SCMFs of the 4 SMCs for the mini-FSSM example.

14.5.3 Calculations Table (1/4) for the Mini-FSSM Example – Software Component's Measurements (SCMs) and Software Component's Feature Measurements (SCFMs)

Table 28 shows the calculations of the SCMs and SCFMs for the mini-FSSM example.

Table 25 Software Component's Feature Points (SCFPs) Consolidation, Addition, and Conversion to the Software Component's Feature Point Counts (SCFPCs) for the Mini-FSSM Example

	Software Component's Feature Point Counts (SCFPCs) Formation from the Software Component's Feature Points (SCFPs) for the Mini-FSSM Example																															
Requirement Identifier	**FPDC**	**FPDA**	**FPDF**	**FPCM**	**FPDM**	**FPDR**	**FPDW**	**FPDI**	**FPDO**	**FPMS**	**FPMR**	**FPFC**	**FPFL**	**FPFD**	**FPFR**	**FPFA**	**FPFO**	**FPFE**	**FPFM**	**FPLM**	**FPLI**	**FPLS**	**FPLG**	**FPUS**	**FPUF**	**FPUO**	**FPUI**	**FPUM**	**FPNM**	**FPMF**	**FPMM**	**Remarks**
LDM																																
LD1	1	25	25	2																												
LD2	1	19	19																													
LD3	1	18	18																													
FE																																
FS1								1								1			3		1											
FS2					7			1	1							2			8		2											
FS3								1								1					1											
FS4								1	2					2		3			3		3		1									
FS5																																
FS6						1		1	1				25	25	1	26		25		1	3		4									
FS7							3	1	2					3		5	3			3	5		4									

FS8							3		3							3	3			3	6		3									
FS8.1						1						44			1	1				1			2									
FS9												3				1							2									
FS10												13				1							2									
FS11												10				1							1									
FS12												4				1							2									
FS13												2				1							2									
FS14												4				1							1									
FS15																																
FS16					1							20				1							2									
FS17					1							33				1							2									
FS18					1							2				1							1									
FS19												3				1							1									
FS20																																
FS21					1							2				1							1									
FS22					1							2				1							1									
FS23												2				1							1									
FS24												2				1							1									
FS25												2				1							1									

(continued)

Table 25 (*Continued*)

Requirement Identifier	Software Component's Feature Point Counts (SCFPCs) Formation from the Software Component's Feature Points (SCFPs) for the Mini-FSSM Example																														
	FPDC	FPDA	FPDF	FPCM	FPDM	FPDR	FPDW	FPDI	FPDO	FPMS	FPMR	FPFC	FPFL	FPFD	FPFR	FPFA	FPFO	FPFE	FPFM	FPLM	FPLI	FPLS	FPLG	FPUS	FPUF	FPUO	FPUI	FPUM	FPNM	FPMF	FPMM	Remarks
FS26												7	4	4		5							8									
FS27												7	4	4		5							8									
FS28												7	4	4		5							8									
FS29												7	4	4		5							8									
FS30												7	4	4		5							8									
FS31												7	4	4		5							8									
FS32												7	4	4		5							8									
FS33												7	4	4		5							8									
FS34												7	4	4		5							8									
FS35												4	3	4		5							5									
FS36												4	3	4		5							5									
FS37												10	4	4		5							8									
FS38												7	4	4		5							8									
FS39												7	4	4		5							8									
FS40												7	4	4		5							8									
FS41												8	4	4		5							8									
FS42												8	4	4		5							8									

FS43												7	4	4		5							8									
UI																																
UI1																								1	2	1		7				
UI2																			1					1	5	1		3				
UI3																			1					1	1			4				
UI4																			1					1	2			5				
UI5																			1					1	57	3		4				
UI6																			1					1	50	1		4				
UI7																			2					1	44	1		6				
UI8																			1					1	40	1		3				
ME																																
SCFPCs	**3**	**62**	**62**	**2**	**12**	**2**	**6**	**6**	**9**	**0**	**0**	**273**	**95**	**102**	**2**	**147**	**6**	**25**	**22**	**8**	**21**	**0**	**173**	**8**	**201**	**8**	**0**	**36**	**0**	**0**	**0**	
	↑FCDC	**↑FCDA**	**↑FCDF**	**↑FCCM**	**↑FCDM**	**↑FCDR**	**↑FCDW**	**↑FCDI**	**↑FCDO**	**↑FCMS**	**↑FCMR**	**↑FCFC**	**↑FCFL**	**↑FCFD**	**↑FCFR**	**↑FCFA**	**↑FCFO**	**↑FCFE**	**↑FCFM**	**↑FCLM**	**↑FCLI**	**↑FCLS**	**↑FCLG**	**↑FCUS**	**↑FCUF**	**↑FCUO**	**↑FCUI**	**↑FCUM**	**↑FCNM**	**↑FCMF**	**↑FCMM**	

Table 26 Results – Software Component's Feature Points (SCFPs) Consolidation, Addition, and Conversion to the Software Component's Feature Point Counts (SCFPCs) for the Mini-FSSM Example

Functional Software Size Measurement Methodology with Effort Estimation and Performance Indication (FSSM 1.0) – Results																																
Software Component's Feature Points (SCFPs) Consolidation, Addition, and Conversion to the Software Component's Feature Point Counts (SCFPCs) for the Mini-FSSM Example																																
SCFP→ Domain↓	FPDC	FPDA	FPDF	FPCM	FPDM	FPDR	FPDW	FPDI	FPDO	FPMS	FPMR	FPFC	FPFL	FPFD	FPFR	FPFA	FPFO	FPFE	FPFM	FPLM	FPLI	FPLS	FPLG	FPUS	FPUF	FPUO	FPUI	FPUM	FPNM	FPMF	FPMM	Remarks
LDM	3	62	62	2																												
FE					12	2	6	6	9	0	0	273	95	102	2	147	6	25	14	8	21	0	173									
UI																			8					8	201	8	0	36				
ME																													0	0	0	
SCFPC→	**3**	**62**	**62**	**2**	**12**	**2**	**6**	**6**	**9**	**0**	**0**	**273**	**95**	**102**	**2**	**147**	**6**	**25**	**22**	**8**	**21**	**0**	**173**	**8**	**201**	**8**	**0**	**36**	**0**	**0**	**0**	
	↑ FCDC	↑ FCDA	↑ FCDF	↑ FCCM	↑ FCDM	↑ FCDR	↑ FCDW	↑ FCDI	↑ FCDO	↑ FCMS	↑ FCMR	↑ FCFC	↑ FCFL	↑ FCFD	↑ FCFR	↑ FCFA	↑ FCFO	↑ FCFE	↑ FCFM	↑ FCLM	↑ FCLI	↑ FCLS	↑ FCLG	↑ FCUS	↑ FCUF	↑ FCUO	↑ FCUI	↑ FCUM	↑ FCNM	↑ FCMF	↑ FCMM	

Table 27 Results – The Software Component's Feature Point Counts (SCFPCs) for the Mini-FSSM Example

Functional Software Size Measurement Methodology with Effort Estimation and Performance Indication (FSSM 1.0) – Results		
Software Component's Feature Point Counts (SCFPCs) for the Mini-FSSM Example		
Software's Measurable Components (SMCs)	**Software Component's Feature Point Counts (SCFPCs)**	**SCFP Value**
Software's Measurable Component 'Functional Data' (CFD)	FCDC (Data Class): Total number of classes (data entity)	3
	FCDA (Data Attribute): Total number of attributes for all the classes (data entity)	62
	FCDF (Data Field): Total number of fields for all the attributes	62
	FCDM (Data Missing): Total number of apparent missing items for all the functional data	12
Software's Measurable Component 'Functionality Execution' (CFE)	FCDR (Data Read): Total number of memory reads for the Data Collections	2
	FCDW (Data Write): Total number of memory writes for the Data Collections	6
	FCDI (Data Input): Total number of data inputs from the input devices for the Data Collections	6
	FCDO (Data Output): Total number of data outputs to the output devices for the Data Collections	9
	FCMS (Message Send): Total number of messages sent to the other programs	0
	FCMR (Message Receive): Total number of messages received from the other programs	0
	FCFC (Function Computational Operation): Total number of computational operations	273
	FCFL (Function Logical Operation): Total number of logical operations – AND, OR, NOT, XOR	95
	FCFD (Function Decision Execution): Total number of conditions checking and taking decisions	102
	FCFR (Function Repeat Execution): Total number of repeats for the action(s)	2
	FCFA (Function Action Execution): Total number of actions to be performed	147
	FCFO (Function Execution Flow Control): Total number of execution flow control operations	6

(continued)

Table 27 (*Continued*)

Functional Software Size Measurement Methodology with Effort Estimation and Performance Indication (FSSM 1.0) – Results		
Software Component's Feature Point Counts (SCFPCs) for the Mini-FSSM Example		
Software's Measurable Components (SMCs)	**Software Component's Feature Point Counts (SCFPCs)**	**SCFP Value**
	FCFE (Function Error Handling): Total number of errors to be treated	25
	FCCM (Class Method): Total number of methods (procedures) for all the classes (data entity)	2
	FCFM (Functionality Missing): Total number of apparent missing items for all the functionality	22
	FCLM (Memory Operations Functional Data): Total number of Data Collections handled in the memory operations	8
	FCLI (Input and Output Operations Functional Data): Total number of Data Collections handled in the input/output operations	21
	FCLS (Message Exchange Operations Functional Data): Total number of Data Collections handled in message communications	0
	FCLG (General Operations Functional Data): Total number of Data Collections handled in the general computational, logical, decision, repeat, and execution flow control operations	173
Software's Measurable Component 'User Interface' (CUI)	FCUS (User Screen): Total number of user screens	8
	FCUF (User Screen Field): Total number of fields for all the user screens	201
	FCUO (User Screen Output Link): Total number of output links for all the user screens	8
	FCUI (User Screen Input Link): Total number of input links for all the user screens	0
	FCUM (User Screen Missing): Total number of apparent missing items for all the user screens	36
Software's Measurable Component 'Message Exchange' (CME)	FCNM (Notifying Message): Total number of messages	0
	FCMF (Message Field): Total number of fields for all the messages	0
	FCMM (Message Missing): Total number of apparent missing items for all the messages	0

Table 28 Calculations (1/4) of the Software Component's Measurements (SCMs) and Software Component's Feature Measurements (SCFMs) for the Mini-FSSM Example

Functional Software Size Measurement Methodology with Effort Estimation and Performance Indication (FSSM 1.0) – Calculations (1/4)		
Software Component's Measurements (SCMs) and Software Component's Feature Measurements (SCFMs) Calculations for the Mini-FSSM Example		
Software's Measurable Components (SMCs)	**Measurement Calculations**	**SCFP Value**
1. Software Component 'Functional Data' Measurement (CFDM)	**a. Data Class Entities (DCE)** = FCDC	3
	b. Data Class Attribute Entities (DAE) = FCDA	62
	c. Data Class Field Entities (DFE) = FCDF	62
	d. CFDM = Data Class Entities (DCE) + Data Class Attribute Entities (DAE) + Data Class Field Entities (DFE)	127
2. Software Component 'Functionality Execution' Measurement (CFEM) a. Functionality Execution Operations Dynamic Measurement (FEODM) b. Functionality Execution Operations Measurement (FEOM) c. Functionality Execution Data Manipulation Measurement (FEDM)	**a. Memory Operations (MO)** = FCDR + FCDW	8
	b. Computational Operations (CO) = FCFC	273
	c. Logical Operations (LO) = FCFL	95
	d. Decision Execution Operations (DEO) = FCFD	102
	e. Repeat Execution Operations (REO) = FCFR	2
	f. Action Execution Operations (AEO) = FCFA	147
	g. Execution Flow Control Operations (EFCO) = FCFO	6
	h. Input and Output Operations (IOO) = FCDI + FCDO	15
	i. Message Exchange Operations (MEO) = FCMS + FCMR	0
	j. Error Handling Operations (EHO) = FCFE	25
	k. Class Method Entities (CMDE) = FCCM	2
	l. Memory Operations Functional Data Entities (MOFE) = FCLM	8
	m. Input and Output Operations Functional Data Entities (IOFE) = FCLI	21
	n. Message Exchange Operations Functional Data Entities (EOFE) = FCLS	0
	o. General Operations Functional Data Entities (GOFE) = FCLG	173
	p. FEODM = Memory Operations (MO) + Computational Operations (CO) + Logical Operations (LO) + Decision Execution Operations (DEO) + Repeat Execution Operations (REO) + Execution Flow Control Operations (EFCO) + Input and Output Operations (IOO) + Message Exchange Operations (MEO)	501

Table 28 (*Continued*)

Functional Software Size Measurement Methodology with Effort Estimation and Performance Indication (FSSM 1.0) – Calculations (1/4)		
Software Component's Measurements (SCMs) and Software Component's Feature Measurements (SCFMs) Calculations for the Mini-FSSM Example		
Software's Measurable Components (SMCs)	**Measurement Calculations**	**SCFP Value**
	q. FEOM = FEODM + Action Execution Operations (AEO) + Class Method Entities (CMDE)	650
	r. FEDM = Memory Operations Functional Data Entities (MOFE) + Input and Output Operations Functional Data Entities (IOFE) + Message Exchange Operations Functional Data Entities (EOFE) + General Operations Functional Data Entities (GOFE)	202
	s. CFEM = FEOM + FEDM	**852**
3. Software Component 'User Interface' Measurement (CUIM)	**a. User Interface Screen Entities (UISE)** = FCUS	8
	b. User Interface Field Entities (UIFE) = FCUF	201
	c. User Interface Input Link Entities (UIIE) = FCUI	8
	d. User Interface Output Link Entities (UIOE) = FCUO	0
	e. CUIM = User Interface Screen Entities (UISE) + User Interface Field Entities (UIFE) + User Interface Input Link Entities (UIIE) + User Interface Output Link Entities (UIOE)	**217**
4. Software Component 'Message Exchange' Measurement (CMEM)	**a. Notifying Message Entities (NME)** = FCNM	0
	b. Message Field Entities (MFE) = FCMF	0
	c. CMEM = Notifying Message Entities (NME) + Message Field Entities (MFE)	0
5. Software Components Requirement Deficiency Measurement (CRDM)	**a. Functional Data Missing Entities (FDME)** = FCDM	12
	b. Functionality Execution Missing Entities (FEME) = FCFM	22
	c. User Interface Missing Entities (UIME) = FCUM	36
	d. Message Exchange Missing Entities (MEME) = FCMM	0
	e. CRDM = Functional Data Missing Entities (FDME) + Functionality Execution Missing Entities (FEME) + User Interface Missing Entities (UIME) + Message Exchange Missing Entities (MEME)	**70**
6. Software Total Components Measurement (STCM)	**a. STCM** = CFDM + CFEM + CUIM + CMEM	**1196**

Table 29 Calculations (2/4) of the Software Size and Effort Estimations (SSEEs) for the Mini-FSSM Example

Functional Software Size Measurement Methodology with Effort Estimation and Performance Indication (FSSM 1.0) – Calculations (2/4)		
Software Size and Effort Estimations (SSEEs) Calculations for the Mini-FSSM Example		
1. Software Logical Size (SLS)	**a. Software Data Statements (SDS)** = 4 × DCE + 2 × DAE + 2 × CMDE + 2 × UISE + UIIE + UIOE + 2 × NME + DFE × (1 + 0.1 × CMDE) + UIFE × (1 + 0.1 × CMDE) + MFE × (1 + 0.1 × CMDE) + 0.1 × (DFE + UIFE + MFE)	506
	b. Software Code Statements (SCDS) = 3 × CMDE + 2 × DEO + 2 × REO + 2 × AEO + 2 × (1 + CMDE) + EFCO + CO + LO + 2 × (MO + IOO + MEO) + MOFE + IOFE + EOFE + GOFE	1136
	c. Software Comment Statements (SCS) = 0.4 × (SDS + SCDS)	657
	d. SLS = SDS + SCDS + SCS	2299
2. Software Analysis, Design, and Coding Effort (SADCE) (including technical specifications documents)	**a. Software Data Analysis and Design Effort (SDADE)** (including technical specifications documents) = ((CFDM + CUIM + CMEM) / 40) person days	9
	b. Software Functionality Analysis and Design Effort (SFADE) (including technical specifications documents) = (CFEM / 80) person days	11
	c. Software Coding Effort (SCE) (including technical specifications documents) = (SLS / 80) person days	29
	d. SADCE = (SDADE + SFADE + SCE) person days	49
3. Software Testing Effort (STE) (including test specifications documents)	**a. STE** = (1.2 × SADCE) person days	59
4. Software Total Development Effort (STDE)	**a. STDE** = (SADCE + STE) person days	108

14.5.4 Calculations Table (2/4) for the Mini-FSSM Example – Software Size and Effort Estimations (SSEEs)

Table 29 shows the calculations of the SSEEs for the mini-FSSM example.

14.5.5 Calculations Table (3/4) for the Mini-FSSM Example – Software Performance Quality Indicators (SPQIs): Software Structural Indicators (SSIs)

Table 30 shows the calculations of the SPQIs – SSIs[5–7] – for the mini-FSSM example.

14.5.6 Calculations Table (4/4) for the Mini-FSSM Example – Software Performance Quality Indicators (SPQIs): Software Operational Indicators (SOIs)

Table 31 shows the calculations of the SPQIs – SOIs[5–7] – for the mini-FSSM example.

Table 30 Calculations (3/4) of the Software Performance Quality Indicators (SPQIs): Software Structural Indicators (SSIs) for the Mini-FSSM Example

Functional Software Size Measurement Methodology with Effort Estimation and Performance Indication (FSSM 1.0) – Calculations (3/4)		
Software Performance Quality Indicators (SPQIs) – Software Structural Indicators (SSIs)[5–7] Calculations for the Mini-FSSM Example		
Software Structural Indicators (SSIs)[5–7] (Nil, Low, Medium, High, Very High)	**Calculation**	**Value**
1. SSIs denoting the Software's Measurable Components (SMCs):		
a. Functional Data Complexity and Size (FDCS)	CFDM	127.0
b. Functionality Execution Complexity and Size (FECS)	CFEM	852.0
c. User Interface Complexity and Size (UICS)	CUIM	217.0
d. Message Exchange Complexity and Size (MECS)	CMEM	0.0
e. Functional Data Component Proportion (FDCP) %	CFDM / STCM	10.6
f. Functionality Execution Component Proportion (FECP) %	CFEM / STCM	71.2
g. User Interface Component Proportion (UICP) %	CUIM / STCM	18.1
h. Message Exchange Component Proportion (MECP) %	CMEM / STCM	0.0
2. SSIs denoting the Functionality Execution (FE) Operations:		
a. Memory Transaction Proportion (MTP) %	MO / STCM	0.7
b. Computational Operation Content Proportion (COCP) %	CO / STCM	22.8
c. Logical Operation Content Proportion (LOCP) %	LO / STCM	7.9
d. Decision Execution Content Proportion (DECP) %	DEO / STCM	8.5
e. Repeat Execution Content Proportion (RECP) %	REO / STCM	0.2
f. Action Execution Content Proportion (AECP) %	AEO / STCM	12.3
g. Execution Flow Control Content Proportion (EFCCP) %	EFCO / STCM	0.5
h. User Interaction Proportion (UIP) %	IOO / STCM	1.3
i. External Communication Proportion (ECP) %	MEO / STCM	0.0
j. Error Handling Proportion (EHP) %	EHO / STCM	2.1
3. SSIs denoting the Functionality Execution (FE) Operations Data Handling:		
a. Memory Operations Functional Data Proportion (MODP) %	MOFE / STCM	0.7
b. Input and Output Operations Functional Data Proportion (IODP) %	IOFE / STCM	1.8
c. Message Exchange Operations Functional Data Proportion (EODP) %	EOFE / STCM	0.0
d. General Operations Functional Data Proportion (GODP) %	GOFE / STCM	14.5
4. SSI denoting the deficiency in the Functional Requirements Specifications (FRS):		
a. Requirements Deficiency Grade (RDG) %	CRDM / STCM	5.9

Table 31 Calculations (4/4) of the Software Performance Quality Indicators (SPQIs): Software Operational Indicators (SOIs) for the Mini-FSSM Example

Functional Software Size Measurement Methodology with Effort Estimation and Performance Indication (FSSM 1.0) – Calculations (4/4)		
Software Performance Quality Indicators (SPQIs) – Software Operational Indicators (SOIs)[5–7] Calculations for the Mini-FSSM Example		
Software Operational Indicators (SOIs)[5–7] (Nil, Low, Medium, High, Very High)	**Calculation**	**Value**
1. SOIs denoting the Functional Operations Execution:		
a. Memory Traffic Level (MTL) %	MO / FEODM	1.6
b. Computational Operations Level (COL) %	CO / FEODM	54.5
c. Logical Operations Level (LOL) %	LO / FEODM	19.0
d. Decision Execution Level (DEL) %	DEO / FEODM	20.4
e. Repeat Execution Level (REL) %	REO / FEODM	0.4
f. Execution Flow Control Level (EFCL) %	EFCO / FEODM	1.2
g. User Interaction Level (UIL) %	IOO / FEODM	3.0
h. External Communication Level (ECL) %	MEO / FEODM	0.0
i. Error Handling Capability (EHC) %	EHO / FEODM	5.0
2. SOIs denoting the Functional Operations Data Handling:		
a. Memory Traffic Functional Data Level (MTDL) %	MOFE / FEDM	4.0
b. User Interaction Functional Data Level (UIDL) %	IOFE / FEDM	10.4
c. External Communication Functional Data Level (ECDL) %	EOFE / FEDM	0.0
d. General Operations Execution Functional Data Level (GODL) %	GOFE / FEDM	85.6

14.5.7 Final Results Table (1/4) for the Mini-FSSM Example – Software Component's Measurements (SCMs) and Software Size and Effort Estimations (SSEEs)

Table 32 shows the final results of the SCMs and SSEEs for the mini-FSSM example.

14.5.8 Final Results Table (2/4) for the Mini-FSSM Example – Software Component's Measurements (SCMs) and Software Component's Feature Measurements (SCFMs)

Table 33 shows the final results of the SCMs and SCFMs for the mini-FSSM example.

14.5.9 Final Results Table (3/4) for the Mini-FSSM Example – Software Performance Quality Indicators (SPQIs): Software Structural Indicators (SSIs)

Table 34 shows the final results of the SPQIs – SSIs[5–7] – for the mini-FSSM example.

Table 32 Final Results (1/4) for the Example mini-FSSM – The Software Component's Measurements (SCMs) and Software Size and Effort Estimations (SSEEs). Adapted from Software Comprehensive Count with Quality Indicators (SCCQI), Jasveer Singh, UKSMA/COSMIC Conference 2012, SMEF 2012, NESMA Autumn Meeting 2012.

Functional Software Size Measurement Methodology with Effort Estimation and Performance Indication (FSSM 1.0) – Final Results (1/4)			
Software Component's Measurements (SCMs) and Software Size and Effort Estimations (SSEEs) Final Results for the Mini-FSSM Example			
Software Component's Measurements (SCMs)	**SCFP Value**	**Software Size and Effort Estimations (SSEEs)**	**Value**
Software Component 'Functional Data' Measurement (CFDM)	**127**	**Software Logical Size (SLS)**	**2299**
Functionality Execution Operations Dynamic Measurement (FEODM)	**501**	**Software Analysis, Design, and Coding Effort (SADCE) (including technical specifications documents) person days**	**49**
Functionality Execution Operations Measurement (FEOM)	**650**	**Software Testing Effort (STE) (including test specifications documents) person days**	**59**
Functionality Execution Data Manipulation Measurement (FEDM)	**202**	**Software Total Development Effort (STDE) person days**	**108**
Software Component 'Functionality Execution' Measurement (CFEM)	**852**		
Software Component 'User Interface' Measurement (CUIM)	**217**		
Software Component 'Message Exchange' Measurement (CMEM)	**0**		
Software Total Components Measurement (STCM)	**1196**		
Software Components Requirement Deficiency Measurement (CRDM)	**70**		

Table 33 Final Results (2/4) for the Example Mini-FSSM – The Software Component's Measurements (SCMs) and Software Component's Feature Measurements (SCFMs)

Functional Software Size Measurement Methodology with Effort Estimation and Performance Indication (FSSM 1.0) – Final Results (2/4)	
Software Component's Measurements (SCMs) and Software Component's Feature Measurements (SCFMs) Final Results for the Mini-FSSM Example	
SCMs and SCFMs	**SCFP Value**
a. Data Class Entities (DCE)	3
b. Data Class Attribute Entities (DAE)	62
c. Data Class Field Entities (DFE)	62
1. Software Component 'Functional Data' Measurement (CFDM)	**127**
a. Memory Operations (MO)	8

(continued)

Table 33 (*Continued*)

Functional Software Size Measurement Methodology with Effort Estimation and Performance Indication (FSSM 1.0) – Final Results (2/4)	
Software Component's Measurements (SCMs) and Software Component's Feature Measurements (SCFMs) Final Results for the Mini-FSSM Example	
SCMs and SCFMs	**SCFP Value**
b. Computational Operations (CO)	273
c. Logical Operations (LO)	95
d. Decision Execution Operations (DEO)	102
e. Repeat Execution Operations (REO)	2
f. Action Execution Operations (AEO)	147
g. Execution Flow Control Operations (EFCO)	6
h. Input and Output Operations (IOO)	15
i. Message Exchange Operations (MEO)	0
j. Error Handling Operations (EHO)	25
k. Class Method Entities (CMDE)	2
l. Memory Operations Functional Data Entities (MOFE)	8
m. Input and Output Operations Functional Data Entities (IOFE)	21
n. Message Exchange Operations Functional Data Entities (EOFE)	0
o. General Operations Functional Data Entities (GOFE)	173
p. Functionality Execution Operations Dynamic Measurement (FEODM)	**501**
q. Functionality Execution Operations Measurement (FEOM)	**650**
r. Functionality Execution Data Manipulation Measurement (FEDM)	**202**
2. Software Component 'Functionality Execution' Measurement (CFEM)	**852**
a. User Interface Screen Entities (UISE)	8
b. User Interface Field Entities (UIFE)	201
c. User Interface Input Link Entities (UIIE)	8
d. User Interface Output Link Entities (UIOE)	0
3. Software Component 'User Interface' Measurement (CUIM)	**217**
a. Notifying Message Entities (NME)	0
b. Message Field Entities (MFE)	0
4. Software Component 'Message Exchange' Measurement (CMEM)	**0**
a. Functional Data Missing Entities (FDME)	12
b. Functionality Execution Missing Entities (FEME)	22
c. User Interface Missing Entities (UIME)	36
d. Message Exchange Missing Entities (MEME)	0
5. Software Components Requirement Deficiency Measurement (CRDM)	**70**
6. Software Total Components Measurement (STCM)	**1196**

Table 34 Final Results (3/4) for the Example mini-FSSM – The Software Performance Quality Indicators (SPQIs): Software Structural Indicators (SSIs). Adapted from Software Comprehensive Count with Quality Indicators (SCCQI), Jasveer Singh, UKSMA/COSMIC Conference 2012[5], SMEF 2012, NESMA Autumn Meeting 2012.

Functional Software Size Measurement Methodology with Effort Estimation and Performance Indication (FSSM 1.0) – Final Results (3/4)	
Software Performance Quality Indicators (SPQIs) – Software Structural Indicators (SSIs)[5–7] Final Results for the Mini-FSSM Example	
Software Structural Indicators (SSIs)[5–7]	**Value**
1. SSIs denoting the Software's Measurable Components (SMCs):	
Functional Data Complexity and Size (FDCS)	Medium
Functionality Execution Complexity and Size (FECS)	Medium
User Interface Complexity and Size (UICS)	Medium
Message Exchange Complexity and Size (MECS)	Nil
Functional Data Component Proportion (FDCP)	Low
Functionality Execution Component Proportion (FECP)	Very High
User Interface Component Proportion (UICP)	Low
Message Exchange Component Proportion (MECP)	Nil
2. SSIs denoting the Functionality Execution (FE) Operations:	
Memory Transaction Proportion (MTP)	Low
Computational Operation Content Proportion (COCP)	Medium
Logical Operation Content Proportion (LOC)	Low
Decision Execution Content Proportion (DECP)	Low
Repeat Execution Content Proportion (RECP)	Low
Action Execution Content Proportion (AECP)	Low
Execution Flow Control Content Proportion (EFCCP)	Low
User Interaction Proportion (UIP)	Low
External Communication Proportion (ECP)	Nil
Error Handling Proportion (EHP)	Low
3. SSIs denoting the Functionality Execution (FE) Operations Data Handling:	
Memory Operations Functional Data Proportion (MODP)	Low
Input and Output Operations Functional Data Proportion (IODP)	Low
Message Exchange Operations Functional Data Proportion (EODP)	Nil
General Operations Functional Data Proportion (GODP)	Low
4. SSI denoting the deficiency in the Functional Requirements Specifications (FRS):	
Requirements Deficiency Grade (RDG)	Low

Table 35 Final Results (4/4) for the Example Mini-FSSM – The Software Performance Quality Indicators (SPQIs): Software Operational Indicators (SOIs). Adapted from Software Comprehensive Count with Quality Indicators (SCCQI), Jasveer Singh, UKSMA/COSMIC Conference 2012, SMEF 2012, NESMA Autumn Meeting 2012.

Functional Software Size Measurement Methodology with Effort Estimation and Performance Indication (FSSM 1.0) – Final Results (4/4)	
Software Performance Quality Indicators (SPQIs) – Software Operational Indicators (SOIs)[5–7] Final Results for the Mini-FSSM Example	
Software Operational Indicators (SOIs)[5–7]	**Value**
1. SOIs denoting the Functional Operations Execution:	
Memory Traffic Level (MTL)	Low
Computational Operations Level (COL)	High
Logical Operations Level (LOL)	Low
Decision Execution Level (DEL)	Low
Repeat Execution Level (REL)	Low
Execution Flow Control Level (EFCL)	Low
User Interaction Level (UIL)	Low
External Communication Level (ECL)	Nil
Error Handling Capability (EHC)	Low
2. SOIs denoting the Functional Operations Data Handling:	
Memory Traffic Functional Data Level (MTDL)	Low
User Interaction Functional Data Level (UIDL)	Low
External Communication Functional Data Level (ECDL)	Nil
General Operations Execution Functional Data Level (GODL)	Very High

14.5.10 Final Results Table (4/4) for the Mini-FSSM Example – Software Performance Quality Indicators (SPQIs): Software Operational Indicators (SOIs)

Table 35 shows the final results of the SPQIs – SOIs[5–7] – for the mini-FSSM example.

14.6 GRAPHICAL REPRESENTATION OF THE FINAL OUTPUT RESULTS FOR THE EXAMPLE MINI-FSSM

Final output results of the Software Component's Measurements (SCMs), Software Component's Feature Measurements (SCFMs), and Software Performance Quality Indicators (SPQIs) for the mini-FSSM example are presented in graphical form next.

14.6.1 Software Component's Measurements (SCMs) Graph for the Mini-FSSM Example

Figure 22 shows the SCMs for the mini-FSSM example in graphical manner.

14.6.2 Software Component's Measurements (SCMs) and Software Component's Feature Measurements (SCFMs) Graph for the Mini-FSSM Example

Figure 23 shows the SCMs and SCFMs for the mini-FSSM example in graphical manner.

14.6.3 Software Structural Indicators (SSIs) Graph for the Mini-FSSM Example

Figure 24 shows the SSIs[5–7] for the mini-FSSM example in graphical manner.

14.6.4 Software Operational Indicators (SOIs) Graph for the Mini-FSSM Example

Figure 25 shows the SOIs[5–7] for the mini-FSSM example in graphical manner.

14.7 CHAPTER SUMMARY

This chapter contains an example to show the usage of the FSSM. The example is of a mini-version of the FSSM called Mini-FSSM Application Software Development (ASD), and it demonstrates how the FSSM methodology is applied for the functional software size measurement, effort estimation, and performance indication.

First, the Functional Requirements Specifications of the mini-FSSM example application for which the software size measurement, effort estimation, and performance indication are performed by using the FSSM are presented. The FRS contain the description of the data, functionality, and user interfaces (screens).

Next, the Software Component's Feature Points (SCFPs) counting table and counting explanations for all the Functional Requirements Specifications of the mini-FSSM example application are presented.

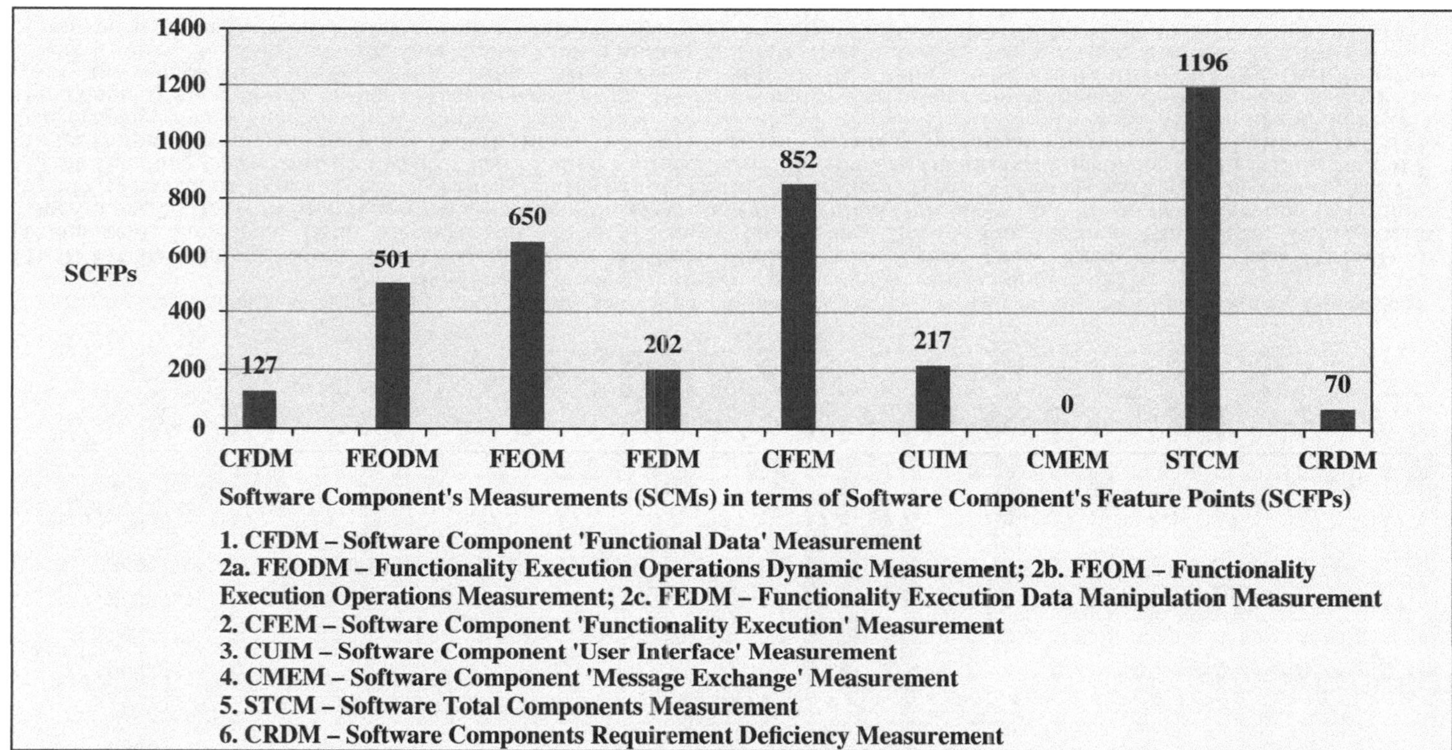

Figure 22 Graphical representation of the Software Component's Measurements (SCMs) for the mini-FSSM example. Adapted from Software Comprehensive Count with Quality Indicators (SCCQI), Jasveer Singh, UKSMA/COSMIC Conference 2012[5], SMEF 2012[6], NESMA Autumn Meeting 2012[7].

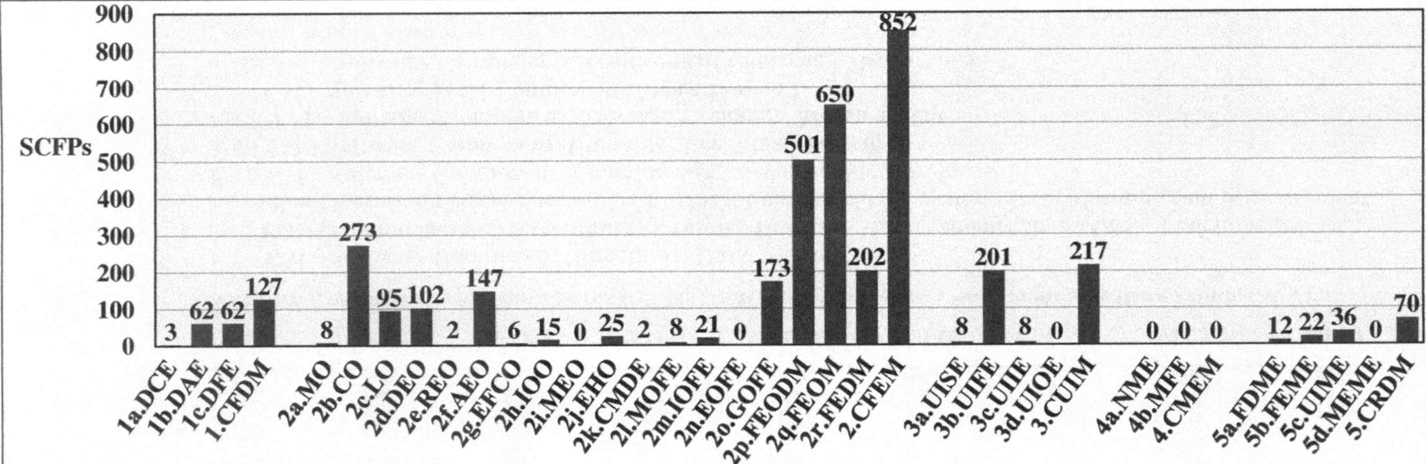

Software Component's Measurements (SCMs) and Software Component's Feature Measurements (SCFMs) (Entities, Operations and Data Handling) in terms of Software Component's Feature Points (SCFPs)

1a.DCE-Data Class Entities, 1b.DAE-Data Class Attribute Entities, 1c.DFE-Data Class Field Entities, 1.CFDM-Software Component 'Functional Data' Measurement; 2a.MO-Memory Operations, 2b.CO-Computational Operations, 2c.LO-Logical Operations, 2d.DEO-Decision Execution Operations, 2e.REO-Repeat Execution Operations, 2f.AEO-Action Execution Operations, 2g.EFCO-Execution Flow Control Operations, 2h.IOO-Input/Output Operations, 2i.MEO-Message Exchange Operations, 2j.EHO-Error Handling Operations, 2k.CMDE-Class Method Entities, 2l.MOFE-Memory Operations Functional Data Entities, 2m.IOFE-Input/Output Operations Functional Data Entities, 2n.EOFE-Message Exchange Operations Functional Data Entities, 2o.GOFE-General Operations Functional Data Entities, 2p.FEODM-Functionality Execution Operations Dynamic Measurement, 2q.FEOM-Functionality Execution Operations Measurement, 2r.FEDM-Functionality Execution Data Manipulation Measurement, 2.CFEM-Software Component 'Functionality Execution' Measurement; 3a.UISE-User Interface Screen Entities, 3b.UIFE-User Interface Field Entities, 3c.UIIE-User Interface Input Link Entities, 3d.UIOE-User Interface Output Link Entities, 3.CUIM-Software Component 'User Interface' Measurement; 4a.NME-Notifying Message Entities, 4b.MFE-Message Field Entities, 4.CMEM-Software Component 'Message Exchange' Measurement; 5a.FDME-Functional Data Missing Entities, 5b.FEME-Functionality Execution Missing Entities, 5c.UIME-User Interface Missing Entities, 5d.MEME-Message Exchange Missing Entities, 5.CRDM-Software Components Requirement Deficiency Measurement.

Figure 23 Graphical representation of the Software Component's Measurements (SCMs) and Software Component's Feature Measurements (SCFMs) for the mini-FSSM example.

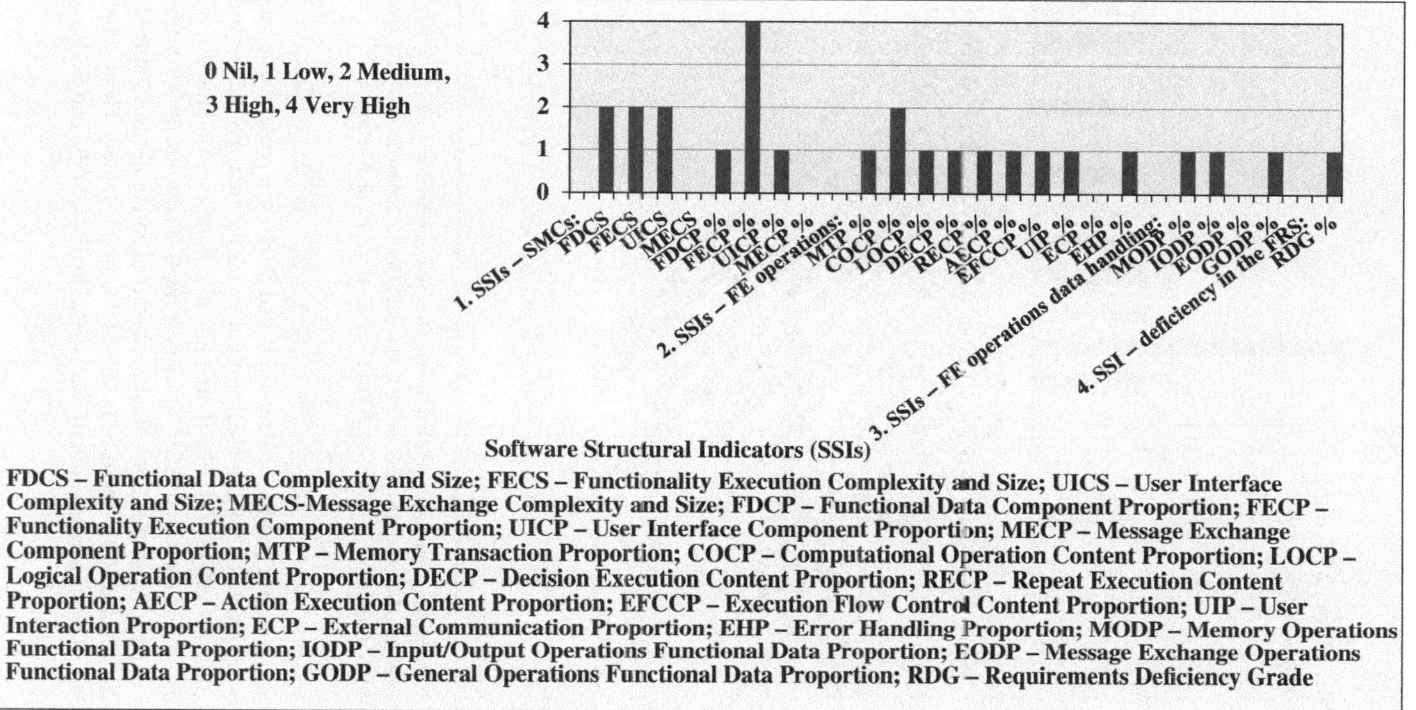

Figure 24 Graphical representation of the Software Structural Indicators (SSIs)[5–7] for the mini-FSSM example. Adapted from Software Comprehensive Count with Quality Indicators (SCCQI), Jasveer Singh, UKSMA/COSMIC Conference 2012[5], SMEF 2012[6], NESMA Autumn Meeting 2012[7].

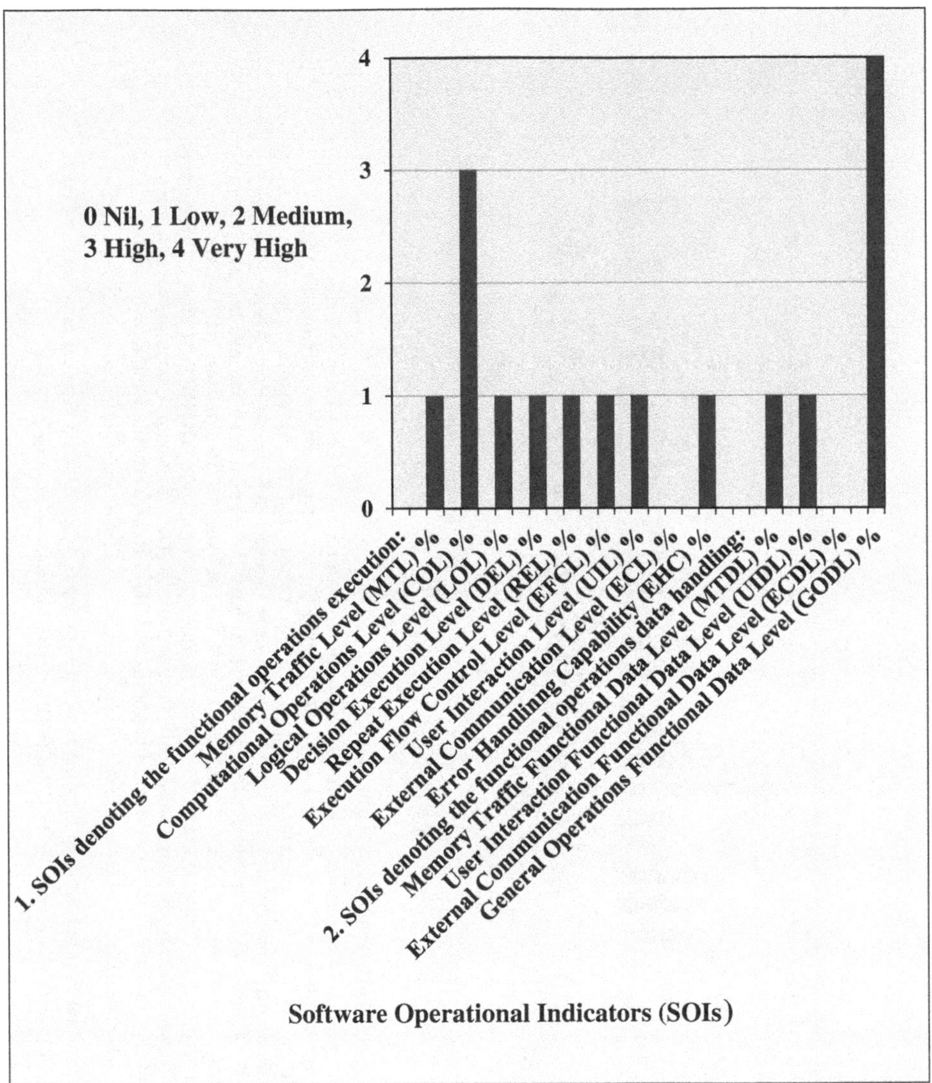

Figure 25 Graphical representation of the Software Operational Indicators (SOIs)[5–7] for the mini-FSSM example. Adapted from Software Comprehensive Count with Quality Indicators (SCCQI), Jasveer Singh, UKSMA/COSMIC Conference 2012[5], SMEF 2012[6], NESMA Autumn Meeting 2012[7].

Finally, the output results – calculations and final – are presented in tabular form, and final results are presented in graphical form also, for the mini-FSSM example.

Regarding the results, first, the input table about the consolidation of SCFPs and their addition and conversion to the SCFPCs is presented. Then, the table for the final SCFPCs status is presented. After that, the calculations tables and final result tables for the SCFMs, SCMs, SSEEs, and SPQIs – both SSIs and SOIs, are presented. These tables are followed by the graphical form presentation of the SCMs, SCFMs, SSIs, and SOIs.

Part Eight

Concluding Information

Chapter 15

Effort Estimate for the Usage of the FSSM

Rough estimation of the approximate effort required for the usage of the FSSM is presented in this chapter.

15.1 SOFTWARE COMPONENT'S FEATURE POINT (SCFP) COUNTING, ANALYSIS, AND REPORT PREPARATION EFFORT ESTIMATE FOR THE USAGE OF THE FSSM

The various phases of the use and application of the Functional Software Size Measurement Methodology with Effort Estimation and Performance Indication (FSSM), and their rough effort estimates are presented next for a fictitious application which has a Functional Requirements Specifications (FRS) description document of about 200 pages (assumed approximately 400 words per page on average including all the words of the text, tables, and figures) describing the Logical Data Model, Functionality Execution, User Interface (screens), and Message Exchange parts.

This estimate assumes that the person using and applying the FSSM is experienced and skilled in the use and application of the FSSM, and has normal, average productivity.

The usage of the FSSM is divided in the following phases:

1. initial reading and preparation;
2. Software Component's Feature Points (SCFPs) counting;
3. consolidation of results;
4. report preparation.

These phases are described next.

15.1.1 Initial Reading and Preparation

During the 'Initial reading and preparation' phase, the following activities would be performed:

a. initial reading of the Functional Requirements Specifications (FRS) document to gain the initial knowledge about the requirements of the software application;

Functional Software Size Measurement Methodology with Effort Estimation and Performance Indication, First Edition. Jasveer Singh.

Companion website: http://booksupport.wiley.com

b. defining the borderline and scope of the measurement;

c. preparing the tables for the next phase 'Software Component's Feature Points (SCFPs) counting'.

All the aforementioned work can be done approximately at an average rate of about 40 pages/day.

So, for a functional requirements document of a total of about 200 pages, it would take about 5 days to complete the work of 'Initial reading and preparatory' phase.

Hence, approximate time required for the 'Initial reading and preparation' activity = 5 days.

15.1.2 Software Component's Feature Points (SCFPs) Counting

'Software Component's Feature Points (SCFPs) counting' phase comprises mainly the following activities:

a. identifying the Software Component's Measurable Features (SCMFs) in the functional requirements;

b. assigning the Software Component's Feature Points (SCFPs) to the identified SCMFs;

c. filling in the SCFP counting table.

All the aforementioned work can be done approximately at an average rate of about 20 pages/day.

So, for a functional requirements document of a total of about 200 pages, it would take about 10 days to complete the work of the 'Software Component's Feature Points (SCFPs) counting' phase.

Hence, approximate time required for the 'Software Component's Feature Points (SCFPs) counting' activity = 10 days.

15.1.3 Consolidation of Results

In the 'Consolidation of results' phase, all the counts need to be consolidated and calculations need to be performed for the results.

This can be done approximately at an average rate of about 70 pages/day.

So, for a functional requirements document of a total of about 200 pages, it would take about 3 days to complete the work of the 'Consolidation of results' phase.

Hence, approximate time required for the 'Consolidation of results' activity = 3 days.

15.1.4 Report Preparation

In the final 'Report preparation' phase, all the results need to be consolidated in a summary report.

This can be done approximately at the average rate of about 100 pages/day.

So, for a functional requirements document of a total of about 200 pages, it would take about 2 days to complete the work of the 'Report preparation' phase.

Hence, approximate time required for the 'Report preparation' activity = 2 days.

15.1.5 Total Effort

Total Effort = addition of the efforts required for the

a. initial reading and preparation;

b. Software Component's Feature Points (SCFPs) counting;

c. consolidation of results;

d. report preparation.

Hence, for a functional requirements document of a total of about 200 pages, the total approximate effort required for using and applying the FSSM would be about $5 + 10 + 3 + 2 = 20$ person days.

15.2 CHAPTER SUMMARY

Effort estimate for the use and application of the FSSM is presented in this chapter. Mainly, there are 4 phases for the use and application of the FSSM and each phase is estimated at the rate of certain pages of the Functional Requirements Specifications document per day:

1. initial reading and preparation at about 40 pages/day;
2. Software Component's Feature Points (SCFPs) counting at about 20 pages/day;
3. consolidation of results at about 70 pages/day;
4. report preparation at about 100 pages/day.

The total of the aforementioned calculated days is the approximate estimated effort required for the use and application of the FSSM.

For an FRS document of about 200 pages, the approximate effort estimate for the usage of the FSSM is calculated as 5, 10, 3, and 2 days, respectively, for the aforementioned 4 phases, resulting in a total of approximately 20 person days.

Chapter 16

Known Limitations, Improvement Scope, and Conclusion

This chapter presents the known limitations of and improvement possibilities in the FSSM, and the conclusion.

16.1 KNOWN LIMITATIONS OF THE FSSM

Following are the known limitations of the FSSM:

1. The actual effort spent on the development/testing activities depends on so many factors: planning, organization, productivity, efficiency, knowledge, experience, etc., and so may not always exactly match with the indicated effort by the FSSM.
2. The FSSM is applicable only for the software development in high-level languages. It cannot be applied for assembly languages.
3. The Software Operational Indicator (SOIs)[5–7] reflect the run-time characteristics calculated with the assumption of the execution of
   - all the repeat loops only once;
   - all the decision (that means both the 'if' condition and 'else' case) simultaneously;
   - all the actions under all the decisions once;
   - all the program once with the above stipulations.
4. No optimization has been considered to calculate the software logical size.
5. While using the SOIs, the facts mentioned about the run-time dynamic characteristics in Section 1.3 should be kept in mind.

16.2 IMPROVEMENT POSSIBILITIES IN THE FSSM

The following features can be tried for improving the output results from the FSSM:

1. Approximate physical data size can also be made available as one of the outputs if the information about the approximate number of instances of the objects of the classes and approximate size of the fields of the classes' attributes is included in the functional requirements specifications.

Functional Software Size Measurement Methodology with Effort Estimation and Performance Indication, First Edition. Jasveer Singh.

Companion website: http://booksupport.wiley.com

This can be done as follows:

Number of tuples for a class or subclass = Number of instances for the class or subclass.

Size of table for a class or subclass = (Total size of fields of all the attributes of the particular class or subclass) × (Number of tuples for the particular class or subclass).

Size of tables should be calculated for all the classes and subclasses.

Total database size = Sum of the size of the tables for all the classes and subclasses.

2. Data usage frequency of the Data Collections (classes, sub-classes) for different operations – memory read/write, input/output, message communications, and general functionality execution (computational, logical, decision, repeat, and execution flow control) – can be collected by recording the use of the Data Collections for these operations while identifying the SCMFs and assigning them the SCFPs in the counting process. This can provide information about the frequency of use of particular data collections in various operations.

16.3 CONCLUSION

The FSSM has many conspicuous, significant, and useful advantages for the Functional Size Measurement[1] of the software, especially in comparison to the currently available software size measurement methodologies. It covers all the important constituents of the software for counting and is therefore very elaborate and comprehensive as it considers and takes into account all the relevant and essential software's measurable components and all the software component's measurable features. So, the size and complexity of all the components can be measured and judged accurately. By using the FSSM, the most realistic effort estimates are directly obtained which can be utilized for a precise project planning. No external multiplication factors based on the past projects statistics are required to be applied for the effort estimation calculations because the effort estimation is an integral part of the FSSM. At the same time, adequate number of vital Software Performance Quality Indicators are made available that help to assess the structural and operational characteristics of the software and to judge the quality of the Functional Requirements Specifications with respect to the error handling and deficiencies. Based on the quality indicators, improvements can be made in the requirements to make them more precise, accurate, and complete, resulting in higher quality of the software. Also, system architecture requirements can be assessed and its design can be improved based on the quality indicators. Both the factors – precise project planning and higher quality software – lead to significant cost savings in the software development process. At the same time, the FSSM is fully compliant with the ISO/IEC 14143-1[1] standards.

The FSSM is designed with a view to helping the software community in improving the quality of the software projects by better methods and techniques, specifically in the area of the software size measurement, by taking into consideration all the constituent parts of the software for the complete software size measurement and thus providing a realistic size determination, development effort estimation, and performance indication of the software. Due to a more precise measurement at an early stage of the software life cycle by using the FSSM, the efficiency of the planning will increase, resources may be used more wisely, and there is a greater chance that projects will be completed within the budget and on time.

To conclude, it is worth using the FSSM because of its multiple, significant strengths and advantages.

16.4 CHAPTER SUMMARY

16.4.1 Known Limitations of the FSSM: Summary

A few know limitations of the FSSM are mentioned in this chapter. They are mainly the following:

- It is not possible to estimate the effort 100% exactly because of various factors like planning, productivity, efficiency, and knowledge.
- The FSSM is applicable only for the software projects for which high-level languages are used.
- Dynamic characteristics determination in the FSSM has a few assumptions attached with it.
- Optimization of the software is not considered in the FSSM.

16.4.2 Improvement Possibilities in the FSSM: Summary

Two possible improvements about the calculations of the physical database size and usage frequency of the Data Collections are suggested.

16.4.3 Conclusion: Summary

The following conclusion is presented in this chapter: it is worth using the FSSM because of multiple, significant strengths and advantages it offers.

Part Nine

Glossary

Chapter 17

Glossary

All the terms used and their significance in the Functional Software Size Measurement Methodology with Effort Estimation and Performance Indication (FSSM) are presented in this chapter. They are arranged alphabetically.

17.1 TERMS AND THEIR SIGNIFICANCE

17.1.1 A

17.1.1.1 Action Execution Content Proportion (AECP)

One of the Software Performance Quality Indicators (SPQIs) of the type Software Structural Indicator (SSI)[5–7]. It gives the indication of the static proportion of the different actions performed in the total software contents.

The AECP is the ratio of the total number of the actions performed, that is, the Action Execution Operations (AEO), to the total software size measurement, that is, the Software Total Components Measurement (STCM), in percentage, and is expressed as Nil, Low, Medium, High, or Very High according to its percentage value.

17.1.1.2 Action Execution Operations (AEO)

The Software Component's Feature Measurement (SCFM) for the Software Component's Measurable Feature 'Function Action Execution' (FFA) in terms of the Software Component's Feature Points (SCFPs).

The AEO (Action Execution Operations) is the measurement for the functional action execution operations which perform different types of actions of the software processing, and which are described in the Functionality Execution (FE) description part of the Functional Requirements Specifications (FRS).

The AEO is calculated from the Software Component's Feature Point Count for 'Function Action Execution' (FCFA), and is used for the following calculations:

a. Software Component's Measurements (SCMs): the Software Total Components Measurement (STCM) through the Software Component 'Functionality Execution' Measurement (CFEM);

Functional Software Size Measurement Methodology with Effort Estimation and Performance Indication, First Edition. Jasveer Singh.

Companion website: http://booksupport.wiley.com

b. Software Size and Effort Estimations (SSEEs): the Software Total Development Effort (STDE) through the Software Logical Size (SLS) and Software Analysis, Design, and Coding Effort (SADCE);

c. Software Performance Quality Indicators (SPQIs): Software Structural Indicators (SSIs)[5–7], that is, the SSIs Functionality Execution Complexity and Size (FECS), Functionality Execution Component Proportion (FECP), and Action Execution Content Proportion (AECP).

17.1.2 C

17.1.2.1 Class Method (CM)

Method belonging to the class or subclass, also known as operation, procedure, or function. It is defined in the class structure description in the Logical Data Model. In the Functional Software Size Measurement Methodology with Effort Estimation and Performance Indication (FSSM), it is one of the Software Component's Measurable Feature (SCMF) known as the Software Component's Measurable Feature 'Class Method' (FCM).

17.1.2.2 Class Method Entities (CMDE)

The Software Component's Feature Measurement (SCFM) for the Software Component's Measurable Feature 'Class Method' (FCM) in terms of the Software Component's Feature Points (SCFPs).

The CMDE (Class Method Entities) is the measurement for the methods of the data classes and subclasses. The methods, classes, and subclasses are described in the Logical Data Model (LDM) part of the Functional Requirements Specifications (FRS).

The CMDE is calculated from the Software Component's Feature Point Count for 'Class Method' (FCCM) and is used for the following calculations:

a. Software Component's Measurements (SCMs): the Software Total Components Measurement (STCM) through the Software Component 'Functionality Execution' Measurement (CFEM);

b. Software Size and Effort Estimations (SSEEs): the Software Total Development Effort (STDE) through the Software Logical Size (SLS) and Software Analysis, Design, and Coding Effort (SADCE);

c. Software Performance Quality Indicators (SPQIs): Software Structural Indicators (SSIs)[5–7], that is, the SSIs Functionality Execution Complexity and Size (FECS) and Functionality Execution Component Proportion (FECP).

17.1.2.3 Common Software Measurement International Consortium (COSMIC)

An existing Functional Size Measurement (FSM)[1] methodology which measures equivalent 4 Software Component's Measurable Features (SCMFs) of 1 Software's Measurable Component (SMC) – Software's Measurable Component 'Functionality Execution' (CFE) – as compared to the 31 Software Component's Measurable Features (SCMFs) of the 4 Software's Measurable Components (SMCs) – Software's Measurable Component 'Functional Data' (CFD), 'Functionality Execution' (CFE), 'User Interface' (CUI), and

'Message Exchange' (CME) – in the case of the Functional Software Size Measurement Methodology with Effort Estimation and Performance Indication (FSSM).

17.1.2.4 Computational Operation Content Proportion (COCP)

One of the Software Performance Quality Indicators (SPQIs) of the type Software Structural Indicator (SSI)[5–7]. It gives the indication of the static proportion of the different computational operations (mathematical calculations) such as addition, subtraction, multiplication, division, log, and power, performed in the total software contents.

The COCP is the ratio of the total number of the computational operations performed, that is, the Computational Operations (CO), to the total software size measurement, that is, the Software Total Components Measurement (STCM), in percentage, and is expressed as Nil, Low, Medium, High, or Very High according to this percentage value.

17.1.2.5 Computational Operations (CO)

The Software Component's Feature Measurement (SCFM) for the Software Component's Measurable Feature 'Function Computational Operation' (FFC) in terms of the Software Component's Feature Points (SCFPs).

The CO (Computational Operations) is the measurement for the mathematical calculation operations, for example, addition, subtraction, multiplication, division, power, log, and equals. These operations are described in the Functionality Execution (FE) description part of the Functional Requirements Specifications (FRS).

The CO is calculated from the Software Component's Feature Point Count for 'Function Computational Operation' (FCFC), and is used for the following calculations:

a. Software Component's Measurements (SCMs): the Software Total Components Measurement (STCM) through the Software Component 'Functionality Execution' Measurement (CFEM);

b. Software Size and Effort Estimations (SSEEs): the Software Total Development Effort (STDE) through the Software Logical Size (SLS) and Software Analysis, Design, and Coding Effort (SADCE);

c. Software Performance Quality Indicators (SPQIs): Software Structural Indicators (SSIs)[5–7], that is, the SSIs Functionality Execution Complexity and Size (FECS), Functionality Execution Component Proportion (FECP), and Computational Operation Content Proportion (COCP); and Software Operational Indicator (SOI)[5–7], that is, the SOI Computational Operations Level (COL).

17.1.2.6 Computational Operations Level (COL)

One of the Software Performance Quality Indicators (SPQIs) of the type Software Operational Indicator (SOI)[5–7]. It gives the indication of the dynamic run-time level of the different computational operations (mathematical calculations) such as addition, subtraction, multiplication, division, log, and power, performed in the software execution.

The COL is the ratio of the total number of the computational operations performed, that is, the Computational Operations (CO), to the dynamic run-time operations performance size of the Software's Measurable Component 'Functionality Execution' (CFE), that is, the Functionality Execution Operations Dynamic Measurement (FEODM), in percentage, and is expressed as Nil, Low, Medium, High, or Very High according to this percentage value.

17.1.3 D

17.1.3.1 Data Class Attribute Entities (DAE)

The Software Component's Feature Measurement (SCFM) for the Software Component's Measurable Feature 'Data Attribute' (FDA) in terms of the Software Component's Feature Points (SCFPs).

The DAE (Data Class Attribute Entities) is the measurement for the attributes of the data classes and subclasses. The attributes, classes, and subclasses are described in the Logical Data Model (LDM) part of the Functional Requirements Specifications (FRS).

The DAE is calculated from the Software Component's Feature Point Count for 'Data Attribute' (FCDA) and is used for the following calculations:

- **a.** Software Component's Measurements (SCMs): the Software Total Components Measurement (STCM) through the Software Component 'Functional Data' Measurement (CFDM);
- **b.** Software Size and Effort Estimations (SSEEs): the Software Total Development Effort (STDE) through the Software Logical Size (SLS) and Software Analysis, Design, and Coding Effort (SADCE);
- **c.** Software Performance Quality Indicators (SPQIs): Software Structural Indicators (SSIs)[5–7], that is, the SSIs Functional Data Complexity and Size (FDCS) and Functional Data Component Proportion (FDCP).

17.1.3.2 Data Class Entities (DCE)

The Software Component's Feature Measurement (SCFM) for the Software Component's Measurable Feature 'Data Class' (FDC) in terms of the Software Component's Feature Points (SCFPs).

The DCE (Data Class Entities) is the measurement for the data classes and subclasses described in the Logical Data Model (LDM) part of the Functional Requirements Specifications (FRS).

The DCE is calculated from the Software Component's Feature Point Count for 'Data Class' (FCDC) and is used for the following calculations:

- **a.** Software Component's Measurements (SCMs): the Software Total Components Measurement (STCM) through the Software Component 'Functional Data' Measurement (CFDM);
- **b.** Software Size and Effort Estimations (SSEEs): the Software Total Development Effort (STDE) through the Software Logical Size (SLS) and Software Analysis, Design, and Coding Effort (SADCE);
- **c.** Software Performance Quality Indicators (SPQIs): Software Structural Indicators (SSIs)[5–7], that is, the SSIs Functional Data Complexity and Size (FDCS) and Functional Data Component Proportion (FDCP).

17.1.3.3 Data Class Field Entities (DFE)

The Software Component's Feature Measurement (SCFM) for the Software Component's Measurable Feature 'Data Field' (FDF) in terms of the Software Component's Feature Points (SCFPs).

The DFE (Data Class Field Entities) is the measurement for the fields of the data classes and subclasses. The fields, classes, and subclasses are described in the Logical Data Model (LDM) part of the Functional Requirements Specifications (FRS).

The DFE is calculated from the Software Component's Feature Point Count for 'Data Field' (FCDF) and is used for the following calculations:

a. Software Component's Measurements (SCMs): the Software Total Components Measurement (STCM) through the Software Component 'Functional Data' Measurement (CFDM);
b. Software Size and Effort Estimations (SSEEs): the Software Total Development Effort (STDE) through the Software Logical Size (SLS) and Software Analysis, Design, and Coding Effort (SADCE);
c. Software Performance Quality Indicators (SPQIs): Software Structural Indicators (SSIs)[5–7], that is, the SSIs Functional Data Complexity and Size (FDCS) and Functional Data Component Proportion (FDCP).

17.1.3.4 Data Collection (DCL)

A group of data that can be handled together independently for the memory read/write, input/output, message exchange, and general functional – computational, logical, decision, repeat, and execution flow control – operations.

The DCL may be either whole class data; or whole subclass data; or single attribute data of a class or subclass; or group of attributes data of a class or subclass.

17.1.3.5 Decision Execution Content Proportion (DECP)

One of the Software Performance Quality Indicators (SPQIs) of the type Software Structural Indicator (SSI)[5–7]. It gives the indication of the static proportion of the different decision operations that are used to check the conditions and take decisions for certain actions according to the conditions, and are performed in the total software contents. These operations are of the type "if the condition is true, then take certain action".

The DECP is the ratio of the total number of the decision operations performed, that is, the Decision Execution Operations (DEO), to the total software size measurement, that is, the Software Total Components Measurement (STCM), in percentage, and is expressed as Nil, Low, Medium, High, or Very High according to this percentage value.

17.1.3.6 Decision Execution Level (DEL)

One of the Software Performance Quality Indicators (SPQIs) of the type Software Operational Indicator (SOI)[5–7]. It gives the indication of the dynamic run-time level of the different decision operations which are conditions checking operations, for example, if the condition is true, take some particular action, and are performed in the software execution.

The DEL is the ratio of the total number of the decision-taking operations performed, that is, the Decision Execution Operations (DEO), to the dynamic run-time operations performance size of the Software's Measurable Component 'Functionality Execution'

(CFE), that is, the Functionality Execution Operations Dynamic Measurement (FEODM), in percentage, and is expressed as Nil, Low, Medium, High, or Very High according to this percentage value.

17.1.3.7 Decision Execution Operations (DEO)

The Software Component's Feature Measurement (SCFM) for the Software Component's Measurable Feature 'Function Decision Execution' (FFD) in terms of the Software Component's Feature Points (SCFPs).

The DEO (Decision Execution Operations) is the measurement for the conditions checking and decision-taking (e.g., if the condition is true, take the action) operations described in the Functionality Execution (FE) description part of the Functional Requirements Specifications (FRS).

The DEO is calculated from the Software Component's Feature Point Count for 'Function Decision Execution' (FCFD), and is used for the following calculations:

a. Software Component's Measurements (SCMs): the Software Total Components Measurement (STCM) through the Software Component 'Functionality Execution' Measurement (CFEM);

b. Software Size and Effort Estimations (SSEEs): the Software Total Development Effort (STDE) through the Software Logical Size (SLS) and Software Analysis, Design, and Coding Effort (SADCE);

c. Software Performance Quality Indicators (SPQIs): Software Structural Indicators (SSIs)[5–7], that is, the SSIs Functionality Execution Complexity and Size (FECS), Functionality Execution Component Proportion (FECP), and Decision Execution Content Proportion (DECP); and Software Operational Indicator (SOI)[5–7], that is, the SOI Decision Execution Level (DEL).

17.1.4 E

17.1.4.1 Error Handling Capability (EHC)

One of the Software Performance Quality Indicators (SPQIs) of the type Software Operational Indicator (SOI)[5–7]. It gives the indication of the dynamic run-time level of the error handling operations, performed in the software execution.

The EHC is the ratio of the total number of the operations used for handling the error conditions in the software, that is, the Error Handling Operations (EHO), to the dynamic run-time operations performance size of the Software's Measurable Component 'Functionality Execution' (CFE), that is, the Functionality Execution Operations Dynamic Measurement (FEODM), in percentage, and is expressed as Nil, Low, Medium, High, or Very High according to this percentage value.

17.1.4.2 Error Handling Operations (EHO)

The Software Component's Feature Measurement (SCFM) for the Software Component's Measurable Feature 'Function Error Handling' (FFE) in terms of the Software Component's Feature Points (SCFPs).

The EHO (Error Handling Operations) is the measurement for the operations which handle error conditions, for example, display error messages, or log error conditions, described in the Functionality Execution (FE) description part of the Functional Requirements Specifications (FRS).

The EHO is calculated from the Software Component's Feature Point Count for 'Function Error Handling' (FCFE), and is used for the following calculations:

a. Software Performance Quality Indicators (SPQIs): Software Structural Indicator (SSI)[5–7], that is, the SSI Error Handling Proportion (EHP); and Software Operational Indicator (SOI)[5–7], that is, the SOI Error Handling Capability (EHC).

17.1.4.3 Error Handling Proportion (EHP)

One of the Software Performance Quality Indicators (SPQIs) of the type Software Structural Indicator (SSI)[5–7]. It gives the indication of the static proportion of the different error handling operations that are used in the case of the error conditions in the Functionality Execution, and are performed in the total software contents.

The EHP is the ratio of the total number of the operations used for handling the error conditions in the software, that is, the Error Handling Operations (EHO), to the total software size measurement, that is, the Software Total Components Measurement (STCM), in percentage, and is expressed as Nil, Low, Medium, High, or Very High according to this percentage value.

17.1.4.4 Execution Flow Control Content Proportion (EFCCP)

One of the Software Performance Quality Indicators (SPQIs) of the type Software Structural Indicator (SSI)[5–7]. It gives the indication of the static proportion of the execution flow control operations that are used to control the flow of the program, and are performed in the total software contents.

The EFCCP is the ratio of the total number of the execution flow control operations performed, that is, the Execution Flow Control Operations (EFCO), to the total software size measurement, that is, the Software Total Components Measurement (STCM), in percentage, and is expressed as Nil, Low, Medium, High, or Very High according to this percentage value.

17.1.4.5 Execution Flow Control Level (EFCL)

One of the Software Performance Quality Indicators (SPQIs) of the type Software Operational Indicator (SOI)[5–7]. It gives the indication of the dynamic run-time level of the execution flow control operations which are used for controlling the flow of the program, and are performed in the software execution.

The EFCL is the ratio of the total number of the execution flow control operations performed, that is, the Execution Flow Control Operations (EFCO), to the dynamic run-time operations performance size of the Software's Measurable Component 'Functionality Execution' (CFE), that is, the Functionality Execution Operations Dynamic Measurement (FEODM), in percentage, and is expressed as Nil, Low, Medium, High, or Very High according to this percentage value.

17.1.4.6 Execution Flow Control Operations (EFCO)

The Software Component's Feature Measurement (SCFM) for the Software Component's Measurable Feature 'Function Execution Flow Control' (FFO) in terms of the Software Component's Feature Points (SCFPs).

The EFCO (Execution Flow Control Operations) is the measurement for the execution flow control operations that perform the program flow control actions described in the Functionality Execution (FE) description part of the Functional Requirements Specifications (FRS).

The EFCO is calculated from the Software Component's Feature Point Count for 'Function Execution Flow Control' (FCFO), and is used for the following calculations:

a. Software Component's Measurements (SCMs): the Software Total Components Measurement (STCM) through the Software Component 'Functionality Execution' Measurement (CFEM);

b. Software Size and Effort Estimations (SSEEs): the Software Total Development Effort (STDE) through the Software Logical Size (SLS) and Software Analysis, Design, and Coding Effort (SADCE);

c. Software Performance Quality Indicators (SPQIs): Software Structural Indicators (SSIs)[5–7], that is, the SSIs Functionality Execution Complexity and Size (FECS), Functionality Execution Component Proportion (FECP), and Execution Flow Control Content Proportion (EFCCP); and Software Operational Indicator (SOI)[5–7], that is, the SOI Execution Flow Control Level (EFCL).

17.1.4.7 External Communication Functional Data Level (ECDL)

One of the Software Performance Quality Indicators (SPQIs) of the type Software Operational Indicator (SOI)[5–7]. It gives the indication of the dynamic run-time functional data handled in the message exchanges (message send/receive operations) with the external application programs in the software execution.

The ECDL is the ratio of the total functional data handled during the message send/receive operations, that is, the Message Exchange Operations Functional Data Entities (EOFE), to the functionality execution data manipulation size of the Software's Measurable Component 'Functionality Execution' (CFE), that is, the Functionality Execution Data Manipulation Measurement (FEDM), in percentage, and is expressed as Nil, Low, Medium, High, or Very High according to this percentage value.

17.1.4.8 External Communication Level (ECL)

One of the Software Performance Quality Indicators (SPQIs) of the type Software Operational Indicator (SOI)[5–7]. It gives the indication of the dynamic run-time level of the external communication through message send/receive operations used for sending/receiving the messages to/from the external application programs or sub-programs of the same application program, performed in the software execution.

The ECL is the ratio of the total number of the message send/receive operations performed, that is, the Message Exchange Operations (MEO), to the dynamic run-time operations performance size of the Software's Measurable Component 'Functionality Execution' (CFE), that is, the Functionality Execution Operations Dynamic Measurement (FEODM), in percentage, and is expressed as Nil, Low, Medium, High, or Very High according to this percentage value.

17.1.4.9 External Communication Proportion (ECP)

One of the Software Performance Quality Indicators (SPQIs) of the type Software Structural Indicator (SSI)[5–7]. It gives the indication of the static proportion of the different message communication operations (message send/receive operations) that are used to communicate with the other programs/sub-programs and are performed in the total software contents.

The ECP is the ratio of the total number of the message send/receive operations performed, that is, the Message Exchange Operations (MEO), to the total software size measurement, that is, the Software Total Components Measurement (STCM), in percentage, and is expressed as Nil, Low, Medium, High, or Very High according to this percentage value.

17.1.5 F

17.1.5.1 Functional Data (FD)

All the data part which is used by the functionality of the software. It is described normally in the Logical Data Model (LDM) part of the Functional Requirements Specifications (FRS). It is characterized as one of the Software's Measurable Components (SMCs) in the Functional Software Size Measurement Methodology with Effort Estimation and Performance Indication (FSSM).

The Functional Data (FD) component is identified in the FSSM as Software's Measurable Component 'Functional Data' (CFD). The CFD is composed of the Software Component's Measurable Features:

- **a.** 'Data Class' (FDC);
- **b.** 'Data Attribute' (FDA);
- **c.** 'Data Field' (FDF);
- **d.** 'Data Missing' (FDM);

which are all measured in the FSSM. The measurement of the CFD is given by the Software Component 'Functional Data' Measurement (CFDM). The CFDM is further used for the calculations of the Software Size and Effort Estimations (SSEEs) and Software Performance Quality Indicators of the type Software Structural Indicators (SSIs)[5–7].

17.1.5.2 Functional Data Complexity and Size (FDCS)

One of the Software Performance Quality Indicators (SPQIs) of the type Software Structural Indicator (SSI)[5–7]. It gives the indication of the size and complexity of the Software's Measurable Component 'Functional Data' (CFD). The CFD comprises number of classes, subclasses, their attributes and fields of the attributes. The measurement for the CFD is the Software Component 'Functional Data' Measurement (CFDM).

The FDCS is evaluated directly based on the value of the CFDM, and is expressed as Nil, Low, Medium, High, or Very High according to the CFDM value.

17.1.5.3 Functional Data Component Proportion (FDCP)

One of the Software Performance Quality Indicators (SPQIs) of the type Software Structural Indicator (SSI)[5–7]. It gives the indication of the static proportion of the functional data size – number of all the classes, subclasses, their attributes and fields of the attributes – in the total software contents.

The FDCP is the ratio of the total functional data size, that is, the Software Component 'Functional Data' Measurement (CFDM), to the total software size measurement, that is, the Software Total Components Measurement (STCM), in percentage, and is expressed as Nil, Low, Medium, High, or Very High according to this percentage value.

17.1.5.4 Functional Data Missing Entities (FDME)

The Software Component's Feature Measurement (SCFM) for the Software Component's Measurable Feature 'Data Missing' (FDM) in terms of the Software Component's Feature Points (SCFPs).

The FDME (Functional Data Missing Entities) is the measurement for the missing data items in the Logical Data Model (LDM) part of the Functional Requirements Specifications (FRS).

The FDME is calculated from the Software Component's Feature Point Count for 'Data Missing' (FCDM) and is used for the following calculations:

- **a.** Software Component's Measurements (SCMs): the Software Components Requirements Deficiency Measurement (CRDM);
- **b.** Software Performance Quality Indicators (SPQIs): Software Structural Indicator (SSI)[5–7], that is, the SSI Requirements Deficiency Grade (RDG).

17.1.5.5 Functional Requirements Specifications (FRS)

The specifications of the functional requirements from the point of view of the user. User can be a human; instrument or equipment; or program, sub-program or module of an application software.

The Functional Requirements Specifications are the same as the Functional User Requirements (FUR)[1] defined in the ISO/IEC 14143–1[1] standards.

In order to apply and use the Functional Software Size Measurement Methodology with Effort Estimation and Performance Indication (FSSM), the FRS should normally have 4 description parts consisting of the

1. Logical Data Model (LDM);
2. Functionality Execution (FE);
3. User Interface (UI);
4. Message Exchange (ME);

that are corresponding to the 4 Software's Measurable Components (SMCs) which are the

1. Software's Measurable Component 'Functional Data' (CFD);
2. Software's Measurable Component 'Functionality Execution' (CFE);
3. Software's Measurable Component 'User Interface' (CUI);
4. Software's Measurable Component 'Message Exchange' (CME);

that are measured in the FSSM.

In the description of the functional requirements, the level of details should be such that it is possible to identify the following Software Component's Measurable Features (SCMFs) of the SMCs:

a. 4 SCMFs of the CFD related with the data classes, subclasses, attributes, and fields;

b. 19 SCMFs of the CFE related with the memory read/write, input/output, message send/receive, computational, logical, decision, repeat, actions, execution flow control, and error handling operations; data handled in the memory read/write, input/output, message exchange and general – computational, logical, decision, repeat, and execution flow control – operations; and class methods;

c. 5 SCMFs of the CUI related with the user screens, fields, and input/output navigational links;

d. 3 SCMFs of the CME related with the messages and their fields.

17.1.5.6 Functional Size Unit (FSU)

The unit used for the software functional size measurement. The FSU in the Functional Software Size Measurement Methodology with Effort Estimation and Performance Indication (FSSM) is the Software Component's Feature Point (SCFP).

All the measurements of the 4 Software's Measurable Components (SMCs) – Software's Measurable Component 'Functional Data' (CFD), 'Functionality Execution' (CFE), 'User Interface' (CUI), and 'Message Exchange' (CME) – and of the 31 Software Component's Measurable Features (SCMFs) of these 4 SMCs are performed by identifying the SCMFs in the Functional Requirements Specifications (FRS) and assigning them the FSU, that is, SCFPs, and by this way producing Software Component's Feature Point Counts (SCFPCs) which are used for the calculations of the 28 Software Component's Feature Measurement (SCFMs). The SCFMs are further used for calculating the 6 Software Component's Measurements (SCMs). The SCMs are the

1. Software Component 'Functional Data' Measurement (CFDM);
2. Software Component 'Functionality Execution' Measurement (CFEM);
3. Software Component 'User Interface' Measurement (CUIM);
4. Software Component 'Message Exchange' Measurement (CMEM);
5. Software Total Components Measurement (STCM);
6. Software Components Requirement Deficiency Measurement (CRDM).

17.1.5.7 Functional Software Size Measurement Methodology with Effort Estimation and Performance Indication (FSSM)

A new, comprehensive Functional Size Measurement[1] methodology for complete software size measurement, development effort estimation, and performance indications presented in this book.

The FSSM overcomes the major limitations of the existing functional software size measurement methodologies and has significant advantages over them. As compared to the currently available methodologies which measure a tiny part of the software, and based on the measurement of the tiny part which does not have any fixed size proportion relationship with the complete size, they try to assess the complete software size by using some assumptive multiplication factors to compensate the lack of the measurement of the remaining unmeasured size, the FSSM measures all the important and relevant features which the software components are composed of, and consequently, it measures all the software components completely of which the software is composed. Hence, the FSSM provides complete and accurate measurement based on which realistic calculations are made for the software development effort and software performance indications.

At the same time, the FSSM is fully compliant with the ISO/IEC 14143–1[1] standards. The following are the complete proceeding steps of the FSSM usage flow process:

1. identification of the following 31 Software Component's Measurable Features (SCMFs) in the 4 Software's Measurable Components (SMCs) – data, functionality, user interfaces/screens, and message communication – corresponding to the 4 description parts – Logical Data Model, Functionality Execution, User Interface, and Message Exchange – in the functional requirements:
   a. classes, subclasses, their attributes and fields of the attributes, and missing data items for the Functional Data component;
   b. memory read/write, input/output, message send/receive, computational, logical, decision execution, repeat execution, action execution, execution flow control, and error handling operations; functional data handled during memory read/write, input/output, message send/receive, computational, logical, decision, repeat, and execution flow control operations; class methods; and missing functionality items for the Functionality Execution component;
   c. user screens, their input/output fields and input/output navigational links, and missing screen items for the User Interface component;
   d. messages and their fields, and missing message items for the Message Exchange component;
2. assignment of the Software Component's Feature Points (SCFPs) to the identified SCMFs creating 31 streams of the SCFPs;
3. summation of the respective SCFPs corresponding to the 31 types of SCMFs to produce the 31 Software Component's Feature Point Counts (SCFPCs);
4. calculations of the 28 Software Component's Feature Measurements (SCFMs) for the SCMFs of the SMCs by using the SCFPCs;
5. using the SCFMs for the calculations of the 4 Software Component's Measurements (SCMs) about the size of the data, functionality, user interface/screen, and message components, their total size, and deficiency in the functional requirements;
6. using the SCFMs and SCMs to calculate the following 4 Software Size and Effort Estimations (SSEEs):
   a. software logical size in number of logical statements;
   b. software analysis, design, and coding effort;
   c. software testing effort;
   d. software total development effort;
7. using the SCFMs and SCMs to calculate the 36 Software Performance Quality Indicators (SPQIs) of which:
   a. the following 23 Software Structural Indicators (SSIs)[5–7] for the software structure indication regarding the sizes and content proportion of the
      i. Functional Data;
      ii. Functionality Execution;

iii. User Interface;
iv. Message Exchange for communication with other programs;

and regarding the content proportion of the

i. memory transactions and their functional data handling;
ii. user interactions and their functional data handling;
iii. external message communications and their functional data handling;
iv. computational operations;
v. logical operations;
vi. decision operations;
vii. repeat operations;
viii. execution flow control operations;
ix. actions performed operations;
x. functional data handling of the computational, logical, decision, repeat, and execution flow control operations;
xi. error handling operations;
xii. requirements deficiencies;

b. the following 13 Software Operational Indicators (SOIs)[5–7] for the dynamic characteristics indication of the software regarding the dynamic run-time levels of the

i. memory transactions and their functional data handling;
ii. user interactions and their functional data handling;
iii. external message communications and their functional data handling;
iv. computational operations;
v. logical operations;
vi. decision operations;
vii. repeat operations;
viii. execution flow control operations;
ix. functional data handling of the computational, logical, decision, repeat, and execution flow control operations;
x. error handling operations.

17.1.5.8 Functional Size (FS)

The size of the software obtained by using the Functional Size Measurement (FSM)[1] techniques whereby the user functionality requirements of the software specified in the Functional Requirements Specifications (FRS) are identified and quantified, and Functional Size Units (FSU) are assigned to the user functional requirements, and thus, the measurements for various components of the software and total software are performed.

In the Functional Software Size Measurement Methodology with Effort Estimation and Performance Indication (FSSM), there are the 6 Software Component's Measurements (SCMs) which provide the Functional Size[1] of the software. They are the

1. Software Component 'Functional Data' Measurement (CFDM);
2. Software Component 'Functionality Execution' Measurement (CFEM);
3. Software Component 'User Interface' Measurement (CUIM);
4. Software Component 'Message Exchange' Measurement (CMEM);
5. Software Total Components Measurement (STCM);
6. Software Components Requirement Deficiency Measurement (CRDM).

Based on the SCMs and the Software Component's Feature Measurements (SCFMs), further Software Size and Effort Estimations (SSEEs), and Software Performance Quality Indicators (SPQIs) of two types – Software Structural Indicators (SSIs)[5–7] and Software Operational Indicators (SOIs)[5–7] are calculated in the FSSM.

17.1.5.9 Functional Size Measurement (FSM)

The process of measuring the functional size of the software. In the Functional Software Size Measurement Methodology with Effort Estimation and Performance Indication (FSSM), the Functional Size Measurement (FSM)[1] is carried out by identifying the Software Component's Measurable Features (SCMFs) of the Software's Measurable Components (SMCs) in the Functional Requirements Specifications (FRS), and then assigning them the FSU (Functional Size Unit), that is, the Software Component's Feature Points (SCFPs), and by this way producing the Software Component's Feature Point Counts (SCFPCs) which are further used to calculate the Software Component's Feature Measurements (SCFMs) which in turn are used to calculate the Software Component's Measurements (SCMs) of the following types:

1. Software Component 'Functional Data' Measurement (CFDM);
2. Software Component 'Functionality Execution' Measurement (CFEM);
3. Software Component 'User Interface' Measurement (CUIM);
4. Software Component 'Message Exchange' Measurement (CMEM);
5. Software Total Components Measurement (STCM);
6. Software Components Requirement Deficiency Measurement (CRDM).

The SCFMs along with the SCMs are also used for further calculation of the Software Size and Effort Estimations (SSEEs) and Software Performance Quality Indicators (SPQIs) of two types – Software Structural Indicators (SSIs)[5–7] and Software Operational Indicators (SOIs)[5–7].

17.1.5.10 Functionality Execution (FE)

All the functionality part which is executed in the software. It is described normally in the Functionality Execution (FE) description part of the Functional Requirements Specifications (FRS). It is characterized as one of the Software's Measurable Components (SMCs) in the Functional Software Size Measurement Methodology with Effort Estimation and Performance Indication (FSSM).

The Functionality Execution (FE) component is identified in the FSSM as Software's Measurable Component 'Functionality Execution' (CFE). The CFE has the Software Component's Measurable Features:

a. 'Data Read' (FDR);
b. 'Data Write' (FDW);
c. 'Memory Operations Functional Data' (FLM);
d. 'Data Input' (FDI);
e. 'Data Output' (FDO);
f. 'Input/Output Operations Functional Data' (FLI);

g. 'Message Send' (FMS);
h. 'Message Receive' (FMR);
i. 'Message Exchange Operations Functional Data' (FLS);
j. 'Function Computational Operation' (FFC);
k. 'Function Logical Operation' (FFL);
l. 'Function Decision Execution' (FFD);
m. 'Function Repeat Execution' (FFR);
n. 'Function Action Execution' (FFA);
o. 'Function Execution Flow Control' (FFO);
p. 'Function Error Handling' (FFE);
q. 'General Operations Functional Data' (FLG);
r. 'Functionality Missing' (FFM);
s. 'Class Method' (FCM);

which are all measured in the FSSM. The measurement of the CFE is given by the Software Component 'Functionality Execution' Measurement (CFEM). The CFEM comprises 3 parts which are the Functionality Execution Operations Dynamic Measurement (FEODM), Functionality Execution Operations Measurement (FEOM), and Functionality Execution Data Manipulation Measurement (FEDM). The FEODM and FEDM are used for the calculations of the Software Performance Quality Indicators of the type Software Operational Indicators (SOIs)[5–7]. The CFEM is further used for the calculations of the Software Size and Effort Estimations (SSEEs) and Software Performance Quality Indicators of the type Software Structural Indicators (SSIs)[5–7].

17.1.5.11 Functionality Execution Complexity and Size (FECS)

One of the Software Performance Quality Indicators (SPQIs) of the type Software Structural Indicator (SSI)[5–7]. It gives the indication of the size and complexity of the Software's Measurable Component 'Functionality Execution' (CFE). The CFE comprises memory read/write, input/output, message exchange, computational, logical, decision execution, repeat execution, action execution, and execution flow control operations; functional data handled during memory read/write, input/output, message exchange, and general – computational, logical, decision, repeat, and execution flow control – operations; and class methods. The measurement for the CFE is the Software Component 'Functionality Execution' Measurement (CFEM).

The FECS is evaluated directly based on the value of the CFEM, and is expressed as Nil, Low, Medium, High, or Very High according to the CFEM value.

17.1.5.12 Functionality Execution Component Proportion (FECP)

One of the Software Performance Quality Indicators (SPQIs) of the type Software Structural Indicator (SSI)[5–7]. It gives the indication of the static proportion of the functionality execution size – number of all the memory read/write, input/output, message exchange, computational, logical, decision execution, repeat execution, action execution, and execution flow control operations; functional data handled during memory read/write, input/output, message exchange, and general (computational, logical, decision, repeat, and execution flow control) operations; and class methods – in the total software contents.

The FECP is the ratio of the total functionality execution size, that is, the Software Component 'Functionality Execution' Measurement (CFEM), to the total software size measurement, that is, the Software Total Components Measurement (STCM), in percentage, and is expressed as Nil, Low, Medium, High, or Very High according to this percentage value.

17.1.5.13 Functionality Execution Data Manipulation Measurement (FEDM)

A measurement in the Functional Software Size Measurement Methodology with Effort Estimation and Performance Indication (FSSM) that measures the magnitude of the functional data handled during the functional operations. The functional data and operations are the

- **a.** Memory Operations Functional Data Entities (MOFE) handled during the Memory Operations (MO);
- **b.** Input/Output Operations Functional Data Entities (IOFE) handled during the Input/Output Operations (IOO);
- **c.** Message Exchange Operations Functional Data Entities (EOFE) handled during the Message Exchange Operations (MEO);
- **d.** General Operations Functional Data Entities (GOFE) handled during the following operations:
  - **i.** computational;
  - **ii.** logical;
  - **iii.** decision execution;
  - **iv.** repeat execution;
  - **v.** execution flow control.

17.1.5.14 Functionality Execution Missing Entities (FEME)

The Software Component's Feature Measurement (SCFM) for the Software Component's Measurable Feature 'Function Missing' (FFM) in terms of the Software Component's Feature Points (SCFPs).

The FEME (Functionality Execution Missing Entities) is the measurement for the missing functionality items in the Functionality Execution (FE) part of the Functional Requirements Specifications (FRS).

The FEME is calculated from the Software Component's Feature Point Count for 'Function Missing' (FCFM) and is used for the following calculations:

- **a.** Software Component's Measurements (SCMs): the Software Components Requirements Deficiency Measurement (CRDM);
- **b.** Software Performance Quality Indicators (SPQIs): Software Structural Indicator (SSI)[5–7], that is, the SSI Requirements Deficiency Grade (RDG).

17.1.5.15 Functionality Execution Operations Dynamic Measurement (FEODM)

A measurement in the Functional Software Size Measurement Methodology with Effort Estimation and Performance Indication (FSSM) that measures the magnitude of the dynamic functionality operations execution and indicates the dynamic run-time behavior of the software. It takes into consideration the functional operations which are the

a. Memory Operations (MO);
b. Computational Operations (CO);
c. Logical Operations (LO);
d. Decision Execution Operations (DEO);
e. Repeat Execution Operations (REO);
f. Execution Flow Control Operations (EFCO);
g. Input/Output Operations (IOO);
h. Message Exchange Operations (MEO);

17.1.5.16 Functionality Execution Operations Measurement (FEOM)

A measurement in the Functional Software Size Measurement Methodology with Effort Estimation and Performance Indication (FSSM) that measures the magnitude of the functional operations which are the

a. Memory Operations (MO);
b. Computational Operations (CO);
c. Logical Operations (LO);
d. Decision Execution Operations (DEO);
e. Repeat Execution Operations (REO);
f. Action Execution Operations (AEO);
g. Execution Flow Control Operations (EFCO);
h. Input/Output Operations (IOO);
i. Message Exchange Operations (MEO);

and the

a. Class Method Entities (CMDE).

17.1.6 G

17.1.6.1 General Operations Execution Functional Data Level (GODL)

One of the Software Performance Quality Indicators (SPQIs) of the type Software Operational Indicator (SOI)[5–7]. It gives the indication of the dynamic run-time functional data handled in the general functional – computational, logical, decision, repeat, and execution flow control – operations in the software execution.

The GODL is the ratio of the total functional data handled during the general functional operations – computational, logical, decision, repeat, and execution flow control, that is, the General Operations Functional Data Entities (GOFE), to the functionality execution data manipulation size of the Software's Measurable Component 'Functionality Execution' (CFE), that is, the Functionality Execution Data Manipulation Measurement (FEDM), in percentage, and is expressed as Nil, Low, Medium, High, or Very High according to this percentage value.

17.1.6.2 General Operations Functional Data Entities (GOFE)

The Software Component's Feature Measurement (SCFM) for the Software Component's Measurable Feature 'General Operations Functional Data' (FLG) in terms of the Software Component's Feature Points (SCFPs).

The GOFE (General Operations Functional Data Entities) is the measurement for the functional data handled, that is, the total number of the Data Collections handled, in the general functional – computational, logical, decision, repeat, and execution flow control – operations described in the Functionality Execution (FE) description part of the Functional Requirements Specifications (FRS).

The GOFE is calculated from the Software Component's Feature Point Count for 'General Operations Functional Data' (FCLG), and is used for the following calculations:

a. Software Component's Measurements (SCMs): the Software Total Components Measurement (STCM) through the Software Component 'Functionality Execution' Measurement (CFEM);

b. Software Size and Effort Estimations (SSEEs): the Software Total Development Effort (STDE) through the Software Logical Size (SLS) and Software Analysis, Design, and Coding Effort (SADCE);

c. Software Performance Quality Indicators (SPQIs): Software Structural Indicators (SSIs)[5–7], that is, the SSIs Functionality Execution Complexity and Size (FECS), Functionality Execution Component Proportion (FECP), and General Operations Functional Data Proportion (GODP); and Software Operational Indicator (SOI)[5–7], that is, the SOI General Operations Execution Functional Data Level (GODL).

17.1.6.3 General Operations Functional Data Proportion (GODP)

One of the Software Performance Quality Indicators (SPQIs) of the type Software Structural Indicator (SSI)[5–7]. It gives the indication of the static proportion of the functional data that is handled during the general operations – computational, logical, decision, repeat, and execution flow control – in the total software contents.

The GODP is the ratio of the total functional data handled during the general functional – computational, logical, decision, repeat, and execution flow control – operations, that is, the General Operations Functional Data Entities (GOFE), to the total software size measurement, that is, the Software Total Components Measurement (STCM), in percentage, and is expressed as Nil, Low, Medium, High, or Very High according to this percentage value.

17.1.7 I

17.1.7.1 Input/Output Operations (IOO)

The Software Component's Feature Measurement (SCFM) for the Software Component's Measurable Feature 'Data Input' (FDI) and 'Data Output' (FDO) combined together in terms of the Software Component's Feature Points (SCFPs).

The IOO (Input/Output Operations) is the measurement for the functional input/output operations which receive the input data from the input devices such as keyboard, and send output data to the output devices such as display. The input/output operations are described in the Functionality Execution (FE) description part of the Functional Requirements Specifications (FRS).

The IOO is calculated from the Software Component's Feature Point Count for 'Data Input' (FCDI) and 'Data Output' (FCDO), and is used for the following calculations:

a. Software Component's Measurements (SCMs): the Software Total Components Measurement (STCM) through the Software Component 'Functionality Execution' Measurement (CFEM);

b. Software Size and Effort Estimations (SSEEs): the Software Total Development Effort (STDE) through the Software Logical Size (SLS) and Software Analysis, Design, and Coding Effort (SADCE);

c. Software Performance Quality Indicators (SPQIs): Software Structural Indicators (SSIs)[5–7], that is, the SSIs Functionality Execution Complexity and Size (FECS), Functionality Execution Component Proportion (FECP), and User Interaction Proportion (UIP); and Software Operational Indicator (SOI)[5–7], that is, the SOI User Interaction Level (UIL).

17.1.7.2 Input/Output Operations Functional Data Entities (IOFE)

The Software Component's Feature Measurement (SCFM) for the Software Component's Measurable Feature 'Input/Output Operations Functional Data' (FLI) in terms of the Software Component's Feature Points (SCFPs).

The IOFE (Input/Output Operations Functional Data Entities) is the measurement for the functional data handled, that is, the total number of the Data Collections handled, in the data input/output operations used for receiving/sending the input/output data from/to the input/output devices. The input/output operations are described in the Functionality Execution (FE) description part of the Functional Requirements Specifications (FRS).

The IOFE is calculated from the Software Component's Feature Point Count for 'Input/Output Operations Functional Data' (FCLI), and is used for the following calculations:

a. Software Component's Measurements (SCMs): the Software Total Components Measurement (STCM) through the Software Component 'Functionality Execution' Measurement (CFEM);

b. Software Size and Effort Estimations (SSEEs): the Software Total Development Effort (STDE) through the Software Logical Size (SLS) and Software Analysis, Design, and Coding Effort (SADCE);

c. Software Performance Quality Indicators (SPQIs): Software Structural Indicators (SSIs)[5–7], that is, the SSIs Functionality Execution Complexity and Size (FECS), Functionality Execution Component Proportion (FECP), and Input/Output Operations Functional Data Proportion (IODP); and Software Operational Indicator (SOI)[5–7], that is, the SOI User Interaction Functional Data Level (UIDL).

17.1.7.3 Input/Output Operations Functional Data Proportion (IODP)

One of the Software Performance Quality Indicators (SPQIs) of the type Software Structural Indicator (SSI)[5–7]. It gives the indication of the static proportion of the functional data that is handled during the input/output operations used for receiving/sending the input/output data from/to the input/output devices in the total software contents.

The IODP is the ratio of the total functional data handled during the input/output operations, that is, the Input/Output Operations Functional Data Entities (IOFE), to the total software size measurement, that is, the Software Total Components Measurement (STCM), in percentage, and is expressed as Nil, Low, Medium, High, or Very High according to this percentage value.

17.1.7.4 International Function Point Users Group (IFPUG)

IFPUG[4] has Function Point Analysis[4] as its standard methodology for the software sizing. It measures roughly equivalent 5 Software Component's Measurable Features (SCMFs) of the 2 Software's Measurable Components (SMCs) – Software's Measurable Component 'Functionality Execution' (CFE) and Software's Measurable Component 'Functional Data' (CFD) – as compared to the 31 Software Component's Measurable Features (SCMFs) of the 4 Software's Measurable Components (SMCs) – Software's Measurable Component 'Functional Data' (CFD), 'Functionality Execution' (CFE), 'User Interface' (CUI), and 'Message Exchange' (CME) – in the case of the Functional Software Size Measurement Methodology with Effort Estimation and Performance Indication (FSSM).

17.1.8 K

17.1.8.1 Key Software Indicator (KSI)

Used in the example Chapter 14. KSI used in the example chapter (Chapter 14) is the same as Software Performance Quality Indicator (SPQI) in the FSSM.

17.1.9 L

17.1.9.1 Logical Data Model (LDM)

Part of the Functional Requirements Specifications (FRS). In the LDM, the information about the functional data used in the software is presented in the form of class structures. The information is composed of mainly the classes and subclasses, their properties, descriptions, diagrams, etc. What is needed in the LDM from the point of view of the FSSM is the information about the classes and subclasses, attributes of the classes/subclasses, fields of the attributes, and class methods. The class structure information about the classes, subclasses, attributes, and fields forms part of the Software's Measurable Component 'Functional Data' (CFD) which is 1 of the 4 Software's Measurable Components (SMCs) measured in the FSSM. Class method forms part of the Software's Measurable Component 'Functionality Execution' (CFE) which is another SMC measured in the FSSM.

17.1.9.2 Logical Operation Content Proportion (LOCP)

One of the Software Performance Quality Indicators (SPQIs) of the type Software Structural Indicator (SSI)[5–7]. It gives the indication of the static proportion of the different logical operations such as AND, OR, and XOR, performed in the total software contents.

The LOCP is the ratio of the total number of the logical operations performed, that is, the Logical Operations (LO), to the total software size measurement, that is, the Software Total Components Measurement (STCM), in percentage, and is expressed as Nil, Low, Medium, High, or Very High according to this percentage value.

17.1.9.3 Logical Operations (LO)

The Software Component's Feature Measurement (SCFM) for the Software Component's Measurable Feature 'Function Logical Operation' (FFL) in terms of the Software Component's Feature Points (SCFPs).

The LO (Logical Operations) is the measurement for the logical operations, for example, AND, OR, and XOR, described in the Functionality Execution (FE) description part of the Functional Requirements Specifications (FRS).

The LO is calculated from the Software Component's Feature Point Count for 'Function Logical Operation' (FCFL), and is used for the following calculations:

a. Software Component's Measurements (SCMs): the Software Total Components Measurement (STCM) through the Software Component 'Functionality Execution' Measurement (CFEM);

b. Software Size and Effort Estimations (SSEEs): the Software Total Development Effort (STDE) through the Software Logical Size (SLS) and Software Analysis, Design, and Coding Effort (SADCE);

c. Software Performance Quality Indicators (SPQIs): Software Structural Indicators (SSIs)[5–7], that is, the SSIs Functionality Execution Complexity and Size (FECS), Functionality Execution Component Proportion (FECP), and Logical Operation Content Proportion (LOCP); and Software Operational Indicator (SOI)[5–7], that is, the SOI Logical Operations Level (LOL).

17.1.9.4 Logical Operations Level (LOL)

One of the Software Performance Quality Indicators (SPQIs) of the type Software Operational Indicator (SOI)[5–7]. It gives the indication of the dynamic run-time level of the different logical operations such as AND and OR, performed in the software execution.

The LOL is the ratio of the total number of logical operations performed, that is, the Logical Operations (LO), to the dynamic run-time operations performance size of the Software's Measurable Component 'Functionality Execution' (CFE), that is, the Functionality Execution Operations Dynamic Measurement (FEODM), in percentage, and is expressed as Nil, Low, Medium, High, or Very High according to this percentage value.

17.1.10 M

17.1.10.1 Memory Operations (MO)

The Software Component's Feature Measurement (SCFM) for the Software Component's Measurable Feature 'Data Read' (FDR) and 'Data Write' (FDW) combined together in terms of the Software Component's Feature Points (SCFPs).

The MO (Memory Operations) is the measurement for the memory data read/write operations from/to the non-volatile permanent storage memory such as disks. The memory read/write operations are described in the Functionality Execution (FE) description part of the Functional Requirements Specifications (FRS).

The MO is calculated from the Software Component's Feature Point Count for 'Data Read' (FCDR) and 'Data Write' (FCDW), and is used for the following calculations:

a. Software Component's Measurements (SCMs): the Software Total Components Measurement (STCM) through the Software Component 'Functionality Execution' Measurement (CFEM);

b. Software Size and Effort Estimations (SSEEs): the Software Total Development Effort (STDE) through the Software Logical Size (SLS) and Software Analysis, Design, and Coding Effort (SADCE);

c. Software Performance Quality Indicators (SPQIs): Software Structural Indicators (SSIs)[5–7], that is, the SSIs Functionality Execution Complexity and Size (FECS), Functionality Execution Component Proportion (FECP), and Memory Transaction Proportion (MTP); and Software Operational Indicator (SOI)[5–7], that is, the SOI Memory Traffic Level (MTL).

17.1.10.2 Memory Operations Functional Data Entities (MOFE)

The Software Component's Feature Measurement (SCFM) for the Software Component's Measurable Feature 'Memory Operations Functional Data' (FLM) in terms of the Software Component's Feature Points (SCFPs).

The MOFE (Memory Operations Functional Data Entities) is the measurement for the functional data handled, that is, the total number of the data collections handled, in the memory read/write operations described in the Functionality Execution (FE) description part of the Functional Requirements Specifications (FRS).

The MOFE is calculated from the Software Component's Feature Point Count for 'Memory Operations Functional Data' (FCLM), and is used for the following calculations:

a. Software Component's Measurements (SCMs): the Software Total Components Measurement (STCM) through the Software Component 'Functionality Execution' Measurement (CFEM);

b. Software Size and Effort Estimations (SSEEs): the Software Total Development Effort (STDE) through the Software Logical Size (SLS) and Software Analysis, Design, and Coding Effort (SADCE);

c. Software Performance Quality Indicators (SPQIs): Software Structural Indicators (SSIs)[5–7], that is, the SSIs Functionality Execution Complexity and Size (FECS), Functionality Execution Component Proportion (FECP), and Memory Operations Functional Data Proportion (MODP); and Software Operational Indicator (SOI)[5–7], that is, the SOI Memory Traffic Functional Data Level (MTDL).

17.1.10.3 Memory Operations Functional Data Proportion (MODP)

One of the Software Performance Quality Indicators (SPQIs) of the type Software Structural Indicator (SSI)[5–7]. It gives the indication of the static proportion of the functional data that is handled during the memory read/write operations in the total software contents.

The MODP is the ratio of the total functional data handled during the memory read/write operations, that is, the Memory Operations Functional Data Entities (MOFE), to the total software size measurement, that is, the Software Total Components Measurement (STCM), in percentage, and is expressed as Nil, Low, Medium, High, or Very High according to this percentage value.

17.1.10.4 Memory Traffic Functional Data Level (MTDL)

One of the Software Performance Quality Indicators (SPQIs) of the type Software Operational Indicator (SOI)[5–7]. It gives the indication of the dynamic run-time functional data handled in the memory traffic (read/write operations used for reading/writing the data from/to the permanent memory, e.g., disk devices) in the software execution.

The MTDL is the ratio of the total functional data handled during the memory read/write operations, that is, the Memory Operations Functional Data Entities (MOFE), to the functionality execution data manipulation size of the Software's Measurable Component 'Functionality Execution' (CFE), that is, the Functionality Execution Data Manipulation Measurement (FEDM), in percentage, and is expressed as Nil, Low, Medium, High, or Very High according to this percentage value.

17.1.10.5 Memory Traffic Level (MTL)

One of the Software Performance Quality Indicators (SPQIs) of the type Software Operational Indicator (SOI)[5–7]. It gives the indication of the dynamic run-time memory traffic level due to the data read/write operations used for reading/writing the data from/to the non-volatile, permanent memory, for example, disk devices, performed in the software execution.

The MTL is the ratio of the total number of the memory data read/write operations performed, that is, the Memory Operations (MO), to the dynamic run-time operations performance size of the Software's Measurable Component 'Functionality Execution' (CFE), that is, the Functionality Execution Operations Dynamic Measurement (FEODM), in percentage, and is expressed as Nil, Low, Medium, High, or Very High according to this percentage value.

17.1.10.6 Memory Transaction Proportion (MTP)

One of the Software Performance Quality Indicators (SPQIs) of the type Software Structural Indicator (SSI)[5–7]. It gives the indication of the static proportion of the memory transaction (read/write) operations functionality used for reading/writing the data from/to the non-volatile, permanent memory, for example, disk devices, performed in the total software contents.

The MTP is the ratio of the total number of the memory read/write operations performed, that is, Memory Operations (MO), to the total software size measurement, that is, the Software Total Components Measurement (STCM), in percentage, and is expressed as Nil, Low, Medium, High, or Very High according to this percentage value.

17.1.10.7 Message Exchange (ME)

All the message exchange part which is used to define the messages and their structures that are used by the functionality of the software for message communications with the external application programs or the sub-programs of the same application program. It is described normally in the Message Exchange (ME) description part of the Functional Requirements Specifications (FRS). It is characterized as one of the Software's Measurable Components (SMCs) in the Functional Software Size Measurement Methodology with Effort Estimation and Performance Indication (FSSM).

The Message Exchange (ME) component is identified in the FSSM as Software's Measurable Component 'Message Exchange' (CME). CME has the Software Component's Measurable Features:

a. 'Notifying Message' (FNM);

b. 'Message Field' (FMF);

which are all measured in the FSSM. The measurement of the CME is given by the Software Component 'Message Exchange' Measurement (CMEM). CMEM is further used for the calculations of the Software Size and Effort Estimations (SSEEs) and Software Performance Quality Indicators of the type Software Structural Indicators (SSIs)[5–7].

17.1.10.8 Message Exchange Complexity and Size (MECS)

One of the Software Performance Quality Indicators (SPQIs) of the type Software Structural Indicator (SSI)[5–7]. It gives the indication of the size and complexity of the Software's Measurable Component 'Message Exchange' (CME). The CME comprises the number of messages and their fields for communication with the external application programs or the sub-programs of the same application program. The measurement for the CME is the Software Component 'Message Exchange' Measurement (CMEM).

The MECS is evaluated directly based on the value of the CMEM, and is expressed as Nil, Low, Medium, High, or Very High according to the CMEM value.

17.1.10.9 Message Exchange Component Proportion (MECP)

One of the Software Performance Quality Indicators (SPQIs) of the type Software Structural Indicator (SSI)[5–7]. It gives the indication of the static proportion of the message exchange size – number of all the messages and their fields – in the total software contents.

The MECP is the ratio of the total message exchange size, that is, Software Component 'Message Exchange' Measurement (CMEM), to the total software size measurement, that is, the Software Total Components Measurement (STCM), in percentage, and is expressed as Nil, Low, Medium, High, or Very High according to this percentage value.

17.1.10.10 Message Exchange Missing Entities (MEME)

The Software Component's Feature Measurement (SCFM) for the Software Component's Measurable Feature 'Message Missing' (FMM) in terms of the Software Component's Feature Points (SCFPs).

The MEME (Message Exchange Missing Entities) is the measurement for the missing message items in the Message Exchange (ME) part of the Functional Requirements Specifications (FRS).

The MEME is calculated from the Software Component's Feature Point Count for 'Message Missing' (FCMM), and is used for the following calculations:

- **a.** Software Component's Measurements (SCMs): the Software Components Requirements Deficiency Measurement (CRDM);
- **b.** Software Performance Quality Indicators (SPQIs): Software Structural Indicator (SSI)[5–7], that is, the SSI Requirements Deficiency Grade (RDG).

17.1.10.11 Message Exchange Operations (MEO)

The Software Component's Feature Measurement (SCFM) for the Software Component's Measurable Feature 'Message Send' (FMS) and 'Message Receive' (FMR) combined together in terms of the Software Component's Feature Points (SCFPs).

The MEO (Message Exchange Operations) is the measurement for the message send/receive operations used for sending/receiving the messages to/from all the external application programs or the sub-programs (modules) of the same application program. The message send/receive operations are described in the Functionality Execution (FE) description part of the Functional Requirements Specifications (FRS).

The MEO is calculated from the Software Component's Feature Point Count for 'Message Send' (FCMS) and 'Message Receive' (FCMR), and is used for the following calculations:

a. Software Component's Measurements (SCMs): the Software Total Components Measurement (STCM) through the Software Component 'Functionality Execution' Measurement (CFEM);

b. Software Size and Effort Estimations (SSEEs): the Software Total Development Effort (STDE) through the Software Logical Size (SLS) and Software Analysis, Design, and Coding Effort (SADCE);

c. Software Performance Quality Indicators (SPQIs): Software Structural Indicators (SSIs)[5–7], that is, the SSIs Functionality Execution Complexity and Size (FECS), Functionality Execution Component Proportion (FECP), and External Communication Proportion (ECP); and Software Operational Indicator (SOI)[5–7], that is, the SOI External Communication Level (ECL).

17.1.10.12 Message Exchange Operations Functional Data Entities (EOFE)

The Software Component's Feature Measurement (SCFM) for the Software Component's Measurable Feature 'Message Exchange Operations Functional Data' (FLS) in terms of the Software Component's Feature Points (SCFPs).

The EOFE (Message Exchange Operations Functional Data Entities) is the measurement for the functional data handled, that is, the total number of the data collections handled, in the message exchange operations which are the message send/receive operations used for sending/receiving the messages to/from the external application programs or the sub-programs/modules of the same application program. The message send/receive operations are described in the Functionality Execution (FE) description part of the Functional Requirements Specifications (FRS).

The EOFE is calculated from the Software Component's Feature Point Count for 'Message Exchange Operations Functional Data' (FCLS), and is used for the following calculations:

a. Software Component's Measurements (SCMs): the Software Total Components Measurement (STCM) through the Software Component 'Functionality Execution' Measurement (CFEM);

b. Software Size and Effort Estimations (SSEEs): the Software Total Development Effort (STDE) through the Software Logical Size (SLS) and Software Analysis, Design, and Coding Effort (SADCE);

c. Software Performance Quality Indicators (SPQIs): Software Structural Indicators (SSIs)[5–7], that is, the SSIs Functionality Execution Complexity and Size (FECS), Functionality Execution Component Proportion (FECP), and Message Exchange Operations Functional Data Proportion (EODP); and Software Operational Indicator (SOI)[5–7], that is, the SOI External Communication Functional Data Level (ECDL).

17.1.10.13 Message Exchange Operations Functional Data Proportion (EODP)

One of the Software Performance Quality Indicators (SPQIs) of the type Software Structural Indicator (SSI)[5–7]. It gives the indication of the static proportion of the functional data that is handled during the message exchange operations (message send/receive) in the total software contents.

The EODP is the ratio of the total functional data handled during the message exchange (message send/receive) operations, that is, the Message Exchange Operations Functional Data Entities (EOFE), to the total software size measurement, that is, the Software Total Components Measurement (STCM), in percentage, and is expressed as Nil, Low, Medium, High, or Very High according to this percentage value.

17.1.10.14 Message Field Entities (MFE)

The Software Component's Feature Measurement (SCFM) for the Software Component's Measurable Feature 'Message Field' (FMF) in terms of the Software Component's Feature Points (SCFPs).

The MFE (Message Field Entities) is the measurement for the fields of the messages described in the Message Exchange (ME) part of the Functional Requirements Specifications (FRS).

The MFE is calculated from the Software Component's Feature Point Count for 'Message Field' (FCMF) and is used for the following calculations:

a. Software Component's Measurements (SCMs): the Software Total Components Measurement (STCM) through the Software Component 'Message Exchange' Measurement (CMEM);

b. Software Size and Effort Estimations (SSEEs): the Software Total Development Effort (STDE) through the Software Logical Size (SLS) and Software Analysis, Design, and Coding Effort (SADCE);

c. Software Performance Quality Indicators (SPQIs): Software Structural Indicators (SSIs)[5–7], that is, the SSIs Message Exchange Complexity and Size (MECS) and Message Exchange Component Proportion (MECP).

17.1.11 N

17.1.11.1 Notifying Message Entities (NME)

The Software Component's Feature Measurement (SCFM) for the Software Component's Measurable Feature 'Notifying Message' (FNM) in terms of the Software Component's Feature Points (SCFPs).

The NME (Notifying Message Entities) is the measurement for the messages described in the Message Exchange (ME) part of the Functional Requirements Specifications (FRS).

The NME is calculated from the Software Component's Feature Point Count for 'Notifying Message (FCNM) and is used for the following calculations:

a. Software Component's Measurements (SCMs): the Software Total Components Measurement (STCM) through the Software Component 'Message Exchange' Measurement (CMEM);

b. Software Size and Effort Estimations (SSEEs): the Software Total Development Effort (STDE) through the Software Logical Size (SLS) and Software Analysis, Design, and Coding Effort (SADCE);
c. Software Performance Quality Indicators (SPQIs): Software Structural Indicators (SSIs)[5–7], that is, the SSIs Message Exchange Complexity and Size (MECS) and Message Exchange Component Proportion (MECP).

17.1.12 Q

17.1.12.1 Quality Requirements (QR)

Document containing the requirements related to the quality aspects of the software project. It is also known as the Quality Requirements Specifications (QRS). It is not required for using the Functional Software Size Measurement Methodology with Effort Estimation and Performance Indication (FSSM) because the FSSM derives all the information for its use from the Functional Requirements Specifications (FRS), that is, the Functional User Requirements (FUR)[1] according to the ISO/IEC 14143-1:2007(E)[1] standards.

17.1.12.2 Quality Requirements Specifications (QRS)

Same as Quality Requirements (QR).

17.1.13 R

17.1.13.1 Repeat Execution Content Proportion (RECP)

One of the Software Performance Quality Indicators (SPQIs) of the type Software Structural Indicator (SSI)[5–7]. It gives the indication of the static proportion of the repeat operations that are used to repeat certain actions and are performed in the total software contents.

The RECP is the ratio of the total number of the repeat operations performed, that is, the Repeat Execution Operations (REO), to the total software size measurement, that is, the Software Total Components Measurement (STCM), in percentage, and is expressed as Nil, Low, Medium, High, or Very High according to this percentage value.

17.1.13.2 Repeat Execution Level (REL)

One of the Software Performance Quality Indicators (SPQIs) of the type Software Operational Indicator (SOI)[5–7]. It gives the indication of the dynamic run-time level of the repeat operations which are used for repeating some actions, and are performed in the software execution.

The REL is the ratio of the total number of the repeat operations performed, that is, the Repeat Execution Operations (REO), to the dynamic run-time operations performance size of the Software's Measurable Component 'Functionality Execution' (CFE), that is, the Functionality Execution Operations Dynamic Measurement (FEODM), in percentage, and is expressed as Nil, Low, Medium, High, or Very High according to this percentage value.

17.1.13.3 Repeat Execution Operations (REO)

The Software Component's Feature Measurement (SCFM) for the Software Component's Measurable Feature 'Function Repeat Execution' (FFR) in terms of the Software Component's Feature Points (SCFPs).

The REO (Repeat Execution Operations) is the measurement for the repeat operations that perform the repeat actions described in the Functionality Execution (FE) description part of the Functional Requirements Specifications (FRS).

The REO is calculated from the Software Component's Feature Point Count for 'Function Repeat Execution' (FCFR), and is used for the following calculations:

a. Software Component's Measurements (SCMs): the Software Total Components Measurement (STCM) through the Software Component 'Functionality Execution' Measurement (CFEM);

b. Software Size and Effort Estimations (SSEEs): the Software Total Development Effort (STDE) through the Software Logical Size (SLS) and Software Analysis, Design, and Coding Effort (SADCE);

c. Software Performance Quality Indicators (SPQIs): Software Structural Indicators (SSIs)[5–7], that is, the SSIs Functionality Execution Complexity and Size (FECS), Functionality Execution Component Proportion (FECP), and Repeat Execution Content Proportion (RECP); and Software Operational Indicator (SOI)[5–7], that is, the SOI Repeat Execution Level (REL).

17.1.13.4 Requirements Deficiency Grade (RDG)

One of the Software Performance Quality Indicators (SPQIs) of the type Software Structural Indicator (SSI)[5–7]. It gives the indication of the static proportion of the apparent deficient part in the functional requirements specifications for the Functional Data, Functionality Execution, User Interface and Message Exchange. The following apparently missing items/features are considered:

In the Functional Data:

a. data classes, subclasses, their attributes, the fields of the attributes, and class methods.

In the Functionality Execution:

a. memory read/write, input/output, message exchange, computational, logical, decision execution, repeat execution, action execution, execution flow control, and error handling operations;

b. functional data handled during memory read/write, input/output, message exchange, and general – computational, logical, decision, repeat, and execution flow control – operations.

In the User Interface part:

a. screens, their input/output fields, and input/output navigational links.

In the Message Exchange part:

a. messages and their fields.

The RDG is the ratio of the total number of the aforementioned apparently missing items/features in the Functional Data, Functionality Execution, User Interface, and Message Exchange, that is, the Software Components Requirement Deficiency Measurement (CRDM), to the total software size, that is, the Software Total Components Measurement (STCM), in percentage, and is expressed as Nil, Low, Medium, High, or Very High according to this percentage value.

17.1.14 S

17.1.14.1 Software Analysis, Design, and Coding Effort (SADCE)

Effort required for the analysis, design, coding, and technical specifications documents preparation in the software development process. It is dependent on the size and complexity of the Software's Measurable Component 'Functional Data' (CFD), 'Functionality Execution' (CFE), 'User Interface' (CUI), and 'Message Exchange' (CME); Software Logical Size; and average productivity for the analysis, design, and coding activities.

The SADCE (Software Analysis, Design, and Coding Effort) is calculated from the following efforts:

a. Software Data Analysis and Design Effort (SDADE) which is calculated from the Software Component 'Functional Data' Measurement (CFDM), Software Component 'User Interface' Measurement (CUIM), Software Component 'Message Exchange' Measurement (CMEM), and average productivity for the data analysis and design activity;

b. Software Functionality Analysis and Design Effort (SFADE) which is calculated from the Software Component 'Functionality Execution' Measurement (CFEM) and average productivity for the functionality analysis and design activity;

c. Software Coding Effort (SCE) which is calculated from the Software Logical Size (SLS) and average productivity for the coding activity.

17.1.14.2 Software Code Statements (SCDS)

Statements used for coding the software programs. They are used to perform various operations of the functionality and are required mainly for the following types of operations:

a. Memory operations used for reading/writing the data from/to the memory devices;

b. Input/output operations used for receiving/sending the input/output data from/to input/output devices;

c. Message exchange operations (message send/receive) used for sending/receiving the messages to/from the external application programs or sub-programs (modules);

d. Functionality execution operations which are the following:

  i. computational;
  ii. logical;
  iii. decision execution;
  iv. repeat execution;
  v. action execution;
  vi. execution flow control;
  vii. error handling;

and the following types of functional data handling during the functionality operations indicated:

- **a.** functional data handled in the memory read/write operations;
- **b.** functional data handled in the input/output operations;
- **c.** functional data handled in the message exchange operations;
- **d.** functional data handled in the functionality execution operations for the following types of functional operations:
  - **i.** computational;
  - **ii.** logical;
  - **iii.** decision execution;
  - **iv.** repeat execution;
  - **v.** execution flow control.

17.1.14.3 Software Coding Effort (SCE)

Effort spent on the coding activity of the software during the software development process. This is calculated based on the Software Logical Size (SLS) and average productivity for the coding activity. It includes the technical documentation part.

17.1.14.4 Software Comment Statements (SCS)

Statements used as comments in the software programs. They provide useful and helpful information about the data declaration statements and code statements. They help greatly to understand the program during the development and maintenance of the software.

17.1.14.5 Software Component 'Functional Data' Measurement (CFDM)

Measurement for the Software's Measurable Component 'Functional Data' (CFD). It indicates the functional data size and complexity, taking into account the class structure by considering the classes and subclasses, their attributes, and their fields.

The CFDM is obtained by adding together the Software Component's Feature Measurements (SCFMs) Data Class Entities (DCE), Data Class Attribute Entities (DAE), and Data Class Field Entities (DFE) which are measured by the Software Component's Feature Point Count for 'Data Class' (FCDC), 'Data Attribute' (FCDA), and 'Data Field' (FCDF), respectively.

Hence, CFDM = DCE + DAE + DFE = FCDC + FCDA + FCDF.

17.1.14.6 Software Component 'Functionality Execution' Measurement (CFEM)

Measurement for the Software's Measurable Component 'Functionality Execution' (CFE). It indicates the Functionality Execution size and complexity, taking into account all the functional operations and functional data handled during these operations by considering:

- **1.** all the functional operations of the
  - **a.** software processing that are the
    - **i.** computational operations;
    - **ii.** logical operations;
    - **iii.** decision-taking operations;

  - **iv.** repeat action operations;
  - **v.** action execution operations;
  - **vi.** execution flow control operations;
- **b.** error handling;
- **c.** memory transactions;
- **d.** input/output device interactions;
- **e.** communications with the external application programs;

2. functional data handled during the

- **a.** memory transactions;
- **b.** input/output device interactions;
- **c.** communications with external application programs;
- **d.** software processing operations which are the
  - **i.** computational;
  - **ii.** logical;
  - **iii.** decision-taking;
  - **iv.** repeat action;
  - **v.** execution flow control;

operations involved in the Functionality Execution, and class methods

The CFEM is obtained by adding together the two parts – functional operations measurement and functional data handling measurement. These two parts measurements are: Functionality Execution Operations Measurement (FEOM) and Functionality Execution Data Manipulation Measurement (FEDM), respectively.

Hence, CFEM = FEOM + FEDM.

17.1.14.7 Software Component 'Message Exchange' Measurement (CMEM)

Measurement for the Software's Measurable Component 'Message Exchange' (CME). It indicates the message size and complexity, taking into account the message structure by considering the messages and their fields.

The CMEM is obtained by adding together the Software Component's Feature Measurements (SCFMs) Notifying Message Entities (NME) and Message Field Entities (MFE) which are measured by the Software Component's Feature Point Count for 'Notifying Message' (FCNM) and 'Message Field' (FCMF), respectively.

Hence, CMEM = NME + NMF = FCNM + FCMF.

17.1.14.8 Software Component 'User Interface' Measurement (CUIM)

Measurement for the Software's Measurable Component 'User Interface' (CUI). It indicates the User Interface size and complexity, taking into account the screens and their size by considering all the screens, their fields, and their input/output navigation links which are used for interconnecting the screens or connecting screens to/from other operations.

The CUIM is obtained by adding together the Software Component's Feature Measurements (SCFMs) User Interface Screen Entities (UISE), User Interface Field Entities (UIFE), User Interface Input Link Entities (UIIE), and User Interface Output Link Entities (UIFE) which are measured by the Software Component's Feature Point Count for 'User Screen' (FCUS), 'User Screen Field' (FCUF), 'User Screen Input Link' (FCUI), and 'User Screen Output Link' (FCUO), respectively.

Hence, CUIM = UISE + UIFE + UIIE + UIOE = FCUS + FCUF + FCUI + FCUO.

17.1.14.9 Software Component's Feature Measurement (SCFM)

Measurement of the Software Component's Measurable Features (SCMFs) in terms of the Software Component's Feature Points (SCFPs) which is the Functional Size Unit (FSU) in the Functional Software Size Measurement Methodology with Effort Estimation and Performance Indication (FSSM). These measurements indicate the size of all the features of the 4 SMCs by measuring the following entities and operations:

A. Software Component Feature Measurements (SCFMs) for the Software's Measurable Component 'Functional Data' (CFD):
  a. Data Class Entities (DCE): it is the measurement of the Software Component's Measurable Feature 'Data Class' (FDC), for all the data classes and subclasses, and is calculated from the Software Component's Feature Point Count for 'Data Class' (FCDC).
  b. Data Class Attribute Entities (DAE): it is the measurement of the Software Component's Measurable Feature 'Data Attribute' (FDA), for all the attributes of all the classes and subclasses, and is calculated from the Software Component's Feature Point Count for 'Data Attribute' (FCDA).
  c. Data Class Field Entities (DFE): it is the measurement of the Software Component's Measurable Feature 'Data Field' (FDF), for all the fields of all the attributes of all the classes and subclasses, and is calculated from the Software Component's Feature Point Count for 'Data Field' (FCDF).
  d. Functional Data Missing Entities (FDME): it is the measurement of the Software Component's Measurable Feature 'Data Missing', for all the missing data items in the Logical Data Model, and is calculated from the Software Component's Feature Point Count for 'Data Missing' (FCDM).

B. Software Component Feature Measurements (SCFMs) for the Software's Measurable Component 'Functionality Execution' (CFE):
  a. Memory Operations (MO): it is the measurement of the Software Component's Measurable Features 'Data Read' (FDR) and 'Data Write' (FDW), for all the memory read/write operations used for reading/writing the data from/to the memory devices, and is calculated from the Software Component's Feature Point Count for 'Data Read' (FCDR) and 'Data Write' (FCDW).
  b. Computational Operations (CO): it is the measurement of the Software Component's Measurable Feature 'Function Computational Operation' (FFC), for all the mathematical computational operations, and is calculated from the Software Component's Feature Point Count for 'Function Computational Operation' (FCFC).
  c. Logical Operations (LO): it is the measurement of the Software Component's Measurable Feature 'Function Logical Operation' (FFL), for all the logical operations of the type AND, OR, etc., and is calculated from the Software Component's Feature Point Count for 'Function Logical Operation' (FCFL).
  d. Decision Execution Operations (DEO): it is the measurement of the Software Component's Measurable Feature 'Function Decision Execution' (FFD), for all the decision-taking operations, such as if, else if and else, and is calculated from the Software Component's Feature Point Count for 'Function Decision Execution' (FCFD).
  e. Repeat Execution Operations (REO): it is the measurement of the Software Component's Measurable Feature 'Function Repeat Execution' (FFR), for all

the repeat operations for actions or group of actions, and is calculated from the Software Component's Feature Point Count for 'Function Repeat Execution (FCFR).

f. Action Execution Operations (AEO): it is the measurement of the Software Component's Measurable Feature 'Function Action Execution' (FFA), for all the actions performing operations, and is calculated from the Software Component's Feature Point Count for 'Function Action Execution (FCFA).

g. Execution Flow Control Operations (EFCO): it is the measurement of the Software Component's Measurable Feature 'Function Execution Flow Control' (FFO), for all the operations which control the execution flow, and is calculated from the Software Component's Feature Point Count for 'Function Execution Flow Control' (FCFO).

h. Error Handling Operations (EHO): it is the measurement of the Software Component's Measurable Feature 'Function Error Handling' (FFE), for all the error handling operations, and is calculated from the Software Component's Feature Point Count for 'Function Error Handling' (FCFE).

i. Input/Output Operations (IOO): it is the measurement of the Software Component's Measurable Features 'Data Input' (FDI) and 'Data Output' (FDO), for all the input/output operations used for receiving/sending the input/output data from/to the input/output devices, and is calculated from the Software Component's Feature Point Count for 'Data Input' (FCDI) and 'Data Output' (FCDO).

j. Message Exchange Operations (MEO): it is the measurement of the Software Component's Measurable Feature 'Message Send' (FMS) and 'Message Receive' (FMR), for all the message send/receive operations used for sending/receiving the messages to/from the other programs/sub-programs, and is calculated from the Software Component's Feature Point Count for 'Message Send' (FCMS) and 'Message Receive' (FCMR).

k. Class Method Entities (CMDE): it is the measurement of the Software Component's Measurable Feature 'Class Method' (FCM), for all the class methods, and is calculated from the Software Component's Feature Point Count for 'Class Method' (FCCM).

l. Memory Operations Functional Data Entities (MOFE): it is the measurement of the Software Component's Measurable Feature 'Memory Operations Functional Data' (FLM), for all the functional data handled during all the memory read/write operations, and is calculated from the Software Component's Feature Point Count for 'Memory Operations Functional Data' (FCLM).

m. Input/Output Operations Functional Data Entities (IOFE): it is the measurement of the Software Component's Measurable Feature 'Input/Output Operations Functional Data' (FLI), for all the functional data handled during all the input/output operations used for receiving/sending the input/output data from/to the input/output devices, and is calculated from the Software Component's Feature Point Count for 'Input/Output Operations Functional Data' (FCLI).

n. Message Exchange Operations Functional Data Entities (EOFE): it is the measurement of the Software Component's Measurable Feature 'Message Exchange Operations Functional Data' (FLS), for all the functional data handled during all the message send/receive operations for sending/receiving the messages to/from the other programs/sub-programs, and is calculated from the Software Component's Feature Point Count for 'Message Exchange Operations Functional Data' (FCLS).

o. General Operations Functional Data Entities (GOFE): it is the measurement of the Software Component's Measurable Feature 'General Operations Functional Data' (FLG), for all the functional data handled during the
  i. mathematical computational operations;
  ii. logical operations;
  iii. decision-taking operations;
  iv. repeat operations for actions/group of actions;
  v. operations controlling the flow of the program;

and is calculated from the Software Component's Feature Point Count for 'General Operations Functional Data' (FCLG).

p. Functionality Execution Missing Entities (FEME): it is the measurement of the Software Component's Measurable Feature 'Function Missing' (FFM), for all the missing items in the Functionality Execution, and is calculated from the Software Component's Feature Point Count for 'Functionality Missing' (FCFM).

C. Software Component Feature Measurements (SCFMs) for the Software's Measurable Component 'User Interface' (CUI):

a. User Interface Screen Entities (UISE): it is the measurement of the Software Component's Measurable Feature 'User Screen' (FUS), for all the user interfaces/screens defined in the User Interface description part, and is calculated from the Software Component's Feature Point Count for 'User Screen' (FCUS).

b. User Interface Field Entities (UIFE): it is the measurement of the Software Component's Measurable Feature 'User Screen Field' (FUF), for all the fields of all the user interfaces/screens, and is calculated from the Software Component's Feature Point Count for 'User Screen Field' (FCUF).

c. User Interface Input Link Entities (UIIE): it is the measurement of the Software Component's Measurable Feature 'User Screen Input Link' (FUI), for all the input navigational links of all the user interfaces/screens, and is calculated from the Software Component's Feature Point Count for 'User Screen Input Link' (FCUI).

d. User Interface Output Link Entities (UIOE): it is the measurement of the Software Component's Measurable Feature 'User Screen Output Link' (FUO), for all the output navigational links of all the user interfaces/screens, and is calculated from the Software Component's Feature Point Count for 'User Screen Output Link' (FCUO).

e. User Interface Missing Entities (UIME): it is the measurement of the Software Component's Measurable Feature 'User Screen Missing' (FUM), for all the missing items in the user interfaces/screens, and is calculated from the Software Component's Feature Point Count for 'User Screen Missing' (FCUM).

D. Software Component Feature Measurements (SCFMs) for the Software's Measurable Component 'Message Exchange' (CME):

a. Notifying Message Entities (NME): it is the measurement of the Software Component's Measurable Feature 'Notifying Messages' (FNM), for all the messages used for communication with the other programs, and is calculated from the Software Component's Feature Point Count for 'Notifying Message' (FCNM).

b. Message Field Entities (MFE): it is the measurement of the Software Component's Measurable Feature 'Message Field' (FMF), for all the fields of all the messages, and is calculated from the Software Component's Feature Point Count for 'Message Field' (FCMF).

c. Message Exchange Missing Entities (MEME): it is the measurement of the Software Component's Measurable Feature 'Message Missing' (FMM), for all the missing items in the message structure, and is calculated from the Software Component's Feature Point Count for 'Message Missing' (FCMM).

17.1.14.10 Software Component's Feature Point (SCFP)

Functional Size Unit (FSU), that is, the unit of measurement in the Functional Software Size Measurement Methodology with Effort Estimation and Performance Indication (FSSM). To carry out the functional software size measurement, measurements of the Software's Measurable Components (SMCs) are performed by identifying the Software Component's Measurable Features (SCMFs) of the SMCs in the Functional Requirements Specifications (FRS), and the SCFPs are assigned to the identified SCMFs. Summation of the assigned SCFPs for the corresponding SCMFs produces Software Component's Feature Point Counts (SCFPCs) which are further used in the calculations to obtain the Software Component's Feature Measurements (SCFMs). The SCFMs are used to calculate the Software Component's Measurements (SCMs). Then, the SCFMs and SCMs are used for the calculations of the Software Size and Effort Estimations (SSEEs) and Software Performance Quality Indicators (SPQIs) of the two types which are the Software Structural Indicators (SSIs)[5–7] and Software Operational Indicators (SOIs)[5–7].

There are 31 SCMFs and so, corresponding to these 31 SCMFs, there are 31 streams of SCFPs and consequently, there are 31 SCFPCs which are used for calculating the 28 SCFMs.

There are 6 Software Component's Measurements (SCMs) calculated from the SCFMs:

1. Software Component 'Functional Data' Measurement (CFDM);
2. Software Component 'Functionality Execution' Measurement (CFEM);
3. Software Component 'User Interface' Measurement (CUIM);
4. Software Component 'Message Exchange' Measurement (CMEM);
5. Software Total Components Measurement (STCM);
6. Software Components Requirement Deficiency Measurement (CRDM).

The values of all the measurements of all the SCMs are in terms of the Software Component's Feature Points (SCFPs).

17.1.14.11 Software Component's Feature Point Count (SCFPC)

Summation of the 31 corresponding Software Component's Feature Points (SCFPs) which are obtained by assigning the SCFPs to the different Software Component's Measurable Features (SCMFs) results in the corresponding Software Component's Feature Point Count (SCFPC). Corresponding to the 31 SCMFs, there are 31 SCFPCs obtained by adding the corresponding assigned SCFPs to the SCMFs.

The SCFPCs are used in the calculations to obtain the 28 Software Component's Feature Measurements (SCFMs) which are used for the calculations of the 6 Software Component's Measurements (SCMs). The SCFMs and SCMs are further used to calculate the 4

Software Size and Effort Estimations (SSEEs) and 36 Software Performance Quality Indicators (SPQIs) of the two types which are the 23 Software Structural Indicators (SSIs)[5–7] and 13 Software Operational Indicators (SOIs)[5–7].

17.1.14.12 Software Component's Feature Point Count for 'Class Method' (FCCM), 'Data Attribute' (FCDA), 'Data Class' (FCDC), and 'Data Field' (FCDF)

Summation of all the corresponding Software Component's Feature Points for 'Class Method' (FPCMs), 'Data Attribute' (FPDAs), 'Data Class' (FPDCs), and 'Data Field' (FPDFs) which are obtained by assigning the Software Component's Feature Points (SCFPs) – Functional Size Unit (FSU) of measurement in the FSSM – to the Software Component's Measurable Feature 'Class Method' (FCM), 'Data Attribute' (FDA), 'Data Class' (FDC), and 'Data Field' (FDF), respectively, are called the Software Component's Feature Point Count for 'Class Method' (FCCM), 'Data Attribute' (FCDA), 'Data Class' (FCDC), and 'Data Field' (FCDF), respectively.

The value of the FCCM (Software Component's Feature Point Count for 'Class Method') signifies the total number of class methods (operation or procedure) and varies according to the quantity of the presence of the FCMs (Software Component's Measurable Features 'Data Class') in the Logical Data Model (LDM) description of the Functional Requirements Specifications (FRS). The more the FCMs, the more the FPCMs and the bigger the FCCM.

Similarly, the values of the FCDA (Software Component's Feature Point Count for 'Data Attribute'), FCDC (Software Component's Feature Point Count for 'Data Class'), and FCDF (Software Component's Feature Point Count for 'Data Field') signify the total number of the data attributes of all the classes and subclasses; the total number of all the classes and subclasses; and the total number of the data fields of all the classes and subclasses; respectively, and vary according to the quantity of the presence of the FDAs (Software Component's Measurable Features 'Data Attribute'), FDCs (Software Component's Measurable Features 'Data Class'), and FDFs (Software Component's Measurable Features 'Data Field'), respectively, in the Logical Data Model (LDM) description of the Functional Requirements Specifications (FRS). The more the FDAs, FDCs, and FDFs, the more the FPDAs, FPDCs, and FPDFs, respectively, and the higher the values of the FCDA, FCDC, and FCDF, respectively.

The FCCM, FCDA, FCDC, and FCDF are used to calculate the following Software Component's Feature Measurements (SCFMs), respectively: Class Method Entities (CMDE), Data Class Attribute Entities (DAE), Data Class Entities (DCE), and Data Class Field Entities (DFE).

17.1.14.13 Software Component's Feature Point Count for 'Data Input' (FCDI), 'Data Missing' (FCDM), and 'Data Output' (FCDO)

Summation of all the corresponding Software Component's Feature Points for 'Data Input' (FPDIs), 'Data Missing' (FPDMs), and 'Data Output' (FPDOs), which are obtained by assigning the Software Component's Feature Points (SCFPs) – Functional Size Unit (FSU) of measurement in the FSSM – to the Software Component's Measurable Feature 'Data Input' (FDI), 'Data Missing' (FDM), and 'Data Output' (FDO), respectively, are called the Software Component's Feature Point Count for 'Data Input' (FCDI), 'Data Missing' (FCDM), and 'Data Output' (FCDO), respectively.

The values of the FCDI (Software Component's Feature Point Count for 'Data Input') and FCDO (Software Component's Feature Point Count for 'Data Output') signify the total number of the input/output operations used for receiving/sending the input/output data from/to the input/output devices in the functionality, respectively; and vary according to the quantity of the presence of the FDIs (Software Component's Measurable Features 'Data Input') and FDOs (Software Component's Measurable Features 'Data Output'), respectively, in the Functionality Execution (FE) description of the Functional Requirements Specifications (FRS). The more the FDIs and FDOs, the more the FPDIs and FPDOs, respectively, and the higher the values of the FCDI and FCDO, respectively.

The value of the FCDM (Software Component's Feature Point Count for 'Data Missing') signifies the total number of missing data items in the Logical Data Model, and varies according to the quantity of the presence of the FDMs (Software Component's Measurable Features 'Data Missing') in the Logical Data Model (LDM) of the Functional Requirements Specifications (FRS). The more the FDMs, the more the FPDMs, and the higher the value of the FCDM.

The FCDI and FCDO are used to calculate the Software Component's Feature Measurement (SCFM) Input and Output Operations (IOO). The FCDM is used to calculate the Software Component's Feature Measurement (SCFM) Functional Data Missing Entities (FDME).

17.1.14.14 Software Component's Feature Point Count for 'Data Read' (FCDR) and 'Data Write' (FCDW)

Summation of all the corresponding Software Component's Feature Points for 'Data Read' (FPDRs) and 'Data Write' (FPDWs) which are obtained by assigning the Software Component's Feature Points (SCFPs) – Functional Size Unit (FSU) of measurement in the FSSM – to the Software Component's Measurable Feature 'Data Read' (FDR) and 'Data Write' (FDW), respectively, are called the Software Component's Feature Point Count for 'Data Read' (FCDR) and 'Data Write' (FCDW), respectively.

The values of the FCDR (Software Component's Feature Point Count for 'Data Read') and FCDW (Software Component's Feature Point Count for 'Data Write') signify the total number of memory read/write operations used to read/write the data from/to the permanent memory devices, for example, disks, respectively, and vary according to the quantity of the presence of the FDRs (Software Component's Measurable Features 'Data Read') and FDWs (Software Component's Measurable Features 'Data Write'), respectively, in the Functionality Execution (FE) description of the Functional Requirements Specifications (FRS). The more the FDRs and FDWs, the more the FPDRs and FPDWs, respectively, and the higher the values of the FCDR and FCDW, respectively.

The FCDR and FCDW are used for the calculation of the Software Component's Feature Measurement (SCFM) Memory Operations (MO).

17.1.14.15 Software Component's Feature Point Count for 'Function Action Execution' (FCFA), 'Function Decision Execution' (FCFD), 'Function Execution Flow Control' (FCFO), and 'Function Repeat Execution' (FCFR)

Summation of all the corresponding Software Component's Feature Points for 'Function Action Execution' (FPFAs), 'Function Decision Execution' (FPFDs), 'Function Execution Flow Control' (FPFOs), and 'Function Repeat Execution' (FPFRs) which are obtained by assigning the Software Component's Feature Points (SCFPs) – Functional Size Unit (FSU) of measurement in the FSSM – to the Software Component's Measurable Feature 'Function Action Execution' (FFA), 'Function Decision Execution' (FFD), 'Function Execution Flow Control' (FFO), and 'Function Repeat Execution' (FFR), respectively, are called the Software Component's Feature Point Count for 'Function Action Execution' (FCFA), 'Function Decision Execution' (FCFD), 'Function Execution Flow Control' (FCFO), and 'Function Repeat Execution' (FCFR), respectively.

The values of the FCFA (Software Component's Feature Point Count for 'Function Action Execution'), FCFD (Software Component's Feature Point Count for 'Function Decision Execution'), FCFO (Software Component's Feature Point Count for 'Function Execution Flow Control'), and FCFR (Software Component's Feature Point Count for 'Function Repeat Execution') signify the total number of the actions performed, decision execution operations, execution flow control operations, and repeat actions, respectively, and vary according to the quantity of the presence of the FFAs (Software Component's Measurable Features 'Function Action Execution'), FFDs (Software Component's Measurable Features 'Function Decision Execution'), FFOs (Software Component's Measurable Features 'Function Execution Flow Control'), and FFRs (Software Component's Measurable Features 'Function Repeat Execution') in the Functionality Execution (FE) description of the Functional Requirements Specifications (FRS), respectively. The more the FFAs, FFDs, FFOs, and FFRs, the more the FPFAs, FPFDs, FPFOs, and FPFRs, respectively, and the higher the values of the FCFA, FCFD, FCFO, and FCFR, respectively.

The FCFA, FCFD, FCFO, and FCFR are used for the calculations of the following Software Component's Feature Measurements (SCFMs), respectively: Action Execution Operations (AEO), Decision Execution Operations (DEO), Execution Flow Control Operations (EFCO), and Repeat Execution Operations (REO).

17.1.14.16 Software Component's Feature Point Count for 'Function Computational Operation' (FCFC) and 'Function Logical Operation' (FCFL)

Summation of all the corresponding Software Component's Feature Points for 'Function Computational Operation' (FPFCs) and 'Function Logical Operation' (FPFLs) which are obtained by assigning the Software Component's Feature Points (SCFPs) – Functional Size Unit (FSU) of measurement in the FSSM – to the Software Component's Measurable Feature 'Function Computational Operation' (FFC) and 'Function Logical Operation' (FFL), respectively, are called the Software Component's Feature Point Count for 'Function Computational Operation' (FCFC) and 'Function Logical Operation' (FCFL), respectively.

The values of the FCFC (Software Component's Feature Point Count for 'Function Computational Operation') and FCFL (Software Component's Feature Point Count for 'Function Logical Operation') signify the total number of the computational operations (addition, subtraction, multiplication, division, and equals, etc.) and logical operations (AND, OR, NOT, and XOR), respectively, and vary according to the quantity of the presence of the FFCs (Software Component's Measurable Features 'Function Computational Operation') and FFLs (Software Component's Measurable Features 'Function Logical Operation') in the Functionality Execution (FE) description of the Functional Requirements Specifications (FRS), respectively. The more the FFCs and FFLs, the more the FPFCs and FPFLs, respectively, and the higher the values of the FCFC and FCFL, respectively.

The FCFC and FCFL are used for the calculation of the following Software Component's Feature Measurements (SCFMs), respectively: Computational Operations (CO) and Logical Operations (LO).

17.1.14.17 Software Component's Feature Point Count for 'Function Error Handling' (FCFE) and 'Functionality Missing' (FCFM)

Summation of all the corresponding Software Component's Feature Points for 'Function Error Handling' (FPFEs) and 'Functionality Missing' (FPFMs) which are obtained by assigning the Software Component's Feature Points (SCFPs) – Functional Size Unit (FSU) of measurement in the FSSM – to the Software Component's Measurable Feature 'Function Error Handling' (FFE) and 'Functionality Missing' (FFM), respectively, are called the Software Component's Feature Point Count for 'Function Error Handling' (FCFE) and 'Functionality Missing' (FCFM), respectively.

The values of the FCFE (Software Component's Feature Point Count for 'Function Error Handling') and FCFM (Software Component's Feature Point Count for 'Functionality Missing') signify the total number of error handling operations and total number of functionality missing items, respectively, and vary according to the quantity of the presence of the FFEs (Software Component's Measurable Features 'Function Error Handling') and FFMs (Software Component's Measurable Features 'Functionality Missing') in the Functionality Execution (FE) description of the Functional Requirements Specifications (FRS), respectively. The more the FFEs and FFMs, the more the FPFEs and FPFMs, respectively, and the higher the values of the FCFE and FCFM, respectively.

The FCFE and FCFM are used to calculate the following Software Component's Feature Measurements (SCFMs), respectively: Error Handling Operations (EHO) and Functionality Execution Missing Entities (FEME).

17.1.14.18 Software Component's Feature Point Count for 'General Operations Functional Data' (FCLG), 'Input/Output Operations Functional Data' (FCLI), 'Memory Operations Functional Data' (FCLM), and 'Message Exchange Operations Functional Data' (FCLS)

Summation of all the corresponding Software Component's Feature Points for 'General Operations Functional Data' (FPLGs), 'Input/Output Operations Functional Data' (FPLIs), 'Memory Operations Functional Data' (FPLMs), and 'Message Exchange Operations Functional Data' (FPLSs) which are obtained by assigning the Software Component's Feature Points (SCFPs) – Functional Size Unit (FSU) of measurement in the FSSM – to the Software Component's Measurable Feature 'General Operations Functional Data' (FLG), 'Input/Output Operations Functional Data' (FLI), 'Memory Operations Functional Data' (FLM), and 'Message Exchange Operations Functional Data' (FLS), respectively, are called the Software Component's Feature Point Count for 'General Operations Functional Data' (FCLG), 'Input/Output Operations Functional Data' (FCLI), 'Memory Operations Functional Data' (FCLM), and 'Message Exchange Operations Functional Data' (FCLS), respectively.

The values of the FCLG (Software Component's Feature Point Count for 'General Operations Functional Data'), FCLI (Software Component's Feature Point Count for 'Input/Output Operations Functional Data'), FCLM (Software Component's Feature Point Count for 'Memory Operations Functional Data'), and FCLS (Software Component's Feature Point Count for 'Message Exchange Operations Functional Data') signify the total number of the Data Collections handled in the general function computational, logical, decision, repeat, and execution flow operations; total number of Data Collections handled in the input/output operations used for receiving/sending the input/output data from/to the input/output devices; total number of Data Collections handled in the memory read/write operations used for reading/writing the data from/to the memory devices; and total number of Data Collections handled in the message send/receive operations used for communication with the external programs; respectively.

The values of the FCLG, FCLI, FCLM, and FCLS vary according to the quantity of the presence of the FLGs (Software Component's Measurable Features 'General Operations Functional Data'), FLIs (Software Component's Measurable Features 'Input/Output Operations Functional Data'), FLMs (Software Component's Measurable Features 'Memory Operations Functional Data'), and FLSs (Software Component's Measurable Features 'Message Exchange Operations Functional Data') in the Functionality Execution (FE) description of the Functional Requirements Specifications (FRS), respectively. The more the FLGs, FLIs, FLMs, and FLSs, the more the FPLGs, FPLIs, FPLMs, and FPLSs, respectively, and the higher the values of the FCLG, FCLI, FCLM, and FCLS, respectively.

The FCLG, FCLI, FCLM, and FCLS are used to calculate the following Software Component's Feature Measurements (SCFMs), respectively: General Operations Functional Data Entities (GOFE), Input and Output Operations Functional Data Entities (IOFE), Memory Operations Functional Data Entities (MOFE), and Message Exchange Operations Functional Data Entities (GOFE).

17.1.14.19 Software Component's Feature Point Count for 'Message Field' (FCMF) and 'Notifying Message' (FCNM)

Summation of all the corresponding Software Component's Feature Points for 'Message Field' (FPMFs) and 'Notifying Message' (FPNMs) which are obtained by assigning the Software Component's Feature Points (SCFPs) – Functional Size Unit (FSU) of measurement in the FSSM – to the Software Component's Measurable Feature 'Message Field' (FMF) and 'Notifying Message' (FNM), respectively, are called the Software Component's Feature Point Count for 'Message Field' (FCMF) and 'Notifying Message' (FCNM), respectively.

The values of the FCMF (Software Component's Feature Point Count for 'Message Field') and FCNM (Software Component's Feature Point Count for 'Notifying Message') signify the total number of the message fields of all the messages and total number of messages, respectively, and vary according to the quantity of the presence of the FMFs (Software Component's Measurable Features 'Message Field') and FNMs (Software Component's Measurable Features 'Notifying Message') in the Message Exchange (ME) description of the Functional Requirements Specifications (FRS), respectively. The more the FMFs and FNMs, the more the FPMFs and FPNMs, respectively, and the higher the values of the FCMF and FCNM, respectively.

The FCMF and FCNM are used to calculate the following Software Component's Feature Measurements (SCFMs), respectively: Message Field Entities (FFE) and Notifying Message Entities (NME).

17.1.14.20 Software Component's Feature Point Count for 'Message Missing' (FCMM), 'Message Receive' (FCMR), and 'Message Send' (FCMS)

Summation of all the corresponding Software Component's Feature Points for 'Message Missing' (FPMMs), 'Message Receive' (FPMRs), and 'Message Send' (FPMSs) which are obtained by assigning the Software Component's Feature Points (SCFPs) – Functional Size Unit (FSU) of measurement in the FSSM – to the Software Component's Measurable Feature 'Message Missing' (FMM), 'Message Receive' (FMR), and 'Message Send' (FMS), respectively, are called the Software Component's Feature Point Count for 'Message Missing' (FCMM), 'Message Receive' (FCMR), and 'Message Send' (FCMS), respectively.

The value of the FCMM (Software Component's Feature Point Count for 'Message Missing') signifies the total number of missing message features, that is, messages and fields of the messages, and varies according to the quantity of the FMMs (Software Component's Measurable Features 'Message Missing') in the Message Exchange (ME) description of the Functional Requirements Specifications (FRS). The more the FMMs, the more the FPMMs, and the higher the value of the FCMM.

The values of the FCMR (Software Component's Feature Point Count for 'Message Receive') and FCMS (Software Component's Feature Point Count for 'Message Send') signify the total number of the messages received/sent from/to the external programs, respectively, and vary according to the quantity of the FMRs (Software Component's Measurable Features 'Message Receive') and FMSs (Software Component's Measurable Features 'Message Send') in the functionality description part of the Functional Requirements Specifications (FRS), respectively. The more the FMRs and FMSs, the more the FPMRs and FMSs, respectively, and the higher the values of the FCMR and FCMS, respectively.

The FCMM is used to calculate the Software Component's Feature Measurement (SCFM) Message Exchange Missing Entities (MEME).

The FCMR and FCMS are used for the calculations of the Software Component's Feature Measurement (SCFM) Message Exchange Operations (MEO).

17.1.14.21 Software Component's Feature Point Count for 'User Screen Field' (FCUF), 'User Screen Input Link' (FCUI), 'User Screen Missing' (FCUM), 'User Screen Output Link' (FCUO), and 'User Screen' (FCUS)

Summation of all the corresponding Software Component's Feature Points for 'User Screen Field' (FPUFs), 'User Screen Input Link' (FPUIs), 'User Screen Missing' (FPUMs), 'User Screen Output Link' (FPUOs), and 'User Screen' (FPUSs) which are obtained by assigning the Software Component's Feature Points (SCFPs) – Functional Size Unit (FSU) of measurement in the FSSM – to the Software Component's Measurable Feature 'User Screen Field' (FUF), 'User Screen Input Link' (FUI), 'User Screen Missing' (FUM), 'User Screen Output Link' (FUO), and 'User Screen' (FUS), respectively, are called the Software Component's Feature Point Count for 'User Screen Field' (FCUF), 'User Screen Input Link' (FCUI), 'User Screen Missing' (FCUM), 'User Screen Output Link' (FCUO), and 'User Screen' (FCUS), respectively.

The values of the FCUF (Software Component's Feature Point Count for 'User Screen Field'), FCUI (Software Component's Feature Point Count for 'User Screen Input Link'), FCUM (Software Component's Feature Point Count for 'User Screen Missing'), FCUO (Software Component's Feature Point Count for 'User Screen Output Link'), and FCUS (Software Component's Feature Point Count for 'User Screen') signify the total number of all the fields of all the user screens; total number of all the input navigational links of all the user screens; total number of all the user screens missing items; total number of all the output navigational links of all the user screens; and total number of all the user screens; respectively, and vary according to the quantity of the presence of the FUFs (Software Component's Measurable Features 'User Screen Field'), FUIs (Software Component's Measurable Features 'User Screen Input Link'), FUMs (Software Component's Measurable Features 'User Screen Missing'), FUOs (Software Component's Measurable Features 'User Screen Output Link'), and FUSs (Software Component's Measurable Features 'User Screen') in the User Interface (UI) description of the Functional Requirements Specifications (FRS), respectively. The more the FUFs, FUIs, FUMs, FUOs, and FUSs, the more the FPUFs, FPUIs, FPUMs, FPUOs, and FPUSs, respectively, and the higher the values of the FCUF, FCUI, FCUM, FCUO, and FCUS, respectively.

The FCUF, FCUI, FCUM, FCUO, and FCUS are used to calculate the following Software Component's Feature Measurements (SCFMs), respectively: User Interface Field Entities (UIFE), User Interface Input Link Entities (UIIE), User Interface Missing Entities (UIME), User Interface Output Link Entities (UIOE), and User Interface Screen Entities (UISE).

17.1.14.22 Software Component's Feature Point for 'Class Method' (FPCM), 'Data Attribute' (FPDA), 'Data Class' (FPDC), and 'Data Field' (FPDF)

An assigned Software Component's Feature Point (SCFP) – Functional Size Unit (FSU) of measurement in the FSSM – to the Software Component's Measurable Feature 'Class Method' (FCM), 'Data Attribute' (FDA), 'Data Class' (FDC), and 'Data Field' (FDF) is called the Software Component's Feature Point for 'Class Method' (FPCM), 'Data Attribute' (FPDA), 'Data Class' (FPDC), and 'Data Field' (FPDF), respectively.

Each FPCM (Software Component's Feature Point for 'Class Method'), FPDA (Software Component's Feature Point for 'Data Attribute'), FPDC (Software Component's Feature Point for 'Data Class'), and FPDF (Software Component's Feature Point for 'Data Field') signifies one class or subclass method; one data attribute of class or subclass; one data class or subclass; and one data field of class or subclass; respectively.

The quantity of the FPCMs, FPDAs, FPDCs, and FPDFs varies according to the magnitude of the presence of the FCMs (Software Component's Measurable Features 'Class Method'), FDAs (Software Component's Measurable Features 'Data Attribute'), FDCs (Software Component's Measurable Features 'Data Class'), and FDFs (Software Component's Measurable Features 'Data Field') in the Logical Data Model (LDM), respectively. The more the FCMs, FDAs, FDCs, and FDFs, the more the FPCMs, FPDAs, FPDCs, and FPDFs, respectively.

The sum of all the corresponding FPCMs, FPDAs, FPDCs, and FPDFs produces the Software Component's Feature Point Count for 'Class Method' (FCCM), 'Data Attribute' (FCDA), 'Data Class' (FCDC), and 'Data Field' (FCDF), respectively.

17.1.14.23 Software Component's Feature Point for 'Data Input' (FPDI), 'Data Missing' (FPDM), and 'Data Output' (FPDO)

An assigned Software Component's Feature Point (SCFP) – Functional Size Unit (FSU) of measurement in the FSSM – to the Software Component's Measurable Feature 'Data Input' (FDI), 'Data Missing' (FDM), and 'Data Output' (FDO) is called the Software Component's Feature Point for 'Data Input' (FPDI), 'Data Missing' (FPDM), and 'Data Output' (FPDO), respectively.

Each FPDI (Software Component's Feature Point for 'Data Input'), FPDM (Software Component's Feature Point for 'Data Missing'), and FPDO (Software Component's Feature Point for 'Data Output') signifies one data input operation for receiving the data from the input device; one missing data feature in the Functional Data description (Logical Data Model) part; and one data output operation for sending the data to the output device; respectively.

The quantity of the FPDIs and FPDOs varies according to the magnitude of the presence of the FDIs (Software Component's Measurable Features 'Data Input') and FDOs

(Software Component's Measurable Features 'Data Output') in the Functionality Execution (FE), respectively. The more the FDIs and FDOs, the more the FPDIs and FPDOs, respectively.

The quantity of the FPDMs varies according to the magnitude of the FDMs (Software Component's Measurable Features 'Data Missing') in the Logical Data Model (LDM). The more the FDMs, the more the FPDMs.

The sum of all the corresponding FPDIs, FPDMs, and FPDOs produces the Software Component's Feature Point Count for 'Data Input' (FCDI), 'Data Missing' (FCDM), and 'Data Output' (FCDO), respectively.

17.1.14.24 Software Component's Feature Point for 'Data Read' (FPDR) and 'Data Write' (FPDW)

An assigned Software Component's Feature Point (SCFP) – Functional Size Unit (FSU) of measurement in the FSSM – to the Software Component's Measurable Feature 'Data Read' (FDR) and 'Data Write' (FDW) is called the Software Component's Feature Point for 'Data Read' (FPDR) and 'Data Write' (FPDW), respectively.

Each FPDR (Software Component's Feature Point for 'Data Read') and FPDW (Software Component's Feature Point for 'Data Write') signifies one memory read and write operation, respectively.

The quantity of the FPDRs and FPDWs varies according to the magnitude of the presence of the FDRs (Software Component's Measurable Features 'Data Read') and FDWs (Software Component's Measurable Features 'Data Write') in the Functionality Execution (FE), respectively. The more the FDRs and FDWs, the more the FPDRs and FPDWs, respectively.

The sum of all the corresponding FPDRs and FPDWs produces the Software Component's Feature Point Count for 'Data Read' (FCDR) and 'Data Write' (FCDW), respectively.

17.1.14.25 Software Component's Feature Point for 'Function Action Execution' (FPFA), 'Function Decision Execution' (FPFD), 'Function Execution Flow Control' (FPFO), and 'Function Repeat Execution' (FPFR)

An assigned Software Component's Feature Point (SCFP) – Functional Size Unit (FSU) of measurement in the FSSM – to the Software Component's Measurable Feature 'Function Action Execution' (FFA), 'Function Decision Execution' (FFD), 'Function Execution Flow Control' (FFO), and 'Function Repeat Execution' (FFR) is called the Software Component's Feature Point for 'Function Action Execution' (FPFA), 'Function Decision Execution' (FPFD), 'Function Execution Flow Control' (FPFO), and 'Function Repeat Execution' (FPFR), respectively.

Each FPFA (Software Component's Feature Point for 'Function Action Execution'), FPFD (Software Component's Feature Point for 'Function Decision Execution'), FPFO (Software Component's Feature Point for 'Function Execution Flow Control'), and FPFR (Software Component's Feature Point for 'Function Repeat Execution') signifies one action performance operation; one decision execution operation; one execution flow control operation; and one repeat execution operation; respectively.

The quantity of the FPFAs, FPFDs, FPFOs, and FPFRs varies according to the magnitude of the presence of the FFAs (Software Component's Measurable Features 'Function

Action Execution'), FFDs (Software Component's Measurable Features 'Function Decision Execution'), FFOs (Software Component's Measurable Features 'Function Execution Flow Control'), and FFRs (Software Component's Measurable Features 'Function Repeat Execution') in the Functionality Execution (FE), respectively. The more the FFAs, FFDs, FFOs, and FFRs, the more the FPFAs, FPFDs, FPFOs, and FPFRs, respectively.

The sum of all the corresponding FPFAs, FPFDs, FPFOs, and FPFRs produces the Software Component's Feature Point Count for 'Function Action Execution' (FCFA), 'Function Decision Execution' (FCFD), 'Function Execution Flow Control' (FCFO), and 'Function Repeat Execution' (FCFR), respectively.

17.1.14.26 Software Component's Feature Point for 'Function Computational Operation' (FPFC) and 'Function Logical Operation' (FPFL)

An assigned Software Component's Feature Point (SCFP) – Functional Size Unit (FSU) of measurement in the FSSM – to the Software Component's Measurable Feature 'Function Computational Operation' (FFC) and 'Function Logical Operation' (FFL) is called the Software Component's Feature Point for 'Function Computational Operation' (FPFC) and 'Function Logical Operation' (FPFL), respectively.

Each FPFC (Software Component's Feature Point for 'Function Computational Operation') and FPFL (Software Component's Feature Point for 'Function Logical Operation') signifies one computational operation – addition, subtraction, multiplication, division, or equals, etc.; and one logical operation – AND, OR, NOT, or XOR; respectively.

The quantity of the FPFCs and FPFLs varies according to the magnitude of the presence of the FFCs (Software Component's Measurable Features 'Function Computational Operation') and FFLs (Software Component's Measurable Features 'Function Logical Operation') in the Functionality Execution (FE), respectively. The more the FFCs and FFLs, the more the FPFCs and FPFLs, respectively.

The sum of all the corresponding FPFCs and FPFLs produces the Software Component's Feature Point Count for 'Function Computational Operation' (FCFC) and 'Function Logical Operation' (FCFL), respectively.

17.1.14.27 Software Component's Feature Point for 'Function Error Handling' (FPFE) and 'Functionality Missing' (FPFM)

An assigned Software Component's Feature Point (SCFP) – Functional Size Unit (FSU) of measurement in the FSSM – to the Software Component's Measurable Feature 'Function Error Handling' (FFE) and 'Functionality Missing' (FFM) is called the Software Component's Feature Point for 'Function Error Handling' (FPFE) and 'Functionality Missing' (FPFM), respectively.

Each FPFE (Software Component's Feature Point for 'Function Error Handling') and FPFM (Software Component's Feature Point for 'Functionality Missing') signifies one error handling operation and one missing functionality feature, respectively.

The quantity of the FPFEs and FPFMs varies according to the magnitude of the presence of the FFEs (Software Component's Measurable Features 'Function Error Handling') and FFMs (Software Component's Measurable Features 'Functionality Missing') in the Functionality Execution (FE), respectively. The more the FFEs and FFMs, the more the FPFEs and FPFMs, respectively.

The sum of all the corresponding FPFEs and FPFMs produces the Software Component's Feature Point Count for 'Function Error Handling' (FCFE) and 'Functionality Missing' (FCFM), respectively.

17.1.14.28 Software Component's Feature Point for 'General Operations Functional Data' (FPLG), 'Input/Output Operations Functional Data' (FPLI), 'Memory Operations Functional Data' (FPLM), and 'Message Exchange Operations Functional Data' (FPLS)

An assigned Software Component's Feature Point (SCFP) – Functional Size Unit (FSU) of measurement in the FSSM – to the Software Component's Measurable Feature 'General Operations Functional Data' (FLG), 'Input/Output Operations Functional Data' (FLI), 'Memory Operations Functional Data' (FLM), and 'Message Exchange Operations Functional Data' (FLS) is called the Software Component's Feature Point for 'General Operations Functional Data' (FPLG), 'Input/Output Operations Functional Data' (FPLI), 'Memory Operations Functional Data' (FPLM), and 'Message Exchange Operations Functional Data' (FPLS), respectively.

Each FPLG (Software Component's Feature Point for 'General Operations Functional Data'), FPLI (Software Component's Feature Point for 'Input/Output Operations Functional Data'), FPLM (Software Component's Feature Point for 'Memory Operations Functional Data'), and FPLS (Software Component's Feature Point for 'Message Exchange Operations Functional Data') signifies one Data Collection handled in a general computational, logical, decision, repeat, or execution flow control operation; one Data Collection handled in an input/output operation used for receiving/sending the input/output data from/to the input/output devices; one Data Collection handled in a memory read/write operation used for reading/writing the data from/to the memory devices; and one Data Collection handled in a message send/receive operation used for sending/receiving the messages to/from the external application programs; respectively.

The quantity of the FPLGs, FPLIs, FPLMs, and FPLSs varies according to the magnitude of the presence of the FLGs (Software Component's Measurable Features 'General Operations Functional Data'), FLIs (Software Component's Measurable Features 'Input/Output Operations Functional Data'), FLMs (Software Component's Measurable Features 'Memory Operations Functional Data'), and FLSs (Software Component's Measurable Features 'Message Exchange Operations Functional Data') in the Functionality Execution (FE), respectively. The more the FLGs, FLIs, FLMs, and FLSs, the more the FPLGs, FPLIs, FPLMs, and FPLSs, respectively.

The sum of all the corresponding FPLGs, FPLIs, FPLMs, and FPLSs produces the Software Component's Feature Point Count for 'General Operations Functional Data' (FCLG), 'Input/Output Operations Functional Data' (FCLI), 'Memory Operations Functional Data' (FCLM), and 'Message Exchange Operations Functional Data' (FCLS), respectively.

17.1.14.29 Software Component's Feature Point for 'Message Field' (FPMF) and 'Notifying Message' (FPNM)

An assigned Software Component's Feature Point (SCFP) – Functional Size Unit (FSU) of measurement in the FSSM – to the Software Component's Measurable Feature 'Message Field' (FMF) and 'Notifying Message' (FNM) is called the Software Component's Feature Point for 'Message Field' (FPMF) and 'Notifying Message' (FPNM), respectively.

Each FPMF (Software Component's Feature Point for 'Message Field') and FPNM (Software Component's Feature Point for 'Notifying Message') signifies one field of a message, and one message, respectively.

The quantity of the FPMFs and FPNMs varies according to the magnitude of the presence of the FMFs (Software Component's Measurable Features 'Message Field') and FNMs (Software Component's Measurable Features 'Notifying Message') in the Message Exchange (ME), respectively. The more the FMFs and FNMs, the more the FPMFs and FPNMs, respectively.

The sum of all the corresponding FPMFs and FPNMs produces the Software Component's Feature Point Count for 'Message Field' (FCMF) and 'Notifying Message' (FCNM), respectively.

17.1.14.30 Software Component's Feature Point for 'Message Missing' (FPMM), 'Message Receive' (FPMR), and 'Message Send' (FPMS)

An assigned Software Component's Feature Point (SCFP) – Functional Size Unit (FSU) of measurement in the FSSM – to the Software Component's Measurable Feature 'Message Missing' (FMM), 'Message Receive' (FMR), and 'Message Send' (FMS) is called the Software Component's Feature Point for 'Message Missing' (FPMM), 'Message Receive' (FPMR), and 'Message Send' (FPMS), respectively.

Each FPMM (Software Component's Feature Point for 'Message Missing'), FPMR (Software Component's Feature Point for 'Message Receive'), and FPMS (Software Component's Feature Point for 'Message Send') signifies one missing message feature; one message send and one message receive operation used for communication with the external programs; respectively

The quantity of the FPMMs, FPMRs, and FPMSs varies according to the magnitude of the FMMs (Software Component's Measurable Features 'Message Missing'), FMRs (Software Component's Measurable Features 'Message Receive'), and FMSs (Software Component's Measurable Features 'Message Send') in the Message Exchange (ME), respectively. The more the FMMs, FMRs, and FMSs, the more the FPMMs, FPMRs, and FPMSs, respectively.

The sum of all the corresponding FPMMs, FPMRs, and FPMSs produces the Software Component's Feature Point Count for 'Message Missing' (FCMM), 'Message Receive' (FCMR), and 'Message Send' (FCMS), respectively.

17.1.14.31 Software Component's Feature Point for 'User Screen Field' (FPUF), 'User Screen Input Link' (FPUI), 'User Screen Missing' (FPUM), 'User Screen Output Link' (FPUO), and 'User Screen' (FPUS)

An assigned Software Component's Feature Point (SCFP) – Functional Size Unit (FSU) of measurement in the FSSM – to the Software Component's Measurable Feature 'User Screen Field' (FUF), 'User Screen Input Link' (FUI), 'User Screen Missing' (FUM), 'User Screen Output Link' (FUO), and 'User Screen' (FUS) is called the Software Component's Feature Point for 'User Screen Field' (FPUF), 'User Screen Input Link' (FPUI), 'User Screen Missing' (FPUM), 'User Screen Output Link' (FPUO), and 'User Screen' (FPUS), respectively.

Each FPUF (Software Component's Feature Point for 'User Screen Field'), FPUI (Software Component's Feature Point for 'User Screen Input Link'), FPUM (Software Component's Feature Point for 'User Screen Missing'), FPUO (Software Component's Feature Point for 'User Screen Output Link'), and FPUS (Software Component's Feature Point for

'User Screen') signifies one field of a user screen; one input navigational link of a user screen; one missing user screen feature; one output navigational link of a user screen; and one user screen; respectively.

The quantity of the FPUFs, FPUIs, FPUMs, FPUOs, and FPUSs varies according to the magnitude of the presence of the FUFs (Software Component's Measurable Features 'User Screen Field'), FUIs (Software Component's Measurable Features 'User Screen Input Link'), FUMs (Software Component's Measurable Features 'User Screen Missing'), FUOs (Software Component's Measurable Features 'User Screen Output Link'), and FUSs (Software Component's Measurable Features 'User Screen') in the User Interface (UI), respectively. The more the FUFs, FUIs, FUMs, FUOs, and FUSs, the more the FPUFs, FPUIs, FPUMs, FPUOs, and FPUSs, respectively.

The sum of all the corresponding FPUFs, FPUIs, FPUMs, FPUOs, and FPUSs produces the Software Component's Feature Point Count for 'User Screen Field' (FCUF), 'User Screen Input Link' (FCUI), 'User Screen Missing' (FCUM), 'User Screen Output Link' (FCUO), and 'User Screen' (FCUS), respectively.

17.1.14.32 Software Component's Measurable Feature (SCMF)

An important and relevant attribute of the Software's Measurable Component (SMC) which can be and should be measured in order to have a comprehensive and correct measurement of the complete software, and it is measured in the FSSM.

Each Software's Measurable Component (SMC), the Base Functional Component (BFC)[1] according to the ISO/IEC 14143-1[1] standards, is composed of several Software Component's Measurable Features (SCMFs). Software Component's Measurable Features (SCMFs) are the Base Functional Component Types (BFC Types)[1] according to the ISO/IEC 14143-1[1] standards. The SCMFs (Software Component's Measurable Features) are identified in the Functional Requirements Specifications (FRS), that is, Functional Users Requirements (FUR)[1] according to the ISO/IEC 14143-1[1] standards. Most of these SCMFs do not have any fixed size proportion relationship amongst themselves for the same software component and with the features of the other software components. Thus, for correct and comprehensive measurement of the complete software, all the important, relevant SCMFs should be measured to obtain the correct size of the complete software. All the SCMFs are measured in the Functional Software Size Measurement Methodology with Effort Estimation and Performance Indication (FSSM).

There are the

A. 4 SCMFs for the Software's Measurable Component 'Functional Data' (CFD). They are the following:
  1. Software Component's Measurable Feature 'Data Class' (FDC):
     They are all the data classes and subclasses;
  2. Software Component's Measurable Feature 'Data Attribute' (FDA):
     They are all the attributes of all the data classes and subclasses;
  3. Software Component's Measurable Feature 'Data Field' (FDF):
     They are all the fields of all the attributes of all the data classes and subclasses;
  4. Software Component's Measurable Feature 'Data Missing' (FDM):
     They are all the apparently missing data classes/subclasses, the missing attributes of the classes/subclasses, or the missing fields of the attributes of the classes/subclasses in the Logical Data Model part;

B. 19 SCMFs for the Software's Measurable Component 'Functionality Execution' (CFE). They are the following:

1. Software Component's Measurable Feature 'Data Read' (FDR):
   They are all the memory data read operations used for reading the data from the memory devices;
2. Software Component's Measurable Feature 'Data Write' (FDW):
   They are all the memory data write operations used for writing the data to the memory devices;
3. Software Component's Measurable Feature 'Memory Operations Functional Data' (FLM):
   They are all the Data Collections handled in the memory data read/write operations used for reading/writing the data from/to the memory devices;
4. Software Component's Measurable Feature 'Data Input' (FDI):
   They are all the data input operations used for receiving the input data from the input devices;
5. Software Component's Measurable Feature 'Data Output' (FDO):
   They are all the data output operations used for sending the output data to the output devices;
6. Software Component's Measurable Feature 'Input/Output Operations Functional Data' (FLI):
   They are all the Data Collections handled in the input/output operations used for receiving/sending the input/output data from/to the input/output devices;
7. Software Component's Measurable Feature 'Message Send' (FMS):
   They are all the message send operations used for sending the messages to the external application programs and to the sub-programs of the same application program;
8. Software Component's Measurable Feature 'Message Receive' (FMR):
   They are all the message receive operations used for receiving the messages from the external application programs and from the sub-programs of the same application program;
9. Software Component's Measurable Feature 'Message Exchange Operations Functional Data' (FLS):
   They are all the Data Collections handled in the message send/receive operations used for sending/receiving the messages to/from the external application programs and to/from the sub-programs of the same application program;
10. Software Component's Measurable Feature 'Function Computational Operation' (FFC):
    They are all the computational (mathematical) operations;
11. Software Component's Measurable Feature 'Function Logical Operation' (FFL):
    They are all the logical (AND, OR, etc.) operations;
12. Software Component's Measurable Feature 'Function Decision Execution' (FFD):
    They are all the decision operations;
13. Software Component's Measurable Feature 'Function Repeat Execution' (FFR):
    They are all the repeat operations;
14. Software Component's Measurable Feature 'Function Action Execution' (FFA):

They are all the action execution operations;

15. Software Component's Measurable Feature 'Function Execution Flow Control' (FFO):
    They are all the execution flow control operations;
16. Software Component's Measurable Feature 'Function Error Handling' (FFE):
    They are all the error handling operations;
17. Software Component's Measurable Feature 'General Operations Functional Data' (FLG):
    They are all the Data Collections handled in the general computational, logical, decision, repeat, and execution flow control operations;
18. Software Component's Measurable Feature 'Class Method' (FCM):
    They are all the class methods of all the data classes and subclasses;
19. Software Component's Measurable Feature 'Functionality Missing' (FFM):
    They are all the apparently missing functional operations and missing functional data handled items in the functionality, and missing class methods in the Logical Data Model;

C. 5 SCMFs for the Software's Measurable Component 'User Interface' (CUI). They are the following:

1. Software Component's Measurable Feature 'User Screen' (FUS):
   They are all the user screens;
2. Software Component's Measurable Feature 'User Screen Field' (FUF):
   They are all the fields of all the user screens;
3. Software Component's Measurable Feature 'User Screen Output Link' (FUO):
   They are all the output navigational links of all the user screens;
4. Software Component's Measurable Feature 'User Screen Input Link' (FUI):
   They are all the input navigational links of all the user screens;
5. Software Component's Measurable Feature 'User Screen Missing' (FUM):
   They are all the missing screens, the missing fields of the screens, or the missing input/output navigational links of the screens in the User Interface part;

D. 3 SCMFs for the Software's Measurable Component 'Message Exchange' (CME). They are the following:

1. Software Component's Measurable Feature 'Notifying Message' (FNM):
   They are all the messages used for the communication with the external application programs and with the sub-programs of the same application program;
2. Software Component's Measurable Feature 'Message Field' (FMF):
   They are all the fields of all the messages used for the communication with the external application programs and with the sub-programs of the same application program;
3. Software Component's Measurable Feature 'Message Missing' (FMM):
   They are all the apparently missing messages or the missing fields of the messages in the Message Exchange part.

The SCMFs are identified in the Logical Data Model (LDM), Functionality Execution (FE), User Interface (UI), and Message Exchange (ME) description parts of the Functional Requirements Specifications (FRS), and the Software Component's Feature Points (SCFPs) – Functional Size Unit (FSU) of the measurement in the FSSM – are assigned to them. Thus, by this assignment, the Software Component's Feature Points (SCFPs) for the corresponding SCMFs are created. The sum of the corresponding SCFPs for respective SCMFs produces the Software Component's Feature Point Counts (SCFPCs) for the respective SCMFs. The SCFPCs are used for the calculations of the Software Component's Feature Measurements (SCFMs) which in turn are used for the calculations of the Software Component's Measurements (SCMs). Then, the SCMFs and SCMs are used for the calculations of the Software Size and Effort Estimations (SSEEs); and Software Performance Quality Indicators (SPQIs) of both the types Software Structural Indicators (SSIs)[5–7] and Software Operational Indicators (SOIs)[5–7].

17.1.14.33 Software Component's Measurable Feature 'Class Method' (FCM)

A Software Component's Measurable Feature (SCMF) of the Software's Measurable Component 'Functionality Execution' (CFE). It signifies the methods (operations) of the classes and subclasses in the class structure defined in the Logical Data Model (LDM) description part of the Functional Requirements Specifications (FRS).

17.1.14.34 Software Component's Measurable Feature 'Data Attribute' (FDA)

A Software Component's Measurable Feature (SCMF) of the Software's Measurable Component 'Functional Data' (CFD). It signifies the attributes of the classes and subclasses in the class structure defined in the Logical Data Model (LDM) description part of the Functional Requirements Specifications (FRS).

17.1.14.35 Software Component's Measurable Feature 'Data Class' (FDC)

A Software Component's Measurable Feature (SCMF) of the Software's Measurable Component 'Functional Data' (CFD). It signifies the classes and subclasses in the class structure defined in the Logical Data Model (LDM) description part of the Functional Requirements Specifications (FRS).

17.1.14.36 Software Component's Measurable Feature 'Data Field' (FDF)

A Software Component's Measurable Feature (SCMF) of the Software's Measurable Component 'Functional Data' (CFD). It signifies the fields of the attributes of the classes and subclasses in the class structure defined in the Logical Data Model (LDM) description part of the Functional Requirements Specifications (FRS).

17.1.14.37 Software Component's Measurable Feature 'Data Input' (FDI)

A Software Component's Measurable Feature (SCMF) of the Software's Measurable Component 'Functionality Execution' (CFE). It signifies the data input operations used for receiving the input data from the input devices such as keyboard. The data input operations are described in the Functionality Execution (FE) description part of the Functional Requirements Specifications (FRS).

17.1.14.38 Software Component's Measurable Feature 'Data Missing' (FDM)

A Software Component's Measurable Feature (SCMF) of the Software's Measurable Component 'Functional Data' (CFD). It signifies the apparent missing items in the functional data class structures, that is, classes, subclasses, their attributes, and the fields of the attributes. The functional data class structures are described in the Logical Data Model (LDM) description part of the Functional Requirements Specifications (FRS).

17.1.14.39 Software Component's Measurable Feature 'Data Output' (FDO)

A Software Component's Measurable Feature (SCMF) of the Software's Measurable Component 'Functionality Execution' (CFE). It signifies the data output operations used for sending the output data to the output devices such as display. The data output operations are described in the Functionality Execution (FE) description part of the Functional Requirements Specifications (FRS).

17.1.14.40 Software Component's Measurable Feature 'Data Read' (FDR)

A Software Component's Measurable Feature (SCMF) of the Software's Measurable Component 'Functionality Execution' (CFE). It signifies the memory data read operations used for reading the data from the non-volatile memory devices such as disk. The data read operations are described in the Functionality Execution (FE) description part of the Functional Requirements Specifications (FRS).

17.1.14.41 Software Component's Measurable Feature 'Data Write' (FDW)

A Software Component's Measurable Feature (SCMF) of the Software's Measurable Component 'Functionality Execution' (CFE). It signifies the memory data write operations used for writing the data to the non-volatile memory devices such as disk. The data write operations are described in the Functionality Execution (FE) description part of the Functional Requirements Specifications (FRS).

17.1.14.42 Software Component's Measurable Feature 'Function Action Execution' (FFA)

A Software Component's Measurable Feature (SCMF) of the Software's Measurable Component 'Functionality Execution' (CFE). It signifies the actions to be performed that are described in the Functionality Execution (FE) description part of the Functional Requirements Specifications (FRS).

17.1.14.43 Software Component's Measurable Feature 'Function Computational Operation' (FFC)

A Software Component's Measurable Feature (SCMF) of the Software's Measurable Component 'Functionality Execution' (CFE). It signifies the computational operations, for example, addition, subtraction, multiplication, division, power, log, and equals. The computational operations are described in the Functionality Execution (FE) description part of the Functional Requirements Specifications (FRS).

17.1.14.44 Software Component's Measurable Feature 'Function Decision Execution' (FFD)

A Software Component's Measurable Feature (SCMF) of the Software's Measurable Component 'Functionality Execution' (CFE). It signifies the conditions checking and decision-taking actions (e.g., if the condition is true, take the action) to be performed that are described in the Functionality Execution (FE) description part of the Functional Requirements Specifications (FRS).

17.1.14.45 Software Component's Measurable Feature 'Function Error Handling' (FFE)

A Software Component's Measurable Feature (SCMF) of the Software's Measurable Component 'Functionality Execution' (CFE). It signifies the error handling operations that are described in the Functionality Execution (FE) description part of the Functional Requirements Specifications (FRS).

17.1.14.46 Software Component's Measurable Feature 'Function Execution Flow Control' (FFO)

A Software Component's Measurable Feature (SCMF) of the Software's Measurable Component 'Functionality Execution' (CFE). It signifies the execution flow control operation (e.g., to execute from various places some part of the functionality which is described at one place) to be performed that are described in the Functionality Execution (FE) description part of the Functional Requirements Specifications (FRS).

17.1.14.47 Software Component's Measurable Feature 'Function Logical Operation' (FFL)

A Software Component's Measurable Feature (SCMF) of the Software's Measurable Component 'Functionality Execution' (CFE). It signifies the logical operations, for example, AND, OR, NOT, and XOR. The logical operations are described in the Functionality Execution (FE) description part of the Functional Requirements Specifications (FRS).

17.1.14.48 Software Component's Measurable Feature 'Function Repeat Execution' (FFR)

A Software Component's Measurable Feature (SCMF) of the Software's Measurable Component 'Functionality Execution' (CFE). It signifies the repeat actions to be performed that are described in the Functionality Execution (FE) description part of the Functional Requirements Specifications (FRS).

17.1.14.49 Software Component's Measurable Feature 'Functionality Missing' (FFM)

A Software Component's Measurable Feature (SCMF) of the Software's Measurable Component 'Functionality Execution' (CFE). It signifies the apparent missing items of the functionality described in the Functionality Execution (FE) description part of the Functional Requirements Specifications (FRS).

17.1.14.50 Software Component's Measurable Feature 'General Operations Functional Data' (FLG)

A Software Component's Measurable Feature (SCMF) of the Software's Measurable Component 'Functionality Execution' (CFE). It signifies the Data Collections handled during the general functional – computational, logical, decision, repeat, and execution flow control – operations described in the Functionality Execution (FE) description part of the Functional Requirements Specifications (FRS).

17.1.14.51 Software Component's Measurable Feature 'Input/Output Operations Functional Data' (FLI)

A Software Component's Measurable Feature (SCMF) of the Software's Measurable Component 'Functionality Execution' (CFE). It signifies the Data Collections handled during the data input and output operations used for receiving/sending the input/output data from/to the input/output devices described in the Functionality Execution (FE) description part of the Functional Requirements Specifications (FRS).

17.1.14.52 Software Component's Measurable Feature 'Memory Operations Functional Data' (FLM)

A Software Component's Measurable Feature (SCMF) of the Software's Measurable Component 'Functionality Execution' (CFE). It signifies the Data Collections handled during the memory read and write operations used for reading/writing the data from/to the memory devices described in the Functionality Execution (FE) description part of the Functional Requirements Specifications (FRS).

17.1.14.53 Software Component's Measurable Feature 'Message Exchange Operations Functional Data' (FLS)

A Software Component's Measurable Feature (SCMF) of the Software's Measurable Component 'Functionality Execution' (CFE). It signifies the Data Dollections handled during the message send/receive operations used for sending/receiving the messages to/from the other programs/sub-program described in the Functionality Execution (FE) description part of the Functional Requirements Specifications (FRS).

17.1.14.54 Software Component's Measurable Feature 'Message Field' (FMF)

A Software Component's Measurable Feature (SCMF) of the Software's Measurable Component 'Message Exchange' (CME). It signifies the fields of the messages that are used for the external communications with other programs/sub-programs and are defined in the Message Exchange (ME) description part of the Functional Requirements Specifications (FRS).

17.1.14.55 Software Component's Measurable Feature 'Notifying Message' (FNM)

A Software Component's Measurable Feature (SCMF) of the Software's Measurable Component 'Message Exchange' (CME). It signifies the messages that are used for the external communications with other programs/sub-programs and are defined in the Message Exchange (ME) description part of the Functional Requirements Specifications (FRS).

17.1.14.56 Software Component's Measurable Feature 'Message Missing' (FMM)

A Software Component's Measurable Feature (SCMF) of the Software's Measurable Component 'Message Exchange' (CME). It signifies the missing items in the message structure described in the Message Exchange part of the Functional Requirements Specifications (FRS).

17.1.14.57 Software Component's Measurable Feature 'Message Receive' (FMR)

A Software Component's Measurable Feature (SCMF) of the Software's Measurable Component 'Functionality Execution' (CFE). It signifies the message receive operations that receive the messages from the external application programs which are either other programs, or sub-programs (modules) of the same application program. The message receive operations are described in the Functionality Execution (FE) description part of the Functional Requirements Specifications (FRS).

17.1.14.58 Software Component's Measurable Feature 'Message Send' (FMS)

A Software Component's Measurable Feature (SCMF) of the Software's Measurable Component 'Functionality Execution' (CFE). It signifies the message send operations that send the messages to the external application programs which are either other programs, or sub-programs (modules) of the same application program. The message send operations are described in the Functionality Execution (FE) description part of the Functional Requirements Specifications (FRS).

17.1.14.59 Software Component's Measurable Feature 'User Screen Field' (FUF)

A Software Component's Measurable Feature (SCMF) of the Software's Measurable Component 'User Interface' (CUI). It signifies the fields of the user screens. Fields of the user screens are used to display the information/data in the output screens or for input of data from the input screens, and are defined in the User Interface (UI) description part of the Functional Requirements Specifications (FRS).

17.1.14.60 Software Component's Measurable Feature 'User Screen Input Link' (FUI)

A Software Component's Measurable Feature (SCMF) of the Software's Measurable Component 'User Interface' (CUI). It signifies the input navigational links of the user screens. Input links of the user screens are used to navigate into the screens either from other screens or from various software operations, and are defined in the User Interface (UI) description part of the Functional Requirements Specifications (FRS).

17.1.14.61 Software Component's Measurable Feature 'User Screen Missing' (FUM)

A Software Component's Measurable Feature (SCMF) of the Software's Measurable Component 'User Interface' (CUI). It signifies the apparent missing items about the user screens in the User Interface (UI) description part of the Functional Requirements Specifications (FRS).

17.1.14.62 Software Component's Measurable Feature 'User Screen Output Link' (FUO)

A Software Component's Measurable Feature (SCMF) of the Software's Measurable Component 'User Interface' (CUI). It signifies the output navigational links of the user screens. Output links of the user screens are used to navigate from the screens either to other screens or to various software operations, and are defined in the User Interface (UI) description part of the Functional Requirements Specifications (FRS).

17.1.14.63 Software Component's Measurable Feature 'User Screen' (FUS)

A Software Component's Measurable Feature (SCMF) of the Software's Measurable Component 'User Interface' (CUI). It signifies the user screens that are used to display the information/data in the screen or for input of data from the screen, and are defined in the User Interface (UI) description part of the Functional Requirements Specifications (FRS).

17.1.14.64 Software Component's Measurement (SCM)

Measurement of the Software's Measurable Components (SMCs) in terms of the Software Component's Feature Points (SCFPs) which is the Functional Size Unit (FSU) in the Functional Software Size Measurement Methodology with Effort Estimation and Performance Indication (FSSM). These measurements indicate the size and complexity of the 4 SMCs, total software size, and extent of the deficiencies in the Functional Requirements Specifications (FRS) by the following measurements:

- **a.** Software's Component 'Functional Data' Measurement (CFDM);
- **b.** Software's Component 'Functionality Execution' Measurement (CFEM);
- **c.** Software's Component 'User Interface' Measurement (CUIM);
- **d.** Software's Component 'Message Exchange' Measurement (CMEM);
- **e.** Software Total Components Measurement (STCM);
- **f.** Software Components Requirement Deficiency Measurement (CRDM).

17.1.14.65 Software Components Requirement Deficiency Measurement (CRDM)

Measurement for the apparently missing items in the 4 Software's Measurable Components which are the

1. Software's Measurable Component 'Functional Data' (CFD);
2. Software's Measurable Component 'Functionality Execution' (CFE);
3. Software's Measurable Component 'User Interface' (CUI);
4. Software's Measurable Component 'Message Exchange' (CME).

The CRDM (Software Components Requirement Deficiency Measurement) is obtained by adding together the Software Component's Feature Measurements (SCFMs) Functional Data Missing Entities (FDME), Functionality Execution Missing Entities (FEME), User Interface Missing Entities (UIME), and Message Exchange Missing Entities (MEME) measured by the Software Component's Feature Point Count for 'Data Missing' (FCDM), 'Functionality Missing' (FCFM), 'User Screen Missing' (FCUM), and 'Message Missing' (FCMM), respectively.

Hence, CRDM = FDME + FEME + UIME + MEME = FCDM + FCFM + FCUM + FCMM.

The CRDM shows the extent of improvements which may be needed to be done in the Functional Requirements Specifications (FRS).

The CRDM is further used to calculate the Software Performance Quality Indicators (SPQIs) of the type Software Structural Indicators (SSIs)[5–7].

17.1.14.66 Software Data Analysis and Design Effort (SDADE)

Effort spent on analyzing the data and designing/defining the data structures (or data tables in database applications) to be used in the program. This is dependent on the size and complexity of the Software's Measurable Component 'Functional Data' (CFD), Software's Measurable Component 'User Interface' (CUI), and Software's Measurable Component 'Message Exchange' (CME); and average productivity for the data analysis and design activity.

The SDADE (Software Data Analysis and Design Effort) is calculated based on the three measurements: the Software Component 'Functional Data' Measurement (CFDM), Software Component 'User Interface' Measurement (CUIM), and Software Component 'Message Exchange' Measurement (CMEM); and average productivity for the data analysis and design activity.

The SDADE includes the effort required for the technical documentation part.

The SDADE is used to calculate the Software Analysis, Design, and Coding Effort (SADCE), Software Testing Effort (STE), and Software Total Development Effort (STDE).

17.1.14.67 Software Data Statements (SDS)

Statements used for the data declarations in the software programs.

They are mainly about the data structures that contain the information about the

a. classes, subclasses, their attributes, and fields of the attributes;

b. input/output screens, their input/output fields, and input/output navigational links;

c. message structures;

d. temporary data storage variables.

The data declaration statements are spread all over the program, that is, in the main program, the class methods, and various subroutines of the program.

The SDS are used for the calculation of the Software Logical Size (SLS) which in turn is used to calculate the Software Coding Effort (SCE), Software Analysis, Design, and Coding Effort (SADCE), Software Testing Effort (STE), and Software Total Development Effort (STDE).

17.1.14.68 Software Functionality Analysis and Design Effort (SFADE)

Effort spent on analyzing the functionality and designing the software code structure. This is dependent on the size and complexity of the Software's Measurable Component 'Functionality Execution' (CFE); and average productivity for the functionality analysis and design activity.

The SFADE (Software Functionality Analysis and Design Effort) is calculated based on the measurement Software Component 'Functionality Execution' Measurement (CFEM); and average productivity for the functionality analysis and design activity.

The SFADE includes the effort required for the technical documentation part.

The SFADE is used to calculate the Software Analysis, Design, and Coding Effort (SADCE), Software Testing Effort (STE), and Software Total Development Effort (STDE).

17.1.14.69 Software Logical Size (SLS)

Logical size in approximate number of statements of the software that is developed to meet the functional requirements described in the Functional Requirements Specifications (FRS). Three types of software statements are considered for the Software Logical Size (SLS): the Software Data Statements (SDS), Software Code Statements (SCDS), and Software Comment Statements (SCS). These statements are calculated based on the Software Component's Feature Measurements (SCFMs). The SCFMs are calculated from the Software Component's Feature Point Counts (SCFPCs) which are obtained by assigning the Software Component's Feature Points (SCFPs) to the Software Component's Measurable Features (SCMFs) of the Software's Measurable Components (SMCs).

17.1.14.70 Software Operational Indicator (SOI)

One of the two sub-categories of the Software Performance Quality Indicators (SPQIs). The SOIs (Software Operational Indicators)[5–7] indicate the operational aspects of the software, that is, the dynamic properties of the software at run-time.

The information about the SOIs is based on the Software Component's Feature Measurements (SCFMs) and Software Component's Measurements (SCMs). The SCFMs are based on the Software Component's Feature Point Counts (SCFPCs) for which the information is derived from the Functional Requirements Specifications (FRS), that is, FUR (Functional Users Requirements)[1] by identifying the Software Component's Measurable Features (SCMFs) and assigning them the Software Component's Feature Points (SCFPs), that is, the FSU (Functional Size Unit).

There are a total of 13 Software Operational Indicators (SOIs)[5–7] which are categorized as

1. 9 SOIs denoting the Functional Operations Execution. They are the
   - **a.** Memory Traffic Level (MTL);
   - **b.** Computational Operations Level (COL);
   - **c.** Logical Operations Level (LOL);
   - **d.** Decision Execution Level (DEL);
   - **e.** Repeat Execution Level (REL);
   - **f.** Execution Flow Control Level (EFCL);
   - **g.** User Interaction Level (UIL);
   - **h.** External Communication Level (ECL);
   - **i.** Error Handling Capability (EHC);

2. 4 SOIs denoting the Functional Operations Data Handling. They are the
   a. Memory Traffic Functional Data Level (MTDL);
   b. User Interaction Functional Data Level (UIDL);
   c. External Communication Functional Data Level (ECDL);
   d. General Operations Execution Functional Data Level (GODL).

The SOIs are categorized in levels of Nil, Low, Medium, High, or Very High so that the areas which are below or above the desired level can accordingly be targeted for improvement, if required.

17.1.14.71 Software Performance Quality Indicator (SPQI)

Indicator which presents the performance quality aspects of the software and deficiency aspects of the functional requirements.

The SPQIs (Software Performance Quality Indicators) give an excellent overview of the most important software characteristics – structural and operational. They are thus divided into two groups: the Software Structural Indicators (SSIs)[5–7] for indicating the static structural characteristics of the software, and Software Operational Indicators (SOIs)[5–7] for indicating the dynamic run-time characteristics of the software.

The SPQIs are categorized in levels of Nil, Low, Medium, High, or Very High so that the areas which are below or above the desired level can accordingly be targeted for improvement, if required.

The complete information about the SPQIs is based on the Software Components Feature Measurements (SCFMs) and Software Components Measurements (SCMs). The SCFMs are based on the Software Component's Feature Point Counts (SCFPCs) for which the information is derived from the Functional Requirements Specifications (FRS), that is, FUR (Functional Users Requirements)[1] by identifying the Software Component's Measurable Features (SCMFs) and assigning them the Software Component's Feature Points (SCFPs), that is, the FSU (Functional Size Unit).

There are a total of 36 Software Performance Quality Indicators (SPQIs) of which

1. 23 Software Structural Indicators (SSIs)[5–7] which are categorized as
   a. 8 SSIs denoting the Software's Measurable Components (SMCs). They are the
      i. Functional Data Complexity and Size (FDCS);
      ii. Functionality Execution Complexity and Size (FECS)
      iii. User Interface Complexity and Size (UICS);
      iv. Message Exchange Complexity and Size (MECS);
      v. Functional Data Component Proportion (FDCP);
      vi. Functionality Execution Component Proportion (FECP);
      vii. User Interface Component Proportion (UICP);
      viii. Message Exchange Component Proportion (MECP);
   b. 10 SSIs denoting the Functionality Execution (FE) Operations. They are the
      i. Memory Transaction Proportion (MTP);
      ii. Computational Operation Content Proportion (COCP);
      iii. Logical Operation Content Proportion (LOCP);
      iv. Decision Execution Content Proportion (DECP);
      v. Repeat Execution Content Proportion (RECP);
      vi. Action Execution Content Proportion (AECP);
      vii. Execution Flow Control Proportion (EFCP);
      viii. User Interaction Proportion (UIP);

   - **ix.** External Communication Proportion (ECP);
   - **x.** Error Handling Proportion (EHP);
- **c.** 4 SSIs denoting the Functionality Execution (FE) Operations Data Handling. They are the
   - **i.** Memory Operations Functional Data Proportion (MODP);
   - **ii.** Input/Output Operations Functional Data Proportion (IODP);
   - **iii.** Message Exchange Operations Functional Data Proportion (EODP);
   - **iv.** General Operations Functional Data Proportion (GODP);
- **d.** 1 SSI denoting the deficiency in the Functional Requirements Specifications (FRS). It is the
   - **i.** Requirements Deficiency Grade (RDG);

2. 13 Software Operational Indicators (SOIs)[5–7] which are categorized as
- **a.** 9 SOIs denoting the Functional Operations Execution. They are the
   - **i.** Memory Traffic Level (MTL);
   - **ii.** Computational Operations Level (COL);
   - **iii.** Logical Operations Level (LOL);
   - **iv.** Decision Execution Level (DEL);
   - **v.** Repeat Execution Level (REL);
   - **vi.** Execution Flow Control Level (EFCL);
   - **vii.** User Interaction Level (UIL);
   - **viii.** External Communication Level (ECL);
   - **ix.** Error Handling Capability (EHC);
- **b.** 4 SOIs denoting the Functional Operations Data Handling. They are the
   - **i.** Memory Traffic Functional Data Level (MTDL);
   - **ii.** User Interaction Functional Data Level (UIDL);
   - **iii.** External Communication Functional Data Level (ECDL);
   - **iv.** General Operations Execution Functional Data Level (GODL).

17.1.14.72 Software Size and Effort Estimation (SSEE)

Estimations about the software's logical size and about the development effort. There are 4 SSEEs (Software Size and Effort Estimations) which are calculated as follows:

1. Software's Logical Size (SLS) is the total logical statements size of the software. It is the sum of 3 types of software statements: the Software Data Statements (SDS), Software Code Statements (SCDS), and Software Comment Statements (SCS). These statements are calculated based on the Software Component's Feature Measurements (SCFMs) which are calculated from the Software Component's Feature Point Counts (SCFPCs). The SCFPCs are obtained by assigning the Software Component's Feature Points (SCFPs) to the Software Component's Measurable Features (SCMFs) of the Software's Measurable Components (SMCs) by the identifications of the SCMFs in the 4 parts – the Logical Data Model (LDM), Functionality Execution (FE), User Interface (UI), and Message Exchange (ME) descriptions – of the Functional Requirements Specifications (FRS).
2. Software Analysis, Design, and Coding Effort (SADCE) is the effort required for analysis, design, and coding of the software including the technical documents preparation. It is calculated from the following efforts:

a. Software Data Analysis and Design Effort (SDADE) is the effort required for the data analysis and design. It is calculated from the Software Component 'Functional Data' Measurement (CFDM), Software Component 'User Interface' Measurement (CUIM), Software Component 'Message Exchange' Measurement (CMEM), and average productivity for the data analysis and design activity.

The measurements CFDM, CUIM, and CMEM are calculated based on the Software Component's Feature Measurements (SCFMs) which are calculated from the Software Component's Feature Point Counts (SCFPCs). The SCFPCs are obtained by assigning the Software Component's Feature Points (SCFPs) to the Software Component's Measurable Features (SCMFs) by their identifications in the 3 parts – the Logical Data Model (LDM), User Interface (UI) and Message Exchange (ME) descriptions – of the Functional Requirements Specifications (FRS).

b. Software Functionality Analysis and Design Effort (SFADE) is the effort required for the functionality analysis and design. It is calculated from the Software Component 'Functionality Execution' Measurement (CFEM) and average productivity for the functionality analysis and design activity.

The measurement CFEM is calculated based on the Software Component's Feature Measurements (SCFMs) which are calculated from the Software Component's Feature Point Counts (SCFPCs). The SCFPCs are obtained by assigning the Software Component's Feature Points (SCFPs) to the Software Component's Measurable Features (SCMFs) by their identifications in the 2 parts – the Logical Data Model (LDM) and Functionality Execution (FE) – of the Functional Requirements Specifications (FRS).

c. Software Coding Effort (SCE) is the effort required for coding the software program. It is calculated from the Software Logical Size (SLS) and average productivity for the coding activity.

3. Software Testing Effort (STE) is the effort required for testing the software including the test specifications documents preparation. It is calculated based on the Software Analysis, Design, and Coding Effort (SADCE) and average productivity for the testing activity.

4. Software Total Development Effort is the total effort required for analysis, design, coding, testing, and technical/test documents preparation. It is the sum of the Software Analysis, Design, and Coding Effort (SADCE) and Software Testing Effort (STE).

17.1.14.73 Software Structural Indicator (SSI)

One of the two sub-categories of the Software Performance Quality Indicators (SPQIs). The SSIs (Software Structural Indicators)[5–7] indicate the structural aspects of the software, that is, the structural size properties of the software from the point of view of its static contents.

The information about the SSIs is based on the Software Components Feature Measurements (SCFMs) and Software Components Measurements (SCMs). The SCFMs are calculated based on the Software Component's Feature Point Counts (SCFPCs) for which the information is derived from the Functional Requirements Specifications (FRS), that is, FUR (Functional Users Requirements)[1] by identifying the Software Component's Measurable Features (SCMFs) and assigning them the Software Component's Feature Points (SCFPs), that is, the FSU (Functional Size Unit).

There are a total of 23 Software Structural Indicators (SSIs)[5–7] which are categorized as

1. 8 SSIs denoting the Software's Measurable Components (SMCs). They are the
   a. Functional Data Complexity and Size (FDCS);
   b. Functionality Execution Complexity and Size (FECS)
   c. User Interface Complexity and Size (UICS);
   d. Message Exchange Complexity and Size (MECS);
   e. Functional Data Component Proportion (FDCP);
   f. Functionality Execution Component Proportion (FECP);
   g. User Interface Component Proportion (UICP);
   h. Message Exchange Component Proportion (MECP);
2. 10 SSIs denoting the Functionality Execution (FE) Operations. They are the
   a. Memory Transaction Proportion (MTP);
   b. Computational Operation Content Proportion (COCP);
   c. Logical Operation Content Proportion (LOCP);
   d. Decision Execution Content Proportion (DECP);
   e. Repeat Execution Content Proportion (RECP);
   f. Action Execution Content Proportion (AECP);
   g. Execution Flow Control Proportion (EFCP);
   h. User Interaction Proportion (UIP);
   i. External Communication Proportion (ECP);
   j. Error Handling Proportion (EHP);
3. 4 SSIs denoting the Functionality Execution (FE) Operations Data Handling. They are the
   a. Memory Operations Functional Data Proportion (MODP);
   b. Input/Output Operations Functional Data Proportion (IODP);
   c. Message Exchange Operations Functional Data Proportion (EODP);
   d. General Operations Functional Data Proportion (GODP);
4. 1 SSI denoting the deficiency in the Functional Requirements Specifications (FRS). It is the
   a. Requirements Deficiency Grade (RDG);

The SSIs are categorized in levels of Nil, Low, Medium, High, or Very High so that the areas which are below or above the desired level can accordingly be targeted for improvement, if required.

17.1.14.74 Software Testing Effort (STE)

Effort required for testing and test specifications documents preparation in the software development process. It is dependent on the size and complexity of the Software's Measurable Component 'Functional Data' (CFD), 'Functionality Execution' (CFE), 'User Interface' (CUI), and 'Message Exchange' (CME); Software Logical Size; and average productivity for the testing activities.

The STE (Software Testing Effort) is calculated from the Software Analysis, Design, and Coding Effort (SADCE) based on the average productivity for the testing activity. The SADCE in turn is calculated from the following efforts:

a. Software Data Analysis and Design Effort (SDADE) which is calculated from the Software Component 'Functional Data' Measurement (CFDM), Software

Component 'User Interface' Measurement (CUIM), Software Component 'Message Exchange' Measurement (CMEM), and average productivity for the data analysis and design activity;

b. Software Functionality Analysis and Design Effort (SFADE) which is calculated from the Software Component 'Functionality Execution' Measurement (CFEM), and average productivity for the functionality analysis and design activity;

c. Software Coding Effort (SCE) which is calculated from the Software Logical Size (SLS) and average productivity for the coding activity.

17.1.14.75 Software Total Components Measurement (STCM)

Measurement for the total software size and complexity. It takes into account the size and complexity of the 4 Software's Measurable Components which are the

1. Software's Measurable Component 'Functional Data' (CFD);
2. Software's Measurable Component 'Functionality Execution' (CFE);
3. Software's Measurable Component 'User Interface' (CUI);
4. Software's Measurable Component 'Message Exchange' (CME).

through the measurements of all the 4 components. The measurements used for the calculation of STCM are the

1. Software Component 'Functional Data' Measurement (CFDM);
2. Software Component 'Functionality Execution' Measurement (CFEM);
3. Software Component 'User Interface' Measurement (CUIM);
4. Software Component 'Message Exchange' Measurement (CMEM).

Thus, STCM = CFDM + CFEM + CUIM + CMEM.

Hence, the STCM shows the enormity, complexity, and size of the total software application.

17.1.14.76 Software Total Development Effort (STDE)

Effort required for the development of the software. It is the effort required for analysis, design, coding, and testing; and for technical specifications documents and test specifications documents preparation in the software development process. It is dependent on the size and complexity of the Software's Measurable Component 'Functional Data' (CFD), 'Functionality Execution' (CFE), 'User Interface' (CUI), and 'Message Exchange' (CME); the Software Logical Size; and average productivity for the development activities.

The STDE (Software Total Development Effort) is calculated from the SADCE (Software Analysis, Design, and Coding Effort), and STE (Software Testing Effort).

The SADCE is calculated from the following efforts:

a. Software Data Analysis and Design Effort (SDADE) which is calculated from the Software Component 'Functional Data' Measurement (CFDM), Software Component 'User Interface' Measurement (CUIM), Software Component 'Message Exchange' Measurement (CMEM), and average productivity for the data analysis and design activity;

   b. Software Functionality Analysis and Design Effort (SFADE) which is calculated from the Software Component 'Functionality Execution' Measurement (CFEM), and average productivity for the functionality analysis and design activity;
   c. Software Coding Effort (SCE) which is calculated from the Software Logical Size (SLS) and average productivity for the coding activity.

The STE is calculated from the SADCE and average productivity for the testing activity.

The STDE is the final effort calculation in the FSSM. It does not include the effort for the project management, deployment, and maintenance activities.

17.1.14.77 Software's Measurable Component (SMC)

An important and relevant constituent part of the software which can be and should be measured in order to have a comprehensive and correct measurement of the complete software, and is measured in the FSSM. An SMC is the same as a Base Functional Component (BFC)[1] of the ISO/IEC 14143-1[1] standards. There are 4 Software's Measurable Components (SMCs) which are measured in the Functional Software Size Measurement Methodology with Effort Estimation and Performance Indication (FSSM). They are the

1. Software's Measurable Component 'Functional Data' (CFD);
2. Software's Measurable Component 'Functionality Execution' (CFE);
3. Software's Measurable Component 'User Interface' (CUI);
4. Software's Measurable Component 'Message Exchange' (CME).

17.1.14.78 Software's Measurable Component 'Functional Data' (CFD)

One of the 4 software's constituent components which is important and relevant to be measured for complete software's measurement and is measured in the Functional Software Size Measurement Methodology with Effort Estimation and Performance Indication (FSSM). The CFD consists of the Functional Data part which is operated upon and handled during the functionality operations. It comprises the data class structure – classes, subclasses, their attributes, and fields of the attributes presented normally in the Logical Data Model (LDM) description part of the Functional Requirements Specifications (FRS) that are the Functional User Requirements (FUR)[1] according to the ISO/IEC 14143-1[1] standards.

17.1.14.79 Software's Measurable Component 'Functionality Execution' (CFE)

One of the 4 software's constituent components which is important and relevant to be measured for complete software's measurement and is measured in the Functional Software Size Measurement Methodology with Effort Estimation and Performance Indication (FSSM). The CFE consists of the Functionality Execution part which comprises the functional operations; functional data handled during these operations; and class methods.

It comprises the following two parts:

1. functionality execution operations which are the
   a. memory operations used for reading/writing the data from/to the memory devices;

   b. input/output operations used for receiving/sending the input/output data from/to the input/output devices;
   c. message exchange operations (message send/receive) used for sending/receiving the messages to/from the external application programs or sub-programs (modules);
   d. error handling operations;
   e. general functionality execution operations which are of the following type:
      i. computational;
      ii. logical;
      iii. decision execution;
      iv. repeat execution;
      v. action execution;
      vi. execution flow control;
2. functional data handling during the following functionality execution operations:
   a. functional data handled in the memory read/write operations;
   b. functional data handled in the input/output operations;
   c. functional data handled in the message exchange operations;
   d. functional data handled in the general functionality execution operations for the following types of functional operations:
      i. computational;
      ii. logical;
      iii. decision execution;
      iv. repeat execution;
      v. execution flow control;

presented normally in the Functionality Execution (FE) description part, and class methods presented normally in the Logical Data Model (LDM) part of the Functional Requirements Specifications (FRS) that are the Functional User Requirements (FUR)[1] according to the ISO/IEC 14143-1[1] standards.

17.1.14.80 Software's Measurable Component 'Message Exchange' (CME)

One of the 4 software's constituent components which is important and relevant to be measured for complete software's measurement and is measured in the Functional Software Size Measurement Methodology with Effort Estimation and Performance Indication (FSSM). The CME consists of the Message Exchange part which defines the messages to be used for communication with the external application programs or the sub-programs (modules) of the same application program through message send/receive operations. It comprises the messages that are sent and received, and fields of the messages, presented normally in the Message Exchange description part of the Functional Requirements Specifications (FRS) that are the Functional User Requirements (FUR)[1] according to the ISO/IEC 14143-1[1] standards.

17.1.14.81 Software's Measurable Component 'User Interface' (CUI)

One of the 4 software's constituent components which is important and relevant to be measured for complete software's measurement and is measured in the Functional Software Size Measurement Methodology with Effort Estimation and Performance Indication (FSSM). The CUI consists of the User Interface part for communication with the input/output devices such as keyboard and display devices. It comprises the structure of the input/output screens: the screens layouts, fields contained in the screens and information about the input/output navigation links of the screens, presented normally in the User Interface description part of the Functional Requirements Specifications (FRS) that are the Functional User Requirements (FUR)[1] according to the ISO/IEC 14143-1[1] standards.

17.1.15 T

17.1.15.1 Technical Design Specifications (TDS)

A document used in the development phase of the software life cycle for presenting the design related technical specifications. It is not required for using the Functional Software Size Measurement Methodology with Effort Estimation and Performance Indication (FSSM) because the FSSM derives all the information from the Functional Requirements Specifications (FRS), that is, the Functional User Requirements (FUR)[1] according to the ISO/IEC 14143-1[1] standards.

17.1.15.2 Technical Requirements (TR)

A document used in the development phase of the software life cycle for presenting the technical requirements of the software project. It is not required for using the Functional Software Size Measurement Methodology with Effort Estimation and Performance Indication (FSSM) because the FSSM derives all the information from the Functional Requirements Specifications (FRS), that is, the Functional User Requirements (FUR)[1] according to the ISO/IEC 14143-1[1] standards.

17.1.16 U

17.1.16.1 User Interaction Functional Data Level (UIDL)

One of the Software Performance Quality Indicators (SPQIs) of the type Software Operational Indicator (SOI)[5–7]. It gives the indication of the dynamic run-time functional data handling in the user interactions (input/output operations used for receiving/sending the input/output data from/to the input/output devices) in the software execution.

The UIDL is the ratio of the total functional data handled during the user interactions input/output operations, that is, the Input/Output Operations Functional Data Entities (IOFE), to the functionality execution data manipulation size of the Software's Measurable Component 'Functionality Execution' (CFE), that is, the Functionality Execution Data Manipulation Measurement (FEDM), in percentage, and is expressed as Nil, Low, Medium, High, or Very High according to this percentage value.

17.1.16.2 User Interaction Level (UIL)

One of the Software Performance Quality Indicators (SPQIs) of the type Software Operational Indicator (SOI)[5–7]. It gives the indication of the dynamic run-time level of the user interaction through input/output operations which are used for receiving/sending data from/to the input/output devices such as keyboard and display, and are performed in the software execution.

The UIL is the ratio of the total number of the input/output operations performed, that is, the Input/Output Operations (IOO), to the dynamic run-time operations performance size of the Software's Measurable Component 'Functionality Execution' (CFE), that is, the Functionality Execution Operations Dynamic Measurement (FEODM), in percentage, and is expressed as Nil, Low, Medium, High, or Very High according to this percentage value.

17.1.16.3 User Interaction Proportion (UIP)

One of the Software Performance Quality Indicators (SPQIs) of the type Software Structural Indicator (SSI)[5–7]. It gives the indication of the static proportion of the user interface related operations (input/output operations used for receiving/sending the input/output data from/to input/output devices), performed in the total software contents.

The UIP is the ratio of the total number of the input/output operations performed, that is, the Input and Output Operations (IOO), to the total software size, that is, the Software Total Components Measurement (STCM), in percentage, and is expressed as Nil, Low, Medium, High, or Very High according to this percentage value.

17.1.16.4 User Interface (UI)

All the User Interface part which is used to define the user interface/screens and is used by the functionality of the software for input/output communications with the input/output devices. It is described normally in the User Interface (UI) description part of the Functional Requirements Specifications (FRS). It is characterized as one of the Software's Measurable Components (SMCs) in the Functional Software Size Measurement Methodology with Effort Estimation and Performance Indication (FSSM).

The User Interface (UI) component is identified in the FSSM as the Software's Measurable Component 'User Interface' (CUI). The CUI has the Software Component's Measurable Features:

- **a.** 'User Screen' (FUS);
- **b.** 'User Screen Field' (FUF);
- **c.** 'User Screen Input Link' (FUI);
- **d.** 'User Screen Output Link' (FUO);

which are all measured in the FSSM. The measurement of the CUI is given by the Software Component 'User Interface' Measurement (CUIM). The CUIM is further used for the calculations of Software Size and Effort Estimations (SSEEs) and Software Performance Quality Indicators of the type Software Structural Indicators (SSIs)[5–7].

17.1.16.5 User Interface Complexity and Size (UICS)

One of the Software Performance Quality Indicators (SPQIs) of the type Software Structural Indicator (SSI)[5–7]. It gives the indication of the size and complexity of the Software's Measurable Component 'User Interface' (CUI). The CUI comprises the user screens, their input/output fields, and their input/output navigational links. The measurement for the CUI is the Software Component 'User Interface' Measurement (CUIM).

The UICS is evaluated directly based on the value of the CUIM, and is expressed as Nil, Low, Medium, High, or Very High according to the CUIM value.

17.1.16.6 User Interface Component Proportion (UICP)

One of the Software Performance Quality Indicators (SPQIs) of the type Software Structural Indicator (SSI)[5–7]. It gives the indication of the static proportion of the User Interface size – number of all the user screens, their input/output fields and their input/output navigational links – in the total software contents.

The UICP is the ratio of the total User Interface size, that is, the Software Component 'User Interface' Measurement (CUIM), to the total software size measurement, that is, the Software Total Components Measurement (STCM), in percentage, and is expressed as Nil, Low, Medium, High, or Very High according to this percentage value.

17.1.16.7 User Interface Field Entities (UIFE)

The Software Component's Feature Measurement (SCFM) for the Software Component's Measurable Feature 'User Screen Field' (FUF) in terms of the Software Component's Feature Points (SCFPs).

The UIFE (User Interface Field Entities) is the measurement for the fields of the user screens described in the User Interface (UI) part of the Functional Requirements Specifications (FRS).

The UIFE is calculated from the Software Component's Feature Point Count for 'User Screen Field' (FCUF) and is used for the following calculations:

a. Software Component's Measurements (SCMs): the Software Total Components Measurement (STCM) through the Software Component 'User Interface' Measurement (CUIM);

b. Software Size and Effort Estimations (SSEEs): the Software Total Development Effort (STDE) through the Software Logical Size (SLS) and Software Analysis, Design, and Coding Effort (SADCE);

c. Software Performance Quality Indicators (SPQIs): Software Structural Indicators (SSIs)[5–7], that is, the SSIs User Interface Complexity and Size (UICS) and User Interface Component Proportion (UICP).

17.1.16.8 User Interface Input Link Entities (UIIE)

The Software Component's Feature Measurement (SCFM) for the Software Component's Measurable Feature 'User Screen Input Link' (FUI) in terms of the Software Component's Feature Points (SCFPs).

The UIIE (User Interface Input Link Entities) is the measurement for the input navigational links of the user screens described in the User Interface (UI) part of the Functional Requirements Specifications (FRS).

The UIIE is calculated from the Software Component's Feature Point Count for 'User Screen Input Link' (FCUI) and is used for the following calculations:

a. Software Component's Measurements (SCMs): the Software Total Components Measurement (STCM) through the Software Component 'User Interface' Measurement (CUIM);

b. Software Size and Effort Estimations (SSEEs): the Software Total Development Effort (STDE) through the Software Logical Size (SLS) and Software Analysis, Design, and Coding Effort (SADCE);

c. Software Performance Quality Indicators (SPQIs): Software Structural Indicators (SSIs)[5–7], that is, the SSIs User Interface Complexity and Size (UICS) and User Interface Component Proportion (UICP).

17.1.16.9 User Interface Missing Entities (UIME)

The Software Component's Feature Measurement (SCFM) for the Software Component's Measurable Feature 'User Screen Missing' (FUM) in terms of the Software Component's Feature Points (SCFPs).

The UIME (User Interface Missing Entities) is the measurement for the missing user interface/screens items in the User Interface (UI) part of the Functional Requirements Specifications (FRS).

The UIME is calculated from the Software Component's Feature Point Count for 'User Screen Missing' (FCUM) and is used for the following calculations:

a. Software Component's Measurements (SCMs): the Software Components Requirements Deficiency Measurement (CRDM);
b. Software Performance Quality Indicators (SPQIs): Software Structural Indicators (SSIs)[5–7], that is, the SSI Requirements Deficiency Grade (RDG).

17.1.16.10 User Interface Output Link Entities (UIOE)

The Software Component's Feature Measurement (SCFM) for the Software Component's Measurable Feature 'User Screen Output Link' (FUO) in terms of the Software Component's Feature Points (SCFPs).

The UIOE (User Interface Output Link Entities) is the measurement for the output navigational links of the user screens described in the User Interface (UI) part of the Functional Requirements Specifications (FRS).

The UIOE is calculated from the Software Component's Feature Point Count for 'User Screen Output Link' (FCUO) and is used for the following calculations:

a. Software Component's Measurements (SCMs): the Software Total Components Measurement (STCM) through the Software Component 'User Interface' Measurement (CUIM);
b. Software Size and Effort Estimations (SSEEs): the Software Total Development Effort (STDE) through the Software Logical Size (SLS) and Software Analysis, Design, and Coding Effort (SADCE);
c. Software Performance Quality Indicators (SPQIs): Software Structural Indicators (SSIs)[5–7], that is, the SSIs User Interface Complexity and Size (UICS) and User Interface Component Proportion (UICP).

17.1.16.11 User Interface Screen Entities (UISE)

The Software Component's Feature Measurement (SCFM) for the Software Component's Measurable Feature 'User Screen' (FUS) in terms of the Software Component's Feature Points (SCFPs).

The UISE (User Interface Screen Entities) is the measurement for the user screens described in the User Interface (UI) part of the Functional Requirements Specifications (FRS).

The UISE is calculated from the Software Component's Feature Point Count for 'User Screen' (FCUS) and is used for the following calculations:

a. Software Component's Measurements (SCMs): the Software Total Components Measurement (STCM) through the Software Component 'User Interface' Measurement (CUIM);

b. Software Size and Effort Estimations (SSEEs): the Software Total Development Effort (STDE) through the Software Logical Size (SLS) and Software Analysis, Design, and Coding Effort (SADCE);

c. Software Performance Quality Indicators (SPQIs): Software Structural Indicators (SSIs)[5–7], that is, the SSIs User Interface Complexity and Size (UICS) and User Interface Component Proportion (UICP).

Part Ten

List of Figures and Answers to Exercises

Chapter 18

List of Figures

Functional Software Size Measurement Methodology with Effort Estimation and Performance Indication, First Edition. Jasveer Singh.

Companion website: http://booksupport.wiley.com

Chapter 19

Answers to Exercises

Answers to the exercises in the chapters are presented next.

19.1 CHAPTER 1 EXERCISES

1.1. A.

1.2. B.

1.3. C.

1.4. C.

1.5. C.

19.2 CHAPTER 2 EXERCISES

2.1. B.

2.2. C.

2.3. D.

2.4. B.

2.5. A.

19.3 CHAPTER 3 EXERCISES

3.1. A.

3.2. C.

3.3. B.

3.4. C.

3.5. B.

Functional Software Size Measurement Methodology with Effort Estimation and Performance Indication, First Edition. Jasveer Singh.

Companion website: http://booksupport.wiley.com

19.4 CHAPTER 4 EXERCISES

4.1. D.
4.2. B.
4.3. C.
4.4. D.
4.5. D.

19.5 CHAPTER 5 EXERCISES

5.1. B.
5.2. C.
5.3. C.

19.6 CHAPTER 6 EXERCISES

6.1. A.
6.2. A.
6.3. B.
6.4. C.

19.7 CHAPTER 7 EXERCISES

7.1. B.
7.2. E.
7.3. E.
7.4. D.

19.8 CHAPTER 8 EXERCISES

8.1. B.
8.2. A.
8.3. B.
8.4. C.

19.9 CHAPTER 9 EXERCISES

9.1. B.
9.2. C.
9.3. A.
9.4. C.

References

[1] ISO/IEC 14143-1:2007(E), Information technology – Software measurement – Functional size measurement, Part 1: Definition of concepts.

[2] ISO/IEC 14143-2:2011(E), Information technology – Software measurement – Functional size measurement, Part 2: Conformity evaluation of software size measurement methods to ISO/IEC 14143-1.

[3] ISO/IEC 19761:2011(E), Software engineering – COSMIC: A functional size measurement method.

[4] The International Function Point Users Group (IFPUG), Function Point Counting Practices Manual, Release 4.3.1.

[5] Software Comprehensive Count with Quality Indicators (SCCQI) – A New Generation, Enhanced and Comprehensive Software Size Measurement Methodology, Jasveer Singh, UKSMA/COSMIC 23rd Annual Conference 2012, 21st Century Metrics, International Conference on Software Metrics and Estimating, London, November 2012, http://www.uksma.co.uk/ConferencePresentations.asp#2012

[6] Software Comprehensive Count with Quality Indicators (SCCQI) – A Comprehensive Approach to Software Size Measurement, Jasveer Singh, SMEF 2012, Proceedings of the 9th Software Measurement European Forum, Rome, 2012, http://www.dpo.it/smef2012/SMEF2012_Proceedings.pdf

[7] Software Comprehensive Count with Quality Indicators (SCCQI) for Software Size Measurement, Jasveer Singh, NESMA 2012 najaarsbijeenkomst (Autumn Meeting), Meten, maar dan anders (Measurement, but then different), ISVW, Leusden, Netherlands, November 2012, http://nesma.org/nesma/meetings/meten-maar-dan-anders-november-2012/

Functional Software Size Measurement Methodology with Effort Estimation and Performance Indication, First Edition. Jasveer Singh.

Companion website: http://booksupport.wiley.com

Index

Functional Software Size Measurement Methodology with Effort Estimation and Performance Indication, First Edition. Jasveer Singh.

Companion website: http://booksupport.wiley.com